A Sociolegal Analysis of Formal Land Tenure Systems

This sociolegal study focuses on the political, legal, and institutional problems and dilemmas of regulating land tenure. By studying the development of the Timorese formal land tenure system, this book engages in the larger debate about the role of state systems in addressing and aggravating social problems such as insecurity, poverty, inequality, destruction of nature, and cultural and social estrangement.

Land tenure issues in Timor-Leste are complex and deeply shaped by the nation's history. Taking an insider's perspective based on the author's experience in Timorese state administration, and through the investigation of five analytical themes—political environment, law-making, legal framework, institutional framework, and social relationships and practices—this book studies the development of the Timorese formal land tenure system from independence in 2002 to 2018. It shows how political, legal, and administrative decisions on land administration are made, what and who influences them, which problems and dilemmas emerge, and how the formal system works in practice. The result is a portrait of a young nation grappling with the enormous task of creating a land tenure system that can address the needs of its citizens in the wake of centuries of socio-political tumult and huge fluctuations in resources. The book concludes by highlighting the importance of law-making and how abuses of power can be curbed by adequate administrative processes and laws. Finally, it argues that land administration is primarily a political matter. The political dimension of technical solutions must be considered if we aim to achieve fairer formal land tenure systems.

The pertinence of the topics covered, the multi-disciplinary perspective, and the research methodology followed make this book appealing to a variety of readers, including international organisations, practitioners, academics, and students engaged in land administration, post-colonial and -conflict issues, law-making, rule of law, public administration, and issues of access and exclusion.

Bernardo Almeida is an Assistant Professor at the Leiden University College and researcher at the Van Vollenhoven Institute (Netherlands), who focuses on land, law, law-making and development.

Part of the
LAW, DEVELOPMENT AND GLOBALIZATION series

series editors
Julio Faundez, University of Warwick, UK
Adriaan Bedner, University of Leiden, The Netherlands

for information about the series and details of previous and forthcoming titles, see https://www.routledge.com/Law-Development-and-Globalization/book-series/CAV30

a GlassHouse book

A Sociolegal Analysis of Formal Land Tenure Systems

Learning from the Political, Legal, and Institutional Struggles of Timor-Leste

Bernardo Almeida

Routledge
Taylor & Francis Group
a GlassHouse Book

First published 2022
by Routledge
4 Park Square, Milton Park, Abingdon, Oxon OX14 4RN

and by Routledge
605 Third Avenue, New York, NY 10158

a GlassHouse book

Routledge is an imprint of the Taylor & Francis Group, an informa business

British Library Cataloguing-in-Publication Data
A catalogue record for this book is available from the British Library

Library of Congress Cataloging-in-Publication Data
A catalog record has been requested for this book

ISBN: 978-1-032-05170-3 (hbk)
ISBN: 978-1-032-05173-4 (pbk)
ISBN: 978-1-003-19639-6 (ebk)

DOI: 10.4324/9781003196396

Typeset in Bembo
by Deanta Global Publishing Services, Chennai, India

For Laurinha and Benjamin

Contents

Maps

Figure

Tables

Abbreviations

ADB	Asian Development Bank
APODETI	Timorese Popular Democratic Association (*Associação Popular Democrática Timorense*)
ASDT	Timorese Social Democrat Association (*Associação Social-Democrata Timorense*)
AUSAID	Australian Agency for International Development
BAL	Indonesian Basic Agrarian Law of 1960—Law 5/1960 (*Undang-Undang Pokok-Pokok Agraria*)
BPN	Indonesian National Land Agency (*Badan Pertanahan Nasional*)
CNRT	National Congress for Timorese Reconstruction (*Congresso Nacional da Reconstrução Timorense*)
CSO(S)	Civil Society Organization(s)
DNTP	National Directorate of Land and Property (*Direcção Nacional de Terras e Propriedades*)
DNTPSC	National Directorate of Land, Property and Cadastral Services (*Direcção Nacional de Terras, Propriedades, e Serviços Cadastrais*)
ESI	Estimated Sustainable Income
FITUN	Always United Front of Timor (*Frente Iha Timor Unidos Nafatin*)
FRETILIN	Revolutionary Front for an Independent East Timor (*Frente Revolucionária de Timor-Leste Independente*)
INR	*Ita Nia Rai* project ('Our Land' in Tetum)
J4P	Justice for the Poor programme (World Bank)
KOTA	Association of Timorese Heroes (*Klibur Oan Timor Asuwain*)
LLP	USAID Land Law Program I and II
LPU	UNTAET Land and Property Unit
MOAFF	Ministry of Agriculture, Forest and Fisheries
MOJ	Ministry of Justice
MP(S)	Member(s) of parliament
NGO(S)	Non-governmental organization(s)
OJECTIL	Organisation of Catholic East Timorese Youth and Students (*Organização Juventude Estudante de Timor-Leste*)

RENETIL	National Resistance of East Timorese Students (*Resistência Nacional dos Estudantes de Timor-Leste*)
SETP	State Secretary for Land and Property (*Secretário de Estado de Terras e Propriedades*)
SNC	National Cadastre System (*Sistema Nacional de Cadastro*)
SSB	Suai Supply Base
UDT	Timorese Democratic Union (*União Democrática Timorense*)
UN	United Nations
UNTAET	United Nations Transitional Administration in East Timor
USAID	United States Agency for International Development
USD	United States Dollar
ZEESM	Special Economic Zone of Social Market Economy of Oecusse (*Zona Especial de Economia Social de Mercado de Oe-Cusse Ambeno*)

Between abstract principles of justice and everyday sticky wickets—a foreword

Law suspends itself between science and craft, between philosophy and the mundane. Law deals with abstract principles of justice as well as everyday sticky wickets like who gets to farm what side of the hedge. Questions of law also range from the legal rules and institutions on the one hand, and the political and historical order in which the doctrinal features of order-making are embedded on the other. Law has proved to be vexingly difficult to define. As a structure of rules or a process of rulemaking, definitions tend to be either over-restrictive and concern only laws passed through a proper legislature, or over-inclusive and look like any other social rule in society. It is, nonetheless, in this field that any scholarly work on law and society must place itself.

A Sociolegal Analysis of Formal Land Tenure Systems defies simplistic classification as either juridical or political; the world is not organised in disciplines (disciplines are probably more a result of university geo-political squabbles over prestige, positions, funding, buildings, and students). Bernardo Ribeiro de Almeida insists, instead, on taking the practical implications of legal principles as seriously as the philosophical implications of people's practice. This is the most remarkable contribution of the book. The author is conscient of the larger principles at stake in any effort at legislating about what people can have and on what conditions, but Almeida is equally aware of where the devil lives. The details of legislation are crucial if law is to be workable and not simply an inert piece of logic. Almeida's experience as a legal adviser to the Timorese land administration has provided him with crucial experience. The process of formulating policy, translating it into legal principles, of operationalising them to be implementable in the bureaucratic practice of government administration in a new country, and, finally, to ensure that law makes sense and is seen as fair and just by the population, is a tall order. Often this process is not offered the attention it deserves in academic literature. It is as if the step from principle to practice is dismissed as a prosaic question of a lesser order than the more philosophical questions of ownership and bundles of rights, of state domain and political authority, of legal subjectivity and representations of property, and so on. However, Almeida's analysis forces us to reckon with bureaucratic practice and capacity, as well as the social and political context in which law must work.

The analysis of the protocol and procedures cast light on the micro-politics of an ostensibly technical process. It shows that at each step, ambiguity, choice, and interpretation turn the technical operation into a negotiated procedure. The book thereby depicts a landscape of institutions which are both instances of authority and arenas of competition.

There is a tendency in some academic writing on developing societies to conduct an implicit comparative analysis between reality and ideals. Often researchers compare the reality of what they find with their expectations of ideal situations in implicit ways. Studies of weak states, for example, have often compared the 'mess' they identify in the data to the rational ideals that theory offers as an index of accomplishment of states. In such cases, reality always falls short of the ideals. Almeida resists this implicit comparison, and his book on building land tenure systems in Timor-Leste is a rare accomplishment. The book provides a forensic analysis of a law-building process at a moment after a societal rupture of independence. Often, land tenure legislation has been fuelled by a vain idea to get institutions right, once and for all. 'Private property, rule of law, and growth' epitomise the ambition and the hope for some causality between them in policies designed by international development organisations. It makes one wonder why nobody had thought of it before if it is so simple. The reason is, of course, that it is not simple at all. His meticulous historical approach allows Almeida to demonstrate that what law is and what law does changes over time. It reflects political agendas in the country and the nature and power of the stakeholders involved. Yet, while getting institutions right, once and for all, is unrealistic, and probably even undesirable, it does not mean that governments should not work to establish a predictable and fair legal environment, even if it will always be provisory. 'Even if there is no truth, man can be truthful, and even if there is no certainty, man can be reliable', Hannah Arendt reminds us in *The Human Condition.* Almeida strikes a fine balance between what society needs law to be and do, and what is practically possible to achieve from the current point in history. Neither the inconsistencies in the legal text nor the improvised approximate implementation are seen as aberrations in the process of building a land tenure system. Rather, they reveal the inevitable tensions in any law-making process. It strikes me as a much bolder position than either a dogged insistence on the implementation of a full and elaborate tenure legislation designed by 'successful countries', or an aloof dismissal of law's role in the development of Timor-Leste, altogether.

Christian Lund, University of Copenhagen

Acknowledgments

This book is the result of my PhD thesis, to which many people and institutions contributed, and to whom I am very grateful. I want to thank all my colleagues and friends at the Fundação das Universidades Portuguesas, Ministry of Justice of Timor-Leste, DNTPSC, UNDP, The Asia Foundation, Rede Ba Rai, Tahan, and other organisations that I had the privilege of working with as legal adviser, consultant, and academic researcher. I'm also thankful to Fundação Oriente, Dutch Research Council, Science for Global Development programmes (NWO-WOTRO), and the Knowledge Platform for Security and Rule of Law for the grants that financed parts of this research.

Many friends that I met in Timor-Leste contributed in all kinds of ways to this research. I want to thank to Lene Østergaard, Ibere Lopes, Miguel Lemos, João Albuquerque, Gobie Rajalingam, Helen Henderson, Ricardo Cunha, Rod Nixon, Meabh Cryan, Rui Feijó, Susana Viegas, Sara Ribeiro, Nigel Thomson, Patrícia Coutinho, Laura Yoder, Susanna Barnes, Todd Wassel, and many others for their friendship and support.

At the Van Vollenhoven Institute of Leiden Law School, where I wrote my PhD thesis, I found my 'academic family'. Running the risk of missing some names, I want to thank Santy, Hoko, Bruno, Annelien, Jan Michiel, Janine, Maartje, Jacqueline, Kari, Kora, Dennis, Pauline, Willem, Laura, Laure, Arshad, Fachrizal, Maryla, Liz, Nadia, Mies, Nick, Suliman, Nienke, Elisabeth, Najib, Yance, Neske, Judith, Daniel, Joseph, Mareike, Danielle, Chase, Rogier, Dorien, Hannah, Bilal, Nada, Feby, and Roxane. My very special thanks go to Adriaan Bedner and Carolien Jacobs, my thesis supervisor and co-supervisor, with whom I had the great luck and privilege of going on this adventure, and from whom I continue to learn so much about the world. I am also very grateful to my PhD committee, which included Janine Ubink, Lorenzo Cotula, Christian Lund, Laura Meitzner Yoder, and Jaqueline Vel for their very valuable feedback and support.

The love, care, and support of my family and close friends in Portugal was paramount to finishing this research, and I'm very grateful for it. My greatest debt is to my wife, Laura Ogden, the most loving and caring partner, wonderful researcher, sharpest peer-reviewer and editor, best friend to share great jokes, and the most dedicated mother of our little Benjamin. Thank you!

Chapter 1

Introduction

Introduction

After lecturing on land rights for one semester in the law degree of the National University of Timor-Leste, I accepted the challenge of returning to the country for six months to work as the legal adviser for the land sector at the Timorese Ministry of Justice (MoJ).[1] The briefing about my tasks was short: we need a legal land adviser to support the ministry and National Directorate of Land, Property and Cadastral Services (DNTPSC)[2] in their daily activities, and to provide technical support to the finalisation and approval process of the new draft Land Law Package. I was told to buy a ticket and come as soon as I could.

In January 2010 I landed in Timor-Leste, ready to start my new job. When introduced to DNTPSC's national director for the very first time, he gave me a strong hug and said *benvindo maun!* ('Welcome brother!' in Tetum). He held my hand, with his fingers interlacing mine, and for the next five minutes talked about the various things he was working on, while I was thinking if leaving my law-firm job back in Portugal had been the best decision. This was the start of a five-year adventure, working as the land adviser for the MoJ of Timor-Leste, which profoundly marked my academic interests and my professional career in land-related issues.

Land tenure issues in Timor-Leste are complex and deeply shaped by the nation's history. Post-colonialism, post-conflict, and the less-mentioned but equally important post-authoritarianism, combined with ambitions of development and prosperity, make land tenure one of the most socially, politically, and legally intricate problems of this young country. Taking my professional experience in the country as the departure point, this book—an adaptation of my PhD thesis—focuses on the processes, problems, and dilemmas of developing

1 My position at MoJ was co-financed by the Justice System Programme of the United Nations Development Programme (UNDP).

2 For simplicity I always refer to this institution as DNTPSC, but this institution has had other names since its creation (Chapter 7).

DOI: 10.4324/9781003196396-1

the Timorese formal land tenure system since the country's formal independence in 2002 until the end of 2017.

Coming from the inside of the state administration, this book shows how political, legal, and administrative decisions on land administration are made, what and who influence them, which problems and dilemmas politicians and state officials face, and how the formal land tenure system works in practice. In other words, I try to lead the reader to see how the state works from the inside. To achieve this objective this book is based on an analytical framework described below, which is composed of five analytical themes: (1) the political environment at the national level; (2) the law-making process; (3) the legal framework (or the law on the books); (4) the institutional framework that implements state legislation; and (5) the social relationships and practices around land tenure. A case study at the end of the book illustrates how all these themes interact with each other: the politics that influence a troubled law-making process, the inapplicable legislation that resulted from that process, the high discretion of state officials, and the limited protection that the formal land tenure system can provide to those that come in the path of the state. The result is a portrait of a young nation grappling with the enormous task of creating a land tenure system that can address the needs of its citizens, in the wake of centuries of cultural and political tumult, huge fluctuations in wealth and resources, and seeking to find its place on the world stage as a new nation.

By studying the design, implementation, and impact of the formal land tenure system, this book enquires into the role of the state in addressing and causing land-related issues in Timor-Leste. The relationship of the Timorese with land, customary land arrangements, and the political economy of land are already well described in the existing literature.[3] However, a perspective that can take into consideration the roles of the formal land tenure system and the problems and dilemmas to implement it, and explain what and who influence political, legal, and administrative decisions on land administration, is still missing. This book aims to fill this gap. Moreover, this book also gives a historical account of the development of the Timorese formal land tenure system.

By describing the case of Timor-Leste this book also intends to contribute to the larger debate about formal land tenure systems and their role in improving people's living conditions in developing countries.[4] First, by proposing

3 Among others, Fitzpatrick, 2002; Urresta and Nixon, 2003, 2004, 2004a; Yoder, 2005; McWilliam and Traube, 2011; Nixon, 2012; Fitzpatrick *et al.*, 2013; Bovensiepen, 2015.

4 The term 'developing country' is controversial, raising questions regarding what development really is and how it can be measured (Heady, 1979: 84; Dann, 2013: 202). The term is loosely used to refer to countries with low gross national product and which are receivers of development assistance from other countries and international organisations (Otto, 2007: 13). Other authors have been using other expressions such as 'the Global South', but these alternatives also raise their own issues. In absence of a better alternative, I use the expression 'developing country', but acknowledging its limitations.

and testing a framework of analysis that allows a clearer comprehension of the roles, influences, functioning, and limitations of formal land tenure systems. Simplified frameworks of analysis, based for instance on the dualistic idea of 'law on the books and law in practice' overlook key factors of a formal land tenure system, and therefore provide only partial overviews. As demonstrated in this book, only a broader analysis can allow us to understand the reasons for the successes and failures of a land tenure system.

Second, this book highlights the assumptions in which the development of formal land tenure systems are based, and the consequences of their practical implementation when these assumptions are not in place (Chapter 2). During colonial times, changes in land tenure were already seen as the solution to improve people's lives. During the post-colonial era, and more recently after De Soto's controversial book 'The Mystery of Capital', land tenure returned to the agendas of politicians, development agencies, and academics as one promising area for tackling development issues. However, the debate around land tenure systems has been marked by wrong assumptions, misconceptions, and hidden agendas. In modern states, the development and territorialisation of formal land tenure systems is done under the assumptions that the state represents the collective will of the people, and its actions will balance collective and individual interests and goals, ultimately providing tenure security and well-being to the people. It is also under these assumptions that formal land tenure systems are promoted in developing countries, with the objective of addressing past injustices, and promoting peace and prosperity. This book provides the literature with another example of how this balance between collective and individual interests is difficult, and how in practice the formal land tenure system can easily be captured by elites, and become a tool of state oppression, inequality, and dispossession.

Finally, this book highlights that land governance is not easy, especially in developing countries. Even when politicians and state officials are genuinely committed to using the formal land tenure system to improve people's living conditions, the development and territorialisation of a formal land tenure system is still difficult. Land tenure, especially in contexts of post-colonialism and post-conflict, is a wicked problem, with multiple interdependencies, influenced by various factors, where the resolution of one problem reveals or creates new ones. While literature is often very critical of land governance choices taken and the results obtained, it frequently fails to acknowledge the difficult problems and dilemmas that lead to those choices and results (Chapter 2). By taking an insider's position this book shows the state from the inside, highlights these problems and dilemmas, and puts the reader in the shoes of politicians and state officials. It shows how formal land tenure systems are much more the result of tensions between different stakeholders, interests, and worldviews than the product of unified and well-thought-through processes. A better knowledge of these problems and dilemmas by researchers and practitioners is paramount for better academic research and interventions on land administration.

Framework of analysis—Land Tenure System Analysis Model

One of the struggles when writing this book was to find an analytical framework that could give a deep understanding of the Timorese formal land tenure system. I wanted to avoid a simple dualist view like the frequently used 'law on the books and law in practice', which does not explain how the law came to be the way it is, and why the law on the books differs from the law in practice. Instead, I wanted a framework that showed how this land tenure system has been formed, the influences that shape it, its relationship with other land tenure systems, and how it impacts the everyday life of the Timorese.

In my search for an adequate analytical framework I came across the framework developed by Benda-Beckmann *et al.* for the study of property (Benda-Beckmann *et al.*, 2006: 14).[5] These authors raise issues with evolutionary frameworks that divide property into what they call 'the big four' categories: private, state, communal, and open access property. Benda-Beckmann *et al.* consider that these categories do not provide useful and consistent criteria for property analysis, and that the study of property should focus instead on different and interrelated 'layers of social organization' (2006: 15), or sub-systems as called by Barry (2015: 28). In other words, they show the importance of looking at the arenas where land gets a social value. These layers are (1) ideology, (2) the legal and institutional systems, and (3) the social relationships and social practices. Benda-Beckmann *et al.* point out that property works very differently in each of these layers of social organisation, and property can only be understood if one looks at each of these layers and the intersections between them. The authors argue that their framework allows for a vision beyond the legal categories of property, eliminates the problems that other approaches have in not distinguishing between categorical and concretised property relationships, and allows for an understanding of property practices in context.

Barry provides a critique of this framework, arguing that while it provides a good tool for explaining and predicting problems, it does not offer any tools for action against the problems the authors describe (2015: 30). Moreover, the complexity of this framework's analysis is not so attractive to international organisations and politicians, who need more simple and digestible messages (ibid.). While Barry's critique is factually correct, it does not diminish the relevance of Benda-Beckmann *et al.*'s framework. First, as this book shows, the initial step to address complex social problems, such as those raised by land tenure, is to have deep knowledge about them and their possible solutions

5 In Chapter 2 I raise some issues with the expression 'property', but I use it here for now. The authors argue that property 'concerns the organization and legitimation of right and obligations with respect to good that are regarded as valuable' (2006: 2). In this book I call the rights and obligations referred by these authors land rights or land tenure, and the mechanisms to organise and legitimise them land tenure systems.

(Seidman and Seidman, 2006; 2008), and a broad framework that provides more knowledge is therefore relevant. Second, the fact that the complexity of a framework of analysis raises low interest from international organisations and politicians says more about the problems of these actors than about the framework. It is correct that governments and international organisations often work in less than ideal scenarios, and limitations such as time and resources can make in-depth research very difficult or even impossible (Chapter 5). But this should not distract them from trying as much as possible to understand the realities in which they are working.

However, while the multi-layered framework of Benda-Beckmann *et al.* provided a good point of departure in my search for an analytical framework, it could not be easily operationalised for the reasons described below. Inspired by this framework, and prompted by its gaps, I have modified it and developed my own framework: the *Land Tenure System Analysis Model.*

The modifications were the following. First, I adjusted the scope and name of the first layer of social organisation from ideology to political environment. The authors do not define ideology, leaving unclear what, in their view, should be analysed. A strict definition of ideology as political theories about societal organisation, the role of the state, and how resources should be shared, such as capitalism, communism, and neoliberalism, provides a very limited scope of analysis (Schwarzmantel, 2008: 36). In Timor-Leste, as in many other countries, political theory plays a very limited role in political debates and decisions. Therefore, focusing the analysis on political theories would provide very limited results. Ideology can also be defined in broader terms, including political theories, less theoretically structured visions and aspirations for the country, and the values that inform those visions and aspirations. But even this broader definition of ideology is limited. Every country has several contextual factors that, in parallel with ideology, influence political debates and decisions around land tenure systems (e.g., historical context, economic situation, rule of law). Focusing only on ideology, even if broadly defined, would overlook these contextual factors and provide a partial view of this layer of analysis. Therefore, Chapter 4 looks into the 'political environment', which encompasses political theories, aspirations, visions and values of the elite but also the contextual factors that guide the political debates around land tenure.

The second modification clarifies the object of the second layer of social ordering—the 'legal-institutional layer'—where the authors look into the categories of rights formed by laws and institutions. However, also in this case the definition of these concepts makes it difficult to set their boundaries. To address this issue, in Chapter 6 I focus on the 'legal framework', where I describe the Timorese legislation relevant for land tenure. In this description I pay attention to the main legal structures and concepts, but also to legislative gaps and contradictions. When possible I also provide the interpretation that courts and state institutions have made of specific legislation. While this conceptualisation of the second layer can, at a first glance, lose some of the analysis proposed by

Benda-Beckmann *et al.*, its object becomes clearer, and the possible losses are compensated by the other changes proposed below. One final detail regarding the layers was to add, as part of the third one, the ideas that people have regarding land tenure.

The third modification was to clearly identify key intersections between the different layers. While Benda-Beckmann *et al.* mention the importance of looking at these intersections, they are less clear in pinpointing them. The first intersection that I identified and included in my model was law-making, as it brings together the political environment and the legal framework; it is through law-making that political debates are translated into laws. Therefore, Chapter 5 is dedicated to the process through which key land-related legislation is idealised, drafted, and approved. The second intersection between layers that I identified and included in the analytical model was the institutional framework responsible for implementing the Timorese formal land tenure system. It is through the practices of these institutions that the laws connect with the social relationships and practices on the ground and, furthermore, law-making is also influenced by the work of these institutions, making their study even more relevant. Therefore, Chapter 7 is dedicated to these institutions. The result is the *Land Tenure System Analysis Model*, where five key analytical themes are identified, as depicted in Figure 1.1.

Based on the Land Tenure System Analysis Model, the structure of this book was designed to study each of these analytical themes, allowing for a comprehensive analysis of the Timorese formal land tenure system beyond simplistic views such as 'the law in the books and the law in practice'.

Research questions

So what is this book about? As described above, departing from the inside of the state administration, this book analyses the development of the Timorese

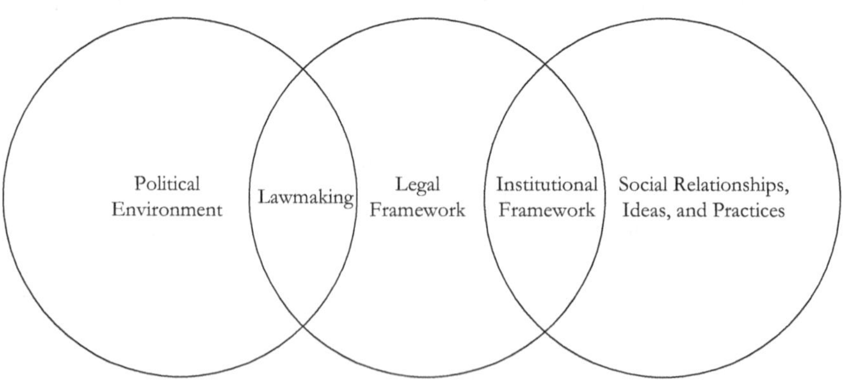

Figure 1.1 The Land Tenure System Analysis Model

formal land tenure system since the country's formal independence in 2002 until the end of 2017. This analysis pays particular attention to the problems and dilemmas of developing this system, and how this system works in practice. This analysis is relevant to better understanding the role of the state in addressing and causing land-related issues in Timor-Leste, but also contributes to the larger debate about formal land tenure systems and their role in improving people's life conditions in developing countries. Therefore, and adopting Timor-Leste as its main scenario, the main research question that guides this book is:

How did Timor-Leste develop its formal land tenure system since independence and which lessons can we learn from this for other developing countries?

The sub-questions that derive from this main question are the following:

1. What land-related problems were caused by past colonial administrations, violence, and displacement?
2. How has the Timorese formal land tenure system dealt with those land-related problems? And how has the formal land tenure system been used to promote the ambitions and visions of development of the Timorese elite?
3. How successful has the Timorese formal land tenure system been in addressing these problems, ambitions, and visions, and what have been the consequences of its implementation?
4. Which key factors contribute to the successes and failures of the Timorese formal land tenure system?
5. What lessons can be drawn from the Timorese case for other developing countries dealing with similar land-related post-colonial, post-conflict, and development problems?

Methodology

This book is the result of a socio-legal research, based on an interdisciplinary approach, which requires the use of several methods. Considering that I am a jurist by training, the easiest methodological choice would have been a legal analysis of the legal problems of the state transition and land-related legislation approved since independence. However, the value of a pure legal analysis would be, in my opinion, much lower than a social-legal approach. I recall a specific episode that strongly pushed me into a social-legal study, instead of a pure legal analysis. Some years ago I was talking with a Portuguese legal scholar that was visiting Timor-Leste for the first time, and I raised some questions about the difficulties of interpreting article 54.3 of the constitution. This article talks about 'the social function of the land', but its real meaning is not clear, and it is often mentioned by politicians and civil servants to justify unlawful dispossessions. In reply to my question this legal scholar dissertated, for several minutes, about the possible interpretations that the German Federal

Constitutional Court would have of such norm. German legal doctrine and jurisprudence has a strong influence in the Portuguese legal system, and this scholar was doing what jurists are trained to do, to find a strictly legal solution for what they see as a strictly legal problem.[6] However, after a few years of working in the country, it was obvious to me that land tenure in Timor-Leste is foremost a social, cultural, and political problem. Legislation plays a role in this problem, but law is only one piece of a very intricate puzzle. My concern was not so much the theoretical debate that a foreign court would have of the Timorese Constitution, but the context that surrounds this norm, the way it is interpreted and applied by state officials and political elites, and the consequences that it has for the Timorese. As this book shows, although land-related legislation impacts the lives of the Timorese, strictly legal research would result in a fairly empty scholarly exercise, with little contribution to understanding and addressing problems of land tenure in Timor-Leste.

Socio-legal studies involve the study of the law, legal doctrine, and jurisprudence, but also include empirical research through quantitative and qualitative methods (Banakar and Travers, 2005). I employed both qualitative and quantitative methods in this book. A considerable part of this book is based on my professional experience in Timor-Leste, which methodologically can be classified as participatory observation (Bernard, 2006: 342). As an observing participant for almost five and an half years (mid 2009 to the end of 2014), I participated in uncountable meetings, public debates, and informal talks from the highest political level to the most remote areas of Timor-Leste.[7] Becoming fairly fluent in Tetum half a year after starting to work with the MoJ was especially important for broadening my integration in the public administration and Timorese society in general, allowing me to communicate in Tetum, Portuguese, and English, depending on the forum and the interlocutors. While daily work experiences were central for forming my views and insights, social events such as weddings, funerals, Christmas parties, and meals were also excellent opportunities to learn more about the other side of the lives of the people I worked with. Car trips with DNTPSC colleagues were also great occasions to chat and learn more about their lives, and a spring of stories from old times, current gossip, stories of witchcraft, their views of Timor-Leste and the world, and a great source of knowledge about different disputes of land parcels along the road.

6 Fernandes's book (2015) is a good example of this legalistic approach. It analyses the Timorese Civil Code—a copy of the Portuguese one—in light of Portuguese legal doctrine, without ever contextualising the code within the Timorese reality or the country's complex history.

7 In practice my work involved a bit of everything: from high-level tasks, such as drafting legislation and presentations at the Council of Ministers, to the most basic tasks such as hanging up event banners or making photocopies; from expected tasks, such as writing legal opinions, to totally unexpected ones such as designing and producing TV commercials. With such a broad spectrum of activities, work was at times chaotic and frequently more about 'putting out fires' than building sustainable processes.

This participatory observation approach resulted in numerous unstructured interviews, quite often informal conversations with key stakeholders from which I made notes afterwards (Bernard, 2006: 211). However, the research is also based on several semi-structured interviews with, among others, politicians, state officials, and civil society representatives, mostly conducted during several visits to Timor-Leste since 2015. Nevertheless, my participatory observation as a government adviser and interviews with work colleagues raise some ethical difficulties that I address in the following section.

For this research I also used around 1,300 newspaper articles.[8] These are great tools to find more details about land-related cases and identify the political discourse on land. However, the Timorese press needs to be analysed with a certain degree of caution. Inexperienced and poorly paid journalists, with limited resources and targeted by political influences, often write articles that lack precision and are misleading or even not true (see also Robie, 2016: 14; IFJ, 2018: 57). I remember, for instance, that on some occasions journalists replied to invitations for an event saying that they would only cover it if transportation and some form of per diem was paid (e.g., money or phone credit). It is also well known among government advisers that distributing a press release at the end of an event would often result in a copy-paste article in the newspapers the next day. To avoid these pitfalls I triangulated information with other articles and sources, contacted informants, and used common sense and experience to assess the reliability of these articles.

Many research findings, especially about the social relationships, ideas, and social practices and the views of the Timorese about land tenure, come from the research project 'Land rights and access to land survey in Timor-Leste: a tool for evidence-based policy and advocacy', implemented by the Van Vollenhoven Institute and The Asia Foundation (Almeida and Wassel, 2016). This research project, funded by the Netherlands Ministry of Foreign Affairs and administered by the Dutch Research Council, Science for Global Development programmes (NWO-WOTRO) in collaboration with the Knowledge Platform on Security and Rule of Law, developed and implemented a pilot land survey to obtain quantitative data regarding land-related issues that were relevant for land policies and legislation, as well as supporting better-informed advocacy by civil society organisations. The inspiration for this research project came from some of my frustrations with many legislative processes in which the participants, including myself, had no access to good scientific research to support their positions (see some examples in Chapters 5 and 9). The survey, written in Tetum through a participatory process, had 126 closed questions about access to land, land use, tenure security, land-related disputes, and expropriation, mostly regarding the land where the household lives. The survey was conducted between 3 and 18 of September 2016, and a random sample of men

8 For parts of this clipping I am thankful to Januário da Silva and Meabh Cryan.

and women aged 17 and above were interviewed in representation of their households in Ainaro, Ermera, and the urban area of Dili. The Timor-Leste Research and Advocacy Network (TRAIN) provided eight enumerators, who conducted a total of 1,152 valid interviews, 384 in each of the selected areas. The sample size and the target population resulted in a 5 percent margin of error for the results which, while not representative of the entire country, allowed some extrapolation for similar areas of the country.[9]

Many findings about civil society organisations are based on my professional experiences while working at the university and as government adviser. However, I also base my findings on semi-structured interviews and two workshops about the Land Law, one in February 2016 and sponsored by The Asia Foundation, and the other in October 2017 sponsored by Oxfam, of which I was a facilitator together with Meabh Cryan. In 2018 and 2019 I also participated in a research project about the National Cadastre System (SNC) conducted by Rede ba Rai, a network of local organisations working on land issues (Rede ba Rai, 2019; see Chapter 3).

The legal part of the research is based on my extensive experience writing legal opinions during my work with the MoJ, and a combination of methods. First, I compiled and reviewed all the relevant Timorese, Indonesian, and Portuguese legislation. Second, I conducted a literature review of the (reduced) academic legal doctrine on Timor-Leste, but also from Portugal and Indonesia, the countries that most inspire the Timorese legal system. Third, I reviewed all the land-related decisions of the Court of Appeal and the district courts that I could find, 70 in total.[10] Finally, I conducted archival research at National Parliament of Timor-Leste, looking for preparatory documents, early drafts, and minutes of debates of the constitution and other relevant legislation. Unfortunately the Council of Ministers, where much of the relevant legislation is approved, does not have an open and organised archive as the parliament.

Ethical considerations

After working for many years with a British development project in India, the anthropologist David Mosse used that experience to write an ethnography on international development, which earned him strong criticism from some of his co-workers, managers, and project funders (Mosse, 2006). As with Mosse, my research also comes from an insider's position, and while this book does not intend to be an ethnography of the Timorese public administration and political world, I was aware of the sensitivity of my research since I wrote my

9 The full questionnaire and results of the survey can be obtained from the authors upon request.

10 Most of these decisions were downloaded from the website of the Court of Appeal (http://www.tribunais.tl), and others were given to me by different people.

first research proposal in 2012. While the role of insider gives one privileged access to otherwise closed worlds, it also challenges the position of researchers in assessing which data they can or should use, where researchers must reflect on the level of consent given by their colleagues/participants and pounder on the impact that their research will have on the social relationships developed, and on their object of study. As described by Mosse, 'the same boundaries that kept us out [keep] us *in*' (2006: 936). To avoid the same problems experienced by Mosse, I took several measures to prevent harming colleagues and to protect information that should not be shared.

First, I informed my close colleagues and hierarchical superiors of my intentions of starting a PhD about the Timorese formal land tenure system and the work of the Timorese administration. From time to time I made a point of bringing up my research in conversation, and I made sure that my hierarchical superiors met one of my supervisors when he visited Timor-Leste in 2014.

Second, I deliberately omitted certain details of episodes described in this book that I observed during my professional experience in Timor-Leste. Names, specific professional positions and affiliations, exact locations, and documents outside the public realm that could somehow harm participants if they were identified or reveal confidential information are not included in the description of many events. I also excluded some episodes due to their sensitivity. There are events in which I provide more information because they were reported by the media, happened in public forums, or the interviewees and informants were keen to mention them during interviews and even provided me with supporting documents. However, even in such situations, I weighed the advantages of providing very specific details against the possible harm that publishing them could bring to the people involved. Finally, the decision on what details to include was also considered in light of their contribution to describing the processes, influences, and difficulties of building the Timorese formal land tenure system.

Third, I carefully considered when to interview specific people. I was not confident that a few of my interviewees would fully understand my parallel roles as a government adviser and an academic researcher, and I worried that this confusion may lead them to provide information that they ultimately would not want to, nor were allowed to, share. As a result, until I finished my role as government adviser, I only formally interviewed people who I was confident could clearly understand my two roles. Only from 2015 onwards, after I finished my work with the MoJ, did I conduct more interviews, and in these cases I made a point of restating my role as researcher. However, it was at times difficult to assess whether interviewees were being open with me because of my skills as a researcher, or if our previous relationship of trust, developed during my time working at MoJ, was leading them to say more than they may have otherwise intended. For this reason, there are several interviewees whose names I do not include, and whose work positions I opted to only generically refer to.

Finally, as happened with Mosse, there is the risk that personal relationships I developed during my work with MoJ are affected because of my research. Here, I found that the best way to address this issue is to try, as much as possible, to put myself in other people's positions and reflect on factors that led to certain decisions, behaviours, and actions. Trying to show the less visible side of each person's position is important for understanding the topics discussed in this book, but also for giving these people a voice in the research. A second step that I took to address the issues arising from the insider's position was to debate with some of my interviewees the conclusions of my research. Finally, I translated the summary of my research into Tetum to make it accessible for my participants who do not speak English. Nevertheless, in line with Mosse, I concluded that there is no set of guidelines that can completely address all ethical issues that come up with writing and publishing research from the insider's perspective, and researchers must be ready to deal with the critiques and ruptures that their work may cause.

Limitations of the research

As in any research, this book has a few limitations that I should acknowledge upfront. Delimiting the scope of this book was probably one of the biggest challenges. Understanding the development of the Timorese formal land tenure system implies deep knowledge about different legal frameworks (i.e., Timor-Leste, Indonesia, and Portugal at least), several areas of study (e.g., law, anthropology, sociology), and different topics (e.g., land tenure, development, public administration, law-making, expropriation). Banakar and Travers alert to the risk of legal scholars engaged in socio-legal research spreading 'their intellectual resources too thin[ly]' over too many areas of knowledge and too many debates (2005: 2), a problem that I felt throughout the research. Each step opened the door for new topics, new theories, and new areas of study, leaving me with the feeling that each chapter of this book deserves its own book. Furthermore, key areas of land administration by the state such as land-use planning, land development, and taxation are not addressed in this book. The solution was to acknowledge that, as an overview and analysis of the development process of the Timorese formal land tenure system, the book would have to incorporate all the key elements that can explain this process but not go as deep as I wanted in any of them. Therefore, a limitation of this book is the depth of each of its chapters, which all deserve further and deeper study.

Another limitation of this book is the narrow analysis of customary land tenure systems. For centuries these systems have been ruling a considerable part of land tenure in Timor-Leste, rather independently of the state and its formal land tenure system, and they are the only systems that a considerable part of the Timorese ever interacted with. Therefore, to understand land tenure in

Timor-Leste it is necessary to understand these systems. However, the focus of the research is on the formal land tenure system. I briefly mention the main characteristics of the customary land tenure systems and the way the formal land tenure system deals with them, but I do not explore their characteristics in detail.

While I think that my position as an insider gave me a perspective and opened certain doors otherwise difficult to achieve, it also brought limitations to my research. For instance, there were a few people that, knowing about my previous role as government adviser, refused to be interviewed. There were also several land-related cases and facts that, while relevant for this book, due to specific episodes of my professional intervention in their formation (both in favour and against), I do not analyse them as deeply as I would like. Finally, due to my deep involvement in the development of the Timorese formal land tenure system, at times it was impossible to remain completely emotionally neutral and objective in my analysis, which is maybe visible in some parts of the book (see here Herzfeld, 2001: 262; Crewe and Axelby, 2013: 38).

Outline

Chapters 2 and 3 play an introductory role in this book. Based on a literature review, Chapter 2 defines the main concepts used throughout the book, and provides an overview of the roles, problems, and dilemmas of formal land tenure systems, highlighting the main academic debates around these topics. Chapter 3 provides the background information necessary to understand land tenure and land tenure systems in Timor-Leste. The first part of the chapter gives a geographical, sociological, and historical overview of the country, and the second part summarises the main steps in the development of formal land tenure systems in Timor-Leste, before and after independence.

It is from Chapter 4 onwards that the framework debated above provides a structure to the book. Chapter 4 looks at the political environment in which the Timorese formal land tenure system is being developed. The first part of this chapter looks at the views of land tenure from the main political parties; the connections between 'development', high-modernistic ideologies, infrastructure, and investment; and finally, the post-authoritarianism and the authoritarian temptation that has marked the country since independence. The second part of the chapter focuses on contextual factors that further influence the political environment. Those are the rule of law; the Indonesian land administration's legacy; corruption, rent-seeking, clientelism, patronage, and elite capture; the affluence of natural resources, oil dependency, and the resource curse; the post-colonial debates; past conflict and potential for violence; and finally the resilience and prevalence of customary land tenure systems.

Chapter 5 analyses the law-making process of key legislation for the Timorese formal land tenure system. This chapter starts by debating the theoretical framework that can better guide this analysis, followed by a description of the main steps in the approval of key Timorese land-related legislation. After this, Chapter 5 focuses on key elements of the law-making process which include the legislative agenda; the knowledge for the law-making process; decision-making; the legal drafters; consultation and transparency mechanisms; drafting options and dilemmas; monitoring and evaluation; and finally, language.

Chapter 6 looks at the legal framework of the Timorese formal land tenure system, describing its main characteristics but also gaps and inconsistencies. The first part of this chapter focuses on topics covered by the fairly recent Land Law, such as the validity of pre-independence land rights; the recognition of customary land rights; long-term possession; state land; land rights of legal entities; and the administrative processes for the identification of formal land rights. The second part of this chapter provides an overview of other relevant topics on land tenure, including a brief overview of formal land rights, and the mechanisms for acquisition and loss of land rights (i.e., transfers, adverse possession, and expropriation).

Chapter 7 dissects the institutions responsible for implementing the Timorese formal land tenure system, with a special focus on DNTPSC. A second part of the chapter briefly describes other institutions that also play a role in the way the formal land tenure system is implemented, including land registration projects, international organisations, and civil society organisations (CSOs) working on land-related issues.

Chapter 8 uses the above-mentioned survey to look at the social relationships, ideas, and practices that regulate land tenure on the ground. By looking at what happens on the ground, this chapter provides a picture of the role and value that, in reality, the formal land tenure system has in Timorese society and what people expect from it. This chapter specifically focuses on the relevance of customary systems; the characteristics of land rights on the ground; legal and perceived land tenure security; land titling; land-related disputes and dispute resolution; and views on development and right to expropriate land.

Chapter 9 describes the case study of the Suai Supply Base. This case study shows how the analytical themes described in previous chapters interact with each other in practice, how these interactions shape the norms, institutions, and practices of the formal land tenure system, and how this system impacts land tenure on the ground.

Chapter 10 provides the conclusions and reflections of this book, as well as a few recommendations and suggestions for future research.

Chapter 2

Formal land tenure systems

Introduction

Land tenure and land tenure systems have been studied by many scholars and practitioners in several fields of study and from very different perspectives. Before taking a deeper look at the case of Timor-Leste, this chapter defines the main concepts used throughout this book and, based on a literature review and examples from other countries, analyses the various roles that formal land tenure systems play in society and the problems and dilemmas that states experience in their implementation. The first part of this chapter focuses on definitions. The second part debates the roles of formal land tenure system, and the third part debates the problems and dilemmas that come with these roles.

Formal land tenure systems and other definitions

Concepts such as land tenure and land tenure systems are used in the literature with very different, and sometimes even contradictory, meanings. It is therefore important to clarify the definition of key concepts used in this book (Shipton, 2001: 8256).[1]

The central object of the book is *land*, a concept that I use to refer to specific parcels of the ground and all structures and plants permanently attached to it, in line with the definition of immovable property established by the Timorese Civil Code (see Serrão, 2014: 7). *Land tenure* is used in this book to mean the legal or non-legal connection that individuals, groups, legal entities, and the state have with land, and which gives them the possibility of holding and benefiting from it, to the exclusion (either in a limited sense or broadly) of others (see FAO, 2002: 7). In other words, land tenure refers to the socially recognised power, independent of its source, to obtain access, hold, and avail of a certain parcel of land, as well as transfer that power to others (Durand-Lasserve

1 My legal background and the civil law basis of the Timorese legal framework played a role in my choice of definitions.

DOI: 10.4324/9781003196396-2

and Selod, 2007: 4; Ubink, 2009: 11; Augustinus, 2010: 171). Others have referred to this as 'land control' (Peluso and Lund, 2011: 668).

Land tenure is expressed through *land rights*, a set of rights and obligations related to land, granted by state law or other source of social control, such as customary norms (Barry, 2015: 5; see also Bruce, 2012: 49).[2] The 'bundle of rights' metaphor is here relevant to clarify the definition of land rights. According to this metaphor, the collection of all possible rights and obligations connected to a property can be grouped in a bundle of 'sticks' (Benda-Beckmann *et al.*, 2006: 15; Delville, 2010: 34; Barry, 2015: 14).[3] The number of 'sticks' (i.e., rights and obligations) in each land right varies, and can change with time, space, and the source that legitimates them. When I mention a *land right*, I am referring to a set of rights and obligations, out of the bundle of all possible rights and obligations. It is possible to have as many land rights as the combinations of rights and obligations (e.g., ownership, usufruct).[4] In some cases, the rights and obligations that compose a land right are pre-established and very well defined; in other cases, land rights are vague and undetermined or are dependent on other rights and obligations. Typically, the land rights based on state law have their bundle of rights and obligations pre-established and are more clearly defined when compared with land rights coming from other sources of authority (e.g., customary systems), but this is not always true. Furthermore, the bundle of rights and obligations over one piece of land can be distributed through more than one person or entity. For instance ownership, usually the strongest land right, can be limited by rights of others such as an encumbrance.

Instead of land rights, some authors use the expression *property rights* (e.g., Deininger, 2003: 22; Benda-Beckmann *et al.*, 2006: 15; Bruce and Holt, 2011: 13), but in my experience this expression is a source of confusion. When authors use the expression *property rights*, they refer to all possible combinations of rights and obligations over land, not necessarily to ownership (Bruce, 1998: 2). However, both the phonetics and spelling of this expression are very similar to *propriété*, *propiedad*, and *propriedade* in French, Spanish, and Portuguese, which mean ownership or freehold.[5] Civil law jurists working with these languages often misinterpret 'property rights' as ownership rights, which becomes a source of confusion (Erp, 2015; Graziadei, 2017; Praduroux, 2017: 53). To avoid this confusion, I use *land rights* instead of property rights to refer to any

2 Barry uses the expression 'land interests' to include both land rights and land claims (2015: 5).

3 The original name of this metaphor—'bundle of rights and duties'—is more accurate because it includes the benefits but also the obligations that come with land rights (Maine, 1861:192; Barry, 2015: 14). Other authors like Ribot and Peluso prefer instead the expression 'bundle of powers' (2003: 158).

4 See a sample list of rights in FAO, 2002: 10.

5 https://dicionario.priberam.org/propriedade; https://dle.rae.es/?id=UOknpDg; www.larousse.fr/dictionnaires/francais/propri%C3%A9t%C3%A9/64421?q=propri%C3%A9t%C3%A9#63694.

specific bundle of rights and obligations over land, independent of its source of authority (FAO, 2002: 46).

A *land tenure system* is a set of norms, institutions, and practices that regulate land tenure (FAO, 2002: 7; Dekker, 2005: 240; Bruce, 2017: 1).[6] A land tenure system originates in some source of authority, and regulates how one can obtain, avail of, and transfer land rights; the characteristics of different land rights; and the institutions of allocation, recognition, and control of the connection that one has with land. Depending on the characteristics of the land tenure system, which other authors call property regimes (Benda-Beckmann *et al.*, 2006: 3), this set of norms, institutions, and practices can be clearly pre-established and defined, or can be more fluid and undefined.

The distinction between formal land tenure system and informal land tenure system is central for this book. With *formal land tenure system*, I refer to norms, institutions, and practices regulating land tenure that are created or recognised as having legal value by the legal framework of the state (Benjaminsen *et al.*, 2008: 28). By contrast, an *informal land tenure system* is a set of norms, institutions, and practices, with a source of legitimacy other than the state, and not recognised by the state's legal framework. In between these two types of land tenure systems there are *semi-formal land tenure systems*, which, despite not having any legal basis, involve the participation of state officials and institutions (Widman, 2015: 112). In semi-formal land tenure systems, the participation of state officials issuing 'official' documents, and a certain consistency in the practices they follow, creates among the people that use these systems an illusion of legality (see Benjaminsen *et al.*, 2008: 30).[7] Formal, semi-formal, and informal land tenure systems can coexist and even compete with each other. It is also possible that, for instance, in times of crisis, there is no land tenure system, and access to and use of land tenure is not based on norms and institutions, but solely on the use of force. Finally, as this book well exemplifies, the distinction between formal, semi-formal, and informal systems does not imply that formal is somehow superior or better organised than the other types (Barry, 2015: 10).

At this point it is important to make some clear distinctions. First, an informal land tenure system and a customary land tenure system are not the same thing. By *informal system* I refer to land tenure systems that have no recognition from state laws. By *customary land tenure system*, I mean a land tenure system that is based on norms, institutions, and practices which are developed outside of the state systems but are nevertheless recognised and followed by a group of

6 The word 'system' refers to a set of parts, in this case norms, institutions, and practices, that work together to provide a certain function, in this case managing land tenure (Barry and Fourie, 2001: 4).

7 See the case of Angola, where in some peri-urban areas a network of public officials and institutions provide documentation that is used by the people for securing and transferring land rights, but with no legal basis to support them (Unruh, 2012: 662; Waldorff, 2016: 364). These systems provide some order and security, but can be suddenly disrupted if the law is enforced or public officials are replaced.

people.[8] In this definition, the expression 'customary' does not refer necessarily to a traditional, old, static or very slowly changing practice; rather, a customary system can be recent and fast-changing. Also, at least in my definition, customary systems are not necessarily limited to rural areas, they can also exist in peri-urban and urban areas (see Santos, 1977). Other authors use other expressions such as 'community-based systems', 'indigenous', or 'traditional rights' (Cotula, 2013; Wily, 2016: 68; see also Benda-Beckmann, 2001: 5705). While in many states customary systems have no recognition by state laws, and therefore these systems are informal, in other cases customary land tenure systems—or at least some of them—are incorporated into state laws and are therefore enforceable by public authority, even against the state.[9] In those cases customary land tenure systems become part of the formal land tenure system. Moreover, the incorporation of a customary land tenure system into the national legal framework does not imply the codification of customary norms; it is enough that the state considers these customary norms applicable and enforceable (Fitzpatrick, 2005: 457; Wily, 2016: 68). In conclusion, customary land tenure systems can be, but are not necessarily, informal (Dekker, 2005: 81).

Another important distinction is between customary tenure and communal tenure (Bruce, 2012: 35). The expression *communal tenure* has been used in the literature to represent different realities, and it is a source of much confusion (Shlager and Ostrom, 1992: 249; Hoekema, 2012: 138). The expression is used to refer to: (1) land that can be used and availed of in open access by everyone; (2) land that is availed of collectively by a community; (3) land that is shared by a more determined group of individuals; or (4) situations in which land tenure is regulated by customary norms (Dekker, 2005: 161; Otto and Hoekema, 2012: 11). In this book, *communal tenure* refers to those situations in which land is availed of collectively by a community. The expression *customary tenure* refers to situations in which land tenure has its origins in a customary land tenure system. A customary land tenure system can, and often does, include communal tenure of some parcels of land, but also individual tenure (Delville, 2010: 86, Wily, 2017: 462). A final distinction is regarding the concept of *individual tenure*, which does not necessarily refer to a Western-like ownership or freehold right, but to any combination of rights and obligations over land of which one person is the beneficiary (Atwood, 1990: 662).

These different concepts of land tenure systems differ from the concept of tenure itself, which can also be divided into formal, semi-formal, and informal types (Reerink, 2011: 15). *Formal tenure*, which is also called legal, formal, or *de jure* right, refers to a specific land right that is recognised and protected by a formal land tenure system (Schlager and Ostrom, 1992: 254; FAO, 2002:

8 Cotula, 2007: 10; Otto, 2007: 36; Peters and Ubink, 2015: 294; Wily, 2017: 461.

9 See, for instance, the example of Ghana in Ubink and Quan, 2008, Mozambique in Tanner, 2002: 28, and Angola in Waldorff, 2016.

45; Barry, 2015: 5). By contrast, *informal tenure*, also called informal or *de facto* rights refers to those cases in which a specific tenure is recognised and protected by an informal land tenure system but not by state law (Schlager and Ostrom, 1992: 254; FAO, 2002: 45).[10] The *semi-formal tenure* is an intermediate category that refers to those cases in which land tenure is not fully recognised and protected by state law, but at least in theory can be converted into formal land tenure (e.g., land in the process of titling). This intermediate definition of semi-formal land tenure allows us to see formality and informality along a continuum (Reerink, 2011: 15; Barry, 2015: 18).

The expression *formalisation* refers to the process through which informal tenure receives recognition by, and therefore protection from, the formal land tenure system (Duran-Lasserve and Selod, 2007: 7; Benjaminsen *et al.*, 2008: 28; Bruce, 2012: 39; Hall, 2013: chap. 5, para. 4).[11] Formalisation is often done through processes that clearly identify the beneficiaries and their respective land parcels (e.g., land registration), but the legal recognition of land tenure by the formal land tenure system can be rather undetermined (see here Wily, 2016: 71). For instance, a law establishing that people occupying state land for more than ten years have the right to remain on that land formalises the land tenure of these occupants, without identifying them nor the parcels they occupy.[12] Importantly, formalisation must not be confused with processes of individualisation or privatisation (Durand-Lasserve and Selod, 2007: 28; Hall, 2013: chap. 5 para. 5).

Land registration, land titling, and land title are three concepts connected with the formalisation process that must be defined to avoid confusion. *Land registration* refers to the process of recording land rights in a public registry, with the registration giving a legal advantage to its beneficiary (FAO, 2002: 46; Dekker, 2005: 240). In different systems, these legal advantages given by registration vary (e.g., incontestable rights or a legal presumption of ownership), as do the approach to registration (e.g., mandatory or optional) and the information that is registered (e.g., some include maps of parcels, others not). In this book, land registration differs from *land titling*, which is the process through which land titles are issued, either on a case-by-case basis or as part of a larger-scale systematic approach. Land titling is often conducted together with land registration, but those activities are not the same and can happen separately. The concept of land title is a source of confusion. Some people

10 Informal tenure does not necessarily mean less-secure tenure (Delville, 2006). See the definition of tenure security below. Some authors use expressions such as 'informal settlers' to refer to cases where houses and other constructions are built without a construction permit or against spatial planning (Duran-Lasserve and Selod, 2007: 6). I do not use the expression 'informal' in that sense in this book.

11 Other authors prefer the expression 'legalisation' (Ubink, 2009: 31), but formalisation avoids this idea that all land tenure that is not recognised by state law is illegal (Bruce, 2012: 34).

12 See the case of Mozambique in Norfolk and Tanner, 2007: 8; McAuslan, 2013: 76.

refer to a land title as the land right that is represented and proved by a document. Others, like myself, define *land title* as the document through which a land right is legally obtained or acknowledged by the legal system, but it is different from the right that it represents.[13] I prefer this second definition because it better represents those situations in which one person or entity has a land right but no document to prove it (e.g., adverse possession without judicial recognition).

A *land registry* or *land register* is an official database where the legal information about land rights is compiled, while a *land cadastre* is a database that contains the geographical description and other relevant information of land parcels, obtained through *cadastral surveys* (FAO, 2002: 44; Deininger, 2003: 118). The cadastre can be incorporated as part of a land registry and can be developed together with a process of land registration, but can also be developed and exist separately from the land registry, for instance for urban planning.

The concept of *land tenure security* can be defined as the protection that land holders have against involuntary removal, and/or the loss of benefits they derive from their land, caused by the state or other persons' intervention, unless due to legal process and adequate compensation (Kanji *et al.*, 2005: 3; Delville, 2006: 29; Reerink, 2011: 1). However, the concept of tenure security can be vague and lead to misunderstandings. In this book I use two sub-concepts of tenure security that further clarify the concept. First, I use *legal tenure security* to refer to the recognition and protection that state law gives to land holders. The second sub-concept is *perceived tenure security*, which refers to land holders feeling that their land tenure is secure (Reerink, 2011: 15). For instance, in a slum area that is de facto ruled by an informal land tenure system, the land holders might not have formal land rights and therefore no legal protection in case of dispossession (i.e., low legal tenure security), but in practice do not fear being displaced by the state or others (i.e., high perceived tenure security). Strangely, while the definitions and solutions for tenure security are profusely discussed in the academic literature, the origin of tenure insecurity is rarely considered (see here Fitzpatrick, 2005: 471). For the sake of this book, I divide the threats to tenure security into public and private, depending on whether the threat is caused by state institutions or private parties (see Reerink, 2011: 2).[14]

The concept of tenure security should not be confused with *precarious tenure*, which refers to the expectation of continuing a specific land tenure through

13 The expression 'obtained or acknowledged' is used deliberately. A land right can be obtained, for instance, through sale, and in that case the land title is the notarised deed that transfers the right between the buyer and seller. But a land title can also recognise an already acquired right, for instance a court decision that acknowledges an acquisition through adverse possession.

14 The concept of the continuum of land rights has been increasingly used but also contested by academics and practitioners (Ubink, 2009: 13; Whittal, 2014). Because this concept is not used throughout the book, I do not debate it further.

the short, medium, and long-term (Delville, 2006: 29). Following Delville's example, a farmer that accesses land through annual land leases can have strong tenure security—a certainty that those one-year leases will not be breached—but this tenure remains precarious because the farmer never knows if the lease will be renewed the following year. Another relevant distinction is between tenure security and *tenure certainty*, which can be defined as the possibility of determining which land rights exist over a certain parcel of land, and who their beneficiaries are (see here Lund, 2000: 15).

All definitions established above are related to land tenure, but land tenure is only one of the four main areas which authors have identified as part of land administration (Deininger and Enemark, 2010: sec. 2 para. 6; UN Habitat, 2012: 3). According to these authors, *land administration* can be divided into: (1) *land tenure*; (2) *land value*; (3) *land use*; and (4) *land development*.

A *land administration system* is a set of norms, institutions, and practices that control the different areas of land administration. While some authors use land administration and *land governance* interchangeably (Borras Jr. and Franco, 2010: 2), others make a distinction between these two concepts. For them, land governance goes beyond the more technical side of land administration, and also includes the development and improvement of policies, processes, laws, and state-society relations (Otto and Hoekema, 2012: 11; Enemark *et al.*, 2014: 13). In this book I use the two terms interchangeably to refer to this second broader definition.

There are two final concepts in this book that are important to define. The first one is *territory*, which is used to refer to the land where a state has its political authority, but also the land that provides identity to that state (Lund, 2008: 69; Hall, 2013: chap. 1, para. 15; Wolford *et al.* 2013: 10). The second relevant definition is *frontier*, which refers to areas over which, despite being integrated in the territory of a state, the state's political authority is exercised either weakly or not at all (Hall, 2013: chap. 3, para. 1; Fitzpatrick *et al.*, 2013: 64). In these areas there is little or no state representation, limited governing and justice structures, and limited control of local activities. It does not mean that the state has no influence in frontier areas, it only means that its political authority is not the primary source of ruling in those areas (Fitzpatrick *et al.*, 2013: 64). However, while the expression is used to refer to a lack of state administration and control, it does not mean that frontier areas are wild and unregulated places, as often these areas have informal mechanisms of social control (Li, 2014: introduction, para. 33).

The roles of land and formal land tenure systems

Virtually all countries in the world have a formal land tenure system. The characteristics and effectiveness of these systems vary considerably from country to country, but all states try, to a certain extent, to regulate and control land tenure. Even in those countries where customary systems play a relevant role regulating land tenure, state authorities attempt to have the last word regarding who has which land rights. This raises the question: why do states care about developing formal land tenure systems?

Based on a literature review, and referring to examples from several countries, this section starts by briefly looking at the characteristics of land and the roles that it plays in people's lives. Next, it looks into the role of formal land tenure systems in the goals of states, followed by the roles of these systems regarding state power.[15] This analysis provides the theoretical foundations for the rest of the book.

The characteristics and roles of land

Land plays a central role in a considerable part of human activity, serving many individual and collective purposes (Shipton, 1994: 349; Hall, 2013: chap. 1, para. 12; Cotula, 2016: 186). First, land is necessary for subsistence, housing, and economic production through agriculture, industry, and services. Second, land is also used for capital accumulation, and it is a source of political and social power (Platteau, 1996: 53; Bruce, 2012: 32; Kerssen, 2013: intro. para. 28). In many cases land is also an element of social identity, spiritual connection, and kinship (Lund 2011: 72; Joireman and Brown, 2013: 166; Dehaibi 2015: 19). Finally, land is necessary for environmental sustainability; the conservation of eco-systems is in part dependent on leaving large tracks of land free from many human activities (Hall *et al.*, 2011: 8). Whether conducted in a more collective or individual way, all these human activities are somehow dependent on access and control of land.

However, land is a limited resource and the use of land by some users for a specific purpose excludes other users and other purposes (Hall *et al.*, 2011: 4, 7). There are examples of shared uses of land and technological innovations that allow for multi-purpose uses, such as communal plantations and multi-story buildings. But even in these cases only a limited number of uses can be combined, and a limited number of users can benefit from that land to the exclusion of others. If land is abundant, the uses and users can be reconciled more easily. But when land becomes scarcer, competition for land becomes stronger, and the need for social ordering mechanisms is more acute (Atwood, 1990: 668). Furthermore, as discussed in more detail below, the visions regarding priorities for the use of land vary substantially. Under the current trends of rapid world population growth, urbanisation, and demand for farmland, competition for land and debate about its priority uses are even more prominent (Deininger and Enemark, 2010: sec. 2 para. 4; Cotula, 2012: 57). As described in the following section, one role of formal land tenure systems is to mediate this competition for land.

15 I deliberately left the literature about Timor-Leste for the following chapters.

Land tenure, formal land tenure systems, and the goals of the state

If we take the assumption that a key goal of the state is to promote a better life for its citizens, one first explanation for the interest states have in formal land tenure systems is that they want to use these systems to improve people's living conditions. Land scarcity generates competition that, once intense enough, needs to be mediated to avoid conflict and to promote an optimal balance between competing private and collective users and uses of land. States want to have the last word in this balance and, through it, promote a better life for its citizens. However, this idea raises a few questions: (1) can states improve people's lives through formal land tenure systems? And (2) do states really want to improve people's living conditions? This section provides some clues to answer these questions.

To respond the first question, I refer to Otto's list of nine key problems that countries must deal with, the goals for each of those problems, and the respective processes for development through which they can be addressed (2009: 190). This list provides a good summary of the main problems that all states must deal with, and interestingly, out of the nine problems Otto identifies, land tenure and land tenure systems play a role both in causing and addressing five of them.

The first problem identified by Otto is insecurity. Competing interests over scarce land are an obvious source of conflict and physical insecurity for the people. For instance, in Afghanistan it is reported that 57 percent of the disputes brought to formal dispute resolution mechanisms are related to land (The Asia Foundation, 2017: 114). By establishing rules about access and rights over land, and providing the mechanisms for a calm resolution of land-related disputes, a formal land tenure system has the potential to decrease and prevent land-related conflict and promote public order (Deininger, 2003: 25). However, in the same way that a formal land tenure system can reduce land-related conflict, it can also create it. For instance, a change in the existing legal framework or a new formalisation process can reignite dormant conflicts (Lund, 2008; Hall, 2013: chap. 5 para. 16; Kerssen, 2013, chap. 3 para 4). Furthermore, for many people land is their most valuable asset and their only source of livelihood (Cotula, 2012: 57; Deininger *et al.*, 2012: 15); losing their land puts their survival at risk, and therefore their reaction to a threat can be quite violent (Shipton, 1994: 347). For instance, dispossession without fair compensation of rural farmers in China, for urbanisation and industry, has led to massive protests against the government (Cao *et al.*, 2008: 22). These examples show that a formal land tenure system can promote security, as well as conflict and instability.

Land tenure is also connected with poverty, the second social problem identified by Otto. As mentioned above, land is necessary for several human activities, including subsistence, housing, and economic production. Even when not intensively exploited, land works for many people as a 'social insurance' against shortages in the labour market (Platteau, 1996: 51; Anderson, 2013: 221). Without some form of access to land, one cannot obtain food and shelter, and most forms of economic production cannot happen. However, while authors and political actors agree that the formal land tenure system can have a central role in promoting prosperity, the configuration in which the land tenure system will achieve that prosperity has been at the heart of most political and economic debates of the last centuries (World Bank, 1975; De Soto, 2000; Deininger, 2003).

In general terms, with the 'victory of capitalism' over communism, the debate is now between those who advocate that the formal land tenure system should serve the neoliberal agenda, and those who caution about the dangers of these views and advocate for alternative paths (Ganti, 2014: 94). In short, neoliberal ideology sees the free market and the private sector as the drivers of prosperity, and 'a condition to which societies naturally progress' (Harvey, 2005: 7; Young, 2011; Crewe and Axelby, 2013: 159). Under a neoliberal agenda, the main objective of a formal land tenure system is the commodification of land to make it available for economic production by a self-regulated market. However, these policies rely on the belief that markets can self-regulate and ignore other roles of land besides economic production (Borras Jr., 2006: 111; Courville and Patel, 2006: 8; Hall *et al.*, 2011: 11). The commodification of land, economic growth (at least for some), and the appetite for controlling land promoted by neoliberal views of the world strongly resonate with the practices and justifications for land tenure systems developed by colonial regimes (Borras Jr. *et al.*, 2011: 209; Peluso and Lund, 2011: 672; Zoomers, 2013: 69). This topic is further debated below.

In developing countries, where globalisation has been strongly influencing changes in formal land tenure systems, neoliberal policies have been implemented in the last decades, often with disastrous results for large groups of people (Crewe and Axelby, 2013: 161; Zoomers, 2013: 68; Dehaibi, 2015: 1). Under neoliberal policies, economic growth becomes the main role of land that states care about, and concentration of wealth in elites is a consequence—if not an understated objective—of neoliberalism (Borras Jr., 2006: 116; Hall *et al.*, 2011: 11; Peluso and Lund, 2011: 672; Kerssen, 2013). For instance, the transfer of control over extensive parcels of land to large corporations, especially in Africa and Asia, justified by neoliberal views of the role of land, has been quite harmful to the livelihoods of local populations and has exacerbated other fragilities of these countries, such as corruption and weak institutions (Borras Jr. *et al.*, 2011; Cotula, 2013; Hall, 2013; Hall, 2013a; Wolford *et al.*, 2013). But there are countless examples; for instance, Stead shows how, in Papua New Guinea, the planning of large-scale industrial investments chronically ignores customary-based land rights and the informal economy that those projects will necessarily destroy (2016: 107). In conclusion, formal tenure systems play a central role in the economy of a country, but in the same way they can stimulate economic growth, they can also contribute to the impoverishment of people.

Connected with economic growth is the third problem identified by Otto: inequality. The way a formal land tenure system recognises and protects land rights can be a major source of inequality, and activities such as formalisation can be used to give further legitimacy to, or even expand situations of, social injustice—a process that Borras Jr. and Franco call *formalisation of inequality* (Borras Jr. and Franco, 2010: 19). On the other hand, well-adjusted land tenure systems can promote redistribution and more equality, both directly through determination of land rights, and indirectly through taxation. The various movements of land reform for a more egalitarian distribution of land rights, although with various approaches and different degrees of success, are clear examples of the use of the formal land tenure system for a more equal society (Borras Jr., 2006; Courville and Patel, 2006). But there are other examples. For instance, authors argue that taxes over inheritances and/or land rights are mechanisms through which land administration and a formal land tenure system can also contribute to more equality (Piketty, 2014). In fact, taxation is pointed out by authors as one of the main incentives for states developing land registration schemes (Scott, 1998: 3).[16]

In combination with economic growth, the role of the formal land tenure system in promoting or hindering social justice and equality has been a central topic of the main political debates of the last centuries, including movements against colonialism, the clashes between socialist and capitalist ideologies, and land reform movements (see Shipton, 2001: 8256; Berry, 2002). The end of colonial projects or the triumph of capitalist political views did not remove land tenure from the political agenda; in recent decades, state-led dispossession for 'development' and movements to protect customary and communal rights to land have again raised the debate about the role of formal land tenure systems in promoting and hindering social justice (Borras Jr., 2006; Wolford *et al.* 2013: 8). For instance, the successive changes in Mexico's land tenure system during the last century—which varied between the *hacienda* system, the protection of the communal *ejidos*, and the promotion of privatisation—are exemplary of the political struggles around the role of land tenure systems as a promoter of equality (Assies and Duhau, 2009).

The destruction of nature is the fourth social problem identified by Otto in which formal land tenure systems play a role (see Deininger, 2003: 41; Shipton, 2001: 8260). The Indonesian Basic Forestry Law from 1967 provides here a good example. In theory, the state monopoly of ownership of the forest established by this law would promote better environmental protection.

16 Research has shown that countries with more egalitarian distribution of land tend to have higher levels of economic growth (Deininger, 2003: 19).

In practice, this contributed little, or even helped deforestation, with the state giving large concessions for logging and agribusiness over areas inhabited by local communities (Bedner, 2016: 70; Krishna *et al.*, 2017: 346). Furthermore, as happened in other countries, this use of the formal land tenure system for conservation initiatives also resulted in weaker legal tenure security, displacement, and loss of livelihoods of local people (Bedner and Huis, 2008: 181; see also Lund, 2008: 142; Li, 2009: 71; Kersen, 2013: chap. 9 para. 1).

The final social problem identified by Otto in which land plays a central role is cultural, and I would also add, social estrangement. For some people land is a fungible asset, with an economic and functional value (e.g., housing), but the asset itself does not have any personal relevance, it can be replaced by any other asset with similar economic value and function. However, in other cases land is part of people's social and self-identity; their view of themselves individually or collectively is intrinsically connected to specific land areas (Platteau, 1996: 51). For some people land is an element of spiritual connection and an integral part of their kin, and loss of their land would result in cultural estrangement (Radin 1993: 71; Lund 2011: 72; Joireman and Brown, 2013: 166; Dehaibi, 2015: 19). But even when this cultural connection with land does not exist, the loss of land can give origin to social estrangement. For instance, large-scale evictions and expropriations often break social networks by physically separating families, long-term neighbours and community members, therefore contributing to their social estrangement (Miltin and Bicknell, 1994: 3; UN Habitat and UNHCR, 2014: 25, 33).

The formal land tenure system can help prevent this cultural and social estrangement by recognising special rights over land and acknowledging cultural and social connections as values that deserve to be protected. The approval of international declarations and treaties regarding indigenous peoples' land rights and their incorporation in and adaptation to national legal frameworks exemplify how formal land tenure systems can protect these special connections to land (Kingsbury, 1999: 326; Shipton, 2001: 8260).[17] However, formal land tenure systems can also further promote cultural and social estrangement, for instance, by allowing evictions in slum areas without taking into consideration the resulting disruption of social networks and proximity of work places (UN Habitat, 2012: 80).

Hence, in reply to the first question raised above, we can say that formal land tenure systems play an important role in addressing insecurity, poverty, inequality, destruction of nature, and cultural and social estrangement, but they can also cause or aggravate these same problems. Moreover, the role of formal land tenure systems in addressing or hindering each of these problems is further complicated by their interconnection; in many cases, the solution to one problem

17 Among others, the 1989 Indigenous and Tribal Peoples Convention (ILO 169) and the 2007 United Nations Declaration on the Rights of Indigenous Peoples.

through the formal land tenure system can aggravate another. For instance, the best way of promoting environmental protection would be to reduce as much as possible all human activity on land, but that would have impacts on economic growth. Therefore, formal land tenure systems not only have to establish a balance between uses and users of land but also between the various problems that states want to address with these systems (Zoomers, 2013: 74).

As was already hinted at above, the balance that each state prescribes for its formal land tenure system is the result of clashes between different ideologies (as defined in Chapter 1), political struggles, and contextual factors. In other words, there is no right balance; rather, it depends on the prevailing political views in the country. Moreover, one must be aware that ideological views are not static, and they are not necessarily or immediately reflected by the state's legal framework, institutions, and practices on the ground (Benda-Beckmann *et al.*, 2006: 22). Using the Land Tenure System Analysis Model described in Chapter 1 as a lens of analysis, one can see that there is often a mismatch between the political environment, the legal framework, and the social relationships, ideas, and social practices on the ground. Additionally, the formal land tenure system can evolve slowly throughout the years, or can change abruptly if there are significant shifts in the dominant state ideology (Dekker, 2005; Borras Jr. and Franco, 2010). This highlights another role of formal land tenure systems; they establish a balance between competing uses and users of land, but by doing so, they are also a tool to spread and implement the dominant political views in a country and affirm the power of the state over the people. This topic is further debated below.

The role formal land tenure systems have in improving people's lives comes with the assumption that the state and ruling elites are working in favour of everyone. By contrast, authors like Marx saw formal land tenure systems as one of the state tools at the disposal of elites to oppress others (Thompson, 2013: 202; Radin, 1993: 49; Harvey, 2004: 74; Campbell, 2015: chap. 3 para. 14). According to Marxist theory, the protection that capitalist systems give to private ownership of land and other means of production allows their accumulation by elites, separating people from land, and converting them into workers that can be exploited by the same elites (Marx, 1887: 507, 513; Hall, 2013a: 1585; Pikkety, 2014: intro. para. 25).[18] Whether Marxist theories are correct or not, it is consensual among authors that, if not by design, at least due to defects of state systems, formal land tenure systems can be abused by elites to the detriment of others. As is debated below, through manipulation, promises of a brighter future, corruption, or rent-seeking, elites often take advantage of the formal land tenure system, and states can use it as a tool of oppression.

18 The concept of 'primitive accumulation' has been reshaped by Harvey's concept of 'accumulation by dispossession' (Harvey, 2004; Hall, 2013a).

In conclusion, formal land tenure systems play a role in addressing insecurity, poverty, inequality, destruction of nature, and cultural and social estrangement, but can also cause or aggravate these same problems. The balance that each state prescribes for its formal land tenure system is the result of clashes between different ideologies, political struggles, and contextual factors, although the legislation and practices on the ground do not necessarily reflect the dominant political ideology. Furthermore, as argued below, formal land tenure systems are used to propagate the dominant ideologies, and can be used by elites for unfair personal gains and oppression of others.

Formal land tenure systems and state power

Although playing a role in achieving state goals, the implementation of formal land tenure systems is not a given. Many countries have areas of frontier inside their territories where the state's political and administrative authority is exercised only weakly or not at all (Hall, 2013: chap. 3, para. 1; Fitzpatrick *et al.*, 2013: 64). These areas can be the result of remoteness, lack of state resources, political instability and threat of violence, or even lack of political interest in those areas.[19] Using the example of Indonesia, Li argues that the fact that 65 million Indonesians live 'illegally' on state forest shows that the state cannot, or chooses not to, implement its own laws (1999: 313). This does not mean that the state is totally absent, nor that there is no authority in those areas as informal systems often take care of social ordering in these places (Li, 2014: intro. para. 33); it simply means that the state is not the dominant authority.

The implementation of formal land tenure systems is dependent on what Vandergeest and Peluso call *internal territorialisation* (Vandergeest and Peluso, 1995), a process through which the state imposes its rule on land tenure inside its territory.[20] In other words, territorialisation refers to the process through which the state enforces its formal land tenure system and therefore affirms its sovereign authority in regulating land tenure, above other sources of power, and obtains the recognition of that authority by the people under the state's authority (Peluso and Lund, 2011: 673; Wolford *et al.*, 2013: 25). In fact, considering the central role that land tenure has in people's lives, imposing the state's formal land tenure system allows the state to affirm not only its superior authority over land tenure but also its political authority in general.

Furthermore, territorialisation is not a one-off process. As said by Lund, '[t]he state is always in the making', the authority of the state is an unfinished product that has to be constantly reaffirmed (2016: 1200). By constantly exercising the

19 Regarding remote areas, see the example of the Brazilian Amazonian region described by Campbell (2015). Regarding the peripheries of the state, see Asad, 2004.

20 Lund does not limit the definition of territorialisation to the state but to any individual or group that asserts control over a geographic area (Lund, 2008: 69).

power to rule a central element of people's lives like land tenure, the state is 'governmentalising' the space (Li, 1999: 296; Foucault, 2007: 144; Peluso and Lund, 2011: 673). In fact, making public services available to frontier areas is a mechanism of state formation through which the state justifies its existence and becomes represented by these services (Li, 1999: 296; Borras Jr., 2006: 101). For instance, the use of land tenure systems to governmentalise the space was an important instrument utilised by colonial ruling to assert its power over colonised territories (Lund, 2008; 12). A formal land tenure system is an especially strong tool for this state formation because it is through it that the state carves its own space to provide state services, for instance by creating public spaces.

Formal land tenure systems are territorialised through several mechanisms: cadastral surveys, land titling, land registration, definition of state land, and land expropriation (Lund, 2016: 1205). By defining boundaries, enclosing land, recognising or denying formal land rights, allocating land, and providing conflict resolution mechanisms, the state is affirming its internal sovereignty over a certain area. By participating in a land registration process, applying for formalisation of land, obtaining documents, and using the courts to enforce formal land rights, the people are acknowledging the authority of the state over their rights to land (Cotula, 2013: chap. 4 para. 7; Campbell, 2015). As stated by Lund, 'the process of recognition works in tandem. Recognition of property rights by an institution simultaneously constitutes a process of recognition of legitimacy of this institution' (2008: 10). In conclusion, the formal land tenure system also works as a tool of legitimation and enforcement of state power. However, as described in the following sections, the exercise of this power faces many problems and dilemmas.

The problems and dilemmas of formal land tenure systems

Assuming that states and their governments work for the best interests of their peoples, the process of territorialisation should be beneficial for peoples' interests. It is this assumption that gives legitimacy to state systems. However, the literature is replete with examples where territorialisation of a formal land tenure system brought disastrous results for the people involved. Instead of the promised order, certainty, and stability, the territorialisation of formal land tenure systems often becomes in practice a source of disorder, insecurity, and uncertainty (Waldorff, 2016: 369). Based on a literature review and examples from different countries, this section debates the main problems and dilemmas that lead such systems to fail in their goal of improving people's living conditions.

Problems of formal land tenure systems

The implementation of formal land tenure systems, especially in developing countries such as Timor-Leste, often faces several interlinked problems.

Although not exhaustive, this section provides an overview of the more common problems that formal land tenure systems face. This overview is divided into three main categories: (1) ideological problems; (2) conceptual problems; and (3) practical problems.

Ideological problems

A first group of problems of a formal land tenure system is related with the ideology that informs it. As discussed above, the dominant political ideology of a state (as defined in Chapter 1) and other contextual factors shape the balance that, through the formal land tenure system, ruling elites aspire to establish between the interests of different land users, land uses, and problems that need to be addressed. This balance always implies some trade-offs that will please certain groups and displease others, which is a normal condition of life in society. However, at times these trade-offs fail to find an acceptable balance and can become problematic, due to the acute inequalities that they cause to most of society, or to specific minority groups.

The failure of ideologies to provide an adequate balance between trade-offs on land tenure can be explained by several interconnected factors. First, if an ideology is based on discriminatory principles, it will result in a discriminatory formal land tenure system. One paradigmatic example is the principles that informed colonial ventures, which too often discriminated against the land rights of local populations, which were viewed as 'non-productive' or land described as 'empty', and therefore resulted in formal land tenure systems that had disastrous consequences for considerable parts of the populations under their rule (Benjaminsen *et al.* 2008: 28; Lund, 2008: 13). Moreover, unequal colonial land tenure systems gave origin to post-colonial 'property monster[s]', in which states claim ownership of vast areas of the country without acknowledging the rights of those using the land (Benda-Beckmann, 2003: 189; see also Cotula, 2016: 195). The formal land tenure system of the colonial and apartheid rule in South Africa is one of the clearest examples of an upfront discriminatory ideology transferred to the formal land tenure system (Wisborg and Rohde, 2005).

Second, there are also situations in which an ideology is not discriminatory upfront, but masks systems designed with a bias in favour of elite groups and their interests, to the detriment of others. The neoliberal ideology that has been shaping a considerable number of formal land tenure systems all over the world is a paradigmatic example. As described above, under this ideology land is primarily an instrument of economic development, and based on the free market, land comes under the control of those that can extract the most economic value out of it, and marginalise those that don't have the same economic power and tools for economic production, or are not only focused on the economic value of land (Ganti, 2014). One recurrent effect of neoliberal ideology on formal land tenure systems is the lack of acknowledgment and protection of indigenous groups and their ways of life, more oriented to the preservation of nature and less dependent on the extraction of natural resources and economic exploitation of the land.[21] However, as pointed out by McAuslan,

> a government that ignores the social aspect of land [...] does so at its peril. At best, there will be clashes on the ground between investors and locals: at worst, ignoring local beliefs and attitudes to land can lead and has led to widespread local violence and civil wars.
>
> (McAuslan, 2010: 203)

Faulty assumptions, misconceptions

Faulty assumptions and misconceptions also contribute to the failure of formal land tenure systems in improving people's lives (see Lund, 2000). The premises that led Hernando De Soto (2000) to promote land titling as a silver bullet to end poverty are a good example of how faulty assumptions result in inefficient, if not harmful, land policies (Benda-Beckmann, 2003; Otto, 2009; Bruce, 2012). Research has proven that, in many circumstances, the land titling promoted by De Soto has perverse effects such as more tenure insecurity and inequality.[22]

Furthermore, the implementation of a formal land tenure system can have unexpected, or at least unintended, side effects. For instance, the commodification of land through land registration tends to solidify and even increase economic inequality among people.[23] Formalisation can also promote landlessness of poor land dwellers due to distress sales of land in a moment of need or market pressures (Platteau, 1996: 51; Deininger, 2003: 94; Duran-Lasserve

21 See, for instance, Brandenburg and Orzel's documentary 'When Two Worlds Collide' (2016), which depicts the clash of indigenous people with the Peruvian government against concessions of indigenous land to oil companies. In the documentary, President Alan García explains to a crowd of supporters how the Amazonian resources such as timber and oil 'are not under the ownership of a group that had the fortune of being born in that area [...], the riches of Peru [the Peruvian Amazonian jungle] belong to all Peruvians'. This speech carries clear political views regarding the connection of those indigenous people with land. First, that economic exploitation of resources prevails over their preservation. Second, that indigenous ways of living, dependent on the preservation of the jungle, deserve less protection than the way of living of others who depend on the economic exploitation of that resource. Third, that no specific group can lay a claim to particular area within a national territory and that cultural connections to land do not deserve special protection.

22 Among many others, see Bruce *et al.*, 1994: 260; Dekker, 2005: 168; Kanji *et al.*, 2005; Durand-Lasserve and Selod, 2007: 12; Benjaminsen *et al.*, 2008; Ubink, 2009: 8; Delville, 2010: 25; Zoomers, 2013: 65.

23 Platteau, 1996: 51; Deininger, 2003: 94; Harvey, 2004; O'Laughlin, 2007: 42; Duran-Lasserve and Selod, 2007: 10; Peluso and Lund, 2011: 674; Bruce, 2012: 43; Wolford *et al.*, 2013: 8; Campbell, 2015: chap. 5 para. 5; Zoomers *et al.*, 2017: 250. Campbell shows how the simple prospect of land titling in rural Brazil, even before the titles are issued, leads to the commodification of land (2015: chap. 5 para. 38).

and Selod, 2007: 10; Campbell, 2015: chap. 5 para. 5). Furthermore, land registration and the commodification of land can, and often does, weaken women's rights to land, which are overlooked or not acknowledged during the registration (Atwood, 1990: 661; Platteau, 1996: 40; Deininger, 2003: 59; Benjaminsen *et al.*, 2008: 33).

Another problem is the common misconception that individual ownership of land is the natural evolution of communal rights, and provides a more economically effective use of land, as well as more tenure security (Platteau, 1996; Dekker; 2005; Lund, 2011). This idea of a 'natural evolutionary process' from communal to individualised land rights has continued since colonial times (Atwood, 1990: 659) and overlooks the role of land in several ways. First, it focuses mostly on economic production, but ignores other roles of land in people's lives (e.g., cultural links with land). Second, it forgets that individualisation tends to concentrate rights in one person and ignore coexisting land rights of others, such as women's secondary rights to land, or grazing rights (Benjaminsen *et al.*, 2008: 31). Third, it overlooks the value of communal systems to address social problems (e.g., less inequality; Barry, 2015: 10), and the economic value produced on land held communally (Atwood, 1990: 662; Lund, 2000: 13; Otto and Hoekema, 2012: 20; Wily, 2012).

One other common misconception is that the loss of land by small farmers for large-scale agriculture, industry, or urban development is compensated by the creation of jobs for those farmers (Li, 2009; Li, 2014: intro. para. 4). Large-scale expropriation and evictions of 'occupied state land' are often politically justified with the promise that new jobs and better lives for those affected will come, but all too often, those affected experience a very different reality (German *et al.*, 2011: 24; Zoomers, 2018: 342). In practice, the jobs created are often much fewer than those initially promised, are badly paid, demand qualifications that those affected by eviction do not have, or the jobs simply disappear with the foreclosure of the investment, leaving those affected with no land and no job (Cotula, 2013: chap. 4 para. 53; Kerssen, 2013: chap. 13 para. 3). People become 'surplus population' (Marx, 1887: 449; Li, 2009: 68). Despite abundant literature pointing out the consequences of these above-mentioned assumptions and misconceptions, they seem to endure as ground principles of many formal land tenure systems.

Practical problems

Even when land policies are well balanced and do not suffer from faulty assumptions and misconceptions, the implementation of formal land tenure systems is affected by many practical problems, especially in the context of weak rule of law and inefficient state systems.

For instance, the implementation of a formal land tenure system is dependent to a larger or smaller degree on an increase in the capacity of administrative and judicial systems to implement and enforce state rules and procedures.

However, when designing their formal land tenure systems, governments often ignore, misjudge, or fail to improve the human, material, and financial resources necessary to implement those systems (see, for instance, Deininger, 2003: 70; Hall, 2013: chap. 5 para. 17; Enemark *et al.*, 2014; Enemark *et al.*, 2015). Furthermore, it is not uncommon for state norms and institutions to lack legitimacy in the eyes of the people they intend to rule, besides competing with well-established and recognised customary norms, institutions, and practices (Platteau, 1996: 69; see Berry, 2002: 663). Misjudgements about other aspects, such as cultural adequacy of administrative procedures and lack of public information also entangle the implementation of the formal land tenure system.

Another common practical problem of formal land tenure systems is that the process of territorialising them opens up opportunities for manipulation and unfair appropriation of land. The design of land policies and legislation in favour of ruling elites is not the only moment in which the formal land tenure system can be used for personal benefit. Even when land legislation is fair, in contexts of weak rule of law, unclear administrative procedures, low legal knowledge, and high corruption, the territorialisation of a formal land tenure system opens up space for personal exploitation of the system (Atwood, 1990: 661; Platteau, 1996: 43; Lund, 2000: 16).[24] Elites and state officials know the gaps and loopholes of legislation and control the state administrative machinery. They can, and often do, take advantage of processes such as land registration to obtain formal rights over land, to the detriment of other individuals or the state (Barry and Fourie, 2001: 2; Dekker, 2005: 133).[25]

Furthermore, state interventions such as new laws and registration processes have the potential to challenge the status quo on a certain area, opening up opportunities to start or reignite land-related disputes (Lund, 2008; 91). These moments of change can represent an opportunity to settle dormant conflicts, but also for outsiders or the more cunning and powerful members of communities to overpower others (Platteau, 1996: 43; Ubink and Quan, 2008; 205). In these situations, instead of tenure security, formalisation becomes a tool of further dispossession and inequality.[26]

The above-mentioned problems are just a summary of the many challenges that the implementation of a formal land tenure system faces, and many other

24 Land-related organisations are often identified among the most corrupt ones (Deininger *et al.*, 2012: 13). As stated by Bruce *et al.*, 'The corruption of the land allocation process seems inevitable when a valuable good is allocated free and rationed administratively' (1994: 261).

25 See, for instance, Fairbairn's conclusion regarding state intervention in land tenure in Mozambique: 'bureaucratic intervention may benefit two groups: the administrators themselves—those in direct contact with the bureaucratic process—and political elites whose connections give them sufficient clout to influence the actions of those administrators' (2013: 151).

26 For instance, Waldorff reports how formalisation is used in Angola as a tool for dispossessing informal settlers (2016: 372).

problems could be listed. Moreover, as the following section shows, many of these problems raise difficult dilemmas, to which there is no right answer.

Dilemmas of a formal land tenure system

Finally, this section provides an overview of recurrent dilemmas that the implementation of a formal land tenure system raises. While the literature reports the many problems that arise with formal land tenure systems (see above), the same literature often fails to acknowledge that land governance is not an easy task. Even the most good-hearted and well-prepared politicians and state officials must deal with several problems to which there are no good answers, solutions for which values have to be prioritised, and decisions whose results cannot be predicted. Dealing with dilemmas is a core part of land administration.

These dilemmas are connected with the kind of problems that formal land tenure systems must address. These systems are designed to deal with problems that result from a plurality of social values and interests, complex and multi-layered governance systems, which cut across many fields of study and to which there is no clear scientific solution (Barry and Fourie, 2001; Deininger *et al.*, 2012: 20; Barry and Augustine, 2015: 18; Head and Alford, 2015: 716). These can be classified as *wicked problems* because they are not possible to clearly define, are constantly evolving, and the solution for part of the problem exposes a new set of problems that need to be addressed (Rittel and Webber, 1973: 160).[27] The solutions for wicked problems cannot be divided into right or wrong and need to be individually customised. Furthermore, there is only so much that can be learned about a wicked problem before a solution is tested, and testing solutions is costly and leaves lasting consequences that can trigger a set of new problems (ibid.; Conklin, 2009: 19). In other words, these problems have an unclear definition, as well as an unclear solution, to which there is no 'right' answer.

The answer for wicked problems can only come from 'shared understandings about possible solutions' (ibid.: 13; Head and Alford, 2015: 717). However, the conflict of interests that land-related issues entail is often at the core of those problems, making collaboration very difficult (ibid.: 727). Often these problems pose dilemmas, and solutions might cause new problems and will not please everyone's interests. Understanding the wicked nature of land-related problems is fundamental to comprehend the difficulty of creating a formal land

27 Rittel and Webber define 'wicked' problems in opposition to 'tame' problems, those problems for which 'an exhaustive formulation can be stated containing all the information the problem-solver needs' (Rittel and Webber, 1973: 161). For instance, a mathematical problem is clearly defined, and even if complex and dependent on research, the information to solve it can be detailed in steps. The same does not apply to many land-related problems.

tenure system; even the best-intentioned and prepared politicians and civil servants will have trouble defining the problems and finding the solutions that the formal land tenure system must address and assessing the full impact that any intervention will have.

These dilemmas can have different origins. They are the result of ideological choices; by prioritising one group, problem, or interest, others will be necessarily excluded (Hall *et al.*, 2011: 6). But these dilemmas are also the result of limitations of different mechanisms and tools adopted by formal land tenure systems and very practical constraints such as lack of human, financial, and material resources. The remainder of this section provides some examples of these different dilemmas.

One example of dilemmas that formal land tenure systems deal with, and which is further explored below in this book, are the cases of land restitution after dispossession and formalisation by previous regimes.[28] In many of these cases, both the arguments of previous and current possessors of land are legitimate and there is no easy answer regarding who should get the land, leaving a dilemma for decision-makers. Vague solutions such as protecting good-faith acquirers of land rights or exclusion of 'friends of the regime' do not take into consideration the complexity of the problems they try to address and often in practice result in more arbitrariness. Most often the solution for these cases will not please all people affected and will raise new problems, such as poverty and conflict.

The recognition and integration of customary systems into formal ones provides another example of a dilemma that confronts politicians and state officials. In the last decades authors have been raising awareness for the value of customary land tenure systems and advocating that governments should keep and recognise these systems, considering their low-cost, social recognition, and adaptability (Deininger, 2003: 62; Fitzpatrick, 2005; Ubink and Quan, 2008: 198; Wily, 2017: 458). However, norms and practices of customary land tenure systems are at times in direct conflict with basic human rights principles, such as equality and protection against discrimination.[29] For instance, the prohibition of women to own land, discriminatory social hierarchies inside customary groups, and exclusion of outsiders are fairly common features of customary systems (Atwood, 1990: 661; Lund, 2000: 5; Hall *et al.*, 2011: 12; Cotula, 2013: chap. 2 para. 30). While defenders of cultural relativism views of human rights can argue that these principles are the result of Western views of the world (see Cowan *et al.*, 2001: 4; Menski, 2006: 41; Crewe and Axelby, 2013: 108), the reality is that most states are legally committed to these principles

28 For instance, the cases of Cambodia, Kosovo, Estonia, Latvia, Lithuania, and Libya. See Fitzpatrick, 2004; Ronen, 2013; Ibrahim, 2017.

29 Among many others, art. 1, 2, 13, and 17 of the Universal Declaration of Human Rights, and art. 15 and 16. 1(h) of the Convention on the Elimination of All Forms of Discrimination against Women.

through international declarations, treaties, covenants, and national constitutions and legislation. Therefore, governments are legally obliged to implement these human rights' principles, which in part means fighting discriminatory practices of customary systems. Also, the legal recognition of customary systems can enhance the power of powerful community members, often the brokers between the state and the community, and the 'source' of customary knowledge (Bruce *et al.*, 1994: 260; Platteau, 1996: 44; Ubink and Quan, 2008: 207). There are middle-ways and incremental approaches to intrinsically discriminatory rules of customary systems (Fitzpatrick, 2005; Ubink, 2009: 9; Cotula, 2012: 66), but they always entail some trade-off between the protection of legal principles and the benefits of using these systems. These trade-offs are dilemmas that politicians have to face, and to which no solution will please all stakeholders.

Formal land tenure systems also pose dilemmas at a more practical level, such as the degree of detail that a particular system can reach. As detailed by James Scott, governance in general, and specifically land governance, implies some level of simplification of reality; state systems cannot understand, process, and adapt their intervention to all complexities on the ground (Scott, 1998). The more complexity a land tenure system must process, the more time and resources are needed to keep that system running. This poses several dilemmas to politicians and state officials: they must choose the degree of complexity that the formal land tenure system will process, and the details that will be ignored by it (Platteau, 1996: 42). For instance, when promoting land registration, governments tend to focus on ownership rights over land, but the registry often does not register other rights such as grazing rights and water rights, therefore strengthening the position of the registered owner to the detriment of holders of other rights. This poses a dilemma of conducting land registration that gives a distorted image of reality on the ground, or land registration not happening at all.

If land-related wicked problems are already intrinsically difficult to address, the role of politicians is further complicated by the conditions in which the decisions are made. We tend to imagine that state rules, institutions, and practices are the result of a logical thought process, originating from a unified government, created with the single objective of the improvement of people's living conditions (Platteau, 1996: 69; Lund, 2008: 178). However, these norms, institutions, and practices are much more the result of competing and conflicting interests of different public institutions, groups, individuals, and even international organisations and states than the result of a unified and well-thought-out effort. They are also designed by governments, parliaments, and state officials, who are under constant pressure to show short-term and visible results, and who have limited capacities, time, and resources for research and policy development. Under these conditions, these dilemmas are even more difficult to address, and the wicked nature of land-related problems becomes even more evident.

Conclusion

This chapter defines several concepts used throughout this book, debates why virtually all countries in the world have a formal land tenure system, and highlights that the implementation of formal land tenure systems is marked by many problems and dilemmas. This analysis, based on a literature review and examples from other countries, provides a starting point for studying the Timorese formal land tenure system.

Formal land tenure systems have a central role in the state's goal of improving people's living conditions. Formal land tenure systems can help to address, but can also cause or aggravate insecurity, poverty, inequality, destruction of nature, and cultural and social estrangement, depending on the balance that these systems establish between land uses, users, and the focus on each of these problems. States are aware of this and want to have the final word on the balance that is established. Consequently, the formal land tenure system is a tool for addressing these problems, but also an instrument to spread and implement the dominant ideology of the state. Some authors challenge the assumption that the state uses the formal land tenure system as a tool for improving people's living conditions, arguing instead that this system is a mechanism for the oppression of people by the dominant elites. Although there is no final answer for the true intentions of the state, at least due to flaws of state administration, there are numerous examples where formal land tenure systems are used by elites for unfair personal gains and oppression of others. The following chapters build on these debates and analyse the motivations for developing the Timorese formal land tenure system, the priorities and the balances (or ideologies) that this system is promoting, and who benefits from their implementation.

However, the implementation of formal land tenure systems is not a given, and many countries have inside their territories areas of frontier where, due to their remoteness, political instability, choice, or resource limitations, the administrative and judicial mechanisms of the state that regulate land tenure have little or no reach. The territorialisation of the formal land tenure system works as a tool of legitimation and enforcement of state power and supremacy over its territory. By defining boundaries, enclosing land, recognising or denying land rights, allocating land, and providing conflict resolution mechanisms, the state is affirming its internal sovereignty over that area, and by participating in these activities, people are acknowledging the authority of the state over their rights to land. The case of Timor-Leste provides a vivid example of the reasons for the existence of these frontier areas and how the state uses the formal land tenure system to deal with them when it needs to affirm state authority over the territory.

While formal land tenure systems are presented by politicians and state officials as a mechanism to improve people's living conditions, ideological, conceptual, and practical problems and unexpected side effects can bring more harm than good to large groups of people. Furthermore, the wicked nature of land-related problems makes the development and management of a formal land tenure system a very difficult task, leaving politicians and state officials with many dilemmas on their hands, for which there are no right decisions, and the solutions to which are inevitably a trade-off between two or more imperfect outcomes. Moreover, the less-than-ideal conditions in which decisions are taken, such as internal and external political pressures and interests, and lack of time and resources, result in decisions that often are far from logical and well thought-through.

In conclusion, land governance is not easy. Without a silver bullet for these issues, the main recommendations that can be found in the literature are to take small incremental steps, based on careful contextual assessments, and with a 'learning by doing' approach (Otto and Hoekema, 2012: 21; Wily, 2012: 93; Enemark *et al.*, 2014). The case of Timor-Leste described in the following chapters provides detailed examples of these problems and dilemmas, viewed through the perspective of the state administration.

Chapter 3

Land tenure systems throughout Timor-Leste's history

Introduction

This chapter sets the scenario for the rest of the book. The history of Timor-Leste, as well as its social and geographical characteristics, are key factors to understand land tenure in the country, the roles that formal and informal land tenure systems have, and the problems and dilemmas that these systems must deal with. Therefore, the first part of this chapter gives a brief account of the geographic and social features of the country, followed by a concise historical account. The second part of the chapter focuses specifically on land tenure and land tenure systems, connecting the history of the country with its main land-related problems, and summarising the steps taken by different administrations, since colonial times until now, to develop a formal land tenure system in the country. This summary provides the context necessary to understand the analysis of the following chapters.

Geographic and social overview

The territory of Timor-Leste is approximately half of the island of Timor, located at the eastern side of the Lesser Sunda Islands, and around 700 kilometres northwest from Darwin, Australia (Map 3.1).[1] Timor-Leste, with around 15,000 square kilometres, ranks 160 out of 252 countries in terms of size, and encompasses the east half of the island of Timor, the smaller islands of Ataúro and Jaco, and the exclave of Oecusse in the west.[2] Administratively the country

1 The now Democratic Republic of Timor-Leste has been referred to by many names throughout history, such as Timor Loro'sae, Portuguese Timor, Timor Timur, and East Timor. The name of the country is a source of controversy among the Timorese (Niner, 2011: 13). For simplicity and consistency, I use Timor-Leste throughout the book, even when referring to periods where the territory was known by another name. I use Timorese to refer to nationals of Timor-Leste.

2 https://www.cia.gov/library/publications/the-world-factbook/rankorder/2147rank.html#tt

DOI: 10.4324/9781003196396-3

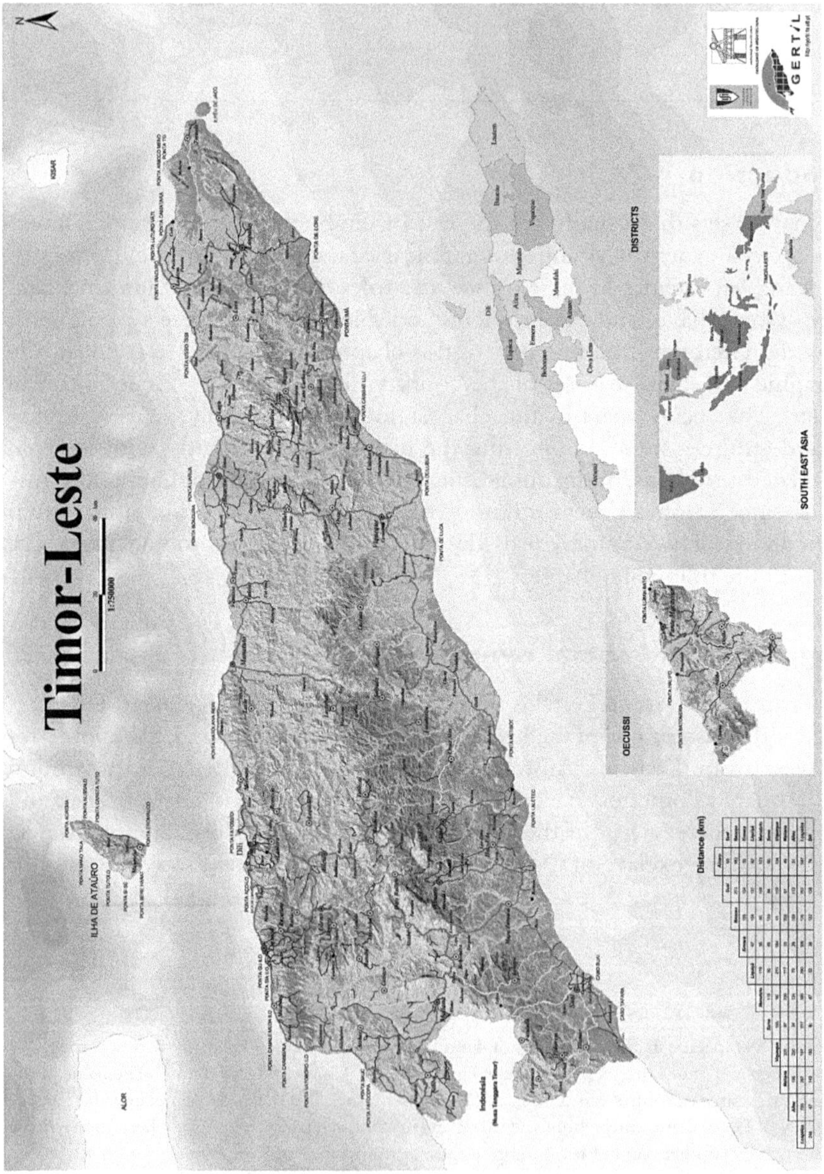

Map 3.1 Timor-Leste. *Source: map produced by GERTIL, available at* https://www.mapsland.com/maps/asia/east-timor/detailed-map-of-timor-leste-with-relief-roads-and-cities.jpg.

is divided into 13 districts, which are further subdivided into *sub-districts*, *suco*, and *aldeia*.[3]

The long history of migrations from different parts of the world to Timor-Leste resulted in a very diverse mosaic of ethnic and linguistic variety (Traube, 1995: 43; Gunn, 1999: 40). Most of the Timorese population is of Austronesian (Malayo-Polynesian) origin (e.g., the Tetum and the Mambae), but there are also groups with Melanesian-Papuan origins, such as the Makasae, Fataluku, and the Bunak (Fox, 2003: 3; GoTL, 2011b: 6; Hägerdal, 2012: 15). There is also a minority Chinese population and a group of mixed Portuguese descent, known as Mestiços (Fox, 2003: 31). However, and despite the different cultural traditions of distinct groups, it is possible to find resemblances between them, as a consequence of centuries of interaction and common practices. Currently Timor-Leste has a population of approximately 1,167,242 inhabitants, with an annual growth rate of 1.81 percent, one of the highest ones in South-East Asia (GoTL, 2015: 13, 15). The population age average is only 16.8 years old, with 70 percent of the population under 30, making the Timorese one of the youngest populations in the word (Palanivel *et al.*, 2016: 28). However, and despite the high population growth, density remains relatively low, with 78 inhabitants per square kilometre, 72 percent of them living in rural areas (GoTL, 2015: 15, 22). The capital Dili is by far the largest city of the country, and its population growth is particularly high. In 1974 Dili had around 20,000 inhabitants. In 2004 its population was 101,551 inhabitants, but it more than doubled to 222,323 in 2015, corresponding to 19 percent of the country's population (GoTL, 2011: 2; GoTL, 2015: 23). Many of these newcomers live in improvised houses on the outskirts of the city and the hills that surround it.

Language is a source of heated debates in Timor-Leste. The constitution establishes Portuguese and Tetum as the two official languages, while Indonesian and English are acknowledged as working languages.[4] Tetum Prasa, a creole version of Tetum is the lingua franca of the country, but linguists identify around 30 other languages spoken nationwide (Klinken and Williams, 2015). While most Timorese speak Tetum, not many can speak Portuguese. In the 2010 census, 39 percent of the population self-reported as 'literate' in Portuguese (GoTL, 2011: 2), but the fluency in this language is in general quite low. Actually, a 2011 survey found that only 1 percent of respondents reported speaking Portuguese as a second language (UNMIT, 2011: 16; see also Simões, 2015: 389, Leach *et al.*, 2012: 5). As discussed in Chapter 5, the low fluency

3 Officially the districts are now called *municipalities*, but this name is misleading because it corresponds mostly to vast, scarcely populated areas. Therefore, I prefer to use the word 'districts'. Each suco and aldeia has an elected leader, the suco chief (*chefe de suco*) and the aldeia chief (*chefe de aldeia*). By law they are considered local representatives, not state officials (Law 9/2016). Often these leadership positions are co-opted by customary leaders or someone appointed by them, but there are examples where these leaders or their appointees lost an election to other candidates (Cummins, 2010: 902).

4 Article 13 and 159 of the constitution.

in Portuguese is especially problematic in the drafting and comprehension of legislation, often written in Portuguese without any official Tetum version. Fluency in Indonesian has been decreasing, especially among younger generations that are no longer schooled in that language (GoTL, 2011: 2). Officially Timor-Leste is a secular state, but almost 97 percent of Timorese identify as Catholic (GoTL, 2011a: xxi).

Historical background

Archaeological studies suggest that human occupation of Timor started more than 30,000 years ago (O'Connor *et al.*, 2002). The first known written accounts of the island of Timor come from fourteenth-century Chinese explorers (Fox, 2003: 6; Hägerdal, 2012: 1), but authors report that 2,000 years before, the island was already known for its sandalwood among Arab, Chinese, and Indian traders (Gunn, 2011: 6; see also Taylor, 1991: 1). While the political arrangements on the island before colonial rule are contested among authors, there is some consensus about a division of the territory into several micro-kingdoms, grouped into the Belu and Servião *confederacies* (Hicks, 2014: 30; see also Gunn, 1999: 32; Hägerdal, 2012: 52).

The first Portuguese contacts with the island of Timor happened in 1515, with the expedition of Afonso de Albuquerque to the Moluccas in search for spices and sandalwood (Figueiredo, 2011: 33). The first centuries of Portuguese engagement with Timor were mostly based on trade, conducted through the *Topasses*—the Portuguese-native mestizo population—first settled on the close-by island of Solor and afterwards on the island of Flores (Gunn, 1999: 92; Taylor, 1999: 3; Fox, 2003: 7). Only in 1702 was a Portuguese settlement established in Lifau (Oecusse), later relocated to Dili due to conflicts with *Topasses*, and a governor was appointed (ibid.: 10; Hägerdal, 2012: 4). From the sixteenth century the Portuguese control over the island was under constant dispute with the Dutch. The dispute was settled through the Lisbon Treaty of 1859, which gave the west side of Timor to the Dutch (now part of Indonesia) and the east side (Timor-Leste) to the Portuguese (Fox, 2003: 13).

During the first centuries of engagement with Timor-Leste, the Portuguese colonial authorities made little progress in consolidating their control over the territory, which was regarded as one of the most remote and least developed Portuguese colonies (Taylor, 1999: 5; Figueiredo, 2011a: 1; Pinto, 2014: 269). The appointment of Governor Celestino da Silva, at the end of the nineteenth century (1884–1908), marked a turning point in the Portuguese administration of Timor-Leste, with an attempt to transform the economy of the colony, mostly based on trade and subsistence agriculture, into a cash crop producer and raw material exporter (Taylor, 1999: 10; Lobato, 2014: 205). These changes required a much tighter political control over the territory, to obtain access to the land and labour essential for large-scale agricultural production (Taylor, 1999: 11). Furthermore, the principle of effective occupation developed in the Conference of Berlin (1884–1885) was becoming doctrine, pressing the Portuguese to expand their control of the Timorese territory (Figueiredo 2011a: 1). The campaigns of 'pacification' and 'occupation', and large-scale plantations of coffee and other crops—some of them in land taken from local producers—were marks of Celestino da Silva's government (Davidson, 1994: 95; Figueiredo, 2011: 70; Lobato, 2014: 205). Also during this period, with the objective of forcing agricultural surplus and raising the income of the colony, a head tax, to be paid in cash or kind by all Timorese males aged from 18 to 60, was created, causing much discontent and revolts against the Portuguese authorities (Taylor, 1999: 11; Figueiredo, 2011: 303). Forced labour and schemes to keep plantation workers in permanent debt were also common practices (Gunn, 1999: 197; Lobato, 2014: 207), as well as efforts to concentrate populations into large and permanent settlements (Fitzpatrick *et al.*, 2013: 37).

Furthermore, together with the abolition of traditional kingdoms, the Portuguese administration established a mechanism of indirect ruling that allowed a tighter control of the territory, by empowering loyal traditional leaders with positions of state officials and military titles, and disempowering uncompliant ones (Taylor, 1999: 11; Ospina and Hohe, 2002: 40–44). However, the objective of converting Timor-Leste into an exporter colony was far from achieved, with only a small percentage of the country's area used for large-scale plantations (ibid.: 15; Lobato, 2014: 205).

The consolidation of the Portuguese administration of Timor-Leste was briefly interrupted during the Second World War when, despite Portugal's neutrality, Japan occupied the territory (1942–1945). Australian and Dutch troops had arrived in Timor before the Japanese, intending to use the island as a buffer zone to prevent attacks against Australia and the Dutch's interests in the region, but they were only able to delay the Japanese invasion (Figueiredo, 2011: 83). The Japanese occupation was marked by numerous atrocities, with the Japanese troops severely punishing the initial support that the Timorese gave to the Australian forces, resulting in the displacement and death of 40,000 to 60,000 Timorese (CAVR, 2005: part 3, 10). Portugal regained control of Timor-Leste after the war, and made use of the disruption created by the Japanese invasion to further spread Portuguese administrative structures throughout the territory (Fitzpatrick *et al.*, 2013: 37). But the control that the Portuguese colonial authorities managed to gain over the territory and the local populations remained weak and was mainly focused on a few areas of agricultural interest. Despite all foreign interference, the resilience of the Timorese social structures allowed them to maintain their main characteristics, only superficially adapting to the imposed colonial administrative structures (Taylor, 1991: 15; Hohe and Nixon, 2003: 26; Soares, 2003a: 266).[5]

5 A more detailed and nuanced vision of the influence of the Portuguese administration can be found in Fitzpatrick *et al.*, 2013: 36–40.

On 25 April 1974 the Carnation Revolution ended 41 years of dictatorship in Portugal and triggered the decolonisation process of all Portuguese colonies, including Timor-Leste. This gave origin to several political parties, and the start of a debate about the different alternatives for the future of Timor-Leste in elections to be held in 1975 (Hicks, 2014: 44). The three main options were represented by the three main political parties: the Democratic Union of Timor-Leste (*União Democrática de Timor-Leste*, UDT) supported a progressive autonomy but a continuous link with Portugal; the Revolutionary Front of Timor-Leste (*Frente Revolucionária de Timor-Leste*, FRETILIN, initially formed as ASDT) wanted full independence; and the Timorese Popular Democratic Association (*Associação Popular Democrática Timorense*, APODETI) campaigned for integration with Indonesia (Shoesmith, 2013: 123; Dovert and Durand, 2016: 330). However, political inexperience and Indonesian interference did not allow a peaceful debate. Encouraged by the Indonesian government and by the strong leftist positions of FRETILIN, UDT attempted a coup against the Portuguese administration still in the territory, which led to a counter-offensive by FRETILIN. Under the inaction of the few Portuguese authorities, the conflict quickly evolved into a short but brutal civil war, in which 1,500 to 3,000 people were killed, and between 10,000 and 30,000 thousand were displaced to West Timor (CAVR, 2005: part 3, 43).[6] The successful counter-offensive of FRETILIN allowed them to take administrative control of territory, but further fuelled the Indonesian argument that a leftist FRETILIN government represented a danger to the region (Lawless, 1976: 953; Dovert and Durand, 2016: 334). On 28 November 1975, under the impending threat of an Indonesian invasion, FRETILIN issued a declaration of independence from Portugal, which had not yet officially ceded power to the Timorese. The day after FRETILIN's declaration of independence, other political parties (UDT, APODETI, KOTA, and Trabalhista) signed a declaration expressing the desire to integrate Timor-Leste within Indonesia, which became known as the 'Declaration of Balibo'. However, many argue that this declaration was actually drafted in Jakarta, and signed by the parties' representatives in Bali under strong pressure of the Indonesians (CAVR, 2005: part 3, 57; Gunn, 2011: 45).

Timor-Leste was invaded by Indonesia only nine days after the declaration of independence and swiftly integrated as the 27th Indonesian province with the name of Timor Timur. During the first years of occupation a large part of the Timorese territory remained outside the control of Indonesian troops due to the armed resistance of FALINTIL (The Armed Forces for the National Liberation of East Timor), which were protected by the mountainous terrain and well-armed with the military equipment left behind by the Portuguese

6 Among other factors, land-related disputes were also in the centre of this civil war (Aditjondro, 1994: 55; Du Plessis and Leckie, 2000: 6; Nixon, 2012: 38).

troops. However, the resistance was progressively suppressed by military offensives and strategies such as the destruction of food crops and massive forced resettlement in 'strategic camps' and 'model villages' of those parts of the population that could provide support to the resistance fighters.[7]

Starvation, illness, death, and misery were widespread during the first years of Indonesian occupation, with 84,000 to 183,000 people dying during this period because of famine and disease caused by the conflict (CAVR, 2005: part 3, 44). With the weakening of the resistance forces in the early 1980s, people were progressively allowed to leave the camps and return to their villages or new resettlement areas. However, brutality and repression continued to characterise the Indonesian administration during the following decades. In the words of the CAVR report:

> [Indonesian security forces] consistently resorted to killings and disappearances during the whole period of its occupation of Timor-Leste. These [...] killings and disappearances had an overall strategic purpose, namely that of eliminating opposition to the occupation by terrorising the general population. [...] The killings committed by the Indonesian security forces had a particularly horrific character.
>
> (Ibid.: part 7, 2, 6)

In the beginning of 1999, after the resignation of Indonesia's President Suharto, and because of increasing internal and international pressure, a referendum to choose between independence or special autonomy within Indonesia was announced by the Indonesian President Habibie. On 30 August 1999, the Timorese overwhelmingly voted for independence, with 78.5 percent of voters rejecting the autonomy option. In response, pro-Indonesia militia, in collaboration with the Indonesian military forces, unleashed widespread destruction, death, and displacement, which was only halted by the intervention of the United Nations peacekeeping force. On 25 October 1999 the UNTAET (United Nations Transitional Administration in East Timor) was established to provisionally manage the territory and prepare the ground for an independent Timor-Leste (Morrow and White, 2002: 4; Gorjão, 2004: 1044).[8]

UNTAET's task was enormous. If before the referendum Timor-Leste was already the poorest province of Indonesia, after the widespread destruction caused by the violent Indonesian withdrawal the situation was appalling. Between 1,400 and 1,500 civilians were killed by the Indonesian military forces and the militia they supported (CAVR, 2005: part 7.2, 245). Around

7 Around 300,000 Timorese were displaced to these camps and model villages in the first years of the occupation (Taylor, 1999: 90).

8 Resolution 1272 (1999) of the United Nations Security Council, mandated UNTAET with legislative and executive powers (art. 1).

250,000 people were forcibly displaced to West Timor and most of the remaining population had to flee their homes (ibid.: part 7.3, 106). The violence also impacted public infrastructure and services; around 80 percent of schools were destroyed or damaged, 80 percent of the high school teachers left the country, and most of the text books were burned; the capacity to supply energy was reduced by 50 to 90 percent in some of the district capitals; most of the telecommunications infrastructure was damaged; and public transportation almost stopped (UNDP, 2002: 57; Cliffe, 2003: 238). While the road network was not deliberately targeted, its use by heavy military vehicles and the lack of maintenance left the roads in poor condition (ibid.: 237). The administrative structures of the state totally collapsed: approximately 70 percent of the administrative buildings were totally or partially destroyed; archives—including the land registry—were burned; senior civil servants, most of them of Indonesian origin, left the country (ibid.; UNDP, 2002: 57). Around three-quarters of the health-care facilities disappeared and 130 out of the nation's 160 practising physicians left the country (Lundahl and Sjöholm, 2005: 8; Cliffe, 2003: 238). The few court rooms in Timor-Leste were destroyed and all judges and public prosecutors—all of Indonesian origin—also left, bringing the judicial system to a grinding halt (Chesterman, 2005: 84; see Chapter 4). The existing banks were looted and destroyed, resulting that for a long time all transactions had to be done in cash (UNDP, 2002: 57). Agriculture was also severely impacted: the agricultural output fell by around 40 percent, and approximately 50 percent of the animal stock was killed (Lundahl and Sjöholm, 2005: 8). The already meagre gross regional product plummeted 25 to 30 percent (ibid.).

Timor-Leste became officially independent on 20 May 2002, after almost three years of UNTAET administration and a progressive transfer of powers to elected Timorese authorities (Morrow and White, 2002: 5).[9] While considerable progress had been achieved during UNTAET's administration, the reconstruction of public infrastructure and state administration had just started, and remained high on the agenda of all of the Timorese governments. The first years of Timor-Leste's independence were marked by reduced state budgets and enormous dependency on international aid (Cotton, 2005: 2; Curtain *et al.*, 2011: 22).

However, the rise of Timor-Leste as an independent country was violently shaken by the political crisis of 2006. The dismissal of 591 soldiers from the army (F-FDTL), most of them from the west side of the country (*loro mono*), resulted in a strike and street protests against alleged discrimination by their eastern (*loro sae*) senior officers. The street protests of these soldiers quickly

9 For some people Independence Day is the day of the declaration of independence from Portugal on 28 November 1975 (article 1.2 of the constitution; Morrow and White, 2002: 3). For simplicity, I use the expression 'independence' to refer to 20 May 2002.

became violent and out-of-control. After two months of civil unrest and clashes between the military and the police, the president and the prime minister requested an external intervention to help restore order. While the numbers are disputed, some authors report that the 2006 events resulted in as much as 200 people killed, 150,000 displaced, and the destruction of 6,000 buildings (Scambary, 2015: 292; see also Kingsbury, 2007).[10] As a consequence of the crisis, Prime Minister Mari Alkatiri resigned. The security situation remained unstable, and in February 2008 tensions reached a new peak with the assassination attempt of President Ramos-Horta and Prime Minister Xanana Gusmão. The fragility of state institutions and the weak rule of law are pointed out as the main causes of the crisis, in which land-related conflict also played a role (Brady and Timberman, 2006: 20; Scambary, 2009: 4).

Since 2006, the country has slowly transitioned to a more stable and peaceful phase of its young history, with the UN peacekeepers leaving at the end of 2012, and no remarkable large-scale violence happening since then. Besides peace, there were other remarkable accomplishments, such as a considerable income raise for part of the population, and the electrification of most of the country (Lundahl and Sjöholm, 2012: 4). A significant part of these achievements are linked with a staggering increase of the public expenditure since 2007, now possible due to oil and gas revenues, which raises doubts among observers about the sustainability of the Timorese economic strategy (ibid.: 3; ICG, 2013, Scheiner, 2015).[11] However, and despite all progress, Timorese society still faces poverty, unemployment, high inequality, and scarcity of basic services, particularly in rural areas (Sahin, 2010; Kingsbury, 2014: 195; Palanivel *et al.*, 2016: 20, 22).

Formal land tenure systems in Timor-Leste

The history of the different formal land tenure systems implemented in Timor-Leste is intimately connected with the history of the country. The Portuguese, Indonesian, UNTAET, and Timorese administrations introduced their own land tenure legislation, institutions, and practices, with different degrees of implementation, complexity, and success. Each of these systems also aimed to address, and were the cause of, a number of different problems. In this section I briefly summarise each of these formal land tenure systems, their objectives, successes, and problems caused. This summary is relevant for the rest of the book because it describes the scenario in which the Timorese formal land tenure system was developed, and in which the analysis of the following chapters unfolds.

10 Reports of different numbers can be found in USAID, 2007.

11 In 2002 the annual state budget was 56 million USD. In 2009 the budget was around 900 million USD, 1.5 billion USD in 2015, and 1.8 billion USD in 2019 (before the veto of the president). This topic is further debated in Chapter 4.

One caveat must be raised. Considering that, besides the vague references to customary practices in land administration, little is known about land tenure systems in Timor-Leste before the arrival of the Portuguese (Martinho, 1943: 230; Taylor, 1999: 6; Du Plessis and Leckie, 2000: 22), and since the debate about state formation is outside of the scope of this book, this analysis starts with the Portuguese colonial administration and does not debate the pre-colonial period.

The Portuguese formal land tenure system in Timor-Leste

While there is some literature about the Portuguese colonial land policies and systems (e.g., Santos, 2004; Direito, 2013), to my knowledge a more detailed account of the Timorese land tenure system during the Portuguese administration has never been published.[12] This section summarises the Portuguese formal land tenure system in Timor-Leste, but a detailed account of this system is out of the scope of this book.

The need to affirm sovereignty over the colonised territories and people, and the ambition of obtaining economic gains through the exploitation of land and natural resources led most colonial powers to, sooner or later, try to control land tenure through the implementation of formal land tenure systems (Serrão, 2014: 9). Portugal was no exception. The successful settlement of a governor in Timor-Leste in 1702 allowed the Portuguese Crown, at least formally, to claim the suzerainty over the Timorese kingdoms, a claim that was further supported by the levy of a tribute (*finta*) and the military support of these kingdoms (Pinto, 2014: 270). However, during the first centuries of the Portuguese colonial rule, the main focus was in Brazil, and limited efforts were made to develop a formal land tenure system for the African and Asian colonies (Cordeiro, 1997: 47; Santos, 2004: 363). Only in 1856 was specific and unified legislation for concessions of state land in all Portuguese colonies approved, and with a few exceptions little was achieved in developing land markets and commercial exploitation of land (*Carta de Lei de 21 de Agosto de 1856*; Santos, 2004: 23; see also Davidson, 1994: 88).

In Timor-Leste it was the government of Celestino da Silva and his 'pacification' campaigns at the end of the nineteenth century that marked a new period of much more intense commercial exploitation of land, through concessions of state land (Davidson, 1994: 276; Figueiredo, 2011: 204; Lobato, 2014: 205). A law from 1901 and its regulations (*Carta de Lei de 09 de Maio de 1901*), contemporary with Celestino's government, became the most relevant milestone for the development of Portuguese colonial formal land

12 Fitzpatrick quotes an unpublished study of Domingos Soares called *Hukum Agraria di Portugal*, from 1989 (Fitzpatrick, 2002: 152). Santos (2004) writes extensively about colonial land legislation, but only until 1945 and without analysing the institutions and practices that implemented these laws.

tenure systems, more prone to commercial use of the land and with clearer rules about concessions of land for economic exploitation.[13] To achieve this objective, this law clearly affirmed the state ownership of all land that was not privately owned, recognising however the right of 'native people' (*indígenas* was the Portuguese word used) to the land that they usually cultivated and used as residential areas. Native people had the possibility of obtaining ownership of land used for more than 20 years of cultivation (Santos, 2004: 203).[14] However, this land could be lost if not used without justification for more than one year.[15] The land around the villages, communally used by the native people, was not considered as theirs but could not be part of a concession. All other 'empty' land, was available for concessions (Silva, 1910: 34). The inheritance of land based on customary norms by native people was allowed, but the transaction of land to non-native was dependent on authorisation of state authorities.[16] These rules were, however, a small part of a large piece of legislation that was mostly focused on attracting investment for economic exploitation of land, although with restrictions for foreign investors (Figueiredo, 2011: 205).[17]

This legislation also established the administrative process and criteria for obtaining land concessions, and created a Land Commission (*Comissão de Terras*) for implementing the concessions' process. The focus on economic exploitation of land continued during this period, with the approval of several pieces of legislation that further expanded the governor's powers to give concessions of large parcels of land. These legal changes resulted in a rush for land, and there were several cases where land of native people was considered empty and taken for concessions (Davidson, 1994: 248; Figueiredo, 2011: 207; see also Kammen, 2016: 112).

The Portuguese legal definition and regulation of customary tenure was influenced by what Direito identifies as the three main ideas that lead early twentieth-century Portuguese legal scholars in the debates on land policy in

13 This law was regulated by a decree (*decreto*) from 2 September 1901 and a Decree from 30 October 1902. See Santos, 2004: 203.

14 The debate about the definition of native land can be found in Santos, 2004: 196. For consistency with the legislation, I use the expressions native people and native Timorese in this section but acknowledging that it is a problematic expression.

15 These rules kept varying along the years. For instance a decree from 5 December 1910 mentioned that at least half of the land had to be cultivated or have a permanent residence and could not be left uncultivated for more than five years.

16 See here art. 1, 2, 3, 4, 5, and 8 of the *Carta de Lei*, and art. 1, 2, 3, 4, 5, 6, 7, 10.2, and 52 of the decree from 2 September 1901.

17 The coffee plantations in the Ermera region, the biggest of them owned by Governor Celestino da Silva (*Sociedade Agrícola Pátria e Trabalho*—SAPT), was the model of the Portuguese authorities' vision for expanding the cash-crop agriculture in the territory. However, concessions of land to large companies was a controversial topic among Portuguese politicians, who feared that the state could lose control of colonial territories to private and foreign companies (Santos, 2004: 194).

colonial Africa (Direito, 2014: 259; see also Martinez, 2010).[18] First, a principle of so-called 'respect for the land held by Africans', which was justified by an ethical obligation of the colonial power and its 'civilizing mission' but also based on past experiences of colonial powers having to deal with rebellions after violently dispossessing native people. However, and as the law (*lei*) from 1901 and its regulations show, the definition of native land was oriented by an economic vision of the land and the need to find 'vacant land' to exploit. Therefore, the definition of native land did not take into consideration the social, spiritual, and political roles of land for these native populations (Direito, 2014: 261).[19]

The second idea of the Portuguese scholars was that the native population needed to be 'protected by the state', which led to legal solutions such as the prohibition of transactions with non-natives. The prevalence of communal tenure in African and Southeast Asian colonies was seen by these scholars and the colonial administrations as a sign of primitive land tenure systems which should progressively evolve into individualised tenure, a vision that was common to other colonial powers (Yoder, 2005: 300; Dekker, 2005: 163). However, the Portuguese scholars argued that this change would have to be slowly introduced, as the native people were not yet prepared for it, and others would take advantage of their naiveté (Direito, 2014: 260). For instance, Júlio Celestino Montalvão e Silva, son of Governor Celestino da Silva, claimed that 'the property regime is being perfected along the evolution of the people, starting from the initial uncertainty until the final individualization' (Silva, 1910: 33; see also Martinho, 1943: 231).

The third idea defended by Portuguese scholars was the need to respect local customs, which should be studied and codified. Based on paternalistic and racist arguments, it was fairly consensual for the Portuguese colonial administration that, due to the very different way of living of the native populations of the colonies, local practices should be respected by law, and special legislation that could accommodate their specificities was necessary. The example of the Netherland Indies was a strong influence on the Portuguese administration, and the idea of respecting local customs even justified the power given to each Portuguese colony to approve specific legislation for that colony (Martinez, 2010; Kammen, 2016: 108). This legislative power was used in Timor-Leste but mostly to adapt national laws to the administrative structure and capacity in Timor-Leste and not to codify customary land tenure systems.

These three ideas continued to be reaffirmed in subsequent legislation. In 1914 the Portuguese administration approved a new regulation that created

18 The fact the literature often only refers to Africa is another example of how Timor-Leste was a mostly disregarded colony for the Portuguese authorities.

19 Castro reports that customary leaders complained about the 1910 law, claiming that they were not anymore consulted nor compensated when a concession was given (Castro, 1944: 124).

what became known as the *alvará indígena*, or the native title (Edit [*portaria*] 193 of 1914). In summary, this regulation established a simplified mechanism for the native Timorese to, individually and optionally, formalise their rights to land by registering them and obtaining a formal land use right (*aforamento*).[20] The introductory text that precedes the preamble of this legislation exemplifies well the 'concerns' about native people losing their land, but also the condescending, racist, and paternalist view of them as prodigal and incapable to navigate 'modern' formal land tenure systems, and therefore the need for state protection. This text also expresses the fear of having native Timorese claiming too much land, and consequently the need to limit the rights that were recognised to them. However, as texts such as the Edit 144 from 8 July 1911 shows, defining who should be considered a native Timorese was problematic, with people claiming this legal status to sell land to other native Timorese, but refusing it to avoid paying the head tax. Nevertheless, the native title legislation had limited success, with few land parcels being registered under this scheme, and it was terminated in the 1950s with the titles issued being recalled by the colonial administration.[21]

The second half of the twentieth century was marked by the end of the Second World War, the growing international pressure for the end of colonial ventures, and the affirmation of self-determination rights of the colonised peoples. In reaction to these movements, the Portuguese authorities started a few reforms that intended to maintain their control of colonial territories, for instance by changing the legal designation of colonies to overseas provinces (*províncias ultramarinas*), and by recognising Portuguese citizenship to native people (Pimenta, 2014: 252).[22] These changes have been reflected in the land-related legislation approved since then.

The Legislative Diploma 865 that approves the Complementary Regulation of the Occupation and Concession of Land in the Timor Province was the last land-related regulation in force in Timor-Leste before 1975.[23] The tone of this legislation is quite different when compared with texts from the beginning of the century, with the previously native people now called residents (*vizinhos de regedorias*), and without any racial considerations. The legislative

20 On *aforamento* see Chapter 6.

21 A document published on 23 November 1918 in the Official Journal (*Boletim Oficial*) states that by then, in Dili, 313 properties had been registered under this programme.

22 The Statute of the Overseas Provinces from 1953 (Law 2066) removed the concept of 'native' (*indígena*) from the legal framework except in Angola, Mozambique, and Guinee. The native statute in these provinces was further regulated by Decree-Law (*decreto-lei*) 39666 from 1954, but latter repealed by Decree-Law 43893 from 1961. This decree-law explicitly states that the native statute was not applicable in Timor-Leste since 1953.

23 Legislative Diploma 865 was regulated Decree 43894 from 1961, and became applicable in Timor-Leste through Edit (*Portaria*) 21 283 from 1965. The new Land Law for the Overseas Provinces from 1973 (Law 6/73) never entered into force in Timor-Leste because the necessary regulatory framework was never approved.

solutions also had some improvements in the protection given to customary land rights. It allowed the delimitation of communal property, used and ruled according to customary practices.[24] It also allowed the individual occupation of land based on customary practices, which could be converted into a land use title (*aforamento*) upon occupation for more than 10 years.[25] The administrative process to formalise these rights was facilitated, allowing oral processes, although transfers of land were still limited. Nevertheless, the process still required time, knowledge about its existence and importance, and in some cases payments. Therefore, few people and communities ever formalised their rights. Furthermore, and in line with the previous legislation, this legal protection focused on housing and cultivation, but ignored other important areas of customary tenure such as grazing, hunting, foresting, sacred areas, and areas reserved for future use. If on one hand housing and cultivated land were more protected, by default other land continued to be legally available for concessions to third parties, as it was classified as 'empty', and therefore belonging to the state. As in previous legislation, the central point of the formal land tenure system remained the concession of land for economic exploitation. This was done through the concession of ownership (*propriedade perfeita*) and land use rights (*aforamento*) that in some cases could later be converted into ownership (Du Plessis and Leckie, 2000: 9).

Despite the efforts of the Portuguese authorities, the implementation of their formal land tenure system had in general limited success. While the exact numbers diverge, it is calculated that only around 3,000 formal land rights were ever issued by the Portuguese authorities, and while there are some large concessions of land in valuable agricultural regions, they represent a relatively small percentage of Timor-Leste's area (Nixon, 2005: 8; Yoder, 2005: 285; Nixon, 2009: 3).[26] The great majority of beneficiaries of the Portuguese formal land tenure system and its formal land rights were those people with links to the Portuguese administration, business interests, the Catholic Church, and some foreigners (Aditjondro, 1994: 55; Du Plessis and Leckie, 2000: 8; Yoder, 2003: 7; Fitzpatrick *et al.*, 2013: 224). Two interviewees that worked closely with the Portuguese administration in its final years said that there was a clear concern in consulting with the local people before giving a concession. However, there are also examples where state concessions took advantage of the limited definition of customary land rights, as well as coercion and legal expedients (Figueiredo, 2011: 207; Kammen, 2016:112). Even today it

24 Art. 284 to 291. See also art. 8 and 9 of Decree 43897 from 1961.

25 Art. 292 to 309.

26 According to Du Plessis and Leckie, the Portuguese authorities issued 2,709 formal rights (2000: 8). Da Cruz reports a total of 2,843, with more than half referring to land in the Dili district (in Fitzpatrick, 2002: 148). The Indonesian Department of Foreign Affairs reported that only 550 formal land rights were issued by the Portuguese administration (Department of Foreign Affairs, 1984: 101). See also Yoder, 2005: 301.

is possible to find complaints about land-related injustices committed by the Portuguese administration to obtain land for public projects and land concessions to companies, individuals, and the church (Matadalan ba Rai and Haburas Foundation, 2010: 154).

In conclusion, the Portuguese formal land tenure system established some rules to formalise and protect existing customary-based land rights, but it was mostly oriented towards providing access to land for commercial exploitation and protecting individual rights to land. By limiting the recognition of customary-based land rights with a narrow definition and establishing a default state ownership over 'empty' land, this system made large tracts of land available for concessions. Nevertheless, its weak territorialisation resulted that, in practice, only a small percentage of the country's area was ever affected by it.

The Portuguese formal land tenure system left a legacy in Timor-Leste that is still relevant today. First, unfair treatment and dispossession caused grievances that still exist and shape the debate about land tenure. Second, the Portuguese formal land tenure system left a few formal land rights that, as described below, are still source of many land claims, but also controversy. Third, principles such as the state being the owner of all 'empty' land, combined with a strict definition and recognition of customary land rights, and a focus on the economic role of land as the central guide of the formal land tenure system are ideas that left a mark in the country, as is debated in Chapter 4.

The Indonesian formal land tenure system in Timor-Leste

After the invasion of Timor-Leste in December 1975 the Indonesian authorities quickly implemented their own political, administrative, and legal structures. Eleven days after the invasion, a provisional government was established and, in the following July, Timor-Leste was officially integrated in Indonesia by the Indonesian People's Representative Council (CAVR 2005: part 4, 37). The implementation of the Indonesian formal land tenure system took longer, but it was a central part of this integration.

The Indonesian formal land tenure system that was applied in Timor-Leste was a mirror of the political situation and the internal contradictions that marked Indonesia during those years. In 1975 the Government of Indonesia was firmly in the hands of General Suharto, after the struggle for independence of the Dutch colonial ruling, the unstable democracy of the 1950s, and the years of fragile balance between the military and the Indonesian Communist Party. Authoritarianism, corruption, suppression of political opposition, and centralisation of power were the main marks of Suharto's New Order, which was well reflected in the way land tenure was managed by the Indonesian authorities.

Land tenure in Indonesia was, and still is, primarily regulated by the Indonesian Agrarian Law of 1960 (*Undang-Undang Pokok-Pokok Agraria*, Law

5/1960, or BAL in its English acronym).[27] The nationalistic, anti-colonial, and socialist principles that guided its drafting, combined with the implementation of the centralistic and authoritarian New Order, resulted in a tenure system where the state took a central and dominant position in land administration (Reerink, 2011: 60; Bedner, 2016: 65). The state granted and registered rights over state land, but also had strong powers to terminate formal land rights whenever it deemed necessary (Fitzpatrick, 2002: 87; Bachriadi and Wiradi, 2013; Bedner, 2016: 66). Under the BAL the recognition of customary (*adat*) rights was very restricted and in practice offered almost no protection against the state, which could always invoke the state interest or consider the uncultivated land as 'unowned' to take the land from the people (Fitzpatrick, 2002: 86; Lucas and Warren, 2013: footnote 13; Bedner, 2016: 65). Additionally, the BAL was not applicable to forest land, which represented around 70 percent of the country's area, and therefore provided no legal tenure security to people living in or near these forest areas (Fitzpatrick, 2002: 86, 126; Bedner, 2016: 70).[28] Furthermore, the formal land tenure system was mostly characterised by discretion, with law being used selectively by the government when deemed necessary to justify its actions and ignored when its application was inconvenient (Bedner, 2016: 68).[29]

The implementation of the Indonesian formal land tenure system in Timor-Leste had to deal with the transition from the Portuguese system, but legal certainty was not a priority for the Indonesian authorities. The law from 1976 that integrated Timor-Leste into Indonesia established that the Indonesian legislation would be applicable in the new Indonesian province, with no special rule regarding land rights.[30] Only in 1979, four years after the invasion and when many properties had already been 'requisitioned' by the army, the military commander issued the SKEP 40 decree (*surat keputusan panglima*), which legally brought under control of the army the abandoned land and land owned by the Portuguese administration (anonymous author, 1991: 10; Fitzpatrick, 2002: 94, 117). Under this decree the army was also entitled to make temporary allocations of these parcels of land until the return of their legal owners, which in practice was unlikely due to the violence and intimidation that became common during that period.

27 The BAL is further regulated by other pieces of legislation such as Government Regulation 24/1997 on Land Registration.

28 Forest land, regulated by the Basic Forestry Law (5/1967) and later replaced by Law 41/1999, refused the recognition of customary-based land rights over forestry land (Lucas and Warren, 2013: 8). Decision No. 35/PUU-X/2012 of the Indonesian Constitutional Court from 2013 recognised customary-based land rights in forestry areas (Bedner, 2016: 76).

29 Despite significant changes since the end of Suharto's dictatorship, state-lead displacement in Indonesia is still a problem for many urban and rural dwellers (Lucas and Warren, 2013; Bedner, 2016).

30 Fitzpatrick mentions that this this law expressly maintained the legality of Portuguese 'legal products', but I cannot find such provision in the law (Fitzpatrick, 2002: 93).

From 1980 onwards military administration was progressively replaced by the Indonesian National Land Agency (*Badan Pertanahan Nasional*—BPN), the Indonesian state institution responsible for managing land tenure, which started with a small local office in Timor-Leste until it was upgraded to a full provincial BPN office. Besides starting to implement the BAL and other relevant Indonesian legislation (see below), BPN also attempted a definitive solution for the transition from the Portuguese system. A regulation for conversion of Portuguese formal land rights into Indonesian ones was approved in 1991 (Government Regulation 18/1991), but it was the cause of much controversy. Some Portuguese formal rights were converted into weaker Indonesian equivalents, and those people that had fled the country were going to lose their rights in the process.[31] Entities such as the church were also going to get weaker land rights. As a result, the implementation of this law and the conversion of Portuguese formal rights into equivalent Indonesian ones had little success.

Despite the complications in dealing with Portuguese formal rights, the Indonesian authorities were more efficient than their Portuguese predecessors in formalising land rights. While there are no definitive numbers, it is estimated that around 44,000 formal rights were issued to individuals and companies, covering around 10 percent of the country's area (Fitzpatrick, 2002: 95, 96).[32] The implementation of large-scale land registration and titling programmes such as the PRONA project (*Proyek Operasi Nasional Agraria*), which was aimed at poor dwellers in rural areas, contributed to this higher number of formalised land rights (Yoder, 2005: 306; Fitzpatrick *et al.*, 2013: 254; Warren and Lucas, 2013). Transmigration programmes that brought people from other areas of Indonesia to Timor-Leste and translocation policies that concentrated Timorese from different areas in one specific location were also at times followed by formalisation schemes (Nixon, 2005: 3).[33] Notably, most formal land rights issued by the Indonesian authorities were temporary (e.g., *hak guna bangunan, hak pakai*), showing a will of the state to keep a tight control over land (Fitzpatrick, 2002: 97). Senior Timorese state officials that worked with BPN during the Indonesian occupation explained to me that *hak milik* rights (ownership rights) were not for everyone, only the people with enough money (and eventually power and connections) were allowed to obtain these titles.[34] One

31 Anonymous author, 1991; Fitzpatrick, 2002: 94; Yoder, 2005: 306. See also Almeida, 2016: 19.

32 Fitzpatrick bases part of his numbers on an unpublished thesis from 1996 written by Baisaku. A table published by the Indonesian Department of Statistics shows that between 1985 and 1996 only around 17,000 formal rights were issued (DKSPTT, 1996: 148). The table does not account, however, for numbers before 1985.

33 As in other places in Indonesia, also in Timor-Leste customary land was claimed as state land and taken for transmigration projects (Yoder, 2003: 9; Bachriadi and Wiradi, 2013: para. 11).

34 However, some of them recall the PRONA project gave *hak milik* rights (see also anonymous author, 1991).

of these state officials also told me that he questioned his BPN Indonesian colleagues about why they were issuing temporary rights to people that owned the land, to which they explained that by doing it state officials would be able to perpetuate their jobs. Furthermore, access to land titles was dependent on the payment of bribes and 'incentives', and it was used as a mechanism to reward the cronies of the regime and to punish those suspected of being connected with the resistance movement (Aditjondro, 1994: 58; Fitzpatrick, 2002: 104, Fitzpatrick *et al.*, 2013: 202; see also Shepherd, 2014: 236).

If the legal protection of land rights was weak, in practice the situation was even worse. Dispossession through intimidation and use of violence especially by the army, combined with a broad interpretation of the definition of state land and state power to expropriate, were largely used to obtain land for private concessions to forcedly resettle displaced populations and to implement state infrastructure projects (Fitzpatrick, 2002: 115; CAVR, 2005: part 7.9, 48). In many cases little or no compensation was paid for these acquisitions, and individuals and communities had few or no mechanisms to safely complain against them (Aditjondro, 1994: 63; ICG, 2010: 4; Fitzpatrick *et al.*, 2013: 41). Some interviewees and DNTPSC staff reported that in the 1990s there was an effort to improve the image of the Indonesian administration and army, which in part restrained abuses in land dispossession, especially when compared with the very militarised period after the invasion. Nevertheless, the situation was far from ideal. When the referendum for independence came in 1999, the territorialisation of the Indonesian formal land tenure system was in full force, but it was marked by corruption, arbitrariness, and dispossession (see Chapters 4 and 7).

The formal land tenure system during the UNTAET administration

The end of the Indonesian administration and the need for international intervention gave origin to another land tenure system, this time from UNTAET. Land-related issues were at that time massive (Goldstone, 2004: 93), and despite the efforts little was achieved in this area by UNTAET (Rohland and Cliffe, 2002: iv; Fitzpatrick and Monson, 2009: 113).[35] The first land-related problem that UNTAET had to face was land occupation. It is estimated that out of a population of around 900,000 people in 1999, 450,000 had been internally displaced, and around 250,000 fled or were forcedly taken to West Timor (Fitzpatrick, 2002a: 6; CAVR, 2005: part 7.3, 106). These displaced people were slowly returning, and many of them were finding their houses destroyed or already occupied by others. Especially in Dili, to where most of the displaced people returned and where many houses were left vacant by

35 Thomson (2003), a former member of staff at UNTAET's Land and Property Unit, gives a detailed account of land administration during this period.

Indonesians that fled the country, a ferocious competition for shelter but also profit opportunities started. Any ruin with a piece of roof left was occupied to shelter entire families. In some cases there where families taking control of several houses expecting to rent, sell, or get some compensation for vacating them (Du Plessis and Leckie, 2000: 10; Fitzpatrick, 2002a: 12; Harrington, 2006: 27; Stead, 2014: 82; Devereux, 2015: 248). This rush for land was a source of conflict, and the lack of a housing policy by UNTAET further complicated this matter (Fitzpatrick, 2002a: 10, 13; Fitzpatrick and Monson, 2009: 111). Moreover, long-term refugees from the Indonesian invasion also returned to claim the land they abandoned in 1975, and people and communities forcedly dispossessed by the Indonesian administration were now reclaiming and repossessing their land.[36] Additionally, the need of land for public administration activities, the arrival of investors, and the influx of thousands of foreign development workers further raised the competition for, and the price of, accessing land.

UNTAET created the Land and Property Unit (LPU) to deal with land tenure problems, but this unit lacked the mechanisms necessary to address them. UNTAET opted for incorporating the Indonesian legislation with some modifications which, in absence of any specific reference, included the Indonesian legal framework on land tenure (Almeida, 2017a: 176). But in practice Indonesian legislation was mostly unknown by UNTAET staff, and this set of rules did not provide solutions for most problems UNTAET was facing (Thomson, 2003: 49). Furthermore, the Indonesian legislation was seen by many Timorese as illegitimate (Fitzpatrick, 2002: 14) and gave little protection to customary land rights.

Moreover, the Indonesian land registry had been mostly destroyed during the violence that followed the referendum, leaving no information to confirm who had which formal rights, or if land occupants were the legitimate owners (ibid.: 7; Thomson, 2003: 10).[37] The loss of personal documentation and the use of forged documents further complicated any recognition of formal rights. Furthermore, there was strong internal opposition from the Timorese

36 See, for instance, the case of Hotel Resende (Almeida, 2017).

37 Parts of the Indonesian property registry might have survived the destruction. Reportedly the book of formal land rights in Dili was saved by the Indonesian head of BPN, but it was never returned to Timor-Leste (Fitzpatrick, 2002: 7). Thomson reports that, when he first arrived in Dili in late January 2000, he found in Dili the Timorese BPN staff working shifts to protect the remaining land records (Thomson, 2003: 10; see also Harrington, 2006: 29). He also reports how, allegedly, land records in Baucau were hidden in a secret cave by a land surveyor during the 1999 violence. I was also told by senior DNTPSC staff that Indonesian records are kept in boxes in DNTPSC headquarters. However, during the period I worked there, I never saw these records, they were not publicly available nor systematically used by DNTPSC. I once asked a senior DNTPSC staff member why Timor-Leste was not asking Indonesia for copies of records that might have been kept. The answer was surprising: 'When we ask the Indonesians for something, they always want something in return. It is better not to negotiate with them'.

cabinet members of UNTAET to re-establish the Indonesian formal land tenure system (ibid.: 17). Finally, humanitarian reasons, the transitory nature of the administration, and the potential for conflict made law enforcement on land tenure a very difficult and sensitive matter. In summary, while in theory the Indonesian legislation remained in place, in practice it ceased to be applied (ibid.: 10; Yoder, 2005: 312).

Changing the legal framework and establishing a land commission, a special court, or any other mechanism to address land-related issues was, from the beginning, identified by UNTAET and many others as a priority for conflict-prevention and state development (Plessi and Leckie, 2000: 28; Morrow and White, 2002: 42; Thomson, 2003: 53). However, and despite having legislative powers, it was not possible for UNTAET to approve any relevant legislation on this matter.[38] Attempts to start debates about, and draft legislation on land-related issues were always halted by the strong opposition part of the Timorese political elite involved in the cabinet of UNTAET administration, which argued that such sensitive topics should be left to a Timorese-elected government and even threatened to resign if land legislation was approved (Fitzpatrick, 2002: 3; Thomson, 2003: 54; Gorjão, 2004: 1059; Yoder, 2005: 313).[39] Furthermore, they argued that UNTAET's legislative mandate did not include the approval of legislation with such lasting impacts like land tenure (Thomson, 2003: 11). Trapped in the dilemma of legislating about this urgent issue, or following the demands of this Timorese elite, UNTAET decided for the second. On 25 October 2000 the Transitional Cabinet agreed on only administering temporary land use and registration of land claims, and deferring any decision on land claims and disputes to a Timorese-elected government.[40] The need to address the lack of legal recognition of customary-based land rights in the draft constitution was also raised but ignored by the politicians involved (Hohe and Nixon, 2003: 41, 51).

As a result of these decisions, UNTAET made minimal use of its legislative powers, and most of its focus became the temporary allocation of state and abandoned land through what was called *temporary use agreements*, similar to lease contracts.[41] However, these agreements were not issued based on Indonesian

38 Articles 1.1, 7.1 and 7.2 of UNTAET Regulation No. 1999/1.

39 According to interviews and literature, Mari Alkatiri, João Carrascalão and Ana Pessoa were the loudest Timorese voices against any UNTAET legislation on land-related issues, but Galbraith, one of the international members of the cabinet was also against this legislation (Gorjão, 2004: 1059; Psychas, 2010: 292; Thomson, 2003: 54; Goldstone, 2004: 93). However, other Timorese were in favour of a UNTAET regulation of this matter. Also, the opposition was not only against interventions regarding land claims but any regulation or policy on housing (Thomson, 2003: 54).

40 http://reliefweb.int/report/timor-leste/untaet-daily-briefing-25-oct-2000. See also the preamble and art. 16.4 of Law 1/2003.

41 Even these temporary use agreements were criticised because some people saw them as a mechanism to formalise inequalities generated by the 1999 violence (Harrington, 2006: 32; Stead, 2016: 130).

law, but on the *Guidelines for the Administration of Public and Abandoned Property by District Administrations*, a UNTAET policy that was applied almost as law, but was never converted into any kind of formal legislation (Thomson, 2003: 11, 18).[42] UNTAET also created an informal process for collecting land claims, but without any legal basis or clear outcome to those claims (Yoder, 2005: 313). The only main land-related piece of legislation approved by UNTAET was Regulation 2000/27, which temporarily forbade transactions of land rights and lease contracts in Timor-Leste by Indonesian citizens not habitually residing in the country, and by Indonesian corporations.[43] Besides land tenure, other parts of land administration were also not addressed in legislation by UNTAET, with exception of a regulation on protected areas (UNTAET Regulation 2000/19).[44]

Without adequate legislation, the LPU worked based on practice, internal guidelines, and common sense, which raised problems of consistency, legitimacy, and transparency (Thomson, 2003: 50).[45] In other words, UNTAET's formal land tenure system was mostly based on institutional practice and not on law, which is surprising in an administration that was in part expected to set an example of rule of law for future Timorese governments. The initial need for pragmatism and the opposition by the Timorese elite in part justified this failure, but independently of whom to blame, the truth is that UNTAET didn't leave a deep legacy for the construction of the Timorese formal land tenure system. During my work with the MoJ, I could experience first-hand this lack of legacy. For instance LPU guidelines were not available in any repository, and I was only able to get them because they were annexed to Thomson's work (2003: 103). Also, any legal reasoning based on violation of principles and rules established by the guidelines is impossible because the guidelines have no legal value outside the public administration. As described in Chapter 7, the legacy of the Indonesian formal land tenure system prevailed over UNTAET's administration.

In closing, it may be said that due to political, legal, and practical limitations UNTAET was not able to leave a legacy regarding land tenure administration in Timor-Leste. Without an adequate legal framework and institutional resources, land tenure administration by UNTAET was mostly reactive and

42 The guidelines were published in February 2000 and revised in August 2000, 2001, and 2002 (Fitzpatrick, 2002a: 15; Thomson, 2003: 21). Directive 2000/6 and Notification 2000/16 established some rules regarding rents.

43 This regulation should be applicable with retroactive effects (art. 5), which raises questions about its legality. A similar provision was later established by Law 1/2003 (art. 13.1).

44 For instance a *Draft Rental Fee Valuation Policy for East Timor* was prepared but never approved as legislation (Thomson, 2003: 40, 41).

45 See for instance Thomson's description of the problematic land acquisition process for the Metinaro military barracks or the evictions of the Dili Market (2003: 55, 66; see also Hohe and Nixon, 2003: 53).

based on internal guidelines and pragmatism, not on law. When Timor-Leste became independent on 20 May 2002, little had been achieved in addressing the land-related problems caused by previous administrations and in establishing the new basis for the formal land tenure system.

The formal land tenure system since independence

After independence, it became the responsibility of the elected Timorese politicians to provide answers to the land-related problems and dilemmas that UNTAET was not able and allowed to solve. The questions were many: which should be the main bases of the Timorese formal land tenure system? What should be the legal validity of formal land rights issued by previous administrations? How to address situations where formal rights issued by Portugal and Indonesia overlap? How to address the problem of formal land rights obtained through nepotism, corruption, and forced displacement? Should customary land tenure systems and rights have legal recognition? If yes, how much and in which format? How to deal with large landowners such as the Catholic Church? Should people forcedly settled on other people's customary land return to their origin place, or should they have the right to remain where they lived for many years? How to deal with the land occupations that occurred before independence? Should the land rights of foreigners be legally recognised? If not, should they be compensated for their loss? And how to answer all these questions with very limited financial resources and administrative capacity? In sum, land tenure posed an extremely complex set of problems and dilemmas to the newly independent Timor-Leste.

This section summarises the main steps taken by the Timorese governments to address these questions and build the Timorese formal land tenure system. To facilitate this summary, the section is divided into three periods, broadly corresponding to three different governments: (a) 2002–2007; (b) 2007–2012; and (c) 2012–2017. Many of the steps and episodes described here are further detailed and analysed in the following chapters.

2002–2007 period—Law 1/2003 and the Land Law Program

The drafting of the Timorese Constitution was the first opportunity to start addressing the above-mentioned questions. But aside from establishing the protection of private property and forbidding foreigners to own land in Timor-Leste, the constitution did little to create the basis of a formal land tenure system that could address past injustices and contribute to address social problems (see Chapter 6; Hohe and Nixon, 2003: 41). The constitution also reaffirmed that Indonesian legislation would continue to be applicable until replaced by Timorese laws, but in practice it was mostly ignored (Almeida, 2017a: 177).

The first main action taken by the newly elected Timorese government was the approval of Law 1/2003. As shown in Chapters 5, 6, and 8, this law was far from successful in addressing the above-mentioned questions and in establishing the new basis for the formal land tenure system. The drafting was marked by lack of background studies, almost no consultation, weak legal drafting, and poor legal solutions. Furthermore, this law was strongly influenced by a state-centric view of land administration, with no real assessment of administrative capacity, and no acknowledgement of the prevalent role of customary systems in land administration. The result was a law that didn't answer most of the above-mentioned questions, and instead strengthened the power of the state to dispossess. In practice, this law gave some, but unclear, legal protection to those Timorese that had a formal land right issued by previous administrations. Those without formal rights, which are the large majority, were in constant risk of seeing their land classified as state land, and being evicted without any compensation. The fact that the approval of complementary legislation was stalled and definitively abandoned due to the 2006 crisis further contributed to the failure of this law in answering the above-mentioned questions and protecting peoples' land rights.

This period was also marked by the creation of what is now DNTPSC, the main administrative institution responsible for implementing the formal land tenure system, which was strongly inspired by the Indonesian BPN (see Chapter 7). Especially from 2004 onwards, the institutional growth of DNTPSC was marked by strong donor support from Australian and American development cooperation agencies (Marquardt *et al.*, 2002: 1; Sousa, 2005: 12; Leigh, 2006: 4). The USAID Land Law Program I and II (LLP) provided DNTPSC with equipment, staff training, research reports developed in coordination with Timorese universities, administrative procedure manuals, and draft legislation (ARD, 2006). However, the impact of these two projects was relatively limited.[46] With the exception of Decree-Law 19/2004 and Law 12/2005 regarding the leases of state and private land respectively, no other legislation drafted by the LLP was approved. During my work with the MoJ and DNTPSC, I could still identify some administrative practices designed during these programmes that were, at least partially, being followed by DNTPSC staff, but a considerable part of the knowledge and momentum created had already been lost. With exception of Urresta and Nixon's studies (2003, 2004, 2004a), most studies, manuals, and other documents produced during this time were also very difficult to obtain, and mostly forgotten.

The political crisis of 2006 stopped the drafting and approval of new legislation, but also highlighted the potential of land disputes to fuel broader conflict, and exposed the difficulties that the government had been having in dealing with land tenure issues (Brady and Timberman, 2006: 20; McWilliam, 2007: 41; Scambary, 2009: 4). The conflict was in part fuelled

46 In the words of Psychas, this project '[was] barely tolerated by the FRETILIN government' (2010: 292).

by tensions around land occupations that happened during 1999 and resulted in a new layer of displacements and occupations (Lopes, 2009: 12; ICG, 2010: 9). DNTPSC national office was one of the many buildings targeted during the 2006 crisis, with its computers destroyed and the building damaged (McWilliam, 2007: 39).

2007–2012 period—Ita Nia Rai and the beginning of the Land Law Package

In the aftermath of the 2006 crisis land tenure came back to the spotlight. Upon request from Prime Minister Ramos-Horta, in 2007 USAID started a new land project that became known as *Ita Nia Rai* (INR, or 'Our Land' in Tetum), designed to address land disputes and create a land registry.[47] In summary, the two main objectives of INR were (1) the development and implementation of a process for systematic collection of land claims that would eventually lead to the development of a land registry, and (2) the approval of the legal framework necessary to legitimise and regulate this systematic process and to formalise the land rights claimed through it.

After a slow beginning the development of a process for systematic collection of land claims went fairly well (see Chapter 7). The initial ambition of registering all land parcels in the country quickly had to be massively scaled down to the registration of the urban areas of the 13 district capitals. Besides the logistical complications and the limited timeframe and budget, the project wanted to focus on areas with higher concentration of people, more individualised rights, land-related disputes, and possible land markets, and avoid the very complex customary arrangements prevalent in rural areas (Haburas Foundation and Rede ba Rai, 2013: 6). Therefore, the methodology developed was mostly designed form urban areas, although there was also room for communal land claims. The process was supported by a strong focus on public information and corruption prevention, and it was fairly simple and transparent (Fella and Boudreaux, 2011; UNMIT, 2011: 33). The main premise was that everyone—individuals, groups, legal entities, communities, and the state—that was considered to own land in an area under survey by the project was entitled to claim that land, for free, independently of having or not a formal right issued by a previous administration. In parallel with the development of a process for collection of land claims, INR also supported the MoJ in drafting legislation that would legally support this process and formalise the rights of land claimants (see Chapter 5).

INR managed to collect more than 50,000 land claims in the urban areas of district capitals. However, these results of INR were overshadowed by

47 The original name of the project was Strengthening Property Rights in Timor-Leste Project (SPRTL).

legislative and institutional problems. The approval of the legal framework necessary to legitimise the claims process remained stalled in parliament for years, and partial solutions such as the Decree-Law 27/2011 experienced a problematic implementation (see below and Chapters 5 and 6). Institutionally, while INR had strong support from the MoJ and DNTPSC district directors, its integration with the national office of DNTPSC was difficult, and in practice the two institutions worked almost separately from each other (see Chapter 7).

At the end of 2011, USAID and the MoJ had not yet agreed on a plan about the future of the project, and in the beginning of 2012 INR started to downsize its staff. Without any clear plan from its counterpart, the MoJ decided to temporarily hire INR's staff, but not its senior managers, who progressively left when their contracts finished (Chapter 7). Without a clear institutional framework, a budget, and a management structure, the activities of INR almost ceased. The land registry that was started under Decree-Law 27/2011 became inaccessible to the public and with no possibility of being updated. The 10 million USD invested in the project and the thousands of work hours invested by hundreds of people became mostly wasted.[48]

In parallel with INR land claims process, key pieces of legislation were being drafted and promoted by MoJ. First, a draft Civil Code was prepared and sent to parliament after approval by the Council of Ministers. This code is mostly a copy of the Portuguese Civil Code, and covers several areas such as legal personality, contracts, family law, inheritance, and land rights. The Civil Code is especially relevant because contains the basis for the normal functioning of the formal land tenure system, such as the characteristics of different land rights (the *bundle of rights and obligations*), the different forms in which they can be transacted, and provisions such as adverse possession (see Chapter 6). For years the draft Civil Code waited for debate by parliament, but in September 2011, without much consultation or public debates, was suddenly approved. Also waiting to be debated by parliament was what became known as the Land Law Package, a group of three laws promoted by MoJ which included the Land Law developed with support of INR, an Expropriation Law, and an Immovable Property Fund Law, each developed by a different Portuguese law firm.

In summary, the Land Law established which formal land rights issued by previous administrations, customary, and communal land rights should be recognised by law, the criteria to address disputes in cases of overlapping rights, and the basis for the systematic collection of land claims.[49] The Expropriation

48 Accounts of the results of INR can be found in Fella and Boudreaux, 2011; Haburas Foundation and Rede ba Rai, 2013.

49 The official name of the law is Special Regime for the Determination of Ownership of Immovable Property (*Regime Especial para a Determinação de Direitos de Propriedade Sobre Bens Imóveis*).

Law established the legal process for the state to expropriate land for public purposes. The Immovable Property Fund Law created a fund for the payment of all the costs and compensations that the implementation of these laws would involve. These drafts also waited almost two years to be debated by parliament and, when finally approved in March 2012, were vetoed by the president (see Chapter 5). Finally, the delays of parliament in approving the Land Law Package led the Council of Ministers to approve the above-mentioned Decree-Law 27/2011 that anticipated some effects of the Land Law, by legalising the process of land claims collection and allowing the registration of ownership rights over undisputed land.

2012–2017 period—SNC and the approval of the Land Law Package

When the government changed in mid-2012, two main questions needed to be addressed. The first was what to do with the INR project, by then under the MoJ's administration, but mostly paralysed without a clear institutional framework, budget, and leadership. The second question was what to do with the vetoed Land Law Package.

Regarding the first question, the solution adopted by the new government for the INR was very controversial. At the end of 2013, through a sole-sourced six-year contract of around 57 million USD (2014–2020), the government awarded the continuation of the land claims' process developed by INR to a Timorese/Portuguese joint venture without any previous experience in this kind of work, which was named National Cadastre System (*Sistema Nacional de Cadastro* or SNC in its Portuguese acronym).[50] The Timorese company was GMN-Holding, a company known for its business in construction, tourism, and media, owned by a Timorese businessman closely connected to Gusmão, at the time prime minister, and his party CNRT. The Portuguese company was ARM-APPRIZE, a small consultancy company without any known experience in land registration or related projects. The terms of reference of this project were never made public, but it was claimed by the government that it was going to register all parcels of land throughout the country.[51]

Conceptually, the idea of re-starting land registration by massively expanding it throughout the country into the more rural areas was the exact opposite

50 The government's efforts to justify the need for this sole-sourced contract and the competency of these companies can be found in Government Resolution 25/2013 and 28/2013. Considering the ethical reasons mentioned in Chapter 1, I abstain from commenting on this process, but I should say that, as MoJ adviser, I strongly advised against this solution. After my negative advice I was detached for the debates about this project. All the findings presented are result of my field work since 2015 and my participation Rede ba Rai's research (2019).

51 I heard from DNTPSC staff that the contract established an objective registering of 200,000 land parcels. Others mentioned 250,000 parcels.

of what all research and best-practices on land registration developed in the previous decades had recommend. A comparison with the conclusions of the seminal work edited by Bruce and Migot-Adholla (1994) provide a good basis for this statement, but it can be further supported by the work of many other authors (Atwood, 1990; Enemark *et al.*, 2014; Enemark *et al.*, 2015). In summary, Bruce *et al.* advised to (1) doubt the wisdom and cost-effectiveness of large-scale, systematic programmes of compulsory titling for smallholders in rural areas; (2) focus on incremental approaches to the local tenure systems; (3) redirect the efforts from systematic individual registration to the effective needs at local level; (4) move away from a 'replacement paradigm' to an 'adaptation paradigm'; (5) focus land registration efforts on valuable areas, subject to intense competition and dispute, where there is no customary system or where the customary system is failing to cope with conflicts, such as urban and peri-urban areas; (6) prevent situations where the formalisation of land rights endangers other secondary rights; and (7) focus on the rehabilitation of existing registry before considering the expansion to new areas (Bruce *et al.*, 1994). SNC contradicted each of these points.

Aside from these conceptual flaws, Rede ba Rai's research (2019), in which I participated, highlighted other serious problems of SNC's work. In summary, SNC's public information was very limited, of poor quality, and at times even wrong. Communities participated in its land registration process without having enough information about their rights, obligations, and the legal impacts of their land claims.[52] Basic legal requisites were ignored, and newly invented requisites and logistical problems made participation in this process very difficult for land claimants.[53] Moreover, SNC worked under a culture of secrecy, refusing to provide information about their methodology, collected data, statistical information about their work, and mechanisms to avoid corruption and alterations in their data.[54] The fact that the great majority of land claims collected by SNC were individual claims, mostly from rural areas, is especially concerning, considering the potential that this type of land registration has to benefit powerful community members to the detriment of others, disrupt customary systems, and further promote gender-based discrimination (Chapter 2).[55] SNC's disregard for these matters was so worrying that, after a

52 For instance, there were cases where the registration was preceded by a 30-minute public meeting.

53 As an example, mandatory publications in the Official Journal were not strictly respected. Also, land claimants were requested to present declarations from two local state officials attesting to the truthfulness of their claims, making the process much more burdensome for participants and more open to bribes.

54 For instance, SNC leadership refused to give me an interview, but also refused to share information about their work with CSOs, donor agencies, diplomatic representatives, and lawyer's offices, claiming that they were not authorised by the government to provide information.

55 Out of the 10,652 land claims analysed by Rede ba Rai, only six were registered as belonging to a community (2019: 56).

visit to Timor-Leste in 2019, the UN Special Rapporteur on the Rights of Indigenous Peoples recommended the temporary suspension of SNC's work (Human Rights Council, 2019: 15).

Moreover, there was no process of updating the land claims collected, which resulted in a progressive outdating of the database, and spikes in land-related conflict caused by the project had already been reported.[56] Finally, as it happened before with INR, the project was set outside DNTPSC structure, which raised concerns about knowledge and data transfer once the project was over (see Chapter 7). SNC ended in early 2020 and, to the best of my knowledge, its activities stopped, the database is not publicly available, and there is no certainty regarding what will be done with the information collected. In conclusion, the nationwide land registration conducted by SNC puts another layer of problems and difficulties on an already complex scenario of land tenure in the country. This topic is further discussed in the following chapters.

The second main question that the new government had to address in the middle of 2012 was what to do with the Land Law Package that had been vetoed by the president. The decision was to revise these laws and re-start the approval process (see Chapter 5). After many delays and episodes, the package was approved at the beginning of 2017.[57] These laws provide answers to many of the questions raised above, but also bring new legal problems, as well as huge implementation challenges, such as the approval of all the complementary regulations, training of the public administration staff, and creation of internal administrative procedures (see Chapter 6). For many years much hope and expectation from the Timorese was put on the approval of these laws (Yoder, 2003: 22), but since their approval little has been done to implement them and provide answers to those expectations.

Finally, it is important to clarify that for many Timorese, all steps taken in the development of a formal land tenure system had little or no impact in their lives. As further debated in Chapters 4 and 8, a considerable part of the Timorese population lives under customary land tenure systems and has little contact with any formal land tenure system. In fact, these self-organised customary systems have proved to be quite resilient despite the many episodes of outside interference. Mechanisms such as ancestral narratives of first possession facilitated the restructuring and adaptation of customary land tenure systems after the several difficult periods experienced in the country (Fitzpatrick and Barnes, 2010; Fitzpatrick *et al.*, 2013).[58] However, the resilience of these

56 Already in 1994, Bruce *et al.* raised awareness of the fact that many systematic registration exercises failed to register transfers and successions, therefore quickly becoming outdated (1994: 261). Regarding spikes in land-related conflict, see Belun, 2015; 2016.

57 In this last version the Immovable Property Fund Law was replaced by the Basic Law on Spatial Planning.

58 For a different perspective on resilience of customary systems, see Stead, 2016: 45.

systems is not a given, and irresponsible state interference such as the one of SNC can seriously endanger it. Furthermore, the still weak protection of customary tenure can be dramatic when people's land becomes of interest to the state or powerful entities (see Chapter 9).

Conclusion

This chapter shows how current land-related problems in Timor-Leste and the difficulties and dilemmas of building its formal land tenure system are closely connected with the colonial experiences, violence, and displacement that the country has experienced throughout history.

The Portuguese colonial ruling and Indonesian military occupation gave Timor-Leste its first experiences with centralised state systems. Despite some nuances and exceptions, these systems were designed to favour a strong state control of land and economic exploitation of land, often by those people with close contact with state authorities. Although a few Timorese managed to get their rights formalised and protected by these land tenure systems, the great majority were in practice excluded from the system. Moreover, these formal systems were also at odds with, and gave little legal recognition to, the customary systems that de facto ruled (and still rule) land tenure throughout most of the country. The forced displacement, violence, corruption, and nepotism experienced in Timor-Leste especially after the violent Indonesian invasion were the source of many long-lasting grievances, and the difficult transition between the Portuguese and Indonesian formal land tenure systems added another layer of confusion about formal land rights.

These land-related problems, further intensified by the violent withdraw of the Indonesian troops and the return of thousands of displaced people, made land tenure one of the most difficult issues to be address by UNTAET. Despite some attempts to address these land-related problems, the work of UNTAET experienced legal, political, and practical limitations, resulting that in practice UNTAET left little legacy on land tenure administration in the country.

Since independence, and despite all efforts, Timor-Leste is still grappling to develop a formal land tenure system that can adequately address the problems inherited from previous administrations and establish an adequate balance between the different land users and uses. There is some progress, such as the approval of the new Land Law and Expropriation Law, which despite their limitations establish a more protective legal framework when compared with the very draconian Law 1/2003. However, several problems and dilemmas show that the formal land tenure system in Timor-Leste is far from achieving its objectives. The lack of implementation of the above-mentioned laws is one example of a vast range of legal, administrative, and political problems still ahead. Moreover, poor decisions with lasting impacts, such as the hiring of SNC, raise serious concerns about the course of the Timorese formal land tenure system. As the above comparison with the recommendations of Bruce *et al.* (1994) exemplifies, the development of the Timorese formal land tenure system has been marked by the same mistakes and wrong assumptions that previously characterised the development of land tenure systems in other developing countries (Chapter 2). The reasons, successes, problems, dilemmas, winners, and losers of the development of the Timorese formal land tenure system are further discussed in the following chapters.

Chapter 4

The political environment

Introduction

This chapter focuses on the political environment in which the Timorese formal land tenure system has been developed. As prescribed in the framework of analysis established for this book (Chapter 1), the political environment is the first layer of social organisation in which one should focus on to understand a land tenure system. The political environment includes ideologies—as broadly defined in Chapter 1—and the contextual factors that, based on the literature but also my personal experience in Timor-Leste, guide the political debates and actions that inform the development of the formal land tenure system.

The first part of this chapter looks at ideology regarding land tenure, visible in the positions of the main political parties on land tenure; the connections between the concept of development, high-modernistic ideology, infrastructure, and investment; and finally, the post-authoritarianism and the authoritarian temptation that has marked the country since independence. This first part of the chapter shows that, for a number of reasons, the political elite tends to favour strong control of land by the state.[1]

The second part of the chapter analyses the contextual and interconnected factors that, together with ideology, play a role in the development of the formal land tenure system. Factors such as the weak rule of law; the Indonesian land administration legacy; and corruption, rent-seeking, clientelism, patronage, and elite capture give politicians and state officials little incentive to improve the formal land tenure system. The effects of the 'resource curse' further constrain improvements in administrative practices. Difficult dilemmas

1 By *political elite* I refer to the group of people that can influence state policies and decisions, by virtue of their positions in political institutions, but also through their social position and economic resources. About this definition see Vel, 2008: 16. The Timorese elite is a diverse group which gained its status from different factors, such as involvement in the Indonesian administration, participation in the guerrilla movement against the occupation, and even advocacy from places of exile during the occupation. These diverse backgrounds are important identity markers that, together with other factors such as local origin and family, play a role in how elite members are perceived and listened to by others. On Timorese elites, see Guterres, 2006; Silva, 2006.

DOI: 10.4324/9781003196396-4

posed by post-colonial and post-conflict debates, the potential for land tenure to ignite violence, and the resilience and prevalence of customary land tenure systems further disincentivise politicians and state officials from improving the formal land tenure system.

There are two points about the chapter that I would like to make upfront. First, I refer to 'government', 'politicians', and 'state officials' in a way that should be read carefully; governments are not monolithic institutions, and politicians and state officials are not all the same. The same happens when I refer to 'political elites'. When I use these expressions, I am referring to a common dynamic among certain groups, but not to every single case from or member of that group. Second, this chapter focuses its analysis at the national level. The study of the political environment can of course go deeper into more localised debates, but such an expansion is beyond the scope of this chapter.

Political parties and land tenure

Political parties are an interesting starting point for the analysis of ideological debates about land tenure. Political science holds that political parties are organised around political theories and visions of the world, and are the institutions where the views and interests of individuals are aggregated, in order to participate in and influence legislative drafting and governance in general (Lindberg, 2007: 218; Ufen, 2008: 328; Ware, quoted by Feijó, 2016: 106). However, analysing Timorese political parties' ideologies is not easy. The Timorese political landscape is still relatively young, with a high number of new parties running in each election, many of whom disappear soon after.[2] Furthermore, many parties do not have a political manifesto or official ideological line and are mostly developed around local figures (Shoesmith, 2013: 125).[3] To limit and simplify the analysis of Timorese political parties, this section centres on the views on land tenure of FRETILIN and CNRT, the two main political parties that have been able to form governments in Timor-Leste since independence.

FRETILIN—Revolutionary Front for an Independent East Timor

FRETILIN (Revolutionary Front for an Independent East Timor or *Frente Revolucionária de Timor-Leste Independente* in Portuguese) was formed in 1974 and is currently the oldest political party with parliamentary representation. FRETILIN's

2 For instance, 21 different parties ran in the 2012 and 2017 parliamentary elections, with six and five new parties, respectively. See http://www.cne.tl/ and https://www.laohamutuk.org/

3 Even the two main political parties, CNRT and FRETILIN, do not have updated manifestos (at least they are not available online), nor webpages through which they can share such documents. However, these political parties are active on social media.

initial ideology is a source of long debate. Some people defined the party at the time of its formation as Marxist-Leninist, a classification that was used by Indonesia to, in part, justify the 1975 invasion (Shoesmith, 2013: 123; Dovert and Durand, 2016; 334, 338). Others argue that FRETILIN was an anti-colonialist party, oriented by social-democratic views, but that it was never Marxist (Kingsbury, 2009: 52; see also Hoadley, 1976: 413). The internal divisions between social-democratic moderates and Marxist radicals remained one main characteristics of the party (Hoadley, 1976: 414; Beuman, 2013: 64; Kammen, 2016: 131). However, the more extremist faction of the party prevailed in the years following its formation, which explains the distinctly Marxist ideas about land tenure proposed then by the party (Nixon, 2012: 53; Shoesmith, 2012: 36). FRETILIN remained internally divided during the Indonesian occupation. In general terms, those members that sought refuge in Mozambique are regarded by academic authors as having strong Marxist ideologies, influenced by the Mozambican political party Frelimo, while other factions in the party are viewed as more moderate (Kingsbury, 2009: 105; Shoesmith, 2012: 36; Scott, 2005: 84).

The Manual and Political Program of FRETILIN from December 1974 established a few key policies on land tenure. First, cooperatives would be the basis of the economic and social life of Timor-Leste. Second, the private farms and plantations which had previously been communal land would be expropriated through agrarian reform and redistributed to the people, to be farmed in cooperatives. Third, unfarmed agricultural land would also be redistributed to the people to be farmed in cooperatives, or alternatively to be used by state-owned farms. Finally, the program determined a shift away from crops for export, such as coffee, to a more diversified production for domestic consumption (FRETILIN, 1974: 11, 29; Hoadley, 1976: 413).[4]

After the 1999 referendum, this more radical faction of FRETILIN, led by Mari Alkatiri, managed to obtain key political positions in the UNTAET administration and later in the first Timorese Government, with Alkatiri assuming the role of prime minister. The control of the party and the government by this faction of FRETILIN earned it the nickname the '*Maputo group*', a reference to their time in the Mozambican capital during the Indonesian occupation and the influences they brought with them on their return (Smith, 2004: 280; Kingsbury, 2009: 105). While this faction of FRETILIN had adopted free-market economy ideas by then, they retained highly top-down, centralised, and authoritarian views of the role of the government, which was the cause of much criticism by the opposition parties (Saldanha, 2006: 71; Kingsbury, 2009: 141; see more below).

4 These ideas directly clashed with the views of UDT, FRETILIN's main rival party in 1974–1975. UDT wanted to: recognise private property, but with the possibility of expropriation in cases of national interest; recognise ownership rights to all land occupied by Timorese; consider vacant land as property of the state until it was occupied; and give foreigners use rights instead of ownership rights (UDT, 1975: 10).

Regarding land tenure, the FRETILIN government abandoned, at least in part, the ideas of agrarian reform, nationalisation of large plantations, and land exploitation under cooperatives (Silva *et. al.*, 2009: 10). Nevertheless, their view was that the state should retain strong control over land, which became clear in Law 1/2003 (Fitzpatrick *et al.*, 2013: 10). Furthermore, the members of this government regarded customary norms and institutions as backward and strongly opposed giving them any legal recognition—a position that led to the rejection of a draft land law in 2005 (Hohe and Nixon, 2003: 41; Fitzpatrick *et al.*, 2013: 102; Grenfell, 2013: 204).[5] Moreover, the FRETILIN government took an 'economic development first' approach, in which democratisation—including more-democratic land administration—was not on the agenda (Kingsbury, 2009: 141; see more below). Moreover, addressing the land-related problems inherited from previous administrations was not a priority of the FRETILIN government, which proved to be a serious mistake when land-related disputes became one of the strongest fuels of the 2006 crisis (Elderton, 2002: 14; Nixon, 2012: 137; see Chapter 3). Nevertheless, the view that the state should retain strong control of land and prevail over individual rights remains to this day among FRETILIN's leadership, even after the party lost control of government after 2007 (with a short hiatus in 2017). These views became clear, for instance, in the positions that FRETILIN representatives took during the debate of the Land Law Package (SAPO24, 13 January 2017) and in the way Alkatiri and other FRETILIN members have been dealing with land-related issues in Oecusse (Almeida, 2018a).

CNRT—National Congress for Timorese Reconstruction

After the 2006 crisis and during the lead-up to the 2007 election, the National Congress for Timorese Reconstruction (*Congresso Nacíonal da Reconstrução Timorense*, or CNRT) was formed and immediately became one of the country's main political parties.[6] Xanana Gusmão, the charismatic leader of the Timorese resistance, was finishing his term as president, and CNRT was created as a vehicle for him to achieve the much more hands-on position of prime minister, with real executive power (Shoesmith, 2012: 38).[7] The political identity of the

5 Ana Pessoa, at the time Minister of Justice, is reported to have dismissed the use of customary law by saying that 'we're not savages and we won't use customary law' (interview reported by Nixon, 2012: 192).

6 The party was cunningly named in order to make its acronym match the previous National Council of Timorese Resistance (initially Maubere National Council), an umbrella organisation that gathered Timorese organisations and individuals against the Indonesian occupation (1986–2001). See Kingsbury, 2009: 163.

7 Gusmão started his political career in FRETILIN, but abandoned the party in 1988 due to disagreements with the party hard-liners, and his conviction that the fight for independence should be detached from political loyalties (Gusmão, 2000: xiv; Niner, 2011: 137).

party remains to this day centred around Gusmão, with economic development, expansion of public infrastructures, increasing social expenditures, and expansion of the oil and gas industries as his main flagship policies (Shoesmith, 2012: 45; ICG, 2013: 2; see below and Chapter 9). While CNRT can be regarded as a free-market liberal party, it is the figure of Gusmão, more than any specific ideology, that orients the party and the governments that he has led or controlled since 2007 (Shoesmith, 2013: 132; Anderson, 2013: 229; Aspinall *et al.*, 2018: 160).[8] The party is so dependent on the figure of Gusmão that his resignation as president of CNRT after the electoral defeat in 2017 was not accepted by the party (Tatoli, 6 August 2017; Diário de Notícias, 4 November 2017).

Regarding land tenure, Gusmão has repeatedly shown that his main priority is quick and cheap access to land by the state for the implementation of infrastructure projects (see below, and Chapter 9). While, to my knowledge, in comparison with FRETILIN, Gusmão's views on land tenure are more open to some recognition of customary land rights and formalisation of land rights, it has never been his priority to create a formal land tenure system that can provide the Timorese with more tenure security and restrain state-led dispossession. For instance, Gusmão did not use his leverage over CNRT's MPs to promote the approval of the Land Law Package during the years that it was awaiting debate in parliament, and at some point he even requested that its approval process be delayed (Chapter 5). And although he supported the SNC project on land registration, his active involvement quickly faded once the contract was signed (Chapter 3). This does not mean that Gusmão actively opposes the development of the formal land tenure system; for instance, the Land Law Package was drafted under his government and approved under a CNRT majority in parliament. But the formal land tenure system is not Gusmão's priority, and protective measures that interfere too much with his infrastructure projects have often received Gusmão's push-back (Chapter 9).

Therefore, although from different backgrounds, the two main political parties favour strong control of and access to land by the state. As described in the following section, a vague concept of 'development' is the main justification for these positions.

'Development', high-modernism, infrastructure, and investment

'Development' has been a key word in the Timorese political environment. What 'development' means is, however, unclear. As argued in the literature, in

8 Although Gusmão resigned from the position of prime minister in 2015 to make room for a new generation of politicians, he has continued to have a substantial influence on subsequent governments, except for the brief 2017 FRETILIN government (Aspinall *et al.*, 2018, 158; The Diplomat, 24 May 2016; Inside Story, 17 February 2016).

recent decades the concept of development has become, for many policymakers around the world, synonymous with trade and economic growth, guided by neoliberal views of the world, and with a strong bias towards a more urban and 'modern' economy (Crewe and Axelby, 2013: 157, 161; Dirlik, 2014: 31). As debated in Chapter 2, under these views, aims to increase the role of land in economic production prevail over all other roles that land can have in public policies. But 'development' is also what David Mosse calls an 'enrolment concept': an expression with a broad meaning, which can be used in vague terms with the objective of bringing together—or 'enrolling'—various stakeholders with very different, and even contradictory, views and agendas (Mosse, 2005: 35). Everyone welcomes development, but only few would agree on what that really means.

These two points about development are quite visible in Timor-Leste. On the one hand, a vague concept of development is often used by politicians and state officials to gather support for state projects and activities, and to condemn detractors of their plans as enemies of development (see for instance Timor Post, 11 November 2014; Tatoli, 18 October 2018; Chapter 9). For many Timorese, development may mean something quite different from the grandiose projects and activities envisioned by politicians, but by evoking 'development' they can keep the debate vague, and therefore more difficult to contest. On the other hand, and following the global trend mentioned above, state policies for development in Timor-Leste have been mostly directed at economic growth, focusing on two areas from which Timorese politicians hope that economic development will come: *infrastructure* and *private investment*. These two areas, which have a strong impact on the way the formal land tenure system has been developed, are analysed in the following sections.

Infrastructure

As described in Chapter 3, the end of the Indonesian administration was marked by massive destruction of the country's infrastructure. Since independence, the need to improve and expand basic infrastructure such as roads, electricity, and the water supply has been constantly mentioned by politicians and the Timorese in general as one of the country's main priorities (see, for instance, GoTL, 2010a: 15). However, especially since 2007 when the economic windfall from oil and gas revenues started (see below), the focus on infrastructure has grown exponentially and shifted from the much-needed basic infrastructure, to large-scale, multi-million dollar projects labelled as 'megaprojects' (World Bank, 2015: 1; Bovensiepen and Yoder, 2018: 382).[9]

9 Referring to Indonesia, Davidson talks about the 'mesmerizing effects' of megaprojects (2015: 5). Flyvbjerg talks about the 'four sublimes of megaprojects': technological, political, economic, and aesthetic sublimes (2017: 7). These concepts are quite applicable in Timor-Leste.

The Strategic Development Plan 2011–2030 approved by Gusmão's first government (2007–2012) became the paradigmatic example of the visions and approaches that have guided the planning and implementation of infrastructure in Timor-Leste. For many observers, the Strategic Development Plan is more of a 'wish-list' than a realistic roadmap for development, and raises many concerns about the need, the economic viability, and the real benefits of many infrastructure projects foreseen in it (Peake, 2013: chapter 8; Scheiner, 2015: 86; Scambary, 2017: 271).[10] Besides listing basic infrastructure, it also includes a myriad of many, much-larger projects such as new sea ports, airports, and the Tasi Mane Project, Gusmão's visionary project of an oil and gas industry corridor on the south coast of the country (Chapter 9). Additionally, in 2014 the Special Economic Zone of Social Market Economy of Oecusse (*Zona Especial de Economia Social de Mercado de Oe-Cusse Ambeno*—ZEESM in its Portuguese acronym), headed by FRETILIN's leader Mari Alkatiri, was added to the list of megaprojects.[11] Megaprojects became the flagship of 'development' for the two top leaders of Timor-Leste, Gusmão with the Tasi Mane Project, and Alkatiri with ZEESM. Moreover, the megaprojects became a new arena for political competition, with these leaders and their supporters promising prosperity through their project and pointing out the failures of the rival in theirs.[12] Despite some progress, much-needed basic infrastructure lost the attention of high-level politicians amidst this fervour around megaprojects, and the implementation of infrastructure projects in general has been marked by poor quality, faulty procurement, and lack of oversight (Scambary, 2015: 285; World Bank, 2015: iv).[13]

The way in which these megaprojects are designed and implemented incorporates some characteristics of the *high-modernism ideology* identified by Scott (1998). These megaprojects also intend to radically change the physical areas of intervention, cutting ties with the past and tradition, and building a new,

10 See also http://www.laohamutuk.org/econ/SDP/10SDPindex.htm

11 The ZEESM is presented as a radical transformation of the poor exclave Oecusse into a regional hub for industry, trade, and tourism. Several state-led infrastructure projects such as roads, an international airport, and a hotel are a central part of ZEESM. This project was seen by many observers as Gusmão's strategy to shut down political opposition (Feijó, 2016a: 7; Aspinall et al., 2018: 158). About ZEESM, see Yoder, 2015; Yoder, 2016; Rose, 2016; Almeida, 2018a; Yoder, 2018.

12 As pointed out by Nygaard-Christensen, this vision of development based on modernist infrastructure closely resembles the political imagery used during the Indonesian New Order (2013: 432). The Indonesian legacy is further debated below.

13 The national budget exemplifies the focus on infrastructure. From the almost 1.4 billion USD of the 2017 budget, 22 million were for agriculture, 128 million USD for education, and 73 million USD for health care. For the ZEESM and the Tasi Mane Project alone, 250 million USD were allocated (http://www.laohamutuk.org/econ/OGE17/LHSubPNOJE2017-7Nov16en.pdf; Doraisami, 2018). The focus on megaprojects is especially concerning when considering that even countries with much stronger planning and control institutions systematically fail to keep these projects on budget, time, and to provide benefits (Flyvbjerg, 2017: 13).

'modern' future. The urban landscape is completely redesigned, with a new grid of large avenues carved over the old city, and new, big, shiny, and futuristic buildings marking the skyline. The state assumes the role of the main motor of these megaprojects, providing the vision, the bureaucracy, and, if necessary, the muscle to implement them. The promotors often mention private investors, but they are a small piece of a bigger puzzle designed by the state.[14] The same happens with the general population, whose role in both the Tasi Mane Project and ZEESM was designed for them (Kammen, 2018: 41). They should follow without questioning, make sacrifices, and accept that these sacrifices are for the good of the country (Chapter 9; Almeida, 2018a). In both projects there is little space, opportunity, or even faith in a more organic development created by the people on the ground.[15]

The developmentalistic ideology and the authoritarian temptation that mark the top national leaders (see below), in combination with the current economic windfall, provide the right ingredients to further fuel these high-modernistic ideas (Scott, 1998: Part 2). However, and contrary to high-modernism ideologies, these megaprojects are not based on a belief in science, but rather derive from the vision of strong leaders. Technical experts such as engineers and planners are involved in the creation process but more as enablers of these visions than their creators.[16]

Basic infrastructure projects need land to be implemented; these high-modernistic megaprojects need even larger tracts of land. The lack of a formal land tenure system that can provide certainty about land rights and legal and administrative tools for land acquisition by the state has been a double-edged sword for infrastructure projects. On the one hand, this lack of legal and administrative mechanisms deprives politicians and state officials of any guidance on land acquisition, raising questions such as when the state can expropriate land, what process to follow, and who should be compensated. On the other hand, this uncertainty regarding land rights, the land acquisition process, and limits for expropriation can be used to the state's advantage. If politicians are willing to move land acquisition processes forward without a clear legal path, then

14 Despite these mega-projects being in part justified as kick-start infrastructure to attract investors, so far no big investor has been announced. I noticed that often politicians and state officials confuse investors with contractors, especially when companies must provide financial guaranties as part of their contracts. On more than one occasion, I heard government representatives proudly saying that a contractor had agreed to invest a certain amount in the country, only to later find out that the 'investment' was a financial guarantee.

15 Besides these mega-projects, many smaller-scale examples of modernistic projects can also be found. See below and, for instance, Kammen, 2009.

16 In the beginning of ZEESM, Alkatiri attempted to create a scientific image of his concept of social market economy by saying that it was a synthesis between the two failed models of communism and capitalism (personal Facebook post from 23 December 2013). This scientific image seems to have since been abandoned; for instance, in 2017 he claimed to use his feelings instead of Excel to manage ZEESM (The Guardian, 25 May 2017).

uncertainty can be used to pressure the people affected to leave the land without compensation or to accept whatever minimal compensation is offered to them.

Since independence, the use of arbitrary administrative processes and exploitation of uncertainty for land acquisition by the state has been the common practice of state authorities.[17] Although the outcomes of land acquisition by the state vary, depending on factors such as the people to be evicted and the promotor of the project, the implementation of infrastructure projects has always taken priority over the development of a formal land tenure system that could allow an adequate and transparent process. Moreover, without an adequate judicial system where this arbitrary approach can be challenged and punished (see below), there is little incentive to develop a formal land tenure system that can protect people's land rights and curb the actions of the state.

Private investment

Private investment is another key factor of development mentioned by politicians. Creating a formal land tenure system that provides investors with legal tenure security and allows land owners to obtain bank credit has been declared by politicians as a priority for the country since the UNTAET administration.[18] While politicians have exaggerated the potential benefits of private investment and relied too heavily on land registration as the tool to tenure security (see the wrong assumptions debated in Chapter 2), the reality is that some degree of tenure security is necessary to attract investment. The very unclear legal framework, and the impossibility of determining who has which land rights over specific plots of land, makes Timor-Leste a difficult place for investors, especially for those with weak knowledge of the informal systems on the ground.[19] During my work with MoJ I saw this first-hand, with potential investors becoming doubtful about the feasibility of their projects after I gave them a brief explanation of land tenure in the country.

However, as also happens with infrastructure, politicians' focus on investment has been quite selective, and strongly influenced by the high-modernism ideology (see above), corruption, rent-seeking, clientelism and patronage (see below), and weak institutional capacity (Chapter 7). Since independence, little has been done to create transparent, fair, and safe mechanisms for investors to access land. Instead, governments have taken a case-by-case approach, in which proposals of

17 Chapters 7 and 9. Among others, Silva and Furusawa, 2014; Cryan, 2015a; Yoder, 2015; Almeida, 2017; Almeida, 2018a; Almeida, 2019. As reported by Davidson, a similar approach was taken by Suharto's regime (2015: 133).

18 See, for instance, Timor Post, 17 May 2014; Timor Post, 28 June 2014; Timor Post, 10 January 2015; UNDP, 2002: 68; Elderton, 2002: 3.

19 Timor-Leste ranked 175th out of 190 countries in the World Bank 2017 *Doing Business Report* (2017: 245). In the category of 'registering property', Timor-Leste has consistently ranked among the last positions. See also Nixon, 2007: 110.

some investors receive political support and move forward, and others do not.[20] The investors with the right contacts, willing to provide the right 'incentives', and promising large-scale investments in skyscrapers, large plantations and futuristic ideas are in general well received by politicians, and the state bureaucracy is put in place to support them.[21] The investors that do not fulfil these requisites have to fend for themselves. The uncertainty of the formal land tenure system turns politicians and state officials into gatekeepers of investment.

The leases of state land are the clearest example of this bias towards the 'right' investors and investments. While the lease of state land is currently the safest way to legally obtain access to land, the rules to get a lease contract with the state, and the clauses of these contracts, are less than clear, and the few that exist are often ignored.[22] For instance, the law demands that in the case of medium- and large-scale investments, the lease of state land must be preceded by a public tender, but this rule is systematically ignored. Also, the regulations with criteria for rent prices were never approved, and state officials use wide discretion in setting the terms of contracts (Almeida, 2016: 19). In practice, the 'right' investor is prioritised before any other and can obtain a contract with optimal clauses. The 'right' investor can even benefit from the wide discretionary declaration of land as state land and have people evicted from the targeted land (Chapter 6). Also, the uncertainty about land rights and a broad interpretation of the power of the state to expropriate land can be made available to the 'right' investor. While the avenues to become the 'right' investor are not clear nor straight-forward, and support from one key political figure or state official can find opposition from others, the general rule is that an investor with a small project and no personal contacts will be in a much worse position to obtain a favourable lease with the state than a well-connected investor with grandiose visions.[23]

20 Therefore, personal status, contacts, and partnerships are important, if not paramount, for obtaining support of state authorities. For instance, claiming, sometimes untruthfully, that Gusmão or another famous war veteran supports an investment project is a common way for investors to open the right doors.

21 Actually, skyscrapers are often pointed to by Timorese politicians as one key symbol of modernity and development, and now and then the construction of a new tower is announced, although so far only the headquarters of the Ministry of Finance have been built (Tatoli, 28 April 2017; Kammen, 2009: 393).

22 The higher security of lease contracts with the state is based on the assumption that state institutions act according to the law and will enforce their authority against third parties if necessary, which normally happens, but not always. I recall a Timorese man that recurrently came to DNTPSC because the land parcel leased to him by the state, and for which he was paying rent, was occupied by others and he could not use it. A solution for the problem was finally reached when, after a couple of visits, he claimed to be a war veteran and said that he was considering the use of violence if the problem was not quickly solved.

23 This lack of transparent processes impacts the quality of investments and investors. Investors that are uncomfortable with shady business practices are less keen to invest in Timor-Leste (see also Fitzpatrick, 2002: 19).

I recall one case that exemplifies all the above. I was asked by DNTPSC to draft a lease contract for a large-scale agricultural investor, which was requesting an area equivalent to 1 percent of the country's entire area, including a large water source. I raised serious concerns about this contract; the land was obviously claimed and used by customary groups, although a DNTPSC report based on a short visit claimed that it was state land because it appeared to be empty. Furthermore, the contract conditions were outrageously unfavourable to the state, and the company's investment plan was not more than a printout of a PowerPoint, with photos of crops and sophisticated agricultural machinery. After writing a legal opinion recommending to not progress with the contract, the case disappeared for a few months. One day, the lawyer of the company appeared again, this time in a role as a government adviser, asking DNTPSC to prepare this lease, which he claimed was a top priority for Prime Minister Gusmão. I advised again against this contract, going beyond my legal adviser role and pointing out the obvious social impacts of the contract, the danger of leaving such a vast area of fertile land in the hands of a single company, the lack of any accreditation of the investor, among other problems. Despite that, the government investment agency kept scheduling meetings with DNTPSC to force the quick signing of this contract, to the point that DNTPSC staff told me that they were quite uncomfortable with this process. They also told me that it was untrue that Gusmão supported this investment, and its promotors were other political figures. There was no clear end to this process when I left MoJ at the end of 2014, but DNTPSC staff told me that the pressure to sign the contract continued.

In conclusion, politicians often claim that private investment is one of the main avenues for developing the country. However, in practice their support for investment is quite biased towards high-modernistic projects and those investors with the right contacts and the right 'incentives'. For these investors, the cumbersome state bureaucracy and uncertainty regarding land rights can even be helpful. On the other hand, smaller investors, without the right contacts and unwilling to participate in shady practices, have a much more difficult experience. Politicians and state officials become, in practice, gatekeepers of investment.

Post-authoritarianism and the authoritarian temptation

All too often, the literature about Timor-Leste overlooks the fact that the country lived for most of the twentieth century under two authoritarian regimes and is a post-authoritarian—not only a post-conflict—state (ICG, 2013: 43).[24]

24 Even the brief rule of FRETILIN in 1975 is regarded by many authors as non-democratic, starting with the fact that the party declared itself as the only legitimate representative of the Timorese

For a considerable part of the Timorese adult population, including many politicians and state officials, democracy—especially the Western-style democracy adopted in Timor-Leste—is still a relatively new experience (Shoesmith, 2013: 126, 128; Feijó, 2016: 99; Arthur, 2019: 176). As a result, there is still no clear understanding in society of key matters such as the limits of governance, the rule of law, constitutional rights, mechanisms of contestation, and the power of politicians. Arguably, democratisation is further complicated by the fact that the norms and procedures of the Western-like democracy implemented in the country do not always align with those of the customary systems deeply rooted in Timorese society (Nixon, 2006: 81; Cummins, 2010). Classism, masculine authority, and hierarchical leadership are common features of many Timorese customary structures, and they influence the way the formal democratic norms and procedures are perceived and enforced (Leach, 2017: 201).

Much has been done since independence to create a democratic country, with various successes being achieved, such as several rounds of elections regarded as free, fair, and peaceful (Aspinall *et al.*, 2018: 153). In fact, Timor-Leste has scored relatively highly in the main rankings of freedom and democracy, and during recent years has been considered the most democratic country of Southeast Asia (The Diplomat, 19 July 2017).[25] Nevertheless, an authoritarian temptation has been a constant presence since independence.

A look at the two top political figures in the country, Gusmão and Alkatiri, illustrates this authoritarian temptation well.[26] The first government of Alkatiri was described by many authors as arrogant and authoritarian, showing little interest in public debates, and reacting strongly against dissenting opinions.[27] Probably inspired by the Mozambican experience of many of its members, including Alkatiri himself, his government was known for its strong-government mentality, trying to implement a 'dominant party' system, and for putting economic development ahead of democratisation (Elderton, 2002: 1). Some authors go so far as to claim that Alkatiri's government managed to highjack the democratic structures and was converting them into mechanisms of repression (Simonsen, 2006; Siapo, 2006; Richmond and Franks, 2009: 95). Land tenure administration reflected this mentality, which was visible, for instance, in the draconian rules for quick and unprotected evictions established in Law 1/2003, approved by Alkatiri's government (Soares, 2007: 198; Chapter 6).

people, without any elections to legitimise such a claim (FRETILIN, 1974: 9, 25; Lawless, 1976: 950; Kingsbury, 2009: 165; Nixon, 2012: 54; Shoesmith, 2012: 41).

25 See http://timor-leste.gov.tl/?p=17298&lang=en. In the 2017 Freedom House ranking, Timor-Leste scored 3 out of 7 (with 7 being the least free) and was considered 'partially free' (2017: 24).

26 The rivalry and tensions between these two political leaders mark a considerable part of the modern Timorese history. Beuman (2013) provides a good summary of several episodes.

27 Among others, see here Soares, 2003: 306; Smith, 2004: 293; Gorjão, 2004: 1054; Saldanha, 2006: 78; Kingsbury, 2007: 364, 371; Kingsbury, 2009: 107; Richmond and Franks, 2009: 98; Psychas, 2010: 48; Shoesmith, 2012: 37; Shoesmith, 2013: 125; Arthur, 2019: 146.

In some cases land tenure administration also became a tool of repression. For instance, after reporting a number of famine deaths, the newspaper Suara Timor Lorosae was threatened by Alkatiri's government with the discontinuation of the lease contract of their headquarters, and a boycott on the government's advertising in the newspaper was declared (The New Internationalist, 1 May 2005; Reporters Without Borders, 3 May 2005; Freedom House, 2006: 92; Saldanha, 2006: 78). An authoritarian approach to land tenure administration by Alkatiri's inner circle continued with the ZEESM in Oecusse (Yoder, 2015; PDHJ, 2016; Rose, 2016; Almeida, 2018a).

In comparison with Alkatiri, Gusmão, the historical leader of the resistance against the Indonesian invasion, is described as more willing to integrate dissenting voices in his governments (Gorjão, 2004: 1054). His role in the resistance movement, unquestionable charisma, and political savviness have made him the predominant political figure of the country, with unparalleled authority over traditional leaders, war veterans, and the population in general (Arthur, 2019: 144). However, as argued by Feijó, a 'charismatic leadership' can lead to authoritarian solutions, with the debate and contestation of the charismatic leader's decisions being crushed by his superior authority (Feijó, 2016: 104). Furthermore, the leadership of the guerrilla movement in which Gusmão gained his authority was not, and could not be, democratic. Gusmão brought the same guerrilla leadership style to his governments, which resulted in a few undemocratic episodes (Kingsbury, 2009: 23; ICG, 2013: 38; Scambary, 2017: 268). To further complicate this matter, the extraordinary increase in public spending under Gusmão's governments further increased his network of 'clients' and supporters, decreasing the space for contestation against his decisions (Shoesmith, 2012: 48; Scambary, 2015: 284; Arthur, 2019: 147). Gusmão's semi-god status allows him to say and do things that no common democratic leader would dare to do—ranging from farcical stunts such as jumping out of his official car to direct traffic, to strong-man demonstrations like interrogating suspected drug-traffickers himself, to seriously authoritarian acts such as giving 48 hours' notice to a number of international judges to leave the country (see below).[28] There are also a number of episodes where Gusmão publicly humiliated members of his own cabinet (Shoesmith, 2013: 132). Executive-style authority is for Gusmão a normal style of governing, and his decisions are put under little scrutiny (Scambary, 2015: 296). Land tenure administration is one of the many areas where this type of leadership trumps rules and processes.[29]

28 Tempo Semanal, 23 October 2012; IPAC, 2015: 4; Grenfell, 2015: 277, and www.facebook.com/moises.dasilva.3591/videos/2507213009504723/. See also the 2019 interview with Major General Lere, the top official of F-FDTL, in which he says that Gusmão is sacred (*lulik* in Tetum) and therefore he cannot criticise him (https://www.youtube.com/watch?v=kA4z2sOugJY).

29 See the case of Hotel Resende, where Gusmão's decision trumped due process regarding the contested ownership of the building (Almeida, 2017).

This authoritarian temptation and the attraction for strong, top-down leadership is not exclusive to top leaders, and can also be found among mid-level politicians, civil servants, and to a certain extent, the general population (Soares, 2013: 89; Shepherd, 2014: 236). One example that marked my view on this matter was a comment I often heard from state officials and politicians expressing exasperation with the fact that nowadays, and contrary to Portuguese and Indonesian times, people were free to move and relocate inside the country, without having to request authorisation from any state official.

While there is no doubt that Timor-Leste is a democracy and much has been done to strengthen it, the influences of past authoritarianism and inexperience with democratic rule, combined with the strong leadership styles of top leaders, make the authoritarian temptation a constant presence, with an inevitable impact on land administration. For instance, it allows that draconian laws such as Law 1/2003 can be proposed and approved with little political scrutiny and public outcry. It also allows top leaders to take decisions on evictions and 'expropriations' against or in absence of law. This authoritarian temptation goes hand-in-hand with the weak rule of law, which is debated in the following section.

Weak rule of law

The weak rule of law that exists in Timor-Leste is another central factor of the political environment that shapes the Timorese formal land tenure system, as it is both a cause and a consequence of all the other factors debated in this chapter.

The definition of rule of law is debated in the literature and ranges from broad and strict definitions to thinner and less demanding ones (Bedner, 2010: 54).[30] Regarding land tenure in Timor-Leste, even under a thin definition that limits rule of law to the obedience of the state to its own rules, it is possible to identify several problems that compromise the success of the country's formal land tenure system. As extensively exemplified throughout this book, it is not uncommon for state institutions, politicians, and state officials to act without the support of, and even against, the country's legislation. As stated by Bedner, 'a state not following its own rules is not a rule of law state' (2010: 56).

Institutional weaknesses of the administrative and judicial institutions can in part explain the problems with the rule of law in Timor-Leste. I debate here the limitations of the judicial system, and leave the administrative institutions, in particular DNTPSC, to Chapter 7. The Portuguese and Indonesian administrations left almost no legacy in the Timorese judicial system.[31] Upon

30 See also the concept of 'autonomy of law' debated in Bedner, 2016a.

31 During Portuguese colonial rule the formal judicial system was mostly used for civil cases between colonial elites and for punishment of serious criminal cases (Hohe and Nixon, 2003: 7, 26;

the withdrawal of the Indonesian administration, in practice the formal judicial system ceased to exist: court buildings were burned down, office equipment was destroyed, and all the Indonesian legal professionals that staffed the formal judicial system left the country (Strohmeyer, 2001: 50, 53; Chesterman, 2005: 84; see also Chapter 3). While the rebuilding and refurbishing of the courts and other judicial infrastructure in the years following the 1999 referendum was a complex logistical enterprise, the selection and training of Timorese judges and prosecutors with adequate professional experience to replace international judicial personnel has been an even more difficult task (Strohmeyer, 2001: 51, 53; IPAC, 2015: 3).[32] Despite UNTAET's efforts, the formal judicial system left in place was of little use to the great majority of Timorese, who continued to recur to their customary systems (Hohe and Nixon, 2003: 37; Grenfell, 2006).[33]

Current data about the judicial system show some progress since its reconstruction started, but also many limitations (CES-OPJ and CRL, 2017). Currently, four district courts serve the 13 districts of the country, together with a program of mobile courts (JSMP, 2014: 21; IPAC, 2015: 8). The Supreme Court of Justice and other courts instituted by the constitution have not yet been established. The number of judicial system staff has consistently risen, reaching 292 at the end of 2014: 40 judges, 40 prosecutors, 36 public defenders, 113 justice officials (bailiffs), 9 translators, and 54 administration staff (JSMP, 2014: 25).[34] At the end of 2014 there were 2,917 pending cases—2,162 criminal cases and 755 civil cases—but the trend has been a growing number of pending cases (JSMP, 2014: 62; see also CES-OPJ and CRL, 2017:

Figueiredo, 2011: 172, 174; IPAC, 2015: 2; Simões, 2015: 382). During the Indonesian occupation the Timorese were in practice banned from any legal professions and the courts were perceived by the population as corrupt and untrustworthy (Strohmeyer, 2001: 53; Hohe and Nixon, 2003: 7, 27, 43; Chesterman, 2005: 85; IPAC, 2015: 2). Village councils created during the Indonesian occupation were responsible for dispute resolution, but mostly disappeared after independence (Hohe and Nixon, 2003: 27; IPAC, 2015: 2).

32 The first Timorese judges and prosecutors were appointed in January 2000 (Strohmeyer, 2001: 52, 54). However, in 2004 all Timorese members of the judiciary appointed by UNTAET were called to a controversial and politicised exam, in which all failed (Marriott, 2013: 107; IPAC, 2015: 3).

33 UNTAET proposed the incorporation of structures and mechanisms of the customary systems in the formal judiciary system, but this idea was strongly opposed by part of the Timorese political elite that saw customary systems as backwards, and the concept of a strictly formal system prevailed (Hohe and Nixon, 2003: 38, 67).

34 IPAC reports lower numbers of prosecutors (35) and judges (34) at the end of 2015, probably due to the termination of contracts of international staff (2015: 8, 9). Until October 2014 the judicial system employed several foreign Portuguese-speaking judges, prosecutors, public defenders, investigators, and justice officials. Gusmão's government, supported by parliament, alleged wrongdoings of these staff and called for the termination of their contracts. The president of the Court of Appeal refused to terminate the judges' contracts and in response, the government revoked the visas of some of the judges, prosecutors, and investigators, and gave them 48 hours to leave the country. Some of the judges and prosecutors expelled were working on the prosecution of eminent politicians, which raised serious concerns about political interference in the judiciary (IPAC, 2015: 4; JSMP, 2014a).

236). In February 2015 there were 84 lawyers registered, many of them international lawyers working with international private law firms established in Timor-Leste and not residing in the country (IPAC, 2015: 13).[35] The Public Defender's Office is responsible for providing legal aid to those who cannot afford a private lawyer, but has only 36 public defenders, spread throughout the four district offices, which raises concerns about the quality of their legal assistance (JSMP, 2014: 25; IPAC, 2015: 19; CES-OPJ and CRL, 2017: 195). The judicial system is still far from providing an ideal service to the Timorese due to its low coverage, difficult access, delays, and poor quality of court decisions (Marriott, 2013; Almeida, 2017a: 185).[36]

The weaknesses of the judicial system have a clear impact on the political environment that surrounds the development of the formal land tenure system. The limited access to, and the quality of, the judicial system provide the Timorese with very limited avenues to challenge illegal land-related decisions and practices of politicians and state officials, who as a result have little incentive to improve their practices.[37] During my work with the MoJ I saw first-hand the consequences of the limitations of the judicial system. In five years working with the MoJ, I do not recall more than a handful of land-related court cases filed against the state. Most people contest wrongful decisions and practices of the administration through letters and requests for meetings with directors, ministers, and MPs, but very rarely do people recur to courts.[38] Although this informal approach sometimes works, it is quite arbitrary—contacts, social, and political position are key factors—and this very imbalanced dispute-resolution approach leaves law to a secondary role. Furthermore, in those few cases that are taken to court, poorly drafted court petitions and weak legal reasoning give the claimants very limited possibility of success against the state. In the end, these court cases against the state result in no meaningful lesson for DNTPSC, ministers, and other state institutions.

However, the weaknesses of the judicial system are not the only explanation for the weak rule of law; other factors further contribute to it. Personal interests, corruption, rent-seeking, clientelism, and patronage are only one part of the explanation (see below). Difficult dilemmas caused by bad legislation (Chapter 6), lack of legal knowledge, weak administrative procedures

35 On the role of legal professionals, especially lawyers, in promoting political liberalism in different countries, see Halliday *et al.*, 2007.

36 For instance, of the 70 court decisions analysed for this book, only seven referred to land disputes outside Dili (Chapter 6).

37 Customary systems are by far preferred by the Timorese and used far more often for conflict resolution (Chapter 8). However, customary systems are of little use when the conflict is between private citizens and the state, but as described in this section, access to courts is very limited.

38 For instance, in 2016 less than 10 percent of the cases started at the district courts were civil cases (CES-OPJ and CRL, 2017: 167). Among these there are number of land-related cases, but the court system is still foreign for most Timorese (ibid.: 210; Chapter 8).

(Chapter 7), and political pressures further explain why state institutions at times do not follow the law.

The weak rule of law does not mean that land tenure is lawless; despite several gaps, the state institutions try to follow the law, and informal practices, informal customary systems, mechanisms of contestation, and good sense often compensate for the flaws of the formal system. But as this book extensively exemplifies, there are many situations in which this weak rule of law is a cause of arbitrariness, injustice, and uncertainty.

Indonesian legacy in land administration

The legacy of the Indonesian land administration has strongly influenced the development of the formal land tenure system in Timor-Leste since independence.[39] As pointed out by Peake *et al.*, authors have been analysing Timor-Leste through the post-conflict lens but often forget the very strong legacy left in the country by the 24 years of Indonesian rule (2014: 2). Under this conflict paradigm, analysis of the country easily gets trapped in a number of pitfalls, such as portraying the Timorese only as 'victims' and the Indonesian period as only negative, focusing too much on the state, and seeing the country as a 'tabula rasa' that only started its history after the 1999 referendum (Bexley, 2010: 9; Peake *et al.*, 2014: 2). The legacy of the Indonesian administration is in general quite influential among politicians, state officials, and most Timorese adults, and it is important to understand this Indonesian legacy to grasp their practices, expectations, and political views (Blunt, 2009: 90; Richmond and Frank, 2009: 90; Nygaard-Christensen, 2013).

The integration of Timor-Leste as an Indonesian province was fast. Eleven days after the full-scale invasion in 1975, a provisional government was established until the approval of the integration law in 1976 (CAVR, 2005: part 4, 37). Government agencies, as well as provincial administrative structures and their links with the central government were quickly put in place (Weatherbee, 1981: 10; Gunn, 2007: 40). While senior positions in the administration were mostly occupied by Indonesians, thousands of lower-level positions were filled by Timorese (ibid.: 42; CAVR, 2005: part 04, 48). In 1997 there were more than 33,600 civil servants, almost twice the national ratio of civil servants in relation to the population in the rest of Indonesia (ibid.: part 04, 48; see also Cliffe, 2003: 238; Tidey, 2012: 40). Many Timorese were trained at universities and provincial offices throughout Indonesia before being integrated into the Indonesian civil service in Timor-Leste (Gunn, 2007: 50). Integration was not just at the administrative level: schools were established and thousands

39 In my research I found fewer traces of the Portuguese administration (see also Leigh, 2006). One obvious reason is the time frame. Another reason is that many more Timorese worked directly with the Indonesian administration.

of students joined the Indonesian educational system; Indonesian media was widespread all over the territory, while Portuguese media was banned;[40] and the migration of people from other parts of Indonesia to Timor-Leste and their integration into Timorese society was promoted, and in the 1990s around 16 percent of the population in Timor-Leste were Indonesians from other provinces (Gunn, 2007: 50, 54; Psychas, 2010: 77). Timorese society became familiar with Indonesian systems, practices, and culture, and despite the past occupation and conflict, the relationship of Timorese with Indonesia is today far from antagonistic (Bexley, 2010: 10; Scambary, 2017: 268).

As in other areas of state administration, the Indonesian administration of Timor-Leste left an indisputable imprint on the way the rules and roles of a formal land tenure system are perceived by politicians, state officials, and the population in general (Elderton, 2002: 2). When I first started working with the MoJ, I encountered practices, opinions, and expectations regarding the formal land tenure system that I simply could not understand. Why were state officials so confident conducting administrative practices that had no legal support in Timorese law? Why were politicians so convinced of the unlimited power of the state to expropriate land? Why would people line up for hours at government offices to talk with state officials instead of sending their cases to court? The answers to these questions became much clearer when I started to understand the Indonesian legacy.

The Indonesian legacy is quite visible at DNTPSC. The Indonesian land agency, BPN, was also established in Timor-Leste, although at a slower pace when compared with other Indonesian institutions, and the Timorese branch was eventually upgraded to a full provincial BPN office (Chapter 3). In 1982 a special course to train 60 Timorese land surveyors was created, and some of the participants continued their university studies and internships around Indonesia before being integrated into the Timorese provincial BPN office. While Indonesians remained the senior staff of BPN in Timor-Leste, the Timorese slowly climbed the institution's hierarchy. These experiences naturally had a profound impact on the way DNTPSC senior staff sees land tenure administration to this day. Belonging to the initial group trained by BPN and having studied in Indonesia is a clear distinctive mark of prestige and knowledge in DNTPSC, and it is invoked from time to time as a sign of authority.[41] The current structure of DNTPSC was designed with the Indonesian BPN in mind (Chapter 7). References to Indonesian times are often used by DNTPSC staff as a guide for administrative practices. For instance, the fact that INR staff were following survey methods and standards different from those learned by

40 Even nowadays Indonesian television channels and other media sources are followed by many Timorese. See UNMIT, 2011.

41 Interestingly, I did not find that professional experience with UNTAET's Land and Property Unit was a source of authority or prestige.

DNTPSC staff during Indonesian administration became a point of great controversy (Chapters 3 and 7).

Unfortunately, the track record of Indonesian BPN is not great, especially during Suharto's rule. A 2003 report from the World Bank describes BPN as 'over-centralised, secretive and unresponsive to landholders; it has been used by the prevailing political and bureaucratic establishment for personal and political gains' (World Bank, 2003: 45). A 2007 survey found BPN to be one of the public institutions in Indonesia with least integrity among 30 institutions surveyed (as cited in Reerink, 2011: 97). Corruption and request for bribes was a common practice in the institution, which was nicknamed as part of the 'wet sector' (Fitzpatrick, 2002: 104; Reerink, 2011: 106). Discretionary and selective use of law and lack of detailed administrative processes were common practices in cases such as land acquisition (Chapter 3). For all of these reasons, BPN is not the best role model of land administration, especially during the years of the Timorese occupation, but nevertheless it is the model that prevails at DNTPSC. Individually, DNTPSC staff are at times critical of specific BPN practices, but in general the institution is still regarded as a model to follow.

The influence of the Indonesian legacy on land administration is not only relevant at DNTPSC, but also has an impact on the expectations, visions, and demands of politicians educated under the Indonesian regime (Nygaard-Christensen, 2013). Suharto's New Order was based on a 'state-centrist developmentalism', oriented towards market expansion and capital-intensive development, where infrastructure and technology were used as symbols of a powerful and developed state.[42] In short, the state and the market were above any individual interest, and land tenure administration was designed to deliver the visions of the country's leader. This was visible, for instance, in the very limited legal recognition of customary-based land rights when land was required for state or private infrastructure projects. The rhetoric around the 'social function of the land' and the 'national interest' were used loosely during Suharto's rule to justify the dispossession of millions of hectares held in customary tenure (Lucas and Warren, 2013: 6). As colonial states had done before, uncultivated land was classified as state land, and if necessary the state would recur to military intimidation for land clearance, with reduced or no compensation nor prior notice (Reerink, 2011: 164; Lucas and Warren, 2013: 6; Davidson, 2015: 42).[43] Furthermore, in a strongly militarised administration like the one in Timor-Leste during the occupation, the involvement of high-ranking military officials in private enterprises resulted in the dispossession of valuable agricultural land (Fitzpatrick, 2002: 116; Gunn, 2007: 48; see also Davidson, 2015: 112).

42 Bachriadi *et al.*, 2013: sec. 10; Warren and Lucas 2013: sec. 3; Nygaard-Christensen, 2013: 432. About developmental states, see Anderson, 2013: 219.

43 Because of these policies, land conflicts with the state were the biggest cause of conflict in Indonesia during the last years of the New Order (Lucas and Warren, 2013: 9).

This legacy of 'state-centrist developmentalism', where the state is above individual interests, is visible in the broad position of many Timorese politicians that the state should keep tight control over land and that the state has almost unlimited power to expropriate land. Some of my interviewees went so far as to say, maybe with some exaggeration, that land acquisition by the state was less respectful of people's rights after independence than during the Indonesian occupation.[44] One clear example of this very broad vision of the power to expropriate is the fact that, when I debated land expropriation with interviewees (mostly state officials and politicians), the right to receive compensation and negotiate land values was mentioned by them, but not a single interviewee referred to the power of individuals and communities to challenge the reasons for the state to expropriate land.

Finally, the Indonesian legacy can even be found in the land lexicon used by the Timorese. For instance, politicians, state officials, and people in general frequently use the Indonesian expression *ganti rugi* to refer to compensation for land acquisition.[45] Customary land in rural areas is often referred as *adat* land (*rai adat* in Tetum) and *Agraria* is used to refer to DNTPSC.

In summary, the strong Indonesian legacy in land administration impacts the development of the Timorese formal land tenure system by providing a model that is far from ideal, based on arbitrary administrative practices, and open to abuses by the state. This model not only normalises current practices, but also provides politicians and state officials with little incentive to develop the formal land tenure system, and dissuades people who have never experienced different practices from demanding for something better. By pointing out this Indonesian influence I do not mean that it impacts everyone equally, nor that those who lived through this administration are not sometimes critical of its flaws. Nevertheless, this influence is notable, and it is not possible to understand the development of the Timorese formal land tenure system without understanding the Indonesian land administration system during occupation as its main source of inspiration.

Corruption, rent-seeking, clientelism, patronage, and elite capture

As already hinted at above, corruption, rent-seeking, clientelism, patronage, and elite capture are also contextual factors that influence the development of the Timorese formal land tenure system. Some authors point out that these are not

44 As mentioned in Chapter 3, there was an effort by the Indonesian authorities to change the image of their violent and militarised administration, especially during the 1990s. This effort included also a more cautious approach to land acquisitions by the state.

45 While still used in Indonesia, the expression 'ganti rugi' is connected with the poor compensations for land acquisition payed by the state during Suharto's regime (Reerink 2011: 171; Davidson, 2015: 136).

new problems, that they are in part a legacy from the Portuguese and Indonesian administrations and even from the Mozambican experience that some Timorese politicians had during the Indonesian occupation (Blunt, 2009: 90; Psychas, 2010: 398, Scambary, 2015: 287). Nevertheless, these problems began to be visible soon after independence and have been present ever since, fuelled by the oil and gas revenues and other factors considered in this chapter.[46] Furthermore, and especially in light of the concentration of power in strong government figures, authors have raised concerns about the formation of a neo-patrimonial state, where state resources are used by patrons to obtain the loyalty and support of their clients and the population in general, albeit masked behind discourses, laws, and institutions that create an appearance of a normal, functioning bureaucracy (Shoesmith, 2012: 48; Scambary, 2015: 8; Feijó, 2016a: 12).[47] Measures to fight these problems have been taken, such as creating an Anti-Corruption Commission, but results are still far from ideal. Timor-Leste currently ranks 105 out of 180 countries in the Index of Perceived Corruption from Transparency International, with a score of 35 out of 100 (Transparency International, 2018).

While debating the reasons for corruption, rent-seeking, clientelism, and patronage is outside the scope of this book, it is important to stress that—in a society shaped by kinship and clandestine resistance ties and strongly marked by reciprocal relationships—it can be difficult for politicians and state officials to refuse requests for illegal favours from family members or other social connections (Butterworth, 2010: 3; Scambary, 2015: 288, 21).[48] The knowledge about what constitutes a legal or illegal activity under the Western laws imported into the country is also limited (Soares, 2013: 88). Moreover, unclear laws and administrative practices make the distinction between irregular and illegal practices more difficult to define. I must also stress that corruption and other illegal practices also exist among the internationals that work with Timorese institutions, including government advisers.[49] While the case of Bobby Boye, a Nigerian-American tax adviser that defrauded the Timorese Government, is perhaps the most famous case of criminal activity by internationals, it is well known among expats that some international advisers are facilitators of shady businesses.[50]

46 See, among others, World Bank, 2006; Lundahl and Sjöholm, 2008: 75; USAID, 2009; ICG, 2013: 5, 35; Soares, 2013; Scambary, 2015: 287; The Diplomat, 17 April 2017.

47 One illustrative example of how a neo-patrimonial state is forming in Timor-Leste is the systematic use of single-source procurement (Scambary, 2015: 300). A report from the Chamber of Auditors found that four of the six most-expensive contracts signed by the government in 2013, including SNC's contract, were single-sourced, with the other two following a public international tender because the Asian Development Bank was involved (Proc. n.° /2014/AUDIT- S/CC: 45, 53. About the Chamber of Auditors, see more below).

48 A similar conclusion about state officials in West Timor (Indonesia) can be found in Tidey, 2012: 9.

49 See here USAID, 2006: 30.

50 About this case, see, for instance, http://laohamutuk.blogspot.nl/2015/10/bobby-boye-sentenced-to-six-years-in.html

The formal land tenure system is a fertile landscape for corruption, rent-seeking, clientelism, and patronage. Authors have mentioned allegations of rent-seeking in the land sector, including by people I worked with, and several stories were also reported to me by various people (Fitzpatrick *et al.*, 2013: 104; IPAC, 2015: 17). While I recall many examples, one was particularly illustrative not only of such illegal practices, but also the difficulties in fighting them. In 2010, a friend asked my advice regarding a land-related problem that her local CSO was facing. For many years, the CSO had been pressured by DNTPSC to either sign a lease contract or leave their headquarters, which DNTPSC considered to be state land. The CSO did not agree with this assessment and remained on the land. Now, one DNTPSC staff member was requesting money to survey their land and issue some unclear documentation that would supposedly secure their tenure. The CSO paid this official for the service, for which he handed over a personal hand-written receipt, but the CSO was feeling tricked and unsure about what to do next. I told my friend that the procedure and documentation offered had no legal basis and that the personal payment was clearly illegal, and she should raise the issue with the MoJ's Office of Inspection and Auditing. However, when the CSO followed my recommendation, this Office told them that of course they would have to pay for this official's work and simply could not understand what the problem was. Sure, they argued, the process and payment were not in the law, but it has been a common practice and the official needed to be compensated for his time and expenses. The case was simply dismissed by this Office and the illegal actions of that DNTPSC member of staff were never punished.[51]

Finally—and in part connected with corruption, rent-seeking, clientelism, and patronage—is the problem of elite capture, which refers to the use of the formal land tenure system by elites to unfairly appropriate land. Elite capture of land in Timor-Leste happens in many ways, such as very favourable leases of state land; occupation of state land without any sanction from state authorities; obtaining documentation to strengthen a land claim; and the granting of privileges and illegal advantages in land registration processes. A number of my interviewees and informants claimed that the lack of progress in approving legislation to clarify tenure rights was because political elites were taking advantage of the unclear legal situation to appropriate land (see also Cryan, 2015: 8). Furthermore, approaches such as the reckless land registration conducted by SNC can further promote elite capture. As argued by several authors, when there are significant differences between the educational levels of the population, and access to state administration is unequal, a process like land registration can be unfairly manipulated by elites to appropriate land (Atwood, 1990: 663; Platteau, 1996: 43; Lund, 2000: 19). Elites' capture of land is a clear example of how formal systems can

51 About other illegal payments, see, for instance, Leigh and Nixon, 2005: 10.

be a double-edged sword: they can promote more equality and prevent conflict, but can also be another tool for elites to keep and obtain more power.

As this section shows, the opaque formal land tenure system gives wide opportunities for politicians and state officials to yield personal benefits through corruption, rent-seeking, clientelism, patronage, and elite capture. Therefore, this factor further disincentivises improvements in the formal land tenure system.

Natural resources' windfall, oil dependency, and the resource curse

The current windfall of revenue from natural resources, oil dependency, and the resource curse are three other factors that deeply influence the way the Timorese formal land tenure system has been developed. Economically, Timor-Leste has for centuries been a poor territory. The Portuguese colonial administration brought minimal economic development to the territory, and despite the heavily subsidised expansion of the public sector during the Indonesian administration, the changes were limited. In 1999 Timor-Leste remained one of the poorest provinces of Indonesia, with no modern private sector and with widespread poverty, illiteracy, and an average life expectancy of just 55 years (Duun, 1996: 41; Hill and Saldanha, 2001: 7; Lundahl and Sjöholm, 2005: 6; Cliffe, 2003: 238). The destruction that followed the 1999 referendum only further complicated the economic situation of the country (Chapter 3). The reconstruction promoted by international aid led to a period of economic revival, but at the end of UNTAET's administration the domestic revenue collection was still very low (UNDP, 2002: 58). The first years of Timor-Leste's independence were marked by minimal state budgets and enormous dependency on international aid (Cotton, 2005: 187).

After 2004, when oil and gas revenues from the Timor Sea started to flow and the boom in oil prices greatly increased profits, the situation changed considerably (Scheiner, 2017: 3). With this new source of income, state expenditure increased rampantly. In 2002 the annual state budget was 56 million USD; by 2009 it was 902 million USD; and in 2015 it was around 1.5 billion USD. Timor-Leste is now one of the most oil-dependent countries in the world, with oil and gas revenues providing around 76 percent of the national Gross Domestic Product (GDP) in 2013, and 93 percent of state revenues in 2014 (Scheiner, 2015: 2, 73). Additionally, a considerable part of the 24 percent of non-oil GDP is dependent on state expenditure, with agriculture and manufacturing representing only 4.7 percent of the country's GDP. Excluding the petroleum sector, the trade deficit in 2013 was close to 2 billion, because of extreme dependency on imports, including basic goods such as rice and eggs (ibid.: 76; IMF, 2017: 25).

Inspired by the Norwegian experience, the Timorese Petroleum Fund was created in 2005 to safeguard the oil and gas revenues for future generations

(Barma, 2012: 347; Doraisami, 2018: 251). The fund retains these revenues and invests them in bonds and stocks. An Estimated Sustainable Income (ESI) benchmark is calculated annually, to limit how much can be withdrawn from the fund to finance the state annual budget without compromising the fund's sustainability. However, since 2008, and with the only exception of 2013, annual withdrawals have exceeded the ESI, with a high percentage of these withdrawn funds being used for infrastructure developments (Scheiner, 2015: 80; Doraisami, 2018: 252). With oil and gas revenues now decreasing, the fund reached its peak of around 17 billion USD in 2015 and has since slowly started to decline (Scheiner, 2017: 2). The country's hydrocarbon dependency and growing expenses are a source of concern for observers, especially considering that the unexploited reserves are estimated to be relatively small (Scheiner, 2015: 88). The massive increase in state expenditure has done little to improve the private sector, and the Petroleum Fund is expected to be depleted within 15 to 30 years (Scheiner, 2017: 3; Doraisami, 2018: 252; see also Petroleum Economist, 28 February 2013).

The access to this relatively large amount of oil and gas revenues for such a small country has raised the problem of the resource curse. The expression 'resource curse' or 'paradox of plenty' refers to the paradox experienced by countries in which the exploitation of natural resources contributes to the decline of economic indicators and the population's standard of living, instead of increasing the country's prosperity (Kolstad and Wiig, 2009: 5317; Castree *et al.*, 2013; Costa and Santos, 2013: 788). In short, the resource curse is economically explained by factors such as an excessive focus on the resource sector and disinvestment in manufacturing, inflation, and increasing imports (Ross, 2012). However, the resource curse is not just an economic, but also an institutional, phenomenon. Authors argue that the exploitation of these resources erodes the quality of governance, administrative and institutional capacity, and contributes to an increase of corruption and rent-seeking (Lundahl and Sjöholm, 2008: 73; Kolstad and Wiig, 2009: 5318; Barma, 2012: 333; Costa and Santos, 2013: 789). Among other factors and effects, authors point out that flows of income remove incentives for more efficient and rigorous planning and functioning of state institutions, and shift the focus of politicians and state officials to rent-seeking opportunities.

The signs of the resource curse in Timorese state institutions have been identified by several authors (Lundahl and Sjöholm, 2008; Barma, 2012; Neves, 2013; Scheiner, 2015).[52] The country's expensive and poorly planned

52 A symbolic example of this resource curse is the scandal involving the Timorese national football team. Despite football being the national sport, the national team's success in international competitions had been understandably low, considering the lack of a professional football industry in the country. Suddenly in 2015, the national team started winning games, but supporters were infuriated. The Timorese Football Federation, through which some politicians had been enhancing their public profiles, was allegedly paying 12 Brazilian players to be naturalised as Timorese and play for

infrastructure projects, the difficulty in executing state budgets, the exponential growth in the number of civil servants, and the low accountability of public expenditure are some examples of the effect of the resource curse in Timorese state institutions (GoTL and World Bank, 2013: 15; ICG, 2013: 29; Aspinall *et al.*, 2018: 158). Furthermore, while legal and administrative mechanisms to prevent the resource curse were put in place in Timor-Leste, many have been undermined (Brama, 2012: 345). The constant withdrawals from the Petroleum Fund above the ESI are one obvious example, but regulatory changes to the Chamber of Auditors are, for me, the most paradigmatic illustration of the institutional effects of the resource curse. This Chamber was created in 2011 to supervise public finances, including the prior verification of state contracts with a value above 500,000 USD. When the Chamber started its work, many contracts were cancelled or delayed because they did not respect the minimum legal requisites (GoTL, 2012). Besides the problems of corruption and patronage, this showed a clear lack of state institutions' capacity to procure contracts according to the law. Confronted with this problem, instead of improving procurement procedures, the government increased the value above which contracts must be checked by the Chamber of Auditors to 5 million USD—ten times the previous threshold—therefore undermining the role of the Chamber in improving governance practices.

As in other parts of state administration, the current natural resources windfall, oil dependency, and the resource curse have a clear impact on the development of the Timorese formal land tenure system in several ways.[53] First, the easy access to oil and gas revenues removes government incentive to promote other sources of revenue. As described in Chapter 2, one of the roles of land is economic production, and formal land tenure systems are pointed to, sometimes exaggeratedly, as necessary tools for increasing private investment, economic production, and state revenues through property taxation. As discussed above, despite the political rhetoric about the importance of developing the formal land tenure system to promote investment and claims about the need to develop land-related taxes, the actions (or inaction) of the political elite have shown that the topic is not a strong priority. Together with other factors mentioned in this chapter, the current availability of oil and gas in part explains this disinterest of using the formal land tenure system to generate state revenue. The same lack of pressure to use land as a source of income happens at

the national team. These players were not even playing in national clubs nor frequently training with the Timorese national team; they were just playing the international games. As stated by a supporter, 'we'd rather lose games with our own talents than win games with foreign players' (The New York Times, 1 October 2015). The scheme has resulted in punishment by FIFA and criminal investigations for the issuing of passports (BBC, 20 July 2017). Like in many other cases, money allowed the purchase of a quick solution, but did not necessarily fix the underlying problem.

53 The effects of the resource curse in the land sector are common to many other countries. See, for instance, Herbertson, 2012 about Uganda.

the administrative level. The budget of DNTPSC is part of the MoJ's budget and is not dependent on any performance standard or independent source of income, such as collection of rents for the use of state land. Therefore, income generation is also not an incentive to develop the administrative practices of DNTPSC. Interestingly, the new Land Law was approved months after the Petroleum Fund had started to decline and the oil fields under exploitation gave the first signs of depletion. One could argue that these factors, at least in part, worked as a wake-up call for politicians about the need to use land as another source of state revenue.

Second, the availability of oil and gas revenues gives politicians more options to address land-related issues, but also allows them to mask these problems with some expensive, short-term, and even inadequate solutions. Advice and oversight by experts and international organisations is easier to dismiss when the government is not dependent on their funds (Psychas, 2010: 348). As observed by Scheiner, 'When a decision-maker has access to money, it seems like the solution for every problem' (2015: 87). Moreover, with the money coming from the Petroleum Fund, and with almost no tax levied on most of the population, the demand for accountability is low (Neves, 2013: 7; Scheiner, 2015: 86). In the land sector, the hiring of SNC is the most paradigmatic example of these wasteful, short-term, and inadequate solutions, without a prior needs assessment nor cost/benefit analysis (Chapters 3 and 7).[54]

In summary, the access to large amounts of money through the exploitation of natural resources has been a blessing for Timor-Leste, but also a curse with real negative consequences on the functioning of state institutions and the state's problem-solving approach. Furthermore, the access to oil and gas revenues has facilitated the high-modernist projects mentioned above. These factors have a clear impact on the development of the formal land tenure system by making its role in providing state revenues secondary, removing incentives for improving institutional capacity and administrative practices, and allowing ill-suited solutions such as SNC.

Post-colonialism debates

The problems left by the colonial rule of Portuguese and Indonesian authorities are another contextual factor influencing the political environment in which the Timorese formal land tenure system is developed. As detailed in Chapter 3, during these administrations there were several episodes of state-led dispossession through violence, intimidation, and legal disempowerment, and formal land rights given to individuals were at times tainted by corruption, discrimination, and usurpation. How to address past injustices and distinguish

54 A comparison between SNC's budget and the average costs of land administration systems clearly shows the wastefulness of this project. See Burns and Fairlie, 2018.

abuses from fair land administration has been a controversial topic for both the Timorese political elite and society in general since independence.

The arguments about how to deal with the colonial legacy have not changed much since independence, and the common positions vary between two extremes. Some people go so far as to claim that land rights should go back to the time before the Portuguese arrived in Timor-Leste. Proponents of this view argue that all formal land rights are the product of colonialism and occupation, and therefore should be erased. I recall one public meeting where, after a participant made this claim, a senior Timorese member of a local CSO asked him about the feasibility of such a solution, and if he was aware of, and willing to go back to, a time where there were local kings, serfs, and slaves. Others have a more moderate position, claiming that only some formal land rights should be recognised. A very common claim is that the rights of powerful families with large tracts of land, such as the Carrascalão, Alkatiri, and Albano families, should not be legally recognised. A more subtle position is that only 'good-faith' or 'fair' rights should be recognised, but the details on these definitions are difficult to reach.[55] In debates in which I participated, land reform was at times mentioned, but the expression was used as a slogan, and people were unclear about what such land reform would entail. Not surprisingly, the elites that obtained formal land rights during previous administrations are more in favour of retaining their legal recognition, basing their position on the fact that those rights were legitimately acquired through the legal system that existed at the time, and that their formal rights are protected by international law regarding succession of states.

Some cases are especially sensitive. For instance, the Catholic Church is reported to be one of the largest land owners in Timor-Leste (Fitzpatrick, 2002: 150), but since independence a number of disputes between individuals, communities, and the state against the Church, and even disputes inside the Church, have been reported.[56] For instance, there are several cases in which people gave land to the Church in order to avoid its confiscation by the Indonesian authorities, but after independence the Church was not willing to give them the land back. However, addressing these disputes is especially sensitive in a strongly Catholic country. I was involved in debates where land ownership by the Church was at stake. I recall politicians and state officials speaking with a certain bravado about the need of curbing the Church's vast possessions, to quickly backtrack on these statements once in the presence of Church representatives.

55 See also Matadalan ba Rai and Haburas Foundation, 2010.

56 According to Indonesian records, the Catholic Church owns at least 4,000 hectares of land, which includes coffee plantations, agricultural fields, urban buildings, and missions in rural areas (Fitzpatrick, 2002: 150). Because these numbers only referred to registered land, and informal land donations of individuals and communities to the Church are a common practice, it is very likely that the Church claims a much larger area (see Suara Timor Lorosae, 21 October 2010; Jornal Nacional Diário, 22 June 2016). Regarding disputes, see Timor Post, 26 August 2011; Timor Post, 5 October 2011; Timor Post, 8 April 2013.

From these debates, one can conclude that post-colonialism brings dilemmas for which there are no clear and unproblematic answers. Naturally, the personal situations shape individual positions in the debate, and finding a consensual solution is simply impossible. Moreover, from all land-related debates in which I participated and the interviews I conducted, it became clear that politicians, state officials, and society in general often did not have a clear overview of the complexity and extent of these problems, which is a symptom of not enough public debate about these issues. This complexity and lack of consensus makes advances in the formal land tenure system difficult to achieve. Nevertheless, as shown in Chapter 6, the 2017 Land Law took a position on many of these questions, although—due to lack of implementation—the solutions established in this law have not yet been tested.

Post-conflict debates and potential for violence

Post-conflict debates and the potential for land-related violence also play a role in the political environment in which the formal land tenure system is developed. As detailed in Chapter 3, violence caused several waves of dispossession and displacement, which became complex problems to which there is no simple solution. A court case, told to me once by a judge, illustrates the complexity of these problems. A woman claimed in court the restitution of her house that was being occupied by another woman. The occupant did not deny the formal land rights of the claimant. However, she argued that the claimant's husband had burned down her house in 1999, and she would only return the house under dispute once proper compensation was paid. The judge could see some reason in both sides, and there was no clear legal nor moral solution for this case.

Also regarding problems caused by post-conflict, I could identify that, in land-related debates, the positions of Timorese politicians and society vary between two extremes. On one side, there are people who support strong protections for land occupants and, for instance, during the debates of the Land Law, would claim that a special adverse possession mechanism should give rights to those that occupied land even after the 1999 violence.[57] On the other side, people claim that no occupation, before or after independence, should ever be protected, and that even long-term occupants should be evicted and returned to their place of origin with no compensation. Some people go so far as to say that occupants had been lucky to have lived on occupied land for free for so long. During the debates of the Land Law in 2012, I recall one MP evoking the Christianity of the Timorese to justify evictions of densely populated areas such as Comoro. He argued (and I paraphrase) that

57 One argument at times used to legitimise or delegitimise occupations of land is to make a distinction between people that left the country during the Indonesian occupation and those that remained fighting for the country (Elderton, 2002: 4; see also Silva, 2006: 186).

'we are all Christians, we should give each thing to its own rightful owner, and God blessed us with oil money to build social housing for these people'. The 2017 Land Law also took a position regarding the dilemmas caused by forced displacement and occupation, by establishing a hierarchy between different land rights (Chapter 6), but for now its solutions remain untested.

Besides these dilemmas, the post-conflict experience also provides the Timorese—politicians and the population in general—with first-hand knowledge of what conflict looks like, both during past administrations and after independence. Especially in 2006, the role of land disputes in sparking and fuelling conflict became quite evident for everyone (Chapter 3), and people are very aware of the conflict potential that land tenure issues have. This first-hand experience with violence, and the potential for land-related interventions to cause more conflict, can in part explain why politicians are generally so reluctant to debate and approve legislation about land. It is true that the same argument could be used the other way around: because people know what violence looks like, they could be keen to address the problem. But in my experience, fear prompted paralysis rather than action.

Resilience and prevalence of customary land tenure systems

As debated in Chapters 3 and 8, customary land tenure systems have been quite resilient and remain a prevalent mechanism of social ordering in Timor-Leste, despite having received limited legal recognition by the different administrations. The resilience and prevalence of customary land tenure systems in Timor-Leste are a further relevant factor of the political environment in which the Timorese formal land tenure system has evolved.

Making a very broad generalisation, we can find the more traditional and ancestral customary land tenure systems in rural areas. These systems are part of complex arrangements of social ordering and are organised around principles of origin, common derivation, and first possession of land (Hohe and Nixon, 2003: 14; Fitzpatrick and Barnes, 2010: 212; Fitzpatrick *et al.*, 2013: 25). One's 'house of origin' (*uma lisan* in Tetum), both through birth and marriage, is a fundamental part of social and communal identity and a source of rights and obligations (Leach *et al.*, 2012: 6; Cryan, 2015b: 148). The traditional social organisation which binds the various cultural groups of Timor-Leste together is based on a complex network of hierarchies and alliances of different *uma lisan*. Customary land tenure systems—including norms for land allocation, rights, and obligations of use and exclusion, rules of inheritance, and share of crops—are established through each group's norms and agreements with allies and neighbours, and are under the rule of customary authorities, usually the senior lineages of the group of origin (Fitzpatrick *et al.*, 2013: 32). In general these systems work quite independently of the formal land tenure system, but at times their paths intersect; for instance, in the case of land tenure disputes that families and customary authorities are not able to address (Chapter 8), or when norms of the formal system are evoked to change customary practices.

However, customary systems are neither exclusive to rural areas, nor based only on ancestral practices. Also in more urban areas, customary norms, practices, and institutions regulate access to and use of land.[58] Generally speaking, these systems coexist more with formal and semi-formal land tenure systems and incorporate more of their elements, but these customary systems exist nevertheless. For instance, people often request permission from suco chiefs to access land that is considered state land.[59] Under the formal land tenure system, the authority to manage state land belongs to DNTPSC; suco chiefs do not have this role, but in practice they are often the authority that the people recur to.

The prevalence of customary land tenure systems in Timor-Leste—and their proven capacity to provide social ordering regarding access to and avail of land, and to adapt to changes and interferences—is well known by Timorese politicians. For legal advisers (like myself) and international organisations focused on investment and the rule of law, the development of a formal land tenure system seems much more urgent and dramatic than for someone who has always lived with this coexistence of formal and informal systems. Timorese politicians know that stalling the development and territorialisation of the formal land tenure system can cause some problems, but will not collapse the country, because the customary systems, despite their problems and limitations, will continue to fill that gap.

Furthermore, while land-related issues are a problem, they are not the main concern of most Timorese (CISR, 2016: 16; The Asia Foundation, 2016: 36).[60] While people complain about land issues that their customary systems cannot address, problems such as access to clean water and good roads are considered much higher priorities. Therefore, social pressure to improve the formal system is not strong, and action only happens when an urgency emerges.

Conclusion

This chapter shows how the political environment that marked Timor-Leste since its independence has not been favourable to the development of a formal land tenure system in general, but especially not to one that can effectively

58 Interestingly, there is much less anthropological work about these systems in urban areas.

59 Suco chiefs are elected local leaders (Chapter 3). Another recurrent practice in which suco chiefs take a role in land administration is the issue of declarations attesting to people's ownership of land and overseeing sales and other transactions (CES-OPJ and CRL, 2017: 226). These declarations are a source of rent-seeking and disputes, their legal value is none, and it is not uncommon that declarations attest to the ownership of more than one owner to a single parcel of land.

60 According to CISR's survey, only 2 percent of the Timorese consider a land law as the most important issue of the country. The Asia Foundation found that 7 percent consider land issues the biggest national problem.

protect people and communities' land tenure. Although some progress has been made since independence—for instance, with the approval or more protective legislation (see Chapter 6)—improving the formal land tenure system is not a priority of the Timorese political elite. A few interconnected ideological and contextual factors that mark the Timorese political environment explain this conclusion.

While coming from different backgrounds, the two main political parties do not see the protection of people and communities' land rights as a priority, and advocate instead for strong control of land by the state. The visions of development of political elites—centred on high-modernistic, state-led infrastructure projects for which large tracts of land are necessary—are especially influential and prevail over the land rights of local populations. Quick and cheap access to land is a priority, and local people are expected to bear the sacrifices of these ambitious national visions. From the perspective of those promoting these visions, a formal land tenure system that could curb the state's access to land would only be an unnecessary obstacle.

Although rhetorically a formal land tenure system that can promote private investment is another part of these visions of development, much less effort has been put into creating it. Instead, politicians and state officials have been the gatekeepers that help investors navigate the very uncertain waters of land rights in the country. A formal land tenure system that can be navigated without 'support' is of little interest to those that benefit from the current chaos.

The post-authoritarian experience, the authoritarian temptation of top political leaders, and cultural features that favour top-down and strong-state approaches further shape interventions in the land sector and limit a more-democratic development of the formal land tenure system. While more-pragmatic, ad hoc land acquisition approaches for basic infrastructure were understandable just after independence, the current paths of land acquisition are at odds with a democratic, rule of law country that effectively protects its people's rights.

A number of contextual factors further undermine improvements in the formal land tenure system. The weak rule of law caused by weaknesses of the judicial system, bad legislation, and lack of administrative processes gives little room for judicial contestation of state actions, and limits legal debates and judicial interpretation of the legal framework. Without legal consequences, state institutions have no incentive to follow the law and improve administrative practices. This lack of incentive to improve the formal land tenure system is further influenced by the Indonesian legacy on land administration, which normalises arbitrary practices of state institutions. Opportunities for corruption, rent-seeking, clientelism, patronage, and elite capture further dissuade politicians and state officials from improving the formal land tenure system. Additionally, the resource curse caused by the windfall of oil and gas revenues removes the need to obtain state revenues through the formal land tenure system and further affects the quality of governance, including land tenure.

Moreover, other contextual factors bring dilemmas that promote inaction regarding the development of the formal land tenure system. Colonialism and conflict left a few dilemmas to which it is not possible to find consensual solutions, and the fear of land-related violence further scares politicians away from trying to improve the formal land tenure system. Finally, the resilience and efficiency of customary systems even in urban areas, and the fact that land tenure issues are not the main priority for most Timorese, further remove pressure from politicians to address the problems of the formal land tenure system. The conclusion to be drawn from this scenario is that there are few incentives in the Timorese political environment to seriously improve the Timorese formal land tenure system.

Chapter 5

The making of land laws

Introduction

This chapter looks at the law-making process of land-related legislation in Timor-Leste. As detailed in Chapter 1, law-making is a key analytical theme in understanding a land tenure system; it is through the law-making process that political debates are translated into the legal framework. Drawing on my experience as legal drafter in Timor-Leste, this chapter describes and analyses how Timorese legislation is drafted, debated, and approved, and how the problems and dilemmas of the law-making process affect the legal framework of the Timorese formal land tenure system. In other words, this chapter tries to explain how the land-related legal framework came to be the way it is.

Law-making is a complex political and legal process, through which a mix of ideologies, policies, and agreements are converted into legislation that must work together within the existing legal framework. This conversion of broad and conflicting ideas into legislation tends to be chaotic, hence legislative institutions throughout the world use procedural devices that help to keep order in the process and ensure the coherence of approved legislation (Waldron, 2006: 24, 28). Detailed rules for drafting and debating legislation, specialised offices for verification of legal compliance, and monitoring and evaluation mechanisms are some examples of the many procedural devices that structure a legislative process. This chapter shows that, in Timor-Leste, a number of these procedural devices are missing or are poorly implemented, which is reflected in the resulting quality of legislation (Chapter 6). Put simply, if the law-making process is bad, the legislation it produces will not be good (Rooij, 2006: 26).

This chapter starts with a brief description of the main steps taken in Timor-Leste to draft and approve key land-related legislation. After, it debates the existing theoretical framework on law-making in developing countries, including what the relevant theories contribute to my analysis as well as their gaps. Next, the chapter takes the theory further by identifying the main characteristics of the law-making process in Timor-Leste. Finally, the chapter analyses each of these aspects as they relate to the approval of key Timorese land-related legislation.

DOI: 10.4324/9781003196396-5

Making land-related laws in Timor-Leste

This section briefly summarises the steps taken in the law-making process of Law 1/2003 and the Land Law Package, the oldest and the most recent Timorese land-related legislation, respectively.[1]

The drafting and approval process of Law 1/2003 was quite basic. The law was drafted by DNTPSC during the first FRETILIN government, to my knowledge without any support study nor public consultation. The draft law was debated and approved by Council of Ministers in August 2002 and sent to parliament in September. A parliamentary commission heard DNTPSC staff, two suco chiefs from Dili, two representatives of the Catholic Church, the Association of Timorese Jurists, the Association of Timorese Businessmen, and two CSOs on their views about the draft law. This draft was then debated by the commission and a few articles were debated in parliament's plenary. With FRETILIN controlling the parliament, the draft law was quickly approved in December 2002.

In comparison with Law 1/2003, the drafting and approval process of the Land Law Package was much more complex. As detailed in Chapter 3, land-related issues were one of the main fuels of the 2006 crisis. Upon a request from Prime Minister Ramos-Horta, in 2007 USAID started the *Ita Nia Rai* project (INR), which aimed to develop a methodology for the systematic collection of land claims and to approve the necessary legal framework to recognise those land claims as land rights. However, the start of INR coincided with the end of FRETILIN's rule and the beginning of Gusmão's first government. The new ministers were distrustful of their predecessors' decisions, and the INR and USAID staff took almost one year to convince Lúcia Lobato, the new minister of justice, of the importance of the project. She eventually got on board and agreed to draft the new Land Law.[2]

A study developed by INR's Brazilian legal adviser, with several years of work experience in Timor-Leste, was the starting point of the Land Law (Lopes, 2008; Cryan, 2015b: 144). The envisioned steps for drafting the Land Law were two-fold: the preparation of a policy options document to be presented in the Council of Ministers, followed by the legal drafting based on the

1 One brief note on legislative powers in Timor-Leste: both parliament and government approve legislation, *laws* and *decree-laws*, respectively. However, on some topics government is dependent on authorisation from the parliament to legislate (e.g., expropriation), and in others it is fully restricted (e.g., fundamental rights). However, the government can approve draft legislation about any topic in Council of Ministers and send it to parliament to be approved as law. Ministers can approve the regulatory framework as *ministerial decrees*. Once approved, laws and decree-laws are sent for promulgation or veto by the president, who can also request the Court of Appeal for constitutional review (Almeida, 2017a: 180).

2 When I interviewed Lúcia Lobato in 2015, she told me that her doubts were in part fuelled by criticisms from DNTPSC officials of the INR, but slowly she became more sceptical of their criticisms, and more aware of the scope of the land problems in Timor-Leste.

results of that presentation. In January 2009, a working group composed of the MoJ's relevant national directors, national and international legal advisers, and the INR legal adviser was formed, with the objective of preparing this policy options document within ten days.[3] The document listed key issues, outlined different options for each of them, and provided the group's recommendation regarding which option to follow. This policy options document was briefly presented in Council of Ministers in February 2009, and the debate with the members of government became the basis for drafting the Land Law.[4] The INR adviser was the lead writer of the draft law, but the working group gathered a few times to analyse and change it. The minister of justice also participated in some of these meetings to finalise decisions on specific points raised by the working group. The main language used during these meetings and in the draft documents was Portuguese, but the policy options document, draft legislation, and other support documents were translated into Tetum once finalised.

The first draft of the Land Law was launched in June 2009 and went through a public consultation phase. The draft law was published on the MoJ's website and distributed to key stakeholders, and one public consultation session, led by the minister of justice, was held in each of the 13 district capitals. Personal invitations were sent to local authorities, but the meetings were open to the public and were well attended. Based on the public consultation results, a second version of the draft law was released in September, together with an explanatory document about the changes to the draft. An additional 17 public consultation sessions were held throughout the country, as well as a final reflection seminar about the results of the public consultation.[5] Representatives of the MoJ also participated in numerous events concerning the law organised by CSOs and international organisations. Stakeholders and participants in public consultations were also encouraged to send written comments about the draft law to MoJ, and a considerable number of submissions were sent. In early January 2010, when I started working with MoJ, one of my first tasks was to help the working group finalise the draft Land Law, which was ready in February 2010.

However, the draft Land Law only covered some of the legal gaps that needed to be addressed (Chapter 6). In 2009, while the Land Law was still being drafted, the MoJ commissioned two Portuguese law firms to draft other

3 Lopes's report, a policy note developed by Fitzpatrick *et al.* (2008), and a report from a mission from the Portuguese Institute of Registration and Notaries are quoted as the basis for this policy options document (available at http://www.mj.gov.tl/files/Relatorio_MinJusticaPortugal.pdf). The policy options document is available at http://www.mj.gov.tl/files/Grupo_de_Trabalho_Opcoes_Terras.pdf.

4 There are no public minutes of this meeting, and therefore no record of the official position of the Council of Ministers on each of the policy options debated.

5 Problems related with dispossession, forced relocation, land occupation, lack of formal rights, customary-based land rights, but also other problems such as inheritance, were the main topics raised in the consultation. About the main debates on land issues, see Chapters 3 and 4.

legal drafts, including the Expropriation Law and the Immovable Property Fund Law, among others. The justification for outsourcing these drafts was that the MoJ did not have enough qualified staff to quickly write these pieces of legislation. These two other draft laws were rapidly debated by the MoJ's working group in the beginning of 2010, but no public consultation was conducted in order to quickly send them together with the draft Land Law to Council of Ministers in February 2010, as what became known as the Land Law Package.

The draft Land Law Package was debated, changed, and approved in three sessions of Council of Ministers in March 2010, and sent to parliament as proposals of law. After an initial presentation to parliament's Commission A in May 2010, and the initial general approval soon after by the parliament's plenary, the draft Land Law Package was sent back to commission A for in-depth debate. However, Commission A did not start the debate of the Land Law Package for almost two years (see the reasons below). Only at the beginning of 2012, during a three-week retreat in Maubara, the three laws of the package were debated and changed by Commission A.[6] The plenary session for final changes and voting took place in February 2012, and after the approval the draft laws were sent to President Ramos-Horta for promulgation. However, he vetoed the draft Land Law Package and sent it back to parliament. The reasons for the veto were, in summary, disagreements with some of the policy options, a few unclear articles, and a lack of national consensus about the Land Law. Quite possibly, the fear of legislating on land-related issues (Chapter 4) also played a role in this veto. By then, the preparations for the legislative elections of July 2012 were underway, and parliament's plenary meetings for re-approving the draft Land Law Package were twice adjourned due to a lack of quorum. With the end of that political cycle, the Land Law Package expired.

After the elections, the new minister of justice, Dionísio Babo Soares, decided to re-start the approval of the draft Land Law Package. I was at the time reading Ann and Robert Seidman's work on law-making and, inspired by them, advised the minister to take a more systematic approach to this approval process. Although it would be impossible to fully implement their complex legislative theory (see below), at least some components could help to better organise the revision of these laws. This included incorporating the lessons learned since the approval of the first draft, addressing the concerns raised in the presidential veto, holding some more public consultation, and publishing

6 The meetings took place at the Carmelite Convent in Maubara, where I participated as the MoJ's legal adviser. The very hot and humid January weather and the frequent power cuts made these meetings extremely exhausting. On the other hand, the fact that all participants were gathered at the same place, sharing meals and coffee-breaks without many distractions, in part due to the lack of cell phone connection, made these meetings a valuable opportunity to understand participants' views and thoughts on land-related issues and politics in general.

a detailed report explaining all changes in the draft laws. My advice was heard, and after an initial revision, the drafts were publicly presented in November 2012, followed by an almost 90-day period for submissions of written comments by CSOs. After receiving a number of submissions, the draft laws were again revised and sent to Council of Ministers, together with a report explaining all the changes made. The draft Expropriation Law in particular, which had been initially drafted by one of the law firms, was considerably altered (see below).

The draft Land Law Package was debated in Council of Ministers in June 2013 and sent again to parliament, but no activity regarding the package was ever scheduled (more details below). By the time I left the MoJ at the end of 2014, nothing more had happened. In February 2015, when Gusmão stepped down as prime minister, the drafts expired again, this time without any debate at all in parliament. In early 2016, a slightly modified version of the drafts was again sent to Council of Ministers, where they were again approved and sent to parliament. In June 2016 Commission A debated the draft Land Law Package, which was approved by parliament in February 2017. President Taur Matan Ruak sent the draft Land Law for constitutional review by the Court of Appeal, but the Court decided that the concerns raised by the president did not violate the constitution. Eight years after the initial drafting, in mid-2017, the Land Law Package was finally approved.

As this description shows, the law-making processes of Law 1/2003 and the Land Law Package were very different, with the latter having gone through a much more thorough process of research and consultation. However, as the following analysis shows, the law-making process in Timor-Leste is still quite problematic. The following sections highlight the problems and dilemmas of drafting and approving legislation and show that the process has a serious impact on the quality of legislation. As mentioned above, if the law-making process is bad, one cannot expect that legislation will be good.

Looking at the law-making process

The study of a complex law-making process like the one described above needs a guiding framework, but finding an adequate theoretical guidance was not easy. As Otto *et al.*'s literature review of legislative theory shows (2008), theories on law-making have generally focused on specific moments and actors of law-making (e.g., agenda-building theory; bureau-politics theory) or related processes such as policymaking. However, few theories provide a framework for a comprehensive analysis of a full law-making process, as well as the factors and actors that influence it (Rooij, 2006: 26; Otto *et al.*, 2008: 57).

The fact that most literature on law-making focuses on countries of the Global North further complicated the search for the right framework of analysis. The assumptions on which these theories are based do not reflect the conditions in which law-making is done in most developing countries (ibid.: 71).

Although there is some common ground between law-making in Timor-Leste and, for instance, the US, these are worlds apart once we look at the apparatus that surrounds law-making in key aspects, such as resources, a detailed and well-tested regulation of the law-making process, legal culture, and political accountability. When reading literature about law-making in the Global North, I can relate my experience in Timor-Leste to some interesting points, but cannot recognise the law-making processes in which I participated.

In this search for a framework of analysis, I considered using the *institutional legislative theory* developed by Ann and Robert Seidman, some of the few authors that have outlined a comprehensive theory on law-making in developing countries (Arnscheidt *et al.*, 2008: 12).[7] However, the Seidmans' theory raised a few problems. First, it prescribes what the authors see as the ideal law-making process, and although it provides some analysis, it does not aim to explain how law-making in developing countries actually happens (Rooij, 2006: 29). Moreover, the ideal scenario that the Seidmans prescribe does account for the many problems and dilemmas that are central characteristics of law-making in developing countries, such as lack of resources, time, and legal and political accountability (Tamanaha, 1999: 152).[8]

Second, the problem-solving methodology proposed by the Seidmans resonates with the concept of *evidence-based policymaking*, trendy among international organisations, but problematic in practice. This concept comes with the belief that, through a scientific approach to a problem, the gaps of knowledge about that problem can be filled, and the 'correct' (or the most correct) policy option can be identified. However, even if applied seriously, the concept comes with naïve and positivist assumptions. First, it ignores the limits to the answers that scientific research can give and the methodological constraints

7 The Seidmans propose a four-step problem-solving methodology for law-making that, according to them, allows for social change through legislation (among others, Seidman, 1992; Seidman and Seidman, 2006, 2008, 2009). The Seidmans say that law-making should start with (1) a description of the social problem that the bill targets, and whose and what behaviours comprise it. Next, (2) a thorough study should explain those behaviours through a multi-layered approach (Seidman and Seidman, 2008: 95; 2009: 453). Only after these two steps the (3) drafting process can start. Finally, they propose (4) monitoring and evaluation of approved legislation. In all these steps, research plays a central role in producing knowledge for law-making.

8 When I first drafted this chapter, I questioned whether I was being fair to the Seidmans. Previously, as a legal drafter, I had tried to use their theory in law-making, and experienced first-hand its disconnection with the limitations of law-making in developing countries, but I still questioned my criticism. My doubts were answered after reading Tamanaha (1999), also an academic with similar experience as a legal drafter, and in whose work I could find, almost point-by-point, the same critiques I had. On the other hand, as also raised by Tamanaha (ibid.: 154), the Seidmans' theory is still valuable because it raises awareness of several relevant points and problems. For instance, they highlight the role of legal drafters in the law-making process (see below) and emphasise the need to start a law-making process by clearly identifying the social problems and behaviours that need to be addressed. Moreover, their ideal scenario for law-making is a good reference for comparison. Therefore, their theory guides some aspects of the analysis, as detailed below.

under which research is conducted (Greenhalegh and Russell, 2009). For instance, many problems that legislation must deal with are eminently political, and no research can give a right answer about how to address them. It can provide knowledge for better-informed decision-making, but ultimately it cannot give *the* right answer. Second, this approach comes with the faulty assumption that research is objective and ideologically neutral, besides ignoring how research is often manipulated by lobby groups and vested interests to promote their own views and agendas (ibid.: 153). In the words of Pawson, '[o]n a bad day, the ivory tower can look awfully like a shopping mall' (2011: 4; see also Santos, 1995: 107; Merry, 2011: 585). The Seidmans' theory fails to acknowledge that research has these limitations. Moreover, and connected with the critique raised above, the research demanded by the Seidmans' theory does not account for all the limitations that characterise law-making in developing countries.

In my search for an adequate theoretical framework for this chapter, I came across the Garbage Can Model, which, although more commonly oriented for policymaking, has been used for the analysis of law-making (Kingdon, 2003: 86; Rooij, 2006: 31; Rooij, 2008: 149). As this chapter shows, decisions in law-making are far from being the result of a well-informed and logical process of analysing problems, possibilities, and consequences. Legislative institutions function as what organisational theorists call *organised anarchies*. They have ill-defined goals; their multiple participants have different identities and conflicting preferences, and each participant takes part in the process inconsistently; and the consequences of different proposals are unclear and disputed. The Garbage Can Model of decision-making proposed by Cohen *et al.* (1972) provides a framework to understand how decisions are made by institutions that work as organised anarchies. In these organisations, the decision-making process is based much more on the intersections of a constant stream of semi-independent *opportunities*, and internal and external *problems*, *solutions*, and *participants*, than on a rational, informed, and structured approach (Cohen *et al.*, 1972; Rooij, 2008: 149; Newmann, 2012). When these streams of opportunities, problems, solutions, and participants connect, fortuitously or through the concerted action of participants, decisions are made (ibid.: 353).[9] The decisions produced by this decision-making process are not ideal for addressing problems, but are the ones made possible by such a complex scenario.

Despite its rather inelegant name, the Garbage Can Model brings two main strong points for the analysis of law-making processes. First, this model provides

9 Cohen *et al.* describe the garbage can metaphor as follows: 'To understand processes within organizations, one can view a choice opportunity as a garbage can into which various kinds of problems and solutions are dumped by participants as they are generated. The mix of garbage in a single can depends on the mix of cans available, on the labels attached to the alternative cans, on what garbage is currently being produced, and on the speed with which garbage is collected and removed from the scene' (1972: 2).

guidance in the analysis of the law-making process, by telling us to look at the interactions between *opportunities*, *problems*, *solutions*, and *participants*. Second, this model provides an adequate framework to highlight and understand why law-making is not the result of a rational process, and to understand the role of problems and dilemmas characteristic of developing countries that legislative theories do not account for. As argued by Cohen *et al.*,

> [t]he great advantage of trying to see garbage can phenomena together as a process is the possibility that that process can be understood, that organisational design and decision making can take account of its existence and that, to some extent, it can be managed.
>
> (1972: 18)

However, this model does not provide a clearer guide regarding where in a law-making process one can see the interactions between *opportunities*, *problems*, *solutions*, and *participants*. I addressed this problem by thinking about the common steps of a law-making process (e.g., drafting, debate, approval) as a main guide, combined with some relevant points raised by the Seidmans' theory and my personal experience as a legal drafter. With these in mind, I identified the key aspects where, in my view, the interactions between *opportunities*, *problems*, *solutions*, and *participants* in the law-making process are most visible, and which are fundamental to understanding the process, and therefore the result, of law-making.[10] Those aspects are: (1) legislative agenda; (2) knowledge production for the law-making process; (3) decision-making; (4) legal drafters; (5) consultation and transparency mechanisms; (6) drafting options and dilemmas; (7) monitoring and evaluation; and (8) language. As the analysis below shows, although some of these aspects overlap with each other due to their different nature, each of them has their own dynamics that need to be singled out and analysed separately. Each of these aspects and their relevance to law-making are discussed in the following sections of this chapter.

In the analysis of each of these aspects, as it is done throughout the book, I pay special attention to the main problems and dilemmas experienced in each of them and, following the example of the pragmatic approach advocated by Tamanaha (1999), I included in the conclusion some brief practical suggestions. While this theoretical approach to studying the law-making process and the related recommendations were designed with the Timorese context in mind, they are relevant for understanding law-making in countries experiencing similar limitations.[11]

10 By *participants* I mean anyone involved in the law-making process, including politicians, legal drafters, experts, CSOs, lobbyists, and others.

11 Regarding law-making in Timor-Leste, see also CRL, 2017, and Cunha, 2018.

Legislative agenda

The first key aspect for analysing law-making in Timor-Leste is the legislative agenda.[12] Legislative institutions are responsible for addressing an endless stream of social problems, but only a few of these problems ever make it onto the legislative agenda, and even fewer go through the approval process. Therefore, understanding the legislative agenda is a key aspect of studying a law-making process. In this section, the study of the Timorese agenda is guided by two questions: (1) which combination of *opportunities*, *participants*, and *solutions* are necessary for a social problem to be addressed by legislation? And (2) which problems and dilemmas are created by the constraints of the legislative agenda?

Regarding the first question, while a myriad of factors influence the legislative agenda, in the Timorese law-making process the line-ministers and their political skills are particularly relevant. In Timor-Leste draft legislation can only be debated in the Council of Ministers or parliament if proposed by a minister or a member of parliament (MP), respectively. Citizens, CSOs, and international organisations can lobby ministers and MPs to start a legislative initiative, but only ministers and MPs can present legislation to be debated. Therefore, they are gatekeepers of the legislative process; without their action, no legislation is approved.

However, the great majority of draft laws debated in parliament are first drafted by a ministry and approved as a proposal of law by Council of Ministers. For a number of reasons, MPs very rarely exercise their right of proposing legislation, which makes ministers the main players in putting a topic on the legislative agenda (UNMIT, 2012: 6).[13] When MPs think that a certain topic needs new legislation, the common approach is to ask the government and the line minister to draft it. What convinces a minister to support and start the drafting process of legislation on a certain topic depends on a myriad of factors, such as personal views about the issue; the scale and visibility of the problem in society and the media; the political and social pressure to address that problem; the tactics used by civil society, interest groups, and international organisations to advocate for the approval of certain legislation; the opportunity to collect political gains and social credit through the approval of legislation; the difficulty of addressing the issue; and the general political environment around the topic.

However, writing and sending draft legislation for approval does not guarantee that the topic will be well positioned in the legislative agenda. The rules (or *regimento* in Portuguese) from Council of Ministers and parliament set guidelines

12 By *legislative agenda* I mean the list of draft legislation that parliament and the government intend to debate and eventually approve. Edelman provides an interesting analysis about how social realities become considered social problems (1988: Chapter 2).

13 See here art. 97 of the constitution, and the rules of parliament and Council of Ministers. On a comparative note, in the Netherlands 97 percent of the legislation is drafted by the government (Veerman, 2015: 22).

about the legislative agenda, but these rules are quite flexible and establish no priority about the order through which legislation is debated (CRL, 2017: 69; Cunha, 2018: 135).[14] Ministers have to compete with each other and with MPs to move the drafts they support up in the legislative agenda and strategise in order to overcome those people that try to block the approval of their drafts. While the relevance of the topic and the social and political pressure for the approval of legislation play a role in this competition, other factors also matter. The political status of each politician, their personal relationships with other relevant politicians, their negotiation skills, their relationship with the media, and the time and effort they invest in pushing the draft forward are paramount. Other factors such as parliament recess periods, the absence of a politician who is blocking the approval process, and the electoral calendar must also be factored into the equation.[15] As argued by Kingdon, in a Garbage Can Model of decision-making there are moments when all factors align and a window of opportunity for acting—in this case approving legislation—can be seized (2003, 166). As I exemplify below, in the Timorese law-making process these opportunities do not depend only on luck, but also skill. Without a skilful minister and a crafty strategy, it is unlikely that draft legislation about a controversial topic is ever approved.

The approval of the Land Law Package depicts the central role of ministers in putting a topic on the legislative agenda. As discussed in Chapter 4, the political environment was never favourable to the approval of legislation on land tenure issues, including the fact that addressing land-related issues was never a priority of the top political leaders like Alkatiri and Gusmão. Furthermore, and despite politicians' public statements on the need to address land-related issues, these draft laws met with strong opposition in Council of Ministers and parliament, with arguments made against the political options in the drafts, and fear expressed that they could reignite conflict (see below).[16] What slowly moved this very controversial legislation through the legislative agenda was the pressure and political savviness of Ministers of Justice Lúcia Lobato and later Dionísio Babo Soares. Both became acutely aware of land-related issues due to their role as ministers, where they received a constant stream of letters from private citizens, business interests, and CSOs with all kinds of complaints and demands. Furthermore, both of them had ambitions of progressing in their political careers, and approving these laws

14 Other countries have different approaches to the legislative agenda. In Indonesia the legislative agenda is set for the five-year term of parliament but adjusted at the beginning of each year (Vel *et al.*, 2017: 7). In the United Kingdom the legislation to be approved each year in parliament is also fixed, while in the Netherlands the legislative agenda can be changed according to the political circumstances (Veerman, 2015: 1).

15 Also relevant is the politicians' personal agenda. A legislative success at the right time can be an important boost for one's political profile (Veerman, 2015: 4).

16 Among many others, Suara Timor Lorosae, 15 June 2009, 3 February 2011, 12 December 2012, 20 February 2013, and 10 January 2017; Jornal Nacional Diário, 15 April 2014.

would show their political strength.[17] Finally, both were well connected inside Council of Ministers and parliament, which allowed them to lobby and strategise for the approval of these draft laws. Most likely, these laws would never have been approved without the skills and connections of these two ministers. Furthermore, some changes in the position of CSOs on these drafts also played a role in pushing their approval forward (Chapter 7).

A few episodes depict well the need for political savviness, strategy, and luck to get these laws approved. According to comments from parliament's staff, in 2010 the draft laws were not being debated in parliament by Commission A because Fernanda Borges, the president of the commission was against them. At the end of 2011, already close to the end of the legislative term, the president of Commission A went on vacation. The vice-president of Commission A (Rui Menezes), from the same party as the speaker of parliament (Fernando Lasama), with whom the minister of justice had a close relationship, quickly booked the time and venue for the commission's debate, leaving the president with no choice when she returned from vacation. A new impasse happened in 2013 when the new speaker of parliament, Vicente Guterres, who was also against these draft laws, simply shelved them. The impasse continued when Gusmão asked parliament to suspend the debate of the Land Law Package.[18] Ultimately, this package of laws was only approved when a number of factors, by chance, happened to line up: the short-lived consensus between FRETILIN and CNRT during the more technocratic government of Rui Araújo (February 2015 to September 2017) reduced political opposition in parliament; the speaker of parliament was replaced; and for the first time, the Petroleum Fund started to decrease, bringing back the debate about land as an alternative source of state revenues (Chapter 4).

As touched upon above, the constraints of the legislative agenda bring several problems and dilemmas to the law-making process. One first problem is the above-mentioned high dependency on a single line-minister. If the legislative process is designed in such a way that the approval of legislation about one topic is dependent on the political skills of a single person, the selection of that person has a significant impact in getting legislation about that topic approved. A second problem caused by the uncertainty of the legislative agenda is the difficulty in planning the implementation of new legislation, both for ministries, other state institutions, and external partners (e.g., international organisations). Implementation steps such as the drafting of regulatory frameworks, trainings, budgets, and procurement are in part dependent on knowing when legislation

17 When the Land Law Package was approved by parliament in 2017, the minister of justice was Ivo Valente—who informants told me was considering retiring from politics—did not show up at the debates in parliament. Instead, Dionísio Babo Soares, at the time Minister of State, Coordinator of State Administration and Justice Affairs and Minister of State Administration, represented the government in parliament.

18 See Timor Post, 29 April 2014, 2 October 2014a, 14 October 2015.

will be approved and what its final content will be. Without this information, planning is difficult and becomes even more problematic when implementation is dependent on development projects with limited timeframes. Moreover, the constraints of the legislative agenda put ministers in difficult dilemmas: when the window of opportunity opens, should they push forward the approval of draft legislation, even if there is not enough research and consultation informing it?[19] Should they rush the approval of the legislation, even if they need to compromise on some policy options in order to do so? In other words, should they compromise on quality to get legislation approved?

The approval of Decree-Law 27/2011 (Chapters 3 and 6) illustrates these problems and dilemmas. By mid-2011 the draft Land Law Package was sitting in parliament, without any prospect of being approved anytime soon. In the meantime, the land-claims collection by INR was progressing without a legal framework to support it, which was becoming problematic for the project's continuation. Furthermore, the initial enthusiasm of international organisations in supporting the drafting and implementation of the Land Law Package was fading, becoming increasingly more conditional on the approval of the laws. Moreover, the MoJ had been budgeting for the implementation of these laws, but without their approval little could be spent, which was damaging for the ministry's reputation. This posed the dilemma of deciding whether to continue including the Land Law implementation in the ministry's budget. With all these problems in mind, the minister of justice asked me and INR for a short-term solution that could anticipate the implementation of the Land Law, put pressure on parliament to approve it, and provide a legal basis for INR's activities. The solution was to draft a decree-law, approved by Council of Ministers, anticipating some effects of the Land Law. While the idea was good, the timeframe for developing the decree-law was short, giving almost no time for internal debate within the ministry nor external consultation about the policy options and the text adopted. These limitations were reflected in the quality of the decree-law, and in the way it was later perceived and poorly implemented (Chapter 6). In conclusion, this decree-law was mostly shaped by the difficulties of moving legislation inside the Timorese legislative agenda, and the outcome was less than ideal.

Knowledge production for the law-making process

Knowledge about the problems that a piece of draft legislation aims to tackle and about the possible solutions to be adopted is the second key element to

19 Managing the window of opportunity is even more complex if one considers the very low productivity of the Timorese Parliament. Since independence parliament has approved an average of 11 laws per year, with a maximum of 17 in 2005. In comparison, the Indonesian Parliament approved 56 laws in 2009, and 24 in 2013 (Vel *et al.*, 2017: 7).

understanding law-making. As discussed above, the impact that research can have as a procedural device to guide law-making is bounded by the limitations of science, the nature of the problems that need to be solved, and contextual factors such as limited time and resources. Within these limitations, research is used by legislatures to guide them through law-making but, as this section shows, the structure and resources for, and interest in, research are not equal everywhere, with clear impacts on the legislation approved. As this section shows, research for law-making in Timor-Leste is limited, with clear impacts on the knowledge about the problems to be addressed and the solutions adopted (Cunha, 2018: 139).

The lack of knowledge about problems and solutions in the Timorese law-making is structural. In other words, neither the government nor the parliament are legally obliged to conduct research before drafting new legislation. The rules of Council of Ministers and parliament require only a *brief* justification note for new draft legislation, which is in practice a one- or two-page document that legal drafters write at the end of the process.[20] Therefore, any research before legislative drafting is dependent on the will of the line minister. For instance, Law 1/2003, to the best of my knowledge, was written without any previous research about the problems that the legislation intended to address, nor the adequacy of the solutions adopted.[21] In comparison, the drafting process of the Land Law was improved with some (limited) research and a policy options document that allowed a better definition and study of problems and solutions. But this change in the process happened mostly due to the intervention of the INR adviser mentioned above, who insisted to the minister of justice that the approach followed in previous drafts—without research and a single drafter working alone—had to be changed.[22] A similar thing happened in 2012 after the first veto of the president, when I convinced the minister to take a more systematic approach to the modifications of the draft laws after having read the work of the Seidmans. In summary, the production of knowledge for law-making in Timor-Leste is not an intrinsic part of the process; it is instead dependent on the will and vision of a few key participants.

This lack of a clear obligation to conduct research before the drafting and approval of legislation is problematic. Politicians are often not aware of, or do not see, the advantages of conducting research before drafting legislation, as they often see the problem and its solutions as self-evident. But even when

20 See the rules of parliament (art. 98.1.d), and the rules of Council of Ministers (art. 27.1.a, of Government Resolution 51/2017). On a comparative note, Indonesia is stricter about the research that precedes the approval of legislation in parliament, demanding for each legal draft a report analysing the parameters of the law and the problems that it intends to address (Vel *et al.*, 2017: 7).

21 From 2004 onwards the government commissioned to the LLP a few studies to inform legislation, but no legislation on the researched topics was approved (LLP, 2004; Chapter 3).

22 Personal communication with Ibere Lopes. For instance, the first draft of the Expropriation Law was not preceded of any research.

politicians agree on conducting some research before drafting legislation, the research often experiences severe limitations of time and resources. As described above, the legislative agenda often gives a very short timeframe for research, as the 10 days given to the MoJ's working group to produce the policy options document that informed the draft Land Law well exemplifies. The fact that the drafting of such an important piece of legislation, although informed by other studies and supported by a working group, depended on the research of a single jurist shows the very limited resources put into research as part of the law-making process.

Another limitation to consider is that research frequently does not reach politicians, even when serious efforts to that end are made. A case in point was the drafting of regulations for community land. In the process of developing the Land Law, it became clear that the topic of community land needed to be regulated separately and would need more research before regulations could be drafted. The World Bank's Justice for the Poor (J4P) programme agreed with the MoJ to conduct comparative legal research for policy options on regulating community land (World Bank, 2010). As part of this study, the MoJ, J4P, and Commission A from parliament organised a seminar specifically targeting MPs to involve them in the research. Considering the relevance of the topic in Timor-Leste, many MPs were expected, and the entire Dili Conventions Centre was reserved. However, out of 65 MPs, only five or six showed up to the seminar. Daniel Fitzpatrick, the main writer of the study, only got one question from the president of Commission A. All other questions were addressed to the minister of justice, on topics with little or nothing to do with community land. The effort to involve MPs in research before the drafting of legislation that they would eventually decide on simply did not work. Ideally, research and presentation of findings should be organised in formats that involve all relevant politicians, but as this example shows, this is more difficult than it seems (ICG, 2013: 14).

Additionally, often politicians and state officials are not interested in reading complex research nor moved by scientific arguments. One episode was especially striking to me. One of the features of the Land Law and the Expropriation Law is the payment of compensation. Based on suggestions from DNTPSC staff, the initial drafts established that the values of compensation would be primarily based on land value tables, which was a methodology that DNTPSC staff knew from Indonesian times. However, DNTPSC had no technical capacity to prepare those tables, and one initial study commissioned by the MoJ to external consultants did not provide a good conclusion, so eventually ADB and the World Bank hired a land valuation specialist to draft these tables. From the first day this specialist pointed out problems with the tables: first, they would be nearly impossible to calculate in a sound way, even in a place with a transparent land market, which was not the case in Timor-Leste. Second, even if the tables were correct, they would soon be outdated, leaving the values of compensation frozen in time. After the 2012 veto of the Land Law Package I was able to use this research to justify the removal of these tables from the revised drafts. But in 2015, when I was no longer at the MoJ and the drafts had to be reapproved, the tables were again introduced at the suggestion of DNTPSC and made it into the final version of the law.

Moreover, some policy options are eminently political, and although research can contribute to a better-informed decision, it cannot provide the 'correct' solution. The Land Law provides another illustrative example. The initial drafts of the Land Law raised concerns among CSOs, politicians, and the population in general that its implementation would result in large-scale evictions. To avoid this problem, subsequent drafts established a mechanism of protection against eviction for poor households.[23] However, this protection was removed from the 2015 drafts. Through the study detailed in Chapter 8, my co-author and I were able to quantify the consequences of this decision, concluding that not having this protection in the draft law would leave at least 28 percent of the Dili population at risk of eviction (Almeida and Wassel, 2016: 28). Although we could estimate the impact of not including this protection in the law, and we managed to reach the right audience through the various ways we shared our research, the decision was ultimately political, and such numbers did not move MPs to reintroduce the protection against eviction in the law.

In summary, the legal framework in Timor-Leste does not require research before law-making, and therefore it is mostly dependent on the will of line-ministers and the influence of other participants. As a result, research for law-making is not a common practice. The case of Timor-Leste is not unique, and adds to the Seidmans' claim that law-making in developing countries is marked by a lack of research about the problems that legislative institutions need to address and the solutions they adopt. But the case of Timor-Leste also shows that a lack of knowledge about the problems, potential solutions to be adopted, and the speculative impacts of those solutions are, to a certain extent, inherent characteristics of organised anarchies (Cohen *et al.*, 1972: 1; Newmann, 2012: 352), and research cannot provide all the answers to law-making. In conclusion, research plays an important role in better-informed decisions in law-making, but should also not be seen as the solution for all problems of law-making.

23 This mechanism raised, however, the problem of determining who should be included in this protection. Very strict criteria would exclude families in need, while excessively broad protections would legitimise cases of abusive occupation of land. The solution was to establish only the main rules in the Land Law and defer the details of this protection to future regulations.

Decision-making

Decision-making is at the heart of the law-making process and it is the third key element to understanding it. Legislation is the result of numerous decisions, such as determining that a problem needs to be regulated, choosing a strategic path to legislate about that problem, and selecting which policy options should be included in the legal text. As debated above, the decisions in law-making are not the result of a very logical and well-informed process, but are rather the encounter of a stream of problems, solutions, participants, and opportunities. To inform the analysis of decision-making in a legislative process, this section looks into: (1) who takes decisions at the different stages of the law-making process; and (2) how those decisions are informed, and their viability, coherence, and legality assessed.

The first question is who takes decisions at the different stages of the Timorese law-making process. Given that line-ministries initially draft most legislation, ministers and, to a certain extent, their legal drafters (see below) play a central role in choosing the policy options that are included in draft legislation. With baseline studies and policy options documents not being a common practice (UNMIT, 2012: 7), first drafts of legislation are quite influential, because they tend to narrow the debate by defining the problem that needs to be addressed and limiting the discussion about policy options (Marriott, 2013: 112).[24] This puts line-ministers in a very powerful position, as they are the ones taking the ultimate decision on what goes in and what stays out of draft legislation written by their ministries.[25] The policy options document for the draft Land Law that was debated in Council of Ministers before the legal drafting was, in this case, an exception.

Once legislation is drafted, it is sent to Council of Ministers for approval. Draft legislation is presented by the line-ministers in the meetings of Council of Ministers and is debated by ministers and the prime minister. During the debate, the participants suggest changes in the draft and, unless the document is sent back for major changes, these meetings are a one-off opportunity to modify draft legislation. Sometimes there are backstage agreements and requests, but in theory modifications must be agreed on during these meetings. If the draft legislation is a decree-law, no more changes are introduced after the Council of Ministers' meetings. If the draft is a proposal of law, it is then sent to parliament for debate and approval. In parliament, MPs can change draft legislation

24 The Seidmans' theory establishes that a law-making process must start with a clear identification of the social problems that need to be addressed. While this can sound self-evident, in practice it is not. For instance, in many countries state officials claim that the main land tenure problem in their countries is the low percentage of registered land. Lack of land registration is not a social problem; land tenure insecurity, landlessness, and inequality are. If lack of registration is identified as a social problem, the next step is to find ways of increasing land registration. If the problem identified is low legal tenure security, then land registration can be seen as one potential solution among many to address this problem, or even as the origin of that problem.

25 Occasionally draft legislation is circulated between ministries for comment, but this is not a standard practice.

at only two moments: during the article-by-article debate by one of parliament commissions and during the final plenary debate.

In short, line-ministers play an especially strong role in the Timorese law-making process, deciding what goes into draft legislation, with other ministers and MPs having relatively limited opportunities to change drafts. As argued below, the way in which these changes are introduced in Council of Ministers and parliament meetings further impacts the result of the law-making process.

The second question is how decisions in the law-making process are informed and their viability, coherence, and legality assessed. As described in the previous section, pre-drafting research in Timor-Leste is not mandatory, and when it happens, it often fails to reach and convince politicians involved in the law-making process. Moreover, while some politicians carefully prepare for the debates, it is not uncommon for ministers and MPs to learn of the topic and the draft legislation during the debate in Council of Ministers or parliament. The consequence is that proposals to change draft legislation during these meetings are often not the result of a well-informed and carefully considered position of a minister or MP and their support staff, but rather an opinion formed on-the-spot. Furthermore, the decision to approve or reject these proposed changes are also often decided on-the-spot, without much time for the draft's promotor, the other participants in the meeting, and support staff to carefully consider the impacts of any modification. Parliament's article-by-article discussions can be particularly chaotic, because a change in one article often implies changes in others to preserve the overall logic of the draft, but the rules do not account for revisiting articles that have already been voted on. Moreover, there are limited mechanisms for assessing the viability, coherence, and legality of decisions in the law-making process. First, as described above, draft legislation is often the product of one or two jurists' work and the decisions of one minister; drafts are rarely circulated within ministries to check for political, legal, and practical coherence. Second, the Council of Ministers and parliament have very few specialists checking draft legislation, and drafts are often debated without a thorough check.[26] As the following examples show, these problems result in ill-considered decisions.

The parliamentary debates of the draft in 2012 provide various examples of poorly informed decisions. Parliament rules allow the government to present the draft laws to Commission A, which, for the first version of the draft Land Law, happened in May 2010, and later at the beginning of the 2012 debates.

26 At times there was only one jurist in Council of Ministers analysing draft legislation coming from ministries (CRL, 2017: 29; art. 28 and 30 of Government Resolution 51/2017). For instance, parliament's Commission A usually has two legal advisers to assist the 12 MPs. The Civil Code, the country's most complex piece of legislation, was debated with one legal adviser assisting the entire commission (JSMP, 2011: 5). The fact that advisers are not allocated to a specific political party gives them some flexibility, but also puts them in strange positions, such as helping one MP to write a change that the MP wants to introduce in a draft legislation, and later providing another MP with legal arguments to defeat that same proposal.

These presentations, done by the minister of justice, lasted for 20 to 30 minutes each, and gave a very brief summary of the complex legal solutions adopted in the draft law. At the time, I suggested to start the debates of these draft laws with a longer presentation about land issues in general, before looking at the content of the law, but the idea was dismissed. The debate by Commission A, article-by-article, started immediately after the minister's summary. The points and questions raised by MPs during the debate made clear that, albeit to different degrees, they had a fairly limited picture of the overall topic of land issues in Timor-Leste, and their positions were mostly based on cases that they personally knew about. Furthermore, they did not have a full understanding of the solutions adopted in the draft laws. This was obvious even for the MPs; after debating all articles of the draft Land Law, they decided to improvise and, against parliament rules, started a second round of discussion article-by-article. However, after debating a few articles for the second time, doubts about the rules of this ad hoc second round led to a long and loud argument among the participants, which only ended when they decided to stop the second round. The changes in the draft introduced during the first round of discussion, which the MPs themselves acknowledged were done without a clear view of the problems and comprehension of the legal solutions adopted, remained in the text.

A final example, this time of the Expropriation Law, links the two questions debated in this section and shows how the factors they refer to can seriously impact the final result of law-making. One of the many changes in the draft Expropriation Law after the 2012 veto and the public consultation that followed was to raise from 30 to 90 days the minimum period that people would be given to vacate land after expropriation. The legal and political reasons for this change, mentioned in the report that detailed the changes in this draft law, was to comply with the *UN Basic Principles and Guidelines on Development-based Evictions and Displacement*. However, during the 2016 debate in Council of Ministers, this provision was changed, without much thought being put into the impact of that decision. The period for vacating land that the state must allow people during expropriation was changed from a *minimum* of 90 days to a *maximum* of 90 days, with no established minimum.[27] The initial purpose of giving people enough time to prepare to leave land was completely subverted, and instead, a notification that gives people a single day to vacate land could be considered legal under this article. With a single decision, a draft law that was protective of people's rights became an extremely oppressive tool. In conclusion, this example shows how a rushed change proposed in the heat of a debate, without mechanisms to assess the impact of that change, can have serious and negative impacts on legislation.

27 The article establishes that 'A reasonable period for vacating the land shall be given to all interested parties, but this period cannot exceed ninety days' (art. 41.2.).

Legal drafters

Legal drafters are the fourth key aspect to understanding a law-making process. As argued by the Seidmans, the literature has focused too much on politicians as the decision-makers of legislative processes, but overlooks the role of legal drafters as more than mere scribes (Seidman and Seidman, 2009: 443).[28] This section builds on the point raised by the Seidmans, showing how the work of legal drafters, and therefore their recruitment, indeed have a significant impact on the final result.

While politicians are the final decision-makers, legal drafters make numerous decisions that impact the text of legislation. Language, technical solutions, and even policy decisions are often left to legal drafters. Moreover, legal drafters are at times also responsible for designing and conducting research that informs draft legislation. Consequently, legal drafters are not mere scribes but key participants in the law-making process, who have a significant impact on draft legislation. This links with a subsequent point: if legal drafters are key participants in the law-making process, their recruitment influences the result of law-making. Legal drafters' knowledge, background, values, and allegiances are reflected in legislation. Moreover, the limitations that legal drafters experience, such as a lack of human resources, excessive workload, short timeframes, and poor lines of communication with politicians, also impact the result of law-making. In no way does this mean that politicians' role in law-making is irrelevant; politicians have the last word in law-making processes and do not always follow the recommendation of legal drafters. Nevertheless, understanding the role of legal drafters is a key step to getting a fuller picture of all participants in, and the final outcome of, law-making.

Given the key role in law-making that legal drafters usually play, one must know who the legal drafters are to understand law-making in Timor-Leste. Most legal drafters in the country are jurists, the great majority foreigners like myself, working as legal advisers. For several reasons, there are few qualified jurists in Timor-Leste, and ministries, parliament, and other state institutions often hire international legal advisers.[29] They tend to come from Portuguese-speaking countries (mostly Portugal, Brazil, and Cape Verde), but sometimes nationals from other countries are also involved in law-making, such as

28 The Seidmans define *drafters* as 'all those who contribute to the detailed design of a bill', including 'experts from the relevant ministry and research institutions as well as legally trained drafters who chain together the final bill's words' (2009: 437). In other words, the drafters are those professionals that provide *legislators* (or 'politicians', as I use throughout the book) with the legal texts.

29 Debating the reasons for few qualified Timorese jurists is beyond the scope of this book, but it is the result of a weak education system (before and after independence), language issues (Chapter 3 and below), and disinvestment from the government and international organisations in raising the quality of national experts, instead of just following the easy road of hiring internationals. See here Massier, 2008: 242; USAID, 2009: 30; Simões, 2015: 393.

Indonesians, Australians, and Americans. When a ministry or (more rarely) parliament wants to draft a new piece of legislation, its first option is to refer to the legal advisers already working with them. Alternatively, these institutions hire a consultant specifically to draft a piece of legislation. International organisations also provide ministries with experts to write or provide advice on a specific draft, as a way of both moving legislation forward and influencing the outcome. Occasionally ministries also hire an (international) law firm to draft a specific piece of legislation. At times, international advisers are paired with national counterparts or drafting teams are created, but this only happens in exceptional cases (UNMIT, 2012: 6). Each legal drafter brings to the drafting process not only their own background, political views, professional experiences, and limitations, but also the values and objectives of the institutions they represent. As exemplified below, all of these elements are reflected in the legislation they ultimately draft.[30]

The drafting of the Expropriation Law provides two clear examples of how the recruitment of legal drafters and the limitations they experience have an impact on the final result of law-making. As described above, the Expropriation Law was first drafted by a Portuguese law firm. Their draft Expropriation Law was a simplified version of the Portuguese law, written without a prior baseline study, with little detail on central elements such as the definition of public purpose and weak protections for people affected by an expropriation. Such elements are not big problems in Portugal, where courts work reasonably well; legal doctrine can reflect on general definitions, and legal aid and other protection mechanisms help people affected by an expropriation. Conversely, in Timor-Leste this lack of detailed definitions and strong protections in the law can quickly open doors to abuses by the state. The draft Expropriation Law written by the hired law firm was briefly debated by the MoJ working group, but there was not enough professional experience in the group to recognise all the problems that the minimal protections would bring, nor time to substantially change the draft in time for the debate in Council of Ministers.[31] Therefore, only minor changes were made to this draft.

After the presidential veto in 2012, I was asked by the minister of justice to make changes to the draft law. By then I was much more aware of land-related practices in Timor-Leste and of the need to strengthen protections in this law. Furthermore, upon consultation with DNTPSC and myself, ADB hired a consultant to advise on the changes made to this draft. Besides being experienced in expropriation processes, this consultant was—contrary to the

30 Fitzpatrick *et al.* (2013) debate the influence of international legal advisers on legal solutions established in legislation.

31 I must include myself in this list of people with little experience in expropriations. When this debate happened, I had just started to work with the MoJ and had limited experience on land rights and public administration practices in Timor-Leste. Therefore, I was not fully prepared to understand all the issues of that draft.

law firm—bound by a strong protective framework, the ADB's Safeguard Policy Statement, which establishes strict rules to avoid, minimise, and mitigate adverse social impacts of expropriation. The support that I, as a legal drafter, got from this consultant was important for providing technical knowledge and a forum for debating ideas. Moreover, it also enabled me to defend the changes I proposed as being in line with international best practices. The result was a new version of the draft Expropriation Law that was the antithesis of its previous version. This was only possible because the right window of opportunity (the veto), participants (in this case legal drafters), and solutions (a more systematic law-making process) happened to line up.

The second example of the role of legal drafters in law-making is connected with the first one, and also refers to the 2012 changes to the draft Expropriation Law. One main change was to add a detailed definition of *public purpose*, which included a long list of categories that are considered to fulfil this legal requirement (e.g., public roads, hospitals). While drafting this list, I had to consider one specific, controversial category: expropriation for a project targeting *economic development* (e.g., building a shopping centre). This kind of expropriation is accepted in some countries, but the results are controversial (Eisenberg, 1995: 220; Wolford *et al.*, 2013; Hoops, 2018: 3). In countries where the judicial system is strong, the nuances regarding how different projects targeting economic development contribute to public purpose can be debated in court, making this kind of expropriation less, but still somewhat, controversial. In countries like Timor-Leste, where the judicial system does not work as a good interpreter of vague legal provisions, allowing expropriation for economic development becomes a Pandora's box for all kinds of abuses, in which the state turns into a land broker of private businesses, often to the detriment of small farmers and urban dwellers (FAO, 2009: 12; Cotula *et al.*, 2016: 36; Hoops, 2016: 4).

When revising the draft Expropriation Law, I was aware of the literature highlighting the abuses that the inclusion of economic development as a valid category of public purpose would lead to. By then, I was also aware of how Timorese politicians are keen to use economic growth as a synonym for 'development' and a go-to justification to impose all kinds of sacrifices on local populations (Chapter 4). Furthermore, expropriation of individual and communal land for private investors was nothing new for Timorese politicians, as it had been standard practice during Suharto's regime (Chapter 4). I was convinced that, if the option of including economic development as a valid category of public purpose was even raised, politicians would include it in the law, despite all recommendations against it. I was conflicted with what to do in this case: in theory, my role as adviser was to lay out all possibilities, explaining their legal arguments and ramifications; however, my own values and professional experience told me that omitting this option would lead to a—by my standards—better result. Ultimately, I decided to simply never raise the option and did not include this debate in the detailed report that I wrote about the changes in the draft Expropriation Law.[32] The topic was never addressed during the debates, and economic development was not included in the definition of public purpose in the law.

In conclusion, these examples illustrate that in law-making legal drafters as more than mere scribes, and their recruitment and contexts in which they work have a real influence on the outcome of law-making.

Consultation and transparency mechanisms

The fifth key aspect of law-making to be considered is public consultation and transparency mechanisms. Access to politicians is relatively limited, especially for those that do not have the right contacts or are not organised in groups with the power to lobby political elites. Public consultations regarding legislation are an especially relevant procedural mechanism to give a voice in law-making to those that otherwise would not have it. Moreover, research has shown that policymaking can significantly benefit from consulting with CSOs and the public, as doing so includes the voices of under-represented people and induces more transparency and accountability among politicians, especially when contact happens face-to-face (see, for instance, Devine, 2002; Jones, 2011: 8).[33]

While the above-mentioned research refers to the broader spectrum of policymaking, the same seems to be valid to law-making. During my work with the MoJ, I saw first-hand the benefits of public consultation in law-making, both in curbing politicians and legal drafters' prejudices and assumptions through direct contact with people, and in making people more conscious of the dilemmas and difficulties of land governance. However, public consultations about legislation are a relatively new practice in Timor-Leste. During the Portuguese and Indonesian dictatorships that ruled the country for most of the twentieth century, law-making was the result of a top-down approach, and people's views and opinions were not a matter of concern for politicians (Massier, 2008: 248; Vel *et al.*, 2017: 6). Since independence there has been a growing awareness of and demand for public consultations on legislation, but they are not an established practice (Marriott, 2013: 112; CRL, 2017: 38). Currently, ministries, government, and parliament are not legally obliged to conduct public consultations before or during law-making. The rules of parliament mention the possibility of its commissions conducting public audiences about specific draft legislation, but these are optional (art. 80 of parliament's rules), and the rules of Council of Ministers say nothing about the topic. Therefore, consultation is dependent only on political will.[34]

32 This raises a number of ethical and theoretical questions that are outside the scope of this chapter, but deserve to be debated in a separate article.

33 However, as raised by Rooij, more participants in the process can also lead to less-certain and less-adequate legislation (2008: 149).

34 A few African countries have successful experiences with participatory approaches to the drafting of land-related legislation, including Mozambique and Tanzania in the 1990s, Burkina Faso

As described above, the draft Land Law had one of the largest public consultations ever conducted in the country, which was a considerable improvement when compared with Law 1/2003, for which there were only brief audiences with CSOs in parliament (Cryan, 2016: 26). The public consultation did allow for considerable discussion of the draft Land Law, and many changes were made because of it (Cryan, 2015b: 150).

Nevertheless, this public consultation was heavily criticised by CSOs (La'o Hamutuk, 2010: 8; ICG, 2010: 13; Cryan, 2015: 5).[35] In fact, this consultation did have a few flaws. First, the consultations were only about the draft Land Law and did not include the Expropriation Law.[36] Second, it would have made more sense to have large public debates before the drafting of the law, allowing for a larger and less-technical discussion about land-related problems and solutions, instead of having those problems and solutions already framed and fixed in the much more complex language of a legal draft (UNMIT, 2012: 7). Third, in Timor-Leste public consultations often seem more like information sessions, where politicians inform participants of what they have already decided and then give some time for comments from the audience. This top-down approach is not the ideal way to consult people, but it is also difficult to break away from.[37] On the other hand, the critiques of the draft Land Law consultations were at times unrealistic. Some critics portrayed the public consultation as if it was a referendum or a public information campaign, criticising a specific policy because it did not ultimately reflect most comments received during the consultation, and complaining that not every single Timorese citizen had been heard nor was aware of the draft law's contents.[38]

Besides consultation, other mechanisms such as public documentation of the process and public access to meetings can increase the transparency of law-making and improve the quality of legislation. As a legal drafter, I experienced first-hand the advantages of drafting a detailed report on a legislative process, while working on the changes to the Land Law Package after the presidential

from 2009–2012, and Mali in 2016 (personal communication with Liz Wily in July 2017; see also Tanner, 2002).

35 See http://www.etan.org/et2009/07july/19/09land.htm and https://www.laohamutuk.org/Agri/land/RedeRecom10Jun09En.pdf

36 Regarding the drafting of the Civil Code, another central law of the Timorese formal land tenure system, one interviewee explained how, at the time of drafting (2008), there was no practice of conducting public consultations at the MoJ. Parliament was also not serious about conducting a good public consultation about the Civil Code, having only a brief session during Christmas vacations (Cryan, 2016: 16. See also JSMP, 2011).

37 It is debatable whether ministers are the best people to conduct public consultations. On one hand, people want to hear and confront them face-to-face, and this contact gives politicians a 'reality check'. On the other hand, their position of authority, especially in the highly hierarchical Timorese society, makes consultations very top-down. More efforts need to be put in designing consultation processes that can overcome these problems.

38 Also, from the legal drafters' perspective, there was a saturation of what could be learned through public consultation, especially if the same approach continued to be followed. See ICG, 2010: 17.

veto. I was at the time reading the Seidmans' work and, inspired by them, convinced the minister of justice that we should write and publish these reports. Although less detailed than what is prescribed by the Seidmans, these reports were quite useful in forcing me to reflect deeply on the rationale for the solutions adopted and the language used, besides documenting the process and the intentions behind the solutions adopted in the draft. However, I also found that not having anyone to co-author or even proof-read the report made the writing—just one of my many tasks—an arduous and time-consuming process and the report's quality less than ideal. Moreover, there was no time nor budget to translate these reports into Tetum, which limited their relevance to the process (see below).

The rules regarding documentation of law-making and access to legislative sessions are different in Council of Ministers and parliament. Agendas, minutes, and records of the meetings of Council of Ministers are, by law, confidential, and its meetings are closed to the public.[39] In parliament the publication of documents is not regulated, but its archives are public, and it is possible to find there most documentation produced about each draft law. The meetings of parliament's commissions can be public, and the meetings of the plenary are always public.[40] On one hand, the higher secrecy of Council of Ministers' documentation and meetings is understandable, because it allows a more open debate of sometimes sensitive topics, but on the other hand it harms the transparency of law-making, leaving no public record about the reasons that justified legislative decisions.

In short, the rules that regulate the law-making process in Timor-Leste provide little space for the participation of the public and civil society. As a result, this participation only happens if and when politicians are willing to open up the law-making process. Moreover, transparency mechanisms such as access to documentation are limited, which further restricts the information people can get about decisions in law-making.

Drafting options and dilemmas

In law-making, the devil is in the details. The options for drafting legislation and the dilemmas that each option brings are the sixth key aspect to understanding law-making, especially in a context where political, judicial, and administrative structures are weak and resource-poor. While not exhaustive, this section provides some examples of these dilemmas and how they affect law-making in Timor-Leste.

39 Art. 20 of Government Resolution 8/2013, and art. 13 and 20 of Government Resolution 51/2017. Despite this rule, much documentation about the Land Law Package was made available on the MoJ's website.

40 Art. 85 and 86 of the rules of parliament (*Regimento do Parlamento*).

One first dilemma that politicians and legal drafters in Timor-Leste face is whether to draft legislation from scratch or transplant and adapt legislation from other countries. The dilemma is not exclusive to Timor-Leste, and there are conflicting positions in the literature. The Seidmans, among other authors, have criticised the use of legal transplants as a legislative technique, saying that too often transplants are blunt copies of other countries' legislation that do not consider the local reality, legal framework, and culture (Seidman and Seidman, 2006; see here Bedner, 2013: 257). However, legal transplants have been a common practice in many countries throughout history (Tamanaha, 1999: 149; Whittaker, 2017: 513), and other authors argue against legislative processes that are too inward-focused, showing that, in certain circumstances, legal transplants can have advantages (Mattei, 1994; Bedner, 2008; Vlies, 2008; Bedner, 2013).

In the Timorese land tenure legal framework, it is possible to find laws specifically designed from scratch for the country, like Law 1/2003 and the Land Law, as well as legal transplants, such as the Civil Code, which is almost an exact copy of the Portuguese one. It is debatable whether copying the Portuguese Civil Code was a good idea. On one hand, several poorly regulated areas, such as legal personality and contracts, gained a clear legal framework quickly and without having to reinvent the wheel, adopting legal solutions already extensively studied and debated in Portuguese legal doctrine and jurisprudence. On the other hand, the Civil Code is a very complex piece of legislation, with many solutions that are quite foreign to Timorese society (e.g., inheritance regulations) and which the administrative and judicial systems are not able to implement (e.g., mandatory notarised deeds for all land sales).[41] While this legal transplant solved some problems, it also created others (Marriott, 2013: 112). Furthermore, even when legal transplants are a good solution, new dilemmas arise. For instance, the prevalence of Portuguese-speaking legal drafters leads to what Mattei calls 'legal parochialism', with too much focus on Portuguese legal solutions that ignore better alternatives from other countries (Mattei, 1994: 11). On the other hand, too much dispersion through different legal traditions also breaks the logic and consistency of the legal system, and can be a source of other problems.

Another dilemma of legal drafting is to strike the right balance between the need for legal certainty and the need for enough flexibility to adapt to changing and unpredictable circumstances. As exemplified below, highly detailed legislation becomes too complex and difficult to implement (Rooij, 2008: 147); conversely, very flexible legislation opens doors to discretionary implementation,

41 The example of inheritance raises another dilemma: should legislation prescribe norms that, while fairer for all heirs and especially women, contradict current practices? The inheritance system established by the Civil Code is much more egalitarian but completely foreign to the current informal norms on inheritance. About this dilemma, see World Bank, 2017: 89.

which can contradict the legislation's initial objectives. The dilemma between certainty and flexibility becomes even more difficult when considering the legislative agenda and its windows of opportunity. Politicians and legal drafters might feel tempted to push through simpler and vaguer legislation, leaving the clarification of details to bylaws, if they feel that the window of opportunity of the legal agenda is closing.[42]

For instance, the article of Law 1/2003 that says that no compensation for eviction from state land shall be paid is quite precise, but it overlooks the complex land tenure reality. In some cases the occupation of state land is clearly opportunistic and unfair, while in other cases the occupation is totally justifiable (e.g., people that were forcibly settled by the Indonesian administration). On the other hand, the vague definitions of state and abandoned land in Law 1/2003 give room to very broad interpretations and are a cause of much tenure insecurity (Chapters 6 and 8). Finally, Law 1/2003 was the first law of a legislation package that, due to political changes, was never completed. Ultimately, the strategy of incrementally approving legislation that clarifies the vagueness of Law 1/2003 failed, causing much confusion and problems in its implementation.[43]

Striking the right balance between adequacy and feasibility of legal solutions is another dilemma that politicians and legal drafters in Timor-Leste experience. The best solutions are often too difficult to implement, and more-realistic approaches might be inadequate for the problems that need to be addressed (Rooij, 2008: 148). I experienced this dilemma when re-drafting the Expropriation Law after the presidential veto. The vetoed version established overly shallow protections for those affected by an expropriation. As detailed above, after the veto, I convinced the new minister of justice that the draft law had to be revised to incorporate lessons learned since the approval of the first draft, to address the concerns raised in the presidential veto, and to adjust the law to international best practices. These changes included, for instance, a clear definition of public purpose, a mandatory impact assessment study, a public consultation phase, and the obligation of the government to clearly justify the public purpose of the expropriation. However, these changes came with a dilemma. While these new rules were adequate to reduce the negative impacts of expropriation on people, they made the expropriation process much more complex, long, and difficult to implement, running the risk that state officials and institutions would simply ignore the law and continue their arbitrary and illegal approaches to expropriation. More than two years after the approval of the law its process had not yet been used—for now with the excuse that complementary legislation remains to

42 Also called a 'piecemeal' approach to legislation (Rooij, 2006: 46).

43 Fitzpatrick *et al.* debate the trade-offs between complexity and simplicity in regulating communal land (2013: 93; see also Fitzpatrick and McWilliam, 2013). To not overextend this already long chapter, I decided not debate their points here, but their argument deserves a separate article.

be approved—and arbitrary processes remain the common practice. One can argue that a simpler and less-protective process, aimed at a more incremental change in behaviours would have been preferable. On the other hand, despite not being fully implemented, the more-protective process at least gives people and CSOs a base over which they can contest arbitrary practices of state officials (World Bank, 2017: 83; Chapter 7). There is no fool proof path for legal drafters.

Another related dilemma of law-making in Timor-Leste is to decide whether legislation should be tailored to a country's current administrative and judicial capacity or instead rely on future improvements in these areas. The answer is trickier than it might seem. First, politicians and legal drafters must take into consideration the windows of opportunity of the legislative agenda, meaning that whatever solution they establish will have to work for a couple of years before they can change the law again. Second, they cannot be sure that the necessary resources will be invested in the development of public administration and the judiciary, nor whether such possible investment will raise capacity to the level required by the drafted legislation.

The capacity of courts to deal with the massive influx of cases caused by the implementation of the Land Law is a good example of this dilemma. This topic raised a chicken-and-egg question: should the law only be approved when the courts are ready to deal with this influx, or should the law be approved to force the courts to prepare? One third option would be to develop simplified mechanisms of dispute resolution, but this would bring a new dilemma: a simplified justice process means in general less protection mechanisms for the parties in dispute. The solution chosen was to create a specialised administrative Land Commission that precedes the court cases, with the intention of reducing the number of cases that get to court; however, the success of this solution is yet to be proven (Chapter 6).

These examples show how politicians and legal drafters in Timor-Leste face difficult dilemmas when drafting legislation. In legal drafting, the devil is in the details, especially in contexts where political, judicial, and administrative structures are weak and resource-poor. With so many dilemmas to deal with, the potential for failure is high.

Monitoring and evaluation

The seventh key aspect to understanding a law-making process are its monitoring and evaluation mechanisms. Although it seems logical that a legislative process must be supervised by monitoring and evaluation mechanisms, in many countries this does not happen (Seidman and Seidman, 2009: 455). Timor-Leste is one of those countries: the implementation of new legislation is not planned and assessed, and its impacts, successes, and failures are not carefully studied (Cunha, 2018: 139). This section briefly highlights the difficulties in establishing monitoring and evaluation mechanisms for law-making in Timor-Leste and illustrates the consequences of not having them in place.

In Timor-Leste, although the government and parliament have a vague formal duty to monitor and evaluate the legislation they approve, there are no institutionalised mechanisms to systematically do this, and attempts to develop these mechanisms have, until now, failed.[44] For instance, in August 2015 the Commission for Legislative Reform was created with the objective of independently studying and evaluating existing legislation in priority areas and providing advice to the government and parliament about possible reforms. However, at the time of writing, the work of the commission has been suspended.[45] Moreover, implementation plans, monitoring mechanisms, and evaluation strategies for each individual piece of legislation are neither mandatory nor common practice.

This lack of institutionalised mechanisms for systematic monitoring and evaluation of legislation in the Timorese law-making process has a number of consequences. For instance, as extensively exemplified in Chapter 6, a considerable proportion of legislation is only partially implemented or not implemented at all (UNMIT, 2012: 2; Cunha, 2018: 138), but there are no systematic mechanisms to flag this problem to government, parliament, CSOs, and society in general. Monitoring and evaluation mechanisms would at least create some awareness of this problem and pressure to address it.

Another example of the lack of monitoring and evaluation mechanisms is linked with the production of knowledge for law-making and documentation of the law-making process raised above. Without systematic monitoring and evaluation of legislation, there is no well-informed research about the successes and failures of each legislative process in Timor-Leste, leaving behind few or no lessons for future legislative processes. This is especially problematic when considering that most legal drafters are foreigners, which sooner or later leave the country, and take with them the knowledge about the laws they helped develop. I experienced this, for instance with Law 1/2003, both as a legal drafter and an academic researcher. With very limited documentation about the drafting process of this law, no access to its legal drafters, and no evaluation of its implementation, it was very difficult to understand why parts of the law were not adequately implemented (Chapter 6).

Language

Procedural devices to deal with language issues are the final aspect of law-making to be analysed. Language can be a difficult problem for law-making,

44 See art. 21.d of Parliament Rules (*Regimento do Parlamento*), and art. 37 of Government Regulation 51/2017.

45 This commission was created during the short-lived consensus between FRETILIN and CNRT (2015–2017). I am not fully aware of the reasons for the suspension of this commission, but the fact that its leadership was connected with FRETILIN might explain it. The work of this commission is available at http://www.crl.gov.tl/pt.

especially in a multi-lingual country like Timor-Leste. Problems such as (in) adequate translation, miscommunication, and difficulties with legal jargon make the process of writing and debating legislation difficult and result in legal texts with gaps and incongruences. This section highlights the role of language in the law-making process and provides a few examples of its impacts on legislation.

As detailed in Chapter 3, Timor-Leste is a multi-lingual country, with Tetum and Portuguese being its two official languages, but with around 30 other languages spoken nationwide. While Tetum is the *lingua franca* of the country, spoken by the majority of (but not all) Timorese, only a small percentage of the population have a good command of Portuguese, even among elites (Marriott, 2013: 113; Simões, 2015: 392). This multiplicity, uneven use, and different statuses of languages is problematic for law-making in a number of ways.

The first main problem that language brings to the law-making process in Timor-Leste is the translation of documents and interpretation of oral discussions. Draft legislation and support documents are usually (if not always) written in Portuguese by foreign legal advisers, and often no Tetum version is provided (UNMIT, 2012: 6; Simões, 2015: 394).[46] The decision to translate draft legislation and support documentation into Tetum is, in practice, dependent on the strategy and will of the line minister. When no Tetum translation is provided, many ministers and MPs simply cannot read the drafts they debate and approve, so their participation is only based on what is said during the debate, and not on the actual text of the law. Moreover, the legal obligation to publish approved legislation in the Official Journal (*Jornal da República*) in both official languages is often ignored by the government and parliament.[47] Furthermore, language is also a problem for informed decision-making. Most academic articles and many reports of international organisations published about Timor-Leste are written in Portuguese or English, with only a few of these translated into Tetum, reducing even more politicians' and state officials' access to information.

The difficulties with translation also limit dialogue and comprehension during debates of draft legislation. The meetings of Council of Ministers and parliament commissions do not have simultaneous interpretations, but rather, presentations and debates are conducted in one of the two official languages. Given some ministers, MPs, and Timorese advisers do not understand

46 Depending on the legal experts hired, sometimes legislation is drafted in English or Indonesian, and later translated into Portuguese. On the problems of translating English drafts into Portuguese, see Pires, 2005: 18. Moreover, many Timorese jurists are trained in Indonesia, therefore being exposed to a very different legal vocabulary.

47 On a positive note, in 2017 the Decree-Law 11/2017 establishing the Regime of the Use of Official Languages in the Justice Sector, showing that inside the government there is some concern about language issues.

Portuguese and some international advisers do not understand Tetum, there are often gaps in the knowledge of, and communication between, the participants in these debates (Soares, 2007: 198). For instance, in the working group created by the MoJ for the drafting of the Land Law, the discussions were mostly conducted in Portuguese, preventing some of its members from understanding and participating in the discussions.

The problem with translation is further complicated by the difficulty of finding good translators. Even official translations have serious errors, as the Land Law exemplifies. In its Portuguese version, article 8.1.g says that mineral deposits belong to the state, but its official Tetum version says that the place (*fatin* in Tetum) where those mineral deposits are located belongs to the state. The fact that both Council of Ministers and parliament do not have a translation unit where consistent legal Tetum language could be slowly developed and unified entraps legal Tetum in a 'catch 22': legal Tetum language is not regularly used because it has not yet developed to cover the range of new legal principles and terminology, but because of this irregular use, it does not have the opportunity to develop (Simões, 2015: 392). Establishing translation units in the Council of Ministers and parliament that can provide consistent legal translations and promote the use of Tetum as a legal language is an important step to break this cycle (Pires, 2005: 18; IPAC, 2015: 17).

A second language problem that often complicates the drafting of legislation is the use of technical language (or legal jargon). Legal language can be difficult for native Portuguese speakers, but is even more difficult for Timorese who are not familiar with many legal concepts, even when adapted to Tetum. However, legal language poses a dilemma: while it can be simplified and adjusted, there are limits to how much technical language can be avoided before legal logic is lost and misinterpretations start to emerge.[48]

Article 9.4 of the Land Law provides a good example of the problems caused by mixing legal terminology and common language. This article establishes that 'the land without a known owner, and the *baldios*, are state land'.[49] The Portuguese word *baldio* was introduced in late versions of the draft and is quite problematic. The noun has two definitions in Portuguese; it can mean (1) uncultivated land, or (2) land that belongs to a community and is used collectively.[50] This second definition is well known by Portuguese rural residents and finds an equivalent meaning in Portuguese legislation that regulates ownership and management of communal land (Portuguese Law 75/2017). In common language, at times the word is used with a third meaning, not covered in the

48 The criticism of legal jargon is for me quite contentious (Marriott, 2013: 114). While I agree that jurists are sometimes keen to make texts undecipherable, critics often ignore that technical language in law exists to give precision to concepts and make the legal system functional.

49 The Portuguese and Tetum versions of this article use the same word, although with different spelling. On the origin of the word *baldio*, see Silva, 2014, 61.

50 https://dicionario.priberam.org/baldio

dictionary nor legislation, to refer to (3) land without a known owner. This raises the question: which meaning does the Land Law refer to when it uses the word *baldio*? If the law refers to the first meaning—uncultivated land—article 9.4 clearly violates the right to private property established in the constitution: that a person or a community can own land that is not cultivated. If the law refers to its second meaning—communally owned land—the article contradicts Chapter VI of the law specifically recognising communally owned land. The third meaning—land with an unknown owner—does not find support in legal language nor the dictionary, and would make article 9.4 of the Land Law repeat the same idea twice. Interestingly, the president raised the problem with the Court of Appeal before promulgating the Land Law, but the court seems to have not understood the problem, defining in its decision *baldio* as 'land without owner, characterised by lack of maintenance, high bush, and trash'.[51] Ultimately, this single word can seriously limit the recognition of communal rights over land, as well as rights over uncultivated land, which can thus be interpreted as belonging to the state.[52]

Conclusion

Based on the analytical framework discussed above, this chapter describes and analyses law-making in Timor-Leste, paying special attention to land-related legislation. This analytical framework bridges some gaps in the literature regarding the study of law-making, namely the lack of a model for a comprehensive analysis of a full law-making process and a lens that takes into consideration the conditions of law-making in developing countries. As such, the proposed model identifies key aspects of law-making to be analysed, and pays special attention to the main problems and dilemmas that affect them.

In summary, this chapter shows how in Timor-Leste ministers have a central role in forming the legislative agenda, considering that most draft legislation is drafted by ministries. A skilful minister and some luck are fundamental to move drafts through the Timorese legislative agenda, and its constraints pose dilemmas regarding how much to compromise in the process. The chapter also shows how in Timor-Leste there is no procedural obligation to conduct research before law-making, making research dependent on the will of ministers and the influence of some participants. The fact that legislation is primarily drafted by ministries, without baseline studies and policy documents, tends to

51 Process n.° 03/Constitucional/17/TR.

52 Even Tetum words are at times problematic. For instance, people give different meanings to terms such as *rai komunidade, rai komunal, rai adat,* and *rai lisan,* which vary between land that is collectively used by a community, land that is claimed collectively by a community but can be individually used, sacred land, and plantations created by the Portuguese administration, and farmed collectively by a community (see here Shepherd, 2014: 62). Furthermore, many of these realities don't find an equivalent land right in Portuguese, which further complicates their translation into law.

narrow the debate by defining the problem that needs to be addressed, and to limit the discussion about policy options because they were already chosen. This narrowing of the debate makes ministers powerful decision-makers, as they have the final word inside their ministries.

Once draft legislation reaches the Timorese Council of Ministers or parliament, changes are often not the result of a well-informed position of a minister or MP, carefully considered with their support staff, but rather an opinion formed on-the-spot during a meeting. Furthermore, the fact that there are few mechanisms for assessing the viability, coherence, and legality of decisions in the legislative process further contributes to contradictions and illogical solutions in legislation, as further illustrated in Chapter 6.

This chapter also shows how legal drafters are more than mere scribes in law-making, and their knowledge, background, values, and allegiances, as well as limitations experienced in the drafting process, tend to be reflected in the legislation they draft. Therefore, their recruitment impacts the final outcome, especially in the Timorese context where only a few drafters are involved in the legislative process.

The chapter highlights how drafting options pose several dilemmas to politicians and legal drafters, which are especially difficult to address when considering the weaknesses of the political, judicial, and administrative structures of the country. Without mechanisms for monitoring and evaluating legislation, problems such as inadequate implementation are not flagged, and few lessons for future legislative processes are learned. Finally, language issues further complicate the debate of draft legislation and the coherence of the texts adopted.

From this analysis, it becomes clear that various procedural devices that help to keep some order and rationality in law-making are missing or are poorly implemented in Timor-Leste, which is reflected in the quality of legislation approved, as this chapter and the following demonstrate. While progress has been made since independence, there is still a lot of room for improvement. Most advances in different procedural devices were promoted by few participants and were not followed up by structural changes, therefore leaving some legacy but no guarantee that these improvements will be consolidated in the future. Steps such as mandatory pre-drafting research and detailed reporting of each legislative process;[53] debate of policy options documents; establishment of minimum criteria for public consultation of draft legislation; mandatory monitoring and evaluation plans for draft legislation; and professional translation units could significantly improve the law-making process and the quality of

53 International organisations could play a role here, for instance, by making research for law-making and detailed reports a standard requirement for their support to legislative processes, and mandatory for the Government advisers paid by them.

legislation.[54] While good legislation is not a guarantee of a better and fairer formal land tenure system, it certainly helps.

Beyond this specific case of Timor-Leste, this chapter also contributes to the larger academic debate on law-making in developing countries in a number of ways that I would like to briefly highlight in this conclusion. The specific characteristics of law-making in developing countries, such as lack of resources, poor regulations of the legislative process, and weak legal culture and political accountability make their legislative processes particular and demand a specific analytical framework to study them. For those interested in studying law-making in developing countries, this chapter provides a possible methodological approach, inspired by the Garbage Can Model, which points out the main aspects to consider in the analysis of law-making and can be easily adapted to other countries.

From this chapter, another lesson that becomes evident is the role and importance of different procedural devices in keeping order in legislative processes, and how each failure of these procedural devices further erodes the quality of law-making, to a point where the outcome can be problematic. Moreover, these procedural devices also give legitimacy to the legislation approved (Waldron, 2006: 31). However, the chapter also shows how even the apparently more-technical sides of law-making are permeated by political decisions. Legal drafters bring to law-making their own political views; research brings political bias and can only inform but not provide an answer to political decisions; and aspects such as the political agenda can affect the political decisions of law-making. Awareness about the political nature of technical decisions in law-making is fundamental to understanding the process.

Finally, this chapter shows how the study of law-making, both to understand and improve it, must take into special consideration the problems and dilemmas that surround a legislative process in developing countries. As the critique to the Seidmans' theory shows, studying or theorising about law-making without taking these problems and dilemmas into account will overlook a central point of law-making in developing countries. As argued by Tamanaha, the law-making process will never be perfect, especially under the conditions of developing countries, and at some point inaction in search of the perfect process is worse than a pragmatic approach to law-making (Tamanaha, 1999: 155). While law-making is burdened by problems and dilemmas for which there are no definitive solutions, it is possible to study this process and find ways to incrementally improve it.

54 I should add one final note on law-making. When revising this chapter, news came out that the Council of Ministers approved a resolution with new rules for enhancing the quality of legal texts (http://timor-leste.gov.tl/?p=21909&lang=en&n=1). Government Resolution 14/2019 identifies various problems in the Timorese law-making process and, in line with what is debated in this chapter, proposes several positive changes.

Chapter 6

Land tenure legislation in Timor-Leste

Introduction

This chapter focuses on the legal framework that regulates the Timorese formal land tenure system. As detailed in Chapter 1, the legal framework is the second layer of social organisation in which one should focus on to understand a land tenure system. One of Timor-Leste's main challenges on the verge of independence was to develop a formal land tenure system that could address the land-related problems inherited from the country's turbulent past and provide answers for its future needs (Chapter 3). Approving adequate legislation was a central step in the development of the Timorese formal land tenure system. The first goal of this chapter is to provide an overview of the legal solutions adopted by the Timorese formal land tenure system. Therefore, this chapter is more legalistic than others in this book and is easier to read once one is familiarised with the Timorese legislation. To help the reader, Table 6.1 lists the most relevant legislation and the date of its entry into force.

The second goal of this chapter is to give an overview of the problems of the Timorese legal framework on land tenure, and the troubles that different professionals and the Timorese in general must deal with. As consequence of the unfavourable political environment and deficient law-making process (Chapters 4 and 5), the approval of new legislation has been slow and its quality problematic, leaving many gaps and contradictions in the legal framework. I got my first glimpse of these problems in 2009, during the semester I worked as a land law lecturer at the Law Faculty of the National University of Timor-Leste (UNTL). While I was developing the course, which was going to be taught for the first time, one main question emerged: which legislation should I teach about? The unapplied Indonesian legislation (Chapter 3)? The insipient, unclear, and incomplete Timorese legislation? Or the complex draft laws that were being circulated but were not yet approved (e.g., Civil Code, Land Law)? My subsequent work as a legal adviser at the MoJ confirmed that the lack of a coherent legal framework was a problem not only for a rooky university lecturer, but also for the public administration, lawyers, judges, and the Timorese in general.

DOI: 10.4324/9781003196396-6

Table 6.1 Most relevant land-related legislation approved since independence

Legislation	*Entry into force*
Constitution of the Democratic Republic of Timor-Leste	20 May 2002
Law 1/2003—Juridical Regime of Real Estate—Part I: Ownership over real estate	10 March 2003[1]
Decree-Law 19/2004—Lease of State Property	18 December 2004
Law 12/2005—Juridical Regime of Real Estate—Part II: Leasing between Individuals	25 May 2005
Decree-Law 6/2011—Compensation for Eviction of State Property	10 February 2011
Decree-Law 27/2011—Ownership of Real Estate in Undisputed Cases	7 July 2011
Ministerial-Decree 16/2011—Cadastral Survey	28 July 2011
Ministerial-Decree 23/2011	24 November 2011
Law 10/2011—Civil Code[2]	14 March 2012
Ministerial-Decree 45/2016—Cadastral Survey	15 September 2016
Ministerial-Decree 46/2016—National Property Cadastre	15 September 2016
Law 8/2017—Expropriation Law	27 April 2017
Law 13/2017—'Land Law' (Special Regime for the Determination of Ownership of Immovable Property)	2 September 2017

[1] The law entered into force on 10 March 2003. The official website (http://jornal.gov.tl/) erroneously mentions 24 December 2003 as the publication date.

[2] The Civil Code was approved through Law 10/2011. I use 'Law 10/2011' to refer to the 19 articles that regulate the approval of the Civil Code and 'the Civil Code' to refer to all the articles that compose it.

To avoid a very extensive chapter, I focus on key topics, features, gaps, problems, and contradictions of the legal framework; in other words, this chapter is not a comprehensive analysis of the land tenure legal framework in Timor-Leste. The first part of this chapter focuses on the key topics regulated by the recently approved Land Law, comparing the situation before and after its approval. The topics covered are (1) the legal status of formal rights issued before independence; (2) the legal recognition of customary land rights; (3) mechanisms to protect long-term possession of land; (4) the definition of state land; (5) the land rights of legal entities; (6) the process for identifying land claims and addressing conflicting ones; and (7) the regulation of evictions. The second part of this chapter looks into other key topics regulated by the Civil Code, including (8) the land rights established by the formal land tenure system, and (9) the legal mechanisms for acquisition and loss of these rights. This chapter's analysis is guided by Rooij's framework to assess the quality of the legal framework, paying special attention to the *adequacy*, *feasibility*, *legal certainty*, and *adaptability* of the studied legislation (Rooij, 2006, 34).

I must add a final note of warning regarding the gap between descriptions of law in this chapter and what happens in reality. This chapter covers both repealed legislation and the current legal framework, and I write in the past tense when referring to the former. However, much new legislation remains unimplemented, and the repealed legislation is still used, alongside many arbitrary practices described below. Therefore, the past tense refers only to changes in the law, not necessarily to actual changes in practice.

Validity of pre-independence rights

After the independence of Timor-Leste, and until the approval of the Land Law in 2017, it was unclear whether the formal land rights issued by the Portuguese and Indonesian administrations remained valid. While some Timorese, usually those with closer connections with the previous administrations, thought these rights should get full recognition in Timorese law, others argued that they were the product of colonialism and occupation, and should therefore not be recognised (Chapters 3 and 4).

As Ederington summarised, in the unclear waters of international law, states have consistently supported the *doctrine of acquired rights*, which establishes that the alteration of sovereignty over a territory does not change previously acquired rights (Ederington, 1997: 266; see also Ronen, 2013: 251). This does not mean, however, that those rights are beyond the jurisdiction of the new sovereign state, which 'can adjust property rights through general, non-discriminatory legislation' (Ederington, 1997: 311; Ronen, 2013: 249). However, the doctrine of acquired rights has been criticised in cases of decolonisation, considering that it gives protection to the injustices caused by colonial land tenure systems (Fitzpatrick, 2002: 143).

When applying the doctrine of acquired rights in Timor-Leste it is necessary to distinguish between Portuguese and Indonesian formal land rights. While this theory is clearly applicable to formal land rights issued by the Portuguese administration, the *international law of belligerent occupation* considers all land rights issued by the Indonesian administration invalid (ibid.: 58). However, not recognising Indonesian formal rights would be extremely unfair to those people who acquired them in good faith, through the legal system that de facto ruled the country at the time (Elderton, 2002: 10). Furthermore, the application of the international law of belligerent occupation conflicts with international norms regarding housing security and protection against unreasonable eviction, received by the Timorese Constitution (art. 9.2 of the constitution).[1] Hence, international law does not give a definitive answer regarding the validity of land rights issued by the Portuguese and Indonesian administrations.

The Timorese Constitution is silent about the validity of formal land rights issued by the Portuguese and Indonesian administrations. Together with the

1 Art. 11 of the Covenant on Economic, Social and Cultural Rights (also considering the General Comments 4 and 7) and art. 25.1 of the Universal Declaration of Human Rights.

international law arguments mentioned above, the constitution's incorporation of Indonesian legislation into the Timorese legal system, with no exceptions regarding land rights, provides another argument in favour of the recognition of these formal rights, but does not address this issue.[2] Law 1/2003 was of little help, establishing contradictory articles about this topic, some hinting that formal rights issued by previous administrations remained valid, while other articles raised doubts about Indonesian formal rights (Almeida, 2016: 8, 22, 28; see also, William, 2009: 585; Ronen, 2013: 289). Under the constitution and Law 1/2003 the courts tended to recognise formal rights issued by previous administrations.[3] The practice within DNTPSC was also to recognise formal rights issued by the Portuguese and Indonesian administrations, although difficulties in accessing past records raised problems in verifying the legitimacy of these rights (Chapter 3). However, the law did not provide a definitive answer to this question.

The situation was even more complex in the case of formal land rights held by foreign citizens. The constitution establishes that '[o]nly national citizens can own land' (art. 54.4), but this provision raises several questions.[4] Does it mean that, (1) after the constitution entered into force, foreigners were no longer allowed to acquire land in Timor-Leste? Or (2) is this prohibition applicable to the rights of foreigners prior to the constitution? If the latter is true, (3) is the state obliged to pay compensation to foreigners for loss of rights?[5] Further, (4) what if a right is claimed by a Timorese national who is an heir of a foreigner? And (5) is this prohibition only applicable to ownership rights, or other land rights, too? Until the approval of the Land Law, the decisions of the Court of Appeal on this topic were inconsistent. Some of its rulings mentioned Timorese nationality as a pre-condition for the recognition of ownership rights, without considering whether those rights were acquired before or

2 The fact that Indonesian law converted Portuguese land titles into Indonesian ones should also be taken into consideration (Almeida, 2016: 11). Fitzpatrick *et al.* mention an equivalent recognition of land rights during UNTAET's administration (2013: 99).

3 In favour of the recognition of all formal rights, see the decisions of the Court of Appeal No. 07/2009 of 2 February 2010; No. 23/01 of 10 March 2010; and No. 06/2003 of 16 July 2009. The decision of the Court of Appeal from 16 July 2008 (without number, regarding Hotel Resende) is an exception. The decision of the Court of Appeal No. 4/Cível/2016/TR, issued after the entry into force of the Land Law, ignores this new legislation and clearly states land use rights issued by Indonesia that already expired are not valid.

4 For more on the land rights of foreigners, see Almeida, 2016: 10, 13. There is widespread confusion in Timorese society about the rules of nationality many people, including top politicians, erroneously think that those Timorese who kept their Indonesian nationality after independence automatically lost their Timorese nationality (Almeida, 2016: 14; Jerónimo, 2017: 19; Timor Post, 16 February 2013).

5 DNTPSC staff told me that it was agreed between Timor-Leste and Indonesia that the Timorese would not seek compensation from Indonesia for the large-scale destruction of the country's infrastructure in 1999, but Indonesia would be responsible for compensating its nationals for their loss of land rights in Timor-Leste. However, no one could tell where that agreement was documented.

after the constitution was adopted.[6] However, at least one ruling clearly states that foreigners cannot be deprived of their property before the approval of specific legislation regarding the rights of foreigners.[7] The common interpretation among politicians and DNTPSC staff was to consider that all rights of foreigners were terminated by the constitution, and that all of their land reverted to state ownership.[8]

The Land Law addresses some of these questions, but leaves others unanswered and creates new problems. According to the law (art. 3.1.b), Timorese citizens that hold valid ownership rights (*propriedade perfeita* or *hak milik*), Portuguese *aforamento* rights, and Indonesian *hak guna-bangunan* and *hak guna usaha* rights, can use them to claim ownership of land or the right to be compensated, in the process established by the Land Law (see below).[9] Conversely, if these formal rights are held by foreigners they revert to the state, but the law does not make completely clear whether foreigners are entitled to compensation (art. 7.2, 47).[10]

However, the recognition of land rights issued by previous administrations has unclear exceptions. The holders of *aforamento*, *hak guna-bangunan*, and *hak guna usaha* rights can only use them to claim land ownership if they possess the land they claim, which can be quite unfair to those that were forcedly dispossessed (art. 3.5). Moreover, the same controversial article of Law 1/2003 that left doubts about the recognition of Indonesian land rights was mostly copy-pasted into the final provisions of the Land Law, obscuring its logic of

6 Decisions No. 23/01 of 10 March 2010, No. 12/2009 of 10 March 2010, and No 07/2009 of 2 February 2010.

7 Decision No. 31/2003 of 13 May 2009.

8 See, for instance, Timor Post, 5 October 2012; Timor Post, 1 December 2014. Sousa, DNTPSC's former director, has a different interpretation, that these rights were not terminated by the constitution (2005: 4). In practice, DNTPSC's recognition or refusal of rights has been made with no clear process and based on various assumptions about one's nationality, with disastrous results. See here the case of Hotel Resende in Almeida, 2017.

9 Ownership rights were called *propriedade perfeita* and *hak milik* during the Portuguese and Indonesian administrations, respectively. The Portuguese *aforamento* right was a land use right, which allowed the transfer of the right of enjoyment of a parcel of land from the state (*senhorio*) to a private person or legal entity (*foreiro*), for a specific purpose, upon the payment of an annual amount (*foro*). The *aforamento* was usually perpetual, and, unless this possibility was restricted in the contract, the *foreiro* was allowed to acquire the property right after 40 years of *aforamento*, upon the payment of 20 *foros*. The Land Law considers valid those *aforamento* that were in force on 28 November 1975 (art. 3.3). *Hak guna usaha* was an Indonesian long-lease right, with a maximum of 25 years for individuals and 35 years for companies, and the *hak guna-bangunan* was a construction right with a maximum term of 30 years (Reerink, 2011: 61). The Land Law considers valid those *hak guna usaha* and *hak guna-bangunan* that were in force on 30 August 1999 (art. 3.4).

10 The 2012 presidential veto mentions the lack of clarity regarding the right of foreigners to receive compensation for loss of land rights. This was corrected in the revised version after the veto (see art. 48.1 of that version). However, in the 2015 approval process, probably inadvertently, the same uncertainty was again introduced.

recognising past formal rights (art. 82. See here Almeida, 2016: 22). Previous versions of the law were much clearer in this topic, but last-minute changes during the approval process create doubts about the validity of land rights issued by previous administrations.

Furthermore, while the Land Law recognises land claims based on formal land rights issued by previous administrations, it does not address issues related to the transfer of those land rights. As detailed below, especially after independence, the great majority of, if not all, transfers of formal land rights have happened without following the formalities established by law, and it is not clear whether these transfers should be considered valid. For instance, can a son claim ownership of land based on the formal right of his deceased father, if the inheritance process established by law was not followed? In summary, while the Land Law provided some answers regarding the validity of formal land rights issued by the Portuguese and Indonesian administrations, several unanswered questions regarding this topic remain and new problems were created.

Legal recognition of customary land rights

The great majority of Timorese have never had a formal land right. Most of the country's territory has always been claimed by individuals, families, and local communities based on customary land tenure systems. But despite their prevalence throughout the country, both the Portuguese and Indonesian legal frameworks gave little recognition to customary land rights (Chapters 3 and 8).

The constitution would have been the ideal legal document to break with this history of weak recognition of customary land rights. However, while it recognises the validity of customary practices that are not contrary to the constitution and other relevant laws (art. 2.4), it makes no reference to customary land rights. The same happened with Law 1/2003, which completely ignored customary land rights and tenure systems (Chapter 4). Combined with the broad definition of state land, this lack of legal recognition of customary land rights has been used to threaten and dispossess people of their land (see below).

Some change came with Law 10/2011, which approves the Civil Code, and which for the first time recognised communal customary-based rights of communities (art. 4).[11] However, this recognition was made in one single article, buried deep in the very complex Civil Code, and without provisions to operationalise it, leaving it unnoticed even by CSOs and academic authors working on the topic (e.g., Fitzpatrick *et al.*, 2013).

11 Decree-Law 5/2016 regarding protected areas also incorporates some customary concepts such as *fatin lulik* (sacred place), *lisuk* (specific customary norms), and *lisan* (system of customary norms), and mentions *customary areas* a few times (art. 8, 11, and 13). The Forest Law (Law 14/2017) also give recognition to customary rules.

The approval of the Land Law significantly changed the recognition of customary land rights in Timor-Leste. This law recognises customary land rights in two ways. First, by creating what the law calls an *informal property right*, which is defined as a right with a customary basis, with characteristics equivalent to an ownership right, and in which the land has been in the possession of the claimant(s) or their predecessors for more than 20 years.[12] This right can be claimed by individuals or a specific group of people (e.g., a number of family members) and gives them a strong claim to ownership of land or the right to compensation in the land-claims process created by the Land Law (see below). The second way in which the Land Law recognises customary land rights is through *community land*, which the law defines as 'land that is considered by a community as part of their communal and shared used, by the collective or some families, and organised according to their customary practices' (art. 27.1). Together with community land, the law also establishes the concept of *community protection zone*, which intends to protect communities by imposing restrictions on land use of private and state land that is important for the livelihoods of these communities (art. 23, 24, and 25).[13]

Despite representing significant progress, the recognition of customary land rights established by the Land Law comes with a few new problems. First, the law does not define 'customary basis', and these two forms of recognition of customary land rights are fairly vague and flexible, which enables land claims to be adapted to the needs and will of groups and individuals, but can also be a source of internal conflict and the concentration of power within communities (Chapter 2). For instance, powerful members of a community can claim the land under their name, in representation of the group, obtaining a legal right that does not represent their obligations towards the community.[14]

Second, the recognition of customary-based land rights in the Land Law is still limited and does not address all problems caused by the past lack of legal protection. For instance, the law establishes that, if one was violently dispossessed after 1999, this interruption of possession shall not be counted when calculating the 20 years necessary for the recognition of a customary-based land right (art. 17). While this exception is good, it does not cover dispossession before 1999, and therefore does not protect many Timorese. Moreover, if narrowly interpreted, the definition of community land can exclude important areas such as forest land or land kept as reserve.[15]

Third, the regulation of many key points of community land and community protection zones are left to subsequent legislation that has not yet been

12 Art. 2.g, 3.1.a, 15, and 18. This right is especially important when considering the problems with adverse possession debated below.

13 On this topic, see Fitzpatrick *et.al*, 2008; World Bank, 2010.

14 This is especially concerning when land registration is done without good public information and legal counselling, as it happened with SNC (Chapter 3; Rede ba Rai, 2019: 40).

15 See what was said in Chapter 5 regarding *baldios*.

approved. As happened before with Law 1/2003, there is the risk that the window of opportunity for legislating about this topic has closed (Chapter 5), and that these rights will remain unregulated for many years, and ignored in practice.

Long-term possession

Long-term possession of land, without a customary basis for the claim, is another complex problem of land tenure in Timor-Leste. As described in Chapter 3, the several waves of conflict and displacement gave origin to many cases of land occupation. While some of these occupations were opportunistic, in many situations they happened because people were forced to settle in a specific place or could not find an alternative after being displaced themselves. In other situations people simply obtained land through informal processes—the only avenue available to them—and, because formalities were not followed, the legality of their land rights can now be challenged.[16] In many of these cases, people have lived on the land for decades without any legal protection for their tenure, and at constant risk of eviction (Chapter 8).

The constitution does little to protect long-term possession or to distinguish fair cases from opportunistic occupation. Only article 161 talks about land occupation, but only to establish the basis for a crime of illegal occupation. As debated below about adverse possession, the Indonesian law also did little to help long-term possessors. Law 1/2003 did not help address this issue either. Besides only focusing on formal rights and ignoring the problem of long-term occupation, the law established a harsh process for evictions (see below) and created the crimes of illegal appropriation and occupation (art. 5 and 6). While in some situations the harsh eviction process and criminalisation could be fair, in many others it became a threat to legitimate long-term possession cases.[17]

The Land Law addresses this problem by establishing a mechanism of *special adverse possession*. Those Timorese who are in peaceful and public possession of land before 1999 are protected by the Land Law, giving them a stronger claim over land or to the right to be compensated if they don't get ownership of the land they possess (art. 19 to 22; see below). However, last-minute changes in parliament introduced some requisites into the law that are not completely clear, and which considerably restrict this mechanism. The special adverse possession is not applicable to cases where occupation occurred due to 'forced displacement during the Indonesian occupation', being instead addressed on a 'case-by-case basis' (art. 20.2 and 75). Also, this mechanism is only applicable in

16 In some of these situations it can be argued that long-term occupation fulfils the definition of customary-based land rights protected by the Land Law.

17 Land possessors are rarely prosecuted for these crimes, but that possibility is at times used by state officials to pressure them to leave the land.

cases where the possessor has 'no other house for living or farming' (art. 21.c). As debated below, the interpretation and implementation of these exceptions have great potential to be problematic, and open doors for arbitrary decisions.

State land

Definition of state land

Together with the weak recognition of customary land rights, the Portuguese and Indonesian administrations also established broad definitions of state land that allowed them to claim vast tracts of land (Chapter 3). In line with other post-colonial countries, this approach was continued in Timor-Leste after independence, transforming the state into a 'property monster' (Benda-Beckmann, 2003: 189).

One main feature and problem of Law 1/2003 was its broad and unclear definition of state land. The law established that '(a) All real estate assets owned by the Portuguese state as of 7 December 1975' and '(b) real estate assets that were acquired by the state by virtue of law or juridical act' are considered state land (art. 4.1). The law also established that any transfer of state land made by the Indonesian administration was invalid, and that all immovable property acquired or built by the Indonesian authorities belonged to the state (art. 16.1 and 16.2). Additionally, the law established a presumption that unclaimed land belonged to the state, despite the incongruences and fragilities of its land-claims process (art. 12.3 and 12.4; see below).[18] Finally, the law also gave the state the power to manage abandoned property (art. 15). The conceptual problems of these provisions, combined with a very broad interpretation by state officials and politicians, gave origin to problems in three main areas: (1) customary land rights; (2) abandoned land; and (3) people unlawfully dispossessed during the Indonesian administration.

As discussed above, the broad definition of state land in Law 1/2003 and the even broader interpretation that politicians and state officials made of its provisions, combined with the almost inexistent legal recognition of customary land rights, allowed state officials and politicians to claim state ownership of land that was customarily claimed by others (Yoder, 2005: 312; Fitzpatrick *et al.*, 2013: 172). There were cases in which state officials acknowledged this legal problem and respected customary-based rights. However, there were many other cases in which state officials classified land as state land and forced holders of customary-based land rights to leave it or to sell it cheaply, because they didn't have Portuguese or Indonesian formal land rights (e.g., Rose, 2016; Almeida, 2018a).

The unclear definition of abandoned land and the mechanisms to identify it were also problematic, allowing the state to claim the right to administer land

18 See below; Almeida, 2016: 28; decision of Court of Appeal No. 12/Cível/2018/TR of 12 July 2018.

without a clearly visible use—such as land under dispute, land kept as a reserve, and grazing land—to the detriment of their customary owners. A simple visit from DNTPSC staff to a seemingly unused field could be enough to classify a piece of land as belonging to the state (Chapter 9). Furthermore, politicians' and state officials' interpretation of Law 1/2003 progressively changed from 'abandoned land *is managed* by the state' to 'abandoned land *is owned* by the state'.[19]

Finally, the provision establishing that all immovable property acquired or built by public entities during the period of the Indonesian occupation automatically became state land was also problematic. While it makes sense that lawfully acquired land by the Indonesian administration reverted to the Timorese state, this provision ignored the many cases of violent dispossession by the Indonesian administration. Many of these 'acquisitions' were legally null or inexistent, and therefore the land belonged to its lawful owner. This provision was in many cases used for expropriation without proven public purpose, nor fair compensation, and was therefore unconstitutional. This provision was a clear example of the priority given by politicians to the land rights of the state, and the little attention put in developing a legal framework that could protect the land rights of the people (Chapter 4).

The Land Law establishes a new, more-detailed, and nuanced definition of state land. The law lists the land that belongs to the public domain of the state (see below), and defines as state land the immovable property that belonged to, or was used by, the Portuguese and Indonesian administrations, but explicitly excludes from this definition customary-based land rights that are protected by the law (art. 8, 9.1, and 9.2). In cases of unlawful dispossession by the state during previous administrations, the Land Law establishes that the land can only remain as state land if it is being used for public administration activities or public purpose, but in these cases the claimant is entitled to compensation (art. 9.3). Land that belonged to foreigners and land for which no owner can be identified belongs to the state (art. 9.1.d, and 9.4). The definition of state land stablished in the Land Law is much clearer than the previous one established by Law 1/2003. However, it can still be problematic, as the example of the use of the word *baldio* analysed in the previous chapter shows. Furthermore, the scope of this definition will depend considerably on how the protection of customary-based land rights is interpreted in practice.

Public and private domain of the state

In several countries state land is divided into two different legal categories: (1) *public domain of the state*, and (2) *private domain of the state*. The public domain encompasses those areas that, due to their strategic importance, should always

19 On the problems with the definition of 'abandoned land', see Almeida, 2016: 24; Almeida, 2017.

belong to the state and be under a more protective legal regime. The private domain of the state encompasses all other areas that belong to the state, but are not considered part of the public domain. Law 1/2003 attempted to establish this legal distinction, but a poor transplantation of legal provisions made the relevant articles simply impossible to implement (Almeida, 2016: 7).

The Land Law brought clarity to the concept by defining public domain and listing those areas that belong to it, such as a strip of 50 meters of the coastline (art. 8 and 9). Also relevant, in cases where the classification of public domain can lead to loss of land rights, the Land Law establishes a right to compensation. Despite this progress, the regime of public and private domain of the state needs subsequent legislation to be fully implemented, but this legislation has not yet been approved.

Land rights of legal entities

The text of the constitution raises doubts regarding the land rights of legal entities when it states that '[o]nly national citizens can own land' in Timor-Leste (art. 54.4). Considering that legal entities are not *national citizens*, this article suggests that the constitution forbids legal entities from owning land in Timor-Leste (Urresta, 2004a: 5). Law 1/2003 gave no answer to this question. Although in practice many legal entities 'owned' land, this question was a source of uncertainty for companies, associations, and foundations.

The Land Law partially addresses this problem by establishing that Timorese legal entities fully owned by Timorese nationals, and non-profit legal entities authorised by law, can own land in Timor-Leste (art. 6.1.b, a.6.1.d).[20] However, the implementation of this provision is dependent on further legislation that has yet not been approved, regulating the identification of legal entities authorised to own land.[21] As with many other topics debated in this chapter, while the Land Law provides answers to previous questions, it leaves others unanswered, and its full implementation is dependent on the approval of further legislation.

Processes for identifying land claims and addressing conflicting ones

One of the main problems of the Timorese formal land tenure system has been the process for identifying land claims and solving conflicting ones. This section looks at the different mechanisms tried since independence until the approval of the Land Law.

20 During the Land Law debate some MPs were against land ownership by legal entities, but quickly backtracked when they realised that such a position would impact the Catholic Church.

21 In the case of the Catholic Church, the 2015 Concordat regulates this matter (art. 12; see Parliament Resolution 18/2015).

The process established by Law 1/2003

Law 1/2003 established the first formal process for people to claim their land rights, stipulating that within one year after the law's entry into force, they had to submit their land claims to DNTPSC, together with all documentary evidence to sustain them (art. 12.1 and 12.2). Unclaimed land would be presumed to be state land, but this presumption could be trumped if successfully challenged in court before 2009 (art. 12.3 and 12.4).

This land-claims process raised several problems. First, it specifically mentioned *ownership* rights, leaving unclear whether it was applicable to other formal land rights, such as *aforamento* and *hak guna-bangunan* (art. 12.1).[22] Furthermore, it only mentioned land that 'has been illegally appropriated or occupied by third parties', therefore excluding those cases where land *had not* been appropriated or occupied, which was at odds with the legal presumption that unclaimed land belonged to the state. Second, this process implicitly excluded customary-based land rights that had not been formalised by demanding documentation proving the right. Third, in many cases, people with formal land rights had lost their documentation during the destruction and displacement of 1999, and therefore their claim could not be filed with any documentation to sustain it. Fourth, due to a lack of public information, in Timor-Leste only 33 and 15 percent of urban and rural families respectively knew about the obligation to claim their land, and therefore very few participated (Urresta and Nixon, 2004a: 29).[23] Finally, the law did not establish an outcome for this land-claims process, which depended on subsequent legislation that was never approved, leaving the claims made under Law 1/2003 in a 'legal limbo' (Fitzpatrick *et al.* 2013: 102).[24] Interestingly, none of the court decisions analysed for this book mentioned this land-claims process.[25] In conclusion, the process established by Law 1/2003 did not solve the problem of identifying land claims and addressing land-related conflicts; it only further complicated the already-difficult land tenure situation in Timor-Leste.

The process established by Decree-Law 27/2011

In mid-2011 the draft Land Law had been waiting for debate in parliament for more than one year and there were no signs of progress. At the same time, the

22 Some holders of land rights other than ownership also claimed land through this process. The lack of distinction that in practice was made in this case between ownership and other land rights is one of many examples of a common misconception in Timorese society regarding characteristics of land rights. For instance, it is common to see court cases in which the holder of a title of *aforamento* claims the recognition of his or her ownership right.

23 Only 12,329 claims were lodged, including around 9,000 claims by foreigners (Sousa, 2005: 5).

24 The process was further complicated by practical problems in the system adopted for the collection of land claims (Almeida, 2016: 31).

25 Law 1/2003 established an even less clear process for land claims by foreigners (Almeida, 2016: 30).

INR project had already collected around 35,000 land claims, 92 percent of them undisputed, but there was no legal basis to support that land-claims process (Chapter 3).[26] To solve this problem, the government approved Decree-Law 27/2011, which provided the legal framework necessary to legitimise INR's work and anticipated some of the effects of the draft Land Law, by strengthening the legal protection given to undisputed land claims.[27]

Decree-Law 27/2011, further regulated by Ministerial-Decree 16/2011, established a land-claims process to be progressively and systematically implemented in relatively small collection areas (e.g., a delimited neighbourhood). In each collection area the process would start with a public information phase that included public meetings, the broadcasting of public information campaigns in the media, and announcements of the process in the Official Journal (art. 2.1 and 2.2 of Ministerial-Decree 16/2011). The second phase of the process was the collection on the ground of geographical information and land claims over each parcel of land inside the collection area (art. 3). The land claims could be presented by individuals, legal entities, communities, groups, and the state. Everyone was entitled to claim any piece of land and to present whatever means of proof they considered relevant, such as documents and testimonials (art. 4.1 and 4.2). After additional public information campaigns and official announcements (art. 2.3), the third phase of the process started with the publication of maps and claimants' lists displayed in the district office of DNTPSC, containing the delimitation of each identified parcel inside the collection area and their claimants (art. 5.1, 5.2, and 5.3). During a pre-established period not shorter than 30 days, any interested party could correct their own claims, present new claims, make counterclaims against claims already presented, and correct possible errors in the boundaries of claimed parcels (art. 5.4).[28]

Ministerial-Decree 23/2011 regulated the following steps of the process. All undisputed claims by individual Timorese were registered as their property in the National Property Cadastre (equivalent to a property registry), and a *registration certificate* was given to them. The other claims remained classified as 'disputed' or waiting for a legal solution to be defined by the Land Law.[29] The

26 Minister of Justice's Ministerial Order No. 229/GM/MJ/VII/2008 allowed the start of the land-claims process and established some criteria for it. However, this ministerial order, by its own nature, had only internal administrative value and was not enforceable outside the structure of the state.

27 A slightly different solution was proposed before by Fitzpatrick (2002a: 25). See also Thomson, 2003: 75; Fitzpatrick *et al.*, 2008: 7.

28 As mentioned above, INR's process started without an adequate legal framework. To address this issue art. 13 of Decree-Law 27/2011 and art. 6 of Ministerial-Decree 16/2011 established that in previously surveyed areas the publication of maps had to be reopened, so all the interested parties could present their land claims.

29 Art. 1.2.a, 1.2.b and 1.2.c of Decree-law 27/2011 and 2.1.a, 2.1.b, 4 and 6 of Ministerial-Decree 23/2011.

registration in the National Property Cadastre did not give beneficiaries the ownership of the registered land, but instead a legal presumption of ownership (art. 4.2 of Decree-Law 27/2011). With this legal presumption of ownership, the beneficiaries were allowed to act as legal owners of the land (e.g., sales), and third parties that acquired registered land in good faith were safeguarded (Almeida, 2016: 34).While this legal presumption could be challenged in court, the challenger had the burden of proving a right that trumped the registered right. This decree-law avoided the most controversial topics such as land rights of legal entities and disputed cases, deferring the legal solutions to the Land Law. Nevertheless, every person and entity that considered themselves to own land had to claim it once the land-claims process was happening in that area, to avoid others securing land rights over it.

This land-claims process differed significantly from the one created by Law 1/2003. First, this process was designed to be implemented progressively around the country, instead of during the one-off period established by Law 1/2003. Second, the land claims were publicly scrutinised through the publication of cadastral maps, which gave more transparency to the process and helped to deter abusive or opportunistic land claims.[30] Third, the state, through DNTPSC district officials, also had to claim its land. The proximity of the district state officials to the local population and local perceptions of existing land rights made these officials less prone to claim areas that were socially acknowledged to belong to individuals or communities as state land. Fourth, by not linking the land-claims process to formalised rights, nor demanding any specific documents, the process was oriented to the social perception of land rights more than previous formalisation attempts. Finally, the presumption of ownership obtained with this process was a significant legal advantage to its participants.

However, the land-claims process of Decree-Law 27/2011 also had its weaknesses. First, as already mentioned, the text of the decree-law was ambiguous on some points; for instance, it was not completely clear for holders of formal rights other than ownership whether they also had to claim their land in the process. Second, the registration of all undisputed claims as ownership rights without looking at the basis of the claims represented a double-edged sword: while it allowed for a better conformation to the local understanding of ownership rights (e.g., customary-based land rights of individuals) and accommodated the diverse realities that exist in Timor-Leste (e.g., loss of documentation), it was also vulnerable to corruption and arbitrariness (e.g., state officials receiving bribes to not claim certain parcels as state land, or presenting selective state counterclaims). Third, this land-claims process was only designed for urban areas and not for rural areas marked by complex customary land tenure

30 INR staff recalled situations in which claimants retracted their land claims after feeling embarrassed for having excessive land claims publicly exposed in their community.

systems; however, this limitation was not explicitly stated in the legal text, which proved to be an error (see below). Finally, the necessary legal framework for formalising transactions of registered land parcels was drafted but never approved. Some of these weaknesses were mitigated by the possibility of contesting the registration in court and the fact that unfair counterclaims by the state would only result in disputed cases, but not in final decisions, with the state having no legal advantage in those disputes.

The troubled end of INR and the controversial SNC project brought new problems to this land-claims process (Chapter 3). Besides SNC's unsound and unprofessional expansion of this process into rural areas for which it was not designed, with dramatic effects on the land rights of individuals and communities (Rede ba Rai, 2019), new problematic regulations were approved (Ministerial-Decree 45/2016 and 46/2016). The most striking example was the new requisite that land claims had to be accompanied by documentation proving ownership of the land or a declaration from two local officials attesting to the right of the claimant (art. 8 of Ministerial-Decree 45/2016). This provision not only put a huge burden on land claimants that had to travel around the district to collect these signatures, but it also gave local officials a de facto power of vetoing land claims by refusing to sign declarations (Rede ba Rai, 2019: 58).[31] Moreover, this new requisite opened the door to extortion and request of bribes by local officials. To add another layer of problems, SNC started issuing new registration certificates, referring to them as the *first registry certificates*, therefore ignoring previous certificates already issued by INR (Diário de Notícias, 8 May 2017). In my visits to Timor-Leste in 2016 and 2017 I asked DNTPSC staff what happened to the parcels already registered by INR but obtained no clear answer. Moreover, SNC kept its database of registered parcels closed to the public.

As someone that was involved in the development of Decree-Law 27/2011, I have mixed feelings about it. On the one hand the idea behind this decree-law was well intentioned, and although it had some flaws, it seemed that it would start to address some important land-related problems in Timor-Leste. On the other hand, its poor implementation by SNC made me question whether approving this decree-law was indeed the best solution.

The process established by the Land Law

Decree-Law 27/2011 was followed by the long-awaited Land Law, approved in 2017. The mechanism for identifying land claims established by the Land Law is similar to the one established previously by Decree-Law 27/2011,

31 The uselessness of these signatures is astonishing; it comes with the assumption that local officials know the history of each parcel of land, have the power and ability to assess the validity of each claim, and do not have any conflict of interest with the land claimants.

except that it expanded the period of publication to 90 days and determined that surveys in community protection zones be regulated separately (art. 29 to 34). The SNC land-claims process has continued as before, adapting only to this 90-day requisite. The Land Law explicitly says that the cadastral survey and the declarations collected under Decree-Law 27/2011 remain valid (art. 80).

The novelty of the Land Law in comparison with Decree-Law 27/2011 is its mechanism to address land-related disputes, which includes a legal classification and prioritisation of different land rights and a process to adjudicate disputes.

The legal classification of land rights is as follows. Claims based on valid formal ownership rights issued by the Portuguese and Indonesian administrations (*propriedade perfeita* and *hak milik*, respectively), informal property rights (as defined above), and community land are classified as *primary rights*. The valid Portuguese *aforamento* rights, and the Indonesian *hak guna-bangunan* and *hak guna usaha* are classified as *secondary rights*. The cases of special adverse possession (see above and below) do not have a special classification, but are also relevant for the prioritisation of different land rights established by the Land Law.

Once land claims are identified through the land-claims process, they are divided into *undisputed* (having one single claim). The undisputed parcels are registered as property of the claimants in the National Property Cadastre, albeit with some restrictions in the case of secondary rights.[32] For the disputed cases, the law establishes a hierarchy based on the classification mentioned above as primary or secondary rights, and on who is currently in possession of the land, determining in each case who is the owner and who is entitled to compensation paid by the state or the other party (art. 39 to 54). This dispute process is primarily adjudicated by the Land Commission at an administrative level, but its decisions can be appealed to the courts (art. 55 to 69).

Finally, the Land Law also clarifies the legal effects of its recognition of land rights. As previously with Decree-Law 27/2011, the registration of land claimants as the owners of a specific land parcel does not necessarily give them the ownership of land but rather a legal presumption of ownership (art. 7.1.1). The novelty is that, after five years, the registered right is acquired through adverse possession if not successfully disputed in court (art. 71.2). This allows

32 As mentioned above, these restrictions exemplify the rushed changes in parliament, without much consideration for the logic of the law. Someone with a secondary land right needs to be currently in possession of the land, have possessed it for at least 20 years, and have acquired the possession in good faith, to become the owner of the land (art. 37); someone with peaceful possession of the land, without any other connection to it, can immediately become its owner, independent of when the possession started (art. 38).

that rights that were not claimed during the land-claims process can still be claimed, but establishes a fairly short period after which the ownership of land can no longer be challenged.[33]

While the mechanism to address land-related disputes provides legal solutions for problems that for many years remained unsolved, the fairness of some political options adopted, and the practical problems of implementing the Land Law are testing its success. One example is a contested political option of protecting long-term possession that started before 1999 through the 'special adverse possession' mechanism. While some people opposed to this date for special adverse possession because it excludes all people displaced during the 1999 conflicts, others believe that no protection should be given to any land occupants (Chapter 4).

Furthermore, if the initial drafts of the Land Law seemed difficult to implement, the changes introduced in the final version bring implementation problems to a completely different level. One example is the provision establishing that special adverse possession is only applicable if the claimant does not have other land for housing or cultivation. This raises important practical questions: (1) how can this requisite be assessed, if the land is not registered? And (2) what happens if claimants own land together with their family or community? Furthermore, if in previous versions of the law the registration of undisputed claims was mostly automatic, now it is necessary to assess and classify every single land claim and, in case of special adverse possession, somehow assess whether the claimant has other land. All these problems significantly complicate the implementation of the Land Law, which has not yet started.

Evictions

Law 1/2003 established a harsh administrative process to evict occupants of state land (art. 7 to 11; see Thomson, 2003: 72; Soares, 2007: 198). In this process, once occupants were notified by DNTPSC that the parcel belonged to the state, occupants had 30 days to leave, and ten days to file an administrative petition against the eviction (art. 7.1 and 7.2).[34] This administrative petition was tacitly considered dismissed if not answered by the minister of justice within 15 days (art. 7.3). After the 30 days, DNTPSC was entitled to vacate the land, if necessary by police force (art. 8.1). The judicial appeal of the eviction order did not halt the eviction (art. 8.2).[35] The evicted people were responsible for paying the expenses of the eviction (art. 8.3) and they were not entitled

33 In case of disputed parcels, the decision of the Land Commission or court is definitive between the parties, but this does not prevent others from claiming rights during the 5-year period (art. 71.3).

34 The 30-day term does not comply with the 90 days prescribed in article 56 (j) of *UN Basic Principles and Guidelines on Development-based Evictions and Displacement*.

35 A preventive action could suspend the eviction until a final decision of the court, but I do not know of a single case where this action was used. No legislation regarding administrative proceedings in

to any compensation, including for any improvements made to the property (art. 8.4).[36]

The problems with this harsh eviction process were many. First, the law provided no detail regarding the process for identifying which land belonged to the state, which was in practice the arbitrary decision of a state official without any due process. Second, the short time-frame to appeal, the limited access to legal aid, and the general population's low levels of literacy and legal knowledge made a meaningful appeal impossible for most Timorese.[37] Third, with the judicial appeal not suspending the eviction, even if occupants could file their appeal on time, they were still in a precarious situation. Fourth, while no right to compensation could be justified in some cases, in many others it was a source of further social exclusion of the people evicted. In practice, some financial compensation was at times paid by the state, but it was based on arbitrary decisions of politicians and state officials, not on legislation (see Chapter 7).[38] In 2011 a special decree-law tried to regulate compensations in case of eviction of state land, but lack of a regulatory framework left this legislation unimplemented (Decree-Law 6/2011). To further complicate the problem of evictions, Decree-Law 4/2014 gave regional authorities the power to start evictions processes of occupants of state land (art. 6.2.c).

The Land Law does not specifically repeal Law 1/2003, but briefly mentions the topic of evictions, establishing some guiding principles and saying that evictions based on the Land Law should be regulated through a specific decree-law that has not yet been approved. Therefore, it is not clear if the eviction process of Law 1/2003 remains applicable, or if no more evictions are allowed until the required decree-law is approved. In fact, the Land Law was a missed opportunity for establishing a more reasonable and protective eviction process, leaving this 'detail' to future regulation.[39] There is the real risk that no improved eviction process will be approved anytime soon.

court has yet been approved, and while the Indonesian law could be used, in practice the courts recur to the Procedural Civil Code (Guerreiro, 2012: 72; Almeida, 2017a: 187).

36 Several constitutional rights could be used to challenge the harshness of this eviction process, but in the young Timorese judicial system there is still little room for this kind of legal analysis and argumentation.

37 See the decision of the Court of Appeal No. 15/Civel/2016/TR of 23 January 2017, where an appeal against an eviction was refused because it was not submitted on time.

38 This arbitrariness can be illustrated with three examples of state-led evictions from land classified by DNTPSC as state land: (1) in 2011, 147 families were evicted from the Brimob neighbourhood; each received 2,000 USD in compensation (Matadalan ba Rai and Haburas Foundation, 2010: 62–64). (2) In 2012 11 families were evicted from the Aitarak Laran neighbourhood; each received between 2,500 USD and 6,500 USD, depending on the size and condition of their houses and plantations (Business Timor, 28 December 2012). (3) In 2013 around 400 occupants of the ruins of Hotel Resende were evicted; they received no compensation (Almeida, 2017).

39 During the revision of the draft Land Law after the 2012 presidential veto, a more detailed and protective process for evictions was introduced, but later removed during the discussion process (Chapter 5).

Land rights in the Timorese formal land tenure system

The Land Law only provides a legal solution to determine who owns land, but it does not define the rights and obligations of landowners, nor regulates other formal land rights. This section summarises the regulation of formal land rights in the Timorese legal framework since independence.

Besides establishing private property as one of the constitutionally protected fundamental rights, the Timorese Constitution did not establish any other regulations on land rights (art. 54).[40] The incorporation of Indonesian legislation into the Timorese legal framework by the constitution meant that, in theory, the law regulating land rights after independence was the Indonesian BAL (Almeida, 2016: 9; Almeida, 2017a: 176). However, Indonesian land-related legislation was in practice mostly ignored by courts and the public administration (Fitzpatrick and Barnes, 2010: 210). The first change to the regulation of land rights came with the approval of Decree-Law 19/2004, establishing the rules and process for the lease of state and abandoned land. Since then, this decree-law has been central to land tenure in Timor-Leste, considering that leases of state land have been one of the safest ways of legally obtaining access to land. However, due to a lack of a regulatory framework (e.g., regarding the price of rents), and DNTPSC's decision to ignore legal obligations (e.g., mandatory public tenders for leases), the implementation of this decree-law is at times arbitrary (Chapter 7; Almeida, 2016: 19). Later, leases between private parties became regulated by Law 11/2005.

The 2011 Civil Code brought significant changes to the legal framework of land rights. Besides regulating ownership rights, the Civil Code also establishes a myriad of other rights *in rem* and further regulates leases.[41] These rights *in rem* can be divided into rights of enjoyment (e.g., ownership rights), real security rights (e.g., mortgages), and rights that give to their holder privileges in the acquisition of specific assets (e.g., preferential rights with real effects; Fernandes, 2009: 153). While a detailed analysis of these rights is outside the scope of this chapter, two specific rights *in rem* are important to highlight here. The usufruct right allows the enjoyment of the asset for a restricted period, which can be at most the life period of the beneficiary or 30 years if the beneficiary is a legal entity (art. 1362, 1366). The surface right allows its beneficiary

40 This provision is often misinterpreted as meaning that the government must give a land parcel to each person (Haburas Foundation and Rede ba Rai, 2013: 18; CEPAD, 2014: 73; Stead, 2016: 157; Almeida, 2016: 12; 2018a: 105;). I participated in public meetings in which even the minimum area of this hypothetical parcel was debated. Indonesian Law 56/1960, establishing the government's obligation to make available a minimum of two hectares of arable land for each farmer's household, is probably the origin of this misinterpretation (Lucas and Warren, 2013: 3).

41 Law 11/2005 on private leases was repealed by Law 10/2011, but Law 19/2004 remains in force.

to build or plant on another person's land, on a temporary or perpetual basis (art. 1414, 1420).[42]

The Civil Code also establishes mechanisms to protect land possessors, which in the case of Timor-Leste are especially relevant, considering that most people do not have formal land rights (art. 1171 to 1206). Those mechanisms can be used as preventive measures in court in case of relevant fear of disturbance or disseizing of possession (art. 1196); direct action and judicial defence of possession (art. 1197); and possessory action for restitution of possession (art. 1198 and 1199). Highly significant is the legal presumption that the possessor of a right *in rem* is the lawful holder of that right, unless other presumptions exist based on registration, established before the possession (art. 1188). This provision can be used in many cases as an effective mechanism to prevent arbitrary dispossession: possessors can challenge an eviction by arguing that they are the presumptive owners of the land, giving the other party the burden to prove their rights.[43]

However, the status of the Civil Code's regulations over land rights is unclear. With the approval of the Civil Code, it was established that 'regarding rights over [land], the new Civil Code is only applicable after the recognition or attribution of the first titles by the Democratic Republic of Timor-Leste' (art. 3 of Law 10/2011). This provision raises a few questions: (1) what is considered a 'first title'? (2) Is the registration created by Decree-Law 27/2011 considered a 'title' for the sake of this article, or is the Civil Code only applicable once land goes through the process established by the Land Law? And (3) considering that the process established by the Land Law is progressively applied throughout the country, does this mean that registered areas are under the regime of the Civil Code, and unregistered areas under the previous regime? The poor legal argumentation of court decisions analysed for this book, and their inconsistent interpretation and use of law do not give a definitive answer to these questions.[44]

42 A surface right is especially relevant, as it can be shaped into a land right very similar to ownership and be used to bypass the constitutional prohibition of land ownership by foreigners. One good example of this bypass was the state transfer of the surface right over a large plot of land to a private company, for the construction of the Pelican Paradise resort (http://timor-leste.gov.tl/?p=14275&lang=en).

43 This provision exemplifies the advantages and disadvantages of legal transplants debated in Chapter 5. On one hand, the copy of the Portuguese Civil Code introduced this provision that automatically gives a significant legal protection for many people who are otherwise not protected by law. On the other hand, this protection is buried in the complexity of this foreign code, which remains mostly unknown to judicial actors and the public. I have not come across a single court case nor administrative process in which this provision was invoked, and CSOs' members were always surprised when I told them about it.

44 A few decisions of the Court of Appeal, issued long after the approval of the Timorese Civil Code, still refer to the provisions about possession of the Indonesian Civil Code that were repealed by the Indonesian BAL in 1960 (Almeida 2018: 9; e.g., decisions of the Court of Appeal No.

Legal mechanisms for acquisition and loss of land rights

Transfers of land rights

At the time of independence the transfers of formal land rights were regulated by the Indonesian legislation incorporated by Timor-Leste, but in practice this legislation was ignored. The Legal Regime of the Notaries (Decree-Law 3/2004) was the first piece of Timorese legislation to regulate transfers of formal land rights, establishing that the recognition, creation, transfer, modification, or extinction of rights over land such as sales, donations, and inheritances had to be done through a notary deed (art. 37.2).[45] However, in the years that followed the approval of this decree-law, there was only one certified notary in the entire country, and in 2016 there were only seven (Almeida, 2016: 35). The result was that, in practice, almost no transaction—if any—was done through a notarised deed. Acknowledging this limitation, Decree-Law 27/2011 suspended the need for a notarised deed for transferring registered land and deferred the regulation of this matter to a subsequent ministerial-decree, which was never approved. With the entry into force of the Civil Code in March 2012, the obligation of a notary deed for transferring land rights was re-established. In practice the great majority of, if not all, transfers of land rights in the country continue to not be done through a notary deed, which makes these transfers legally void. This is one clear case of a complete disconnection between the law and reality, and it puts in the hands of the courts a difficult decision: declare these land transfers void, even if in practice it is practically impossible to follow the legal obligation of a notarised deed, or recognise the validity of these transfers, therefore ignoring the existing law.[46]

Adverse possession and legal protection of possessors

Adverse possession is the legal mechanism that allows the acquisition of a land right by its continuous possession for a period established by law (Prata, 2005: 1241; Fernandes, 2009: 241). Although this mechanism plays an important

4/Civel/2016/TR of 29 December 2017; No. 05/2016/TR of 10 April 2017; and No. 07/Civel/2016/TR of 6 February 2017). Other decisions apply the Timorese Civil Code without questioning the issue of entry into force (e.g., No. 20/Civel/2017/TR of 11 December 2017; No. 24/Civel/2016/TR of 12 September 2017). I found one decision where the Court of Appeal assesses this issue and says that the entry into force of the Land Law makes the rules of the Timorese Civil Code applicable (No. 28/Cível/2015/TR of 5 September 2018).

45 Decree-Law 3/2004 was later changed by Decree-Law 24/2009 and 25/2009.

46 For instance, Penha, a former Portuguese judge in the Court of Appeal, writes that these transactions should not be considered valid (Penha, 2012: 19). Following this interpretation, Court of Appeal, in its decision No. 25/Civel/2016/TR of 18 September 2017, decided that a donation without a notarised deed was void.

role in providing legal certainty to a formal land tenure system, its regulation is Timor-Leste is quite complicated (Almeida, 2018).

Since independence, and until the entry into force of the Civil Code, adverse possession was regulated by the Indonesian legislation that was incorporated into the Timorese legal system. The Indonesian Civil Code from 1847 regulates adverse possession, but Book Two of this code, containing the main provisions that justify adverse possession, was repealed by the BAL in 1960. Furthermore, the BAL regulates the basis for acquisition of land rights and never mentions adverse possession. Scholars say clearly that Indonesian law does not allow adverse possession (Fitzpatrick, 2002: 83; Reerink and Gleder, 2010: 80; Reerink, 2011: 90; Bedner, 2016: 68).[47] Nevertheless, the Timorese courts have been applying the adverse possession provisions established in the Indonesian Civil Code, without discussing whether adverse possession is admissible in Indonesia, quoting articles of the repealed Book Two of the Indonesian Civil Code, and ignoring the literature about the topic (Almeida, 2018).[48] This is one clear example of the problem raised in Chapter 3 about the lack of knowledge, both of national and international advisers and justice actors, of the Indonesian law that was incorporated into the Timorese legal system.

The approval of the Timorese Civil Code introduced adverse possession into the Timorese land tenure system (art. 1213 to 1217). Acquisition through adverse possession is not allowed if the possession is violent or not public and, depending on the characteristics of the possession and its registration, the right *in rem* can be acquired with 10 to 25 years of possession. However, the application of the Civil Code's rules on adverse possession raises at least two main sets of questions (Almeida, 2018: 11). The first is caused by the provision discussed above about the entry into force of the rules on land rights established by the Civil Code (art. 3 of Law 10/2011): (1) are the Civil Code rules on adverse possession dependent on the 'recognition or attribution of the first titles by the Democratic Republic of Timor-Leste', as established in article 3? And if so, (2) are the rules of adverse possession only progressively applicable to those areas where those titles are issued? The second set of questions revolves around when to begin counting the years for adverse possession: (3) should the counting start when possession started, (4) only after the entry into force of the Civil

47 Adverse possession should not be mistaken with the provision of article 24 of the Indonesian Government Regulation No. 24/1997, which allows the registration of land rights without the necessary documents, if the person applying for registration has had possession of the land, publicly and in good faith, for more than 20 consecutive years.

48 See, for instance, the decisions of the Court of Appeal No 14/Cível/2013/TR of 30 July 2013, No 56/2003 of 30 March 2009, No 56/2004 of 1 June 2009. This is also visible in Penha, 2012: 80. Decision No. 28/Cível/2015/TR of 5 September 2018 is an exception, explicitly referring that Book Two of the Indonesian Civil Code was repealed by the BAL.

Code, or (5) only after the 'first title'? The jurisprudence consulted does not look into these questions.[49]

Expropriation

Another way through which land rights can be transferred is through expropriation, in this case always from private parties to the state. The constitution establishes the basic criteria for expropriation: (1) public purpose of the expropriation; (2) payment of fair compensation; and (3) the need for a legal process established by law (art. 54.3; Almeida, 2018b). Since independence until the approval of the Expropriation Law in 2017, the Indonesian Expropriation Law was the legislation in force, but it was never applied.[50] In practice expropriations were conducted through arbitrary and informal processes, often with disastrous results for the people affected (see, for instance, Silva and Furusawa, 2014; Almeida, 2019; Chapter 9). As I pointed out in previous publications, the failure of the state to address its constitutional obligation to protect people's land rights and develop a formal process for expropriation was used in practice by the state to quickly and cheaply dispossess people of their land (Almeida, 2018a; Almeida, 2018b).

Despite some flaws (Chapter 5), the Expropriation Law creates a detailed administrative process for expropriation, and defines central concepts such as public purpose (art. 4). However, it is not clear if this complex and fairly protective process will be ever put into practice. For now, the law has been simply ignored by the public administration, which continues to implement the same arbitrary and improvised processes that were used before the approval of the law (Tatoli 16/05/2019).

Conclusion

As a result of Timor-Leste's history, at the time of independence the land tenure scenario in the country was extremely complex, with many legal gaps, problems, and questions which the national legal framework was unable to answer. Since then legislation has gradually been approved, and some of these gaps, problems, and questions have been addressed. However, as this chapter demonstrates, every new piece of legislation has also resulted in new gaps, problems, and questions. In part, this is the nature of wicked problems such as land tenure, they don't have perfect solutions and solving one problem

49 In my opinion the period for adverse possession must be counted only after the entry into force of the Civil Code, otherwise the Civil Code would be applied with retroactive effects (Almeida, 2018: 12; see also Penha, 2012: 103).

50 See art. 18 of the Indonesian BAL and Law 20/1961. However, even in Indonesia this law was rarely used, with the state resorting to 'voluntary' acquisitions instead (Bedner, 2016: 68).

gives rise to others (Chapter 2). However, the less-than-favourable political environment for legislating about land tenure and the problems of the law-making process analysed in the previous chapters further contribute to this situation (Chapters 4 and 5). If the political will to address land-related problems is not strong, and if the process to draft and approve legislation is far from ideal, it is only natural that the resulting legal framework will be far from perfect.

The problems of the Timorese legal framework on land tenure identified in this chapter are many: legislation that is unimplementable because the necessary regulatory framework is not approved, as happened with the land-claims process of Law 1/2003; profound discrepancies between legal requisites, social practices, and administrative capacity, such as the legal requisite of notarised deeds in all transactions of land rights; unclear legal provisions that leave questions about their interpretation and application, such as the doubts regarding the application of the Civil Code; legal concepts that are wrongly used, such as the definition of public domain established by Law 1/2003; unclear repealing of legislation that leaves doubts regarding which legislation regulates a certain topic, as happened with the rules for eviction after the approval of the Land Law.

The lack of a strong judiciary able to adequately debate these questions and establish clear jurisprudence about these gaps and problems further complicate the Timorese formal land tenure system (Chapter 4). The analysis of courts' jurisprudence made for this book highlights the fragilities of the judicial system, showing the weak legal argumentation used by lawyers, but also the difficulties judges have, even at the Court of Appeal, in providing sound and comprehensive legal argumentation.

This very unclear legal scenario has real consequences in land administration and people's lives. Gaps in legislation, contradictions, unrealistic requirements, and a lack of a regulatory framework legitimise arbitrary approaches of state institutions to land administration (Chapter 7) and result in legal tenure insecurity for most Timorese (Chapter 8). For many of them the lack of legal tenure security will never be a problem, considering that state institutions and laws are just a distant reality; but for those that happen to be in the path of the state, legal tenure security can make a difference in their livelihoods (Chapter 9). While better legislation is not a guarantee of better land administration and more tenure security for the people, it is an important step in that direction.

In this conclusion I must highlight the approval of the Land Law Package in 2017, the biggest landmark in the development of the Timorese legal framework on land tenure since independence. These laws fill major legal gaps and reduce the strong bias in favour of the state control of the land promoted by Law 1/2003. They do this by giving more rights to people and communities and establishing clearer processes for state interventions. However, the Land Law Package also has serious flaws, such as a lack of regulations on central topics like evictions and community land, and dubious provisions such as the ownership of *baldios* (Chapter 5). Furthermore, if initial drafts would be difficult to implement, poorly considered last-minute changes introduced in the final version of these laws raised implementation difficulties to another level (Chapter 5). Moreover, the capacity and preparedness of public administration to implement these laws is quite limited (Chapter 7).

The approval of the Land Law Package did little to change the 'waiting for the law' mentality that has marked land administration in Timor-Leste since independence (Yoder, 2003: 22; Fitzpatrick and McWilliam, 2005). Before, everyone was waiting for the approval of the Land Law for something to change; now everyone is waiting for the approval of the regulatory framework necessary to implement the Land Law Package. For now, the laws of the package remain unimplemented, and although the law on the books can play a role influencing behaviours even without much implementation (Aubert, 1967), the positive impacts of these laws are, for now, unclear. Hopefully, these problems will be addressed and these laws can be implemented to the benefit of the Timorese. But there is also the risk that partial and selective implementation, as happened with previous legislation, will fuel more confusion, dispossession, and conflict.

Chapter 7

Land institutions

Introduction

This chapter looks at the institutions responsible for implementing the Timorese formal land tenure system.[1] As described in Chapter 1, the institutional framework is one key analytical theme to understanding the formal land tenure system. These institutions link the legal framework that delimits the land tenure system, and the social relationships, ideas, and practices that regulate land tenure on the ground. As argued by Lund, while legislation works as a social marker, the conditions in which legislation is implemented bring limitations, which in practice result in new informal norms that differ from those established in law (2016: 1209). Understanding the institutions responsible for implementing legislation and the environment in which they work is key to grasping how the Timorese formal land tenure system works in practice.

In Timor-Leste, DNTPSC is the state institution responsible for the administrative implementation of the formal land tenure system, and most of this chapter provides an insider overview of its intricate functioning and explains what the institution does in practice and why. The courts, due to their limited interventions in land-related issues, play a less important role, and because they are already briefly analysed in Chapter 4 and their decisions in Chapter 6, they are not studied in this chapter. But a few institutions external to the state also participate in the implementation of the formal land tenure system. For instance, DNTPSC's role in land registration was assigned first to INR and later to SNC; international organisations have supported some of DNTPSC activities; and CSOs working on land-related issues monitor the work of DNTPSC. Although in less detail, these institutions external to the state are also analysed here.

This chapter concludes that DNTPSC's structure, resources, and procedures are inadequate for its tasks, and its staff have great discretion in their work. The

1 Avoiding the debate around the different definitions of 'institution', I use the term here to refer to what others call 'organisation'. On this debate see, for instance, Blase, 1973: 255; North, 1990: 4; Building, 2010: 13.

DOI: 10.4324/9781003196396-7

law functions more as a rough guide for their tasks and as a tool for imposing their views when necessary. Although this discretion works at times as a safety valve of the system, more often it is a source of injustice, insecurity, corruption, and rent-seeking. Moreover, the external institutions that participate in the implementation of the formal land tenure system have considerable limitations regarding the support and guidance they can provide to DNTPSC. With these points in mind, it becomes easier to understand the problems and deficiencies of the implementation of the formal land tenure system in Timor-Leste.

This chapter is divided into three main parts. The first section debates the theoretical framework adopted for this institutional analysis. The second section, the largest of this chapter, is structured by the framework of analysis described below and examines DNTPSC in depth. The third and final section of this chapter briefly analyses the other institutions mentioned above.

Looking at institutions

The study of bureaucracies and public administration institutions has been one of the topics researched by the vast field of organisational theory (Crozier, 1964; Riggs, 1964; Esman, 1967; Wilson, 1989; Weber, 2013). The complexity of these institutions, composed by a myriad of people, technologies, and processes, makes them difficult objects of study, for which the guidance of academic theory is necessary.

Otto's Institution-Citizen Model builds on Milton Esman's theories and, combining *institutional*, *target group*, and *contextual* variables, provides a framework of analysis to understand how public institutions work and why (Otto, 1992). As part of the institutional variable, this model looks at the personal, material, and financial *resources* of the institution; the *internal structure*, comprising formal design, working methods, working conditions, informal division of tasks, and motivation; and finally, the *leadership* of the institution. As part of the target group variable (i.e., the citizens), Otto's model takes into account the *interest* of the target group of the institution (i.e., needs, alternatives, preferences, and values); their *access* to the institution (i.e., financial hurdles, geographic distance, costs, socio-psychological gap, and knowledge); the *reach* of the institution; and its *enforcement* capabilities. Regarding the contextual variables, Otto identifies as the main elements of study the *social*, *economic*, and *political* contexts in which the institution works. The analysis of the institution *tasks* is the starting point of the analysis.

While this model provides a good point of departure to study DNTPSC, some adaptations were necessary. First, I added a new element of analysis which I call *origins and influences*.[2] As argued by Wilson, 'every organisation has a culture, that is, a persistent, patterned way of thinking about the central

2 In contrast to its initial versions, the diagram of Otto's model from 2007 includes *influences*.

tasks of human relationships within an organisation. Culture is to an organisation what personality is to an individual' (Wilson, 1989: 91). Studying the history and influences of an institution is paramount to understanding its work and way of thinking, and this new element of origin and influences provides the space for this element. Second, the analysis of tasks is expanded into *goals and tasks*, therefore also including the main objectives of the institution. Third, due to space limitations, I compressed the elements of the target group variable into a single section called *DNTPSC clients*. Finally, this chapter skips the contextual variable, as its elements were already considered in Chapters 3 and 4.

In parallel with Otto's model, in this analysis I pay special attention to the human side of the institution, and I highlight the problems and dilemmas that DNTPSC staff experience in their day-to-day work. Too often scholars fail to put themselves in the shoes of those working in state institutions and criticise them without fully knowing and acknowledging their background, the context and restrictions in which their work is developed, and what they really do in practice (Wilson, 1989: 12).[3] Lipsky's study of *street-level bureaucrats*—state officials that, due to the nature of their job, have direct contact with citizens and significant discretion in exercising their authority—is especially relevant in this chapter (Lipsky, 2010: pref. para. 26).[4] His work is useful to analyse the material, structural, and even personal limitations that street-level bureaucrats must deal with, and the considerable discretion they employ in their work.

However, the analysis of discretion in the work of DNTPSC staff raises a terminological question that I should briefly debate here. Their discretion goes beyond the classic meaning, which defines discretion as the power of state officials, bounded by the law, to choose between different courses of action.[5] As extensively exemplified in this book, the circumstances in which the work of DNTPSC staff is developed allows for and promotes the use of their powers in absence of, and even against, the law. Therefore, discretion is used here with a broad meaning, to refer to the exercise of administrative powers, not necessarily supported and delimited by law.

In summary, the modified version of Otto's model provides the roadmap for this chapter, indicating the institutional points to study. Lipsky's study of street-level bureaucrats provides a good point of departure for my analysis of the human side of institutions, highlighting the limitations and dilemmas experienced by state officials, and especially the role of discretion in their work.

3 In a slightly different perspective, see the concept of *citizen-agent* by Maynard-Moody and Musheno, 2000: 348.

4 Alternatively, the concept of *operators* promoted by Wilson would also work here (1989: 33).

5 On the definition of debates around discretion, see Kanstroom, 1997: 720; Woude, 2015: 9.

State institutions—the National Directorate of Land and Property and Cadastral Services (DNTPSC)

The DNTPSC is the Timorese state institution responsible for the administrative implementation of the formal land tenure system, but surprisingly very little has been written about this institution. This section, with a structure based on the model described above, provides an analysis of DNTPSC, and it is the core part of this chapter. For this analysis, it is important to know that DNTPSC is one of the six national directorates of the MoJ, and it is comprised of 13 district offices (one in each district capital) and a national directorate office located in Dili.

The DNTPSC is also the institution with which I worked most closely during my five years with the MoJ. My office was at the DNTPSC national headquarters, and it is where I spent most of my time and established numerous personal connections. Therefore, I feel an even stronger responsibility to be fair in my analysis. In this chapter I make several generalisations. Naturally, these do not reflect the personal position of all staff members, and this caveat needs to be kept in mind. Nevertheless, I hope that the chapter does justice to the colleagues I worked so closely with.

The origins and influences of DNTPSC

As argued above, exploring the origins of and influences on an institution is critical to understanding it. Institutionally, DNTPSC has its origin in two institutions created during the UNTAET administration: the Land and Property Unit (LPU), responsible for land management, and the National Geodesy and Mapping Institute (NGMI), in charge of maps and other geographical support. Both institutions were mostly run by international staff, although they also had some Timorese working with them (Leigh, 2006: 3).

Following independence in 2002, most of international staff left and the LPU became part of the MoJ, first with the name of Research Office (*Gabinete de Estudos*), but soon changed to National Directorate of Land and Property (*Direcção Nacional de Terras e Propriedades*—DNTP).[6] The NGMI was integrated into the Ministry of Agriculture, Forest and Fisheries (MoAFF), with the name of Directorate of Cadastral Services (*Direcção dos Serviços de Cadastro*).[7] In 2004 this directorate was transferred to the MoJ, but remained an autonomous structure with the name of National Cartography Division (*Divisão de Cartografia Nacional*), until it was integrated into the DNTP (LLP, 2004a: 11;

6 Art. 12 of the Government Decree 3/2003. The Studies Office was never officially created, but had its own budget line in Law 3/2002.

7 The MoAFF was responsible for the 'organisation of the cadastre' (art. 12.1 of Decree-Law 3/2002). This directorate is not mentioned in the Organic Law of MoAFF (Government Decree 4/2003), but had its own budget line in Annex 1 of Law 3/2002 and Law 6/2002.

GoTL, 2007: 41), with the name of Department of Land Management and Development of Spatial Data (*Departamento de Gestão de Terras e Desenvolvimento de Dados Espaciais*).[8] With the approval of Ministerial-Decree 035/2009, the DNTP was again re-named to its current title: National Directorate of Land, Property, and Cadastral Services (*Direcção Nacional de Terras, Propriedades e Serviços Cadastrais*—DNTPSC).

Despite having part of its institutional origin in the LPU, this unit left little legacy in DNTPSC, which is much more influenced by the Indonesian National Land Agency (*Badan Pertanahan Nasional*—BPN; see Elderton, 2002: 2). A few reasons explain the BPN's much stronger influence on DNTPSC. First, the Timorese staff hired by LPU were trained by, and worked many years for, BPN (Chapter 4 and below). While these Timorese staff were not the majority, nor were they in the leadership of LPU, they became the key staff of DNTPSC after independence, when most international staff left. The merger with the Cartography Division and the hiring of more staff brought in more people trained and hired by BPN. For all of them, their previous work with BPN is their common language and their main formative professional experience. Second, the LPU left almost no legal footprint in the country (Chapter 3). Its role, structure, and processes were not regulated by any legislation, and its work was mostly bounded by internal guidelines (Chapter 3). When the LPU's international staff left after independence, most of the institution's knowledge and processes left with them. The expectations and assumptions that national staff, but also politicians and the general population, had about the role, powers, and functioning of the institution aligned much closer with their 25 years of experience with BPN than with the LPU.

This strong influence of BPN is openly acknowledged by DNTPSC's leadership, and it even inspires ongoing changes in the structure of the institution. The paramount example is the ambition of making DNTPSC independent from the MoJ, just like BPN (GoTL, 2010: 26). Unfortunately, as described in Chapter 3 and as will be visible in this chapter again, BPN—especially the BPN that the Timorese got to know during the Indonesian occupation—is not the ideal role model.

DNTPSC's goals and tasks

The goals of state institutions are not always easy to define, often being quite general and vague, and allowing for a high degree of discretion in the definition of the tasks its bureaucrats must perform (Wilson, 1989: 26, 48; Lipsky, 2010: 40). Moreover, undefined goals also leave the definition of these bureaucrats' tasks more exposed to peer and external pressures (Wilson, 1989: 48). The weak rule-of-law environment further contributes to significant discretion in

8 Art. 3.1.f and 13 of the Ministerial-Decree 035/2009.

the definition of tasks (Chapter 4). This section provides a first look at the definition of DNTPSC's goals and tasks, the high level of discretion that its staff have, and the reasons for this. These topics are further detailed below in the analysis of the structure and work of each department of DNTPSC.

The law establishes two main goals for DNTPSC: (1) the establishment of a land registry; and (2) the implementation of an efficient system of management of state property.[9] These goals are translated into a number of tasks listed in the MoJ's organic law, including establishing administrative processes for addressing land-related conflicts; managing abandoned property; developing geographical services; and promoting the drafting of land-related legislation.[10] Although with some gaps and incongruences, the tasks of each of DNTPSC's departments are further detailed in DNTPSC's Organic Law.[11]

While DNTPSC's tasks are fairly well defined in law, they do not fully match what is expected from the institution. Politicians, DNTPSC staff, and the Timorese in general assume that everything related to land tenure is DNTPSC's responsibility, paying little attention to what is written in legislation. The 'assumed' goals and tasks of the institution are even broader than the ones established in law. Adjudicating land disputes, instead of just mediating them, is in my experience the task outside DNTPSC's legal mandate most often requested. Very frequently people write letters and book appointments with DNTPSC staff, leadership, and even the minister of justice (as DNTPSC's hierarchical superior), asking them to decide in their favour in a land dispute.[12] Writing internal legal notes and external letters explaining that the minister of justice and DNTPSC staff have no power to decide land disputes, even when they have personal knowledge of the facts and details of that dispute, was a very common task in my role as legal adviser. DNTPSC can mediate land disputes (with the problems regarding formality raised below), but only the courts can adjudicate them. While DNTPSC's limited role regarding land disputes was becoming progressively clear to its staff, the letters, meetings, and frustrated expectations of outsiders remained common.[13] Whereas this 'extra-legal' task

9 Art. 1 of Ministerial Decree 035/2009. This is an MoJ's goal, delegated to DNTPSC. Among others, art. 22.1.i and 22.1.l of Decree-Law 06/2015, art. 2.l and 2.m of Decree-Law 25/2015, art. 22.1.e and 22.1.g of Decree-Law 7/2007.

10 See, among others, art. 7.1 of Decree-Law 3/2002, art. 18.2 of Decree-Law 25/2015, and Ministerial-Decree 035/2009 that establishes the Organic Law of DNTPSC. With the approval of Decree-law 4/2014, followed by Decree-Law 3/2016, some of these tasks where formally transferred to district authorities (art. 17.1.c and 17.1.d), but at the time of writing these provisions had not yet been implemented.

11 Ministerial-Decree 035/2009 that establishes the Organic Law of DNTPSC.

12 One day, I saw a tearful lady waiting at the door of DNTPSC's director office. Worried, I asked her why she was crying. She unwrapped the newspaper she had around her hand, and showing me a still bleeding hand, told me that her neighbour had bitten her due to a land dispute, and she was there to ask DNTPSC director to intervene in the case.

13 See, for instance, Suara Timor Lorosae, 16 November 2012.

was more clearly refused by DNTPSC staff, others were not, as detailed in the following sections.

Moreover, especially politicians expect and demand that DNTPSC perform its tasks all over the country. As debated in Chapter 2, the territorialisation of a formal land tenure system plays a central role in affirming the state's authority over the territory, and there is an expectation that DNTPSC can exert that authority. As this chapter shows, this expectation does not match the capacity of the institution, and results in criticisms, disappointments, and arbitrary processes when results need to be shown. The following sections provide more details about DNTPSC's goals, tasks and the discretion of its staff.

Resources

This section provides an overview of the personal, material, and financial resources available to DNTPSC. These elements highlight the conditions and limitations in which the formal land tenure system is implemented, and the outcomes of those limitations.

Human resources

Perhaps more than any other element, a look at DNTPSC's human resources can explain how the institution works and why. DNTPSC staff are the motor of the institution's day-to-day activities, but also the main creators of its institutional culture. Moreover, for many Timorese, DNTPSC staff are the only contact they have with land-related state institutions, considering that political and judicial institutions are in practice out of their reach; for many Timorese, DNTPSC staff are the face of the formal land tenure system.

The number of DNTPSC staff has been constantly growing since independence. In 2004 DNTPSC employed around 65 people, half of them working in the district offices; in 2006 it had 82 staff members (LLP, 2004a: 12; Leigh, 2006: 4). In 2019 DNTPSC had grown to 206 staff members. Contrary to what happened with the LPU before independence, and contrary to other departments in the Timorese Government, few internationals work at DNTPSC.[14] Donor projects such as the USAID LLP and INR brought internationals into DNTPSC's orbit, but they were in separate projects and only occasionally participated in DNTPSC's day-to-day activities. In 2006 there were only two AusAID foreign advisers working with DNTPSC (ibid.: 4). During the five years that I worked for the MoJ at DNTPSC (2010–2014), I was the only international working there, except for a few short-term consultants that were occasionally brought in by donors for specific tasks or studies.

Informal and formal distinctions between DNTPSC staff can help to explain its internal functioning, politics, and hierarchies. The most relevant

14 UNTAET's LPU had 15 international staff (Leigh, 2006: 3).

distinction is based on past experiences with the Indonesian BPN. Belonging to the group of Timorese that was trained by and worked with BPN during the Indonesian administration is a distinctive mark of prestige and knowledge among DNTPSC staff, and this status is invoked from time to time as a sign of authority.[15] While the members of this group make distinctions among them based on the training obtained, hierarchical level achieved during Indonesian administration, experiences, and personal quarrels, it is in general quite a close-knit group. Their specialisations vary between land management, cartography, and topography. The members of this group rotate through the leadership of different departments and district offices, have a more authoritative voice inside the institution, and also enjoy more leeway to dismiss the decisions and positions of outsiders of the group. They are also involved in the most difficult cases, even when the task commissioned is outside the competencies of the department for which they are working. Moreover, they are the main influencers on the institutional culture and the main source of socialisation for new staff (see here Lipsky, 2010: 203).

Another relevant distinction amongst DNTPSC staff is between men and women. While the DNTPSC staff includes some women (58 in 2019, around 28 percent), few of them are in leadership positions (see below), and they often are not involved in the institution's decision-making. In simple words, DNTPSC leadership is a boys club. Some examples of how this affects the work of the institution are described below.

Political affiliations also play a role in internal divisions among the staff, and while the influence of these affiliations was less visible to me, they are mentioned internally and externally as an explanation for behaviours of staff and decisions of the leadership. For instance, disagreements between the DNTPSC and MoJ's leadership were at times explained by the staff as the result of different political affiliations. A final distinction amongst DNTPSC staff is between the *permanents* and the *temporaries*, respectively, those with a permanent contract as a civil servant and those with a temporary one. In 2019 there were 139 permanent and 67 temporary staff. While it is difficult for me to say what role this distinction plays, it is definitely a marker and a source of conversations regarding who can become a permanent staff member.

The DNTPSC staff receive the normal civil servants' salary, which currently varies between 115 USD per month for the lowest rank employees and 1,880 USD for a senior national director.[16] As in other state institutions, DNTPSC *per diems* play an important role as a complement to salary and are often an incentive for something to happen. Any work trip outside of the

15 As mentioned in Chapter 4, I did not find that professional experience with LPU was a source of authority or prestige among DNTPSC staff. See Suara Timor Lorosae, 22 November 2012.

16 Decree-Law 22/2017, 24/1016, and 25/2016.

district entitles the staff to a *per diem* of 20 USD to 60 USD per day, which is a considerable bonus when compared to salaries, especially for short trips where no expenses for accommodation and meals are necessary.[17]

As in many other state institutions, staff qualifications are a major problem. Among DNTPSC staff it is possible to find graduates with land management, cartography, topography, and public administration degrees, but these qualifications are often not accompanied by the equivalent skills.[18] Especially complicated is the total mismatch between some DNTPSC's tasks and the profile and skills of the people it employs. As the sections on DNTPSC's tasks above and on internal structure below show, a considerable part of DNTPSC's work is highly dependent on legal skills (e.g., drafting lease contracts, assessing land rights, reporting cases to the court). Nevertheless, since the formation of DNTPSC, the main investment has been in people with geography-related skills such as surveyors, with little attention paid to the development of the institution's legal capacity. My personal experience was a paramount example. During the first two-and-a-half years I worked there, I was the only jurist at DNTPSC. At some point two jurists from another MoJ directorate were allocated to DNTPC but, without clear guidance from the leadership about their role, they soon went back to their original directorate. In the second half of 2013, one of these two jurists was again allocated to DNTPSC, this time with a clear mandate to work closely with me. He was a young Timorese, fluent in Tetum and Indonesian, and quite knowledgeable about the Indonesian legal system. However, his Portuguese was very limited, and he had no knowledge of English. These limitations made his work very difficult; he had difficulties understanding legislation that was not translated into Tetum (see here Chapter 5), as well as the many contracts, letters, and other documents written in Portuguese and English that were part of the daily work of DNTPSC. Moreover, he was employed as an external consultant and, for some unclear reason, instead of a long-term position he had consecutive three-month contracts, which implied a constant saga to get it renewed. Furthermore, little value was given to his work by other Timorese colleagues. We had a good working relationship, but I could see the frustration that these problems were causing him, and a new opportunity took him on a different path. When I visited Timor-Leste in 2016, 2017, and 2018, a new legal adviser had not yet been hired, so DNTPSC was working without any legal assistance. I was quickly ambushed by former colleagues with legal questions and requests, and I could only imagine how much the legality of DNTPSC's procedures had decreased.

The difficulties of finding (skilled) jurists in the country can only partially explain this mismatch between tasks and skills. A look at DNTPSC's leadership

17 Art. 11 of Decree-Law 20/2010.

18 On the mismatch between qualifications and skills, see Psychas, 2010: 80.

further explains it. This leadership is mostly formed by the initial group that worked for BPN, all trained in geography-related skills such as surveying. As the saying goes, for a man with a hammer, everything looks like a nail. Based on their own skills, DNTPSC's leadership sees land administration much more based on maps and land surveys than on laws, contracts, and rule of law. This vision is reflected in the people they hire and how tasks are performed. I do not mean with this that DNTPSC leadership completely ignores the need for jurists in their ranks, but jurists and laws are not their top priorities. Wilson states that '[staff members of an institution] are not blank slates on which the organisation can write at will'; their performance and their impact on the institution will be in part influenced by their past experiences (1989: 55). The DNTPSC is a living example of the influence of past experiences.

Material resources

The work of DNTPSC is dependent on material resources such as buildings, office equipment, specific gear for the geographic work (e.g., GPSs, total-stations, theodolites), and vehicles for field trips. While, since 2007, the supply of material resources has improved with the growing access to oil and gas money (Chapter 4), problems with planning, procurement, and maintenance still complicate the work of the institution.[19]

DNTPSC's headquarters provides a good example of the problems with material resources, and a good allegory about the institution.[20] The building, built from scratch in 2010, was designed with little consideration for the tasks of the institution, its internal structure and functioning, and its future needs. Less than five years after construction, the number of staff had already out-grown the capacity of the building, and one department was working in prefabricated houses installed in the backyard. Furthermore, with the number of staff growing annually, people became more and more encroached on by additional desks, cabinets, and colleagues. Important documents and equipment were

19 DNTPSC's 2006 budget was around 245,000 USD while in 2015 was close to 1.7 million USD (excluding SNC's costs).

20 The design of public administration buildings in Timor-Leste could be the topic of a thesis. I became aware of this when I visited the office of the Dili district notary. It had just been built from scratch, in the middle of a large plot of urban land, with a floorplan more suited to a normal house than an office. For some reason, most staff were crowded into a single room, together with desks, cabinets, and piles of paper, while the rest of the building was nearly empty. Moreover, clients were not allowed inside; instead, they had to line up outside, without shelter from rain or sun, and were served through an awning window kept open with a stick. During my short visit, the window slammed shut on several customers who inadvertently touched the stick keeping it open. In summary, a building designed from scratch had no consideration for the work done there, nor the wellbeing of its staff and clients. To my shock, I was informed that 12 identical buildings had been built in the other district capitals.

also stored in shipping containers at the back of the building.[21] Maybe more importantly, DNTPSC headquarters was not designed with its clients in mind. The national headquarters should mostly coordinate the district activities, but in practice a considerable part of the work happens there, especially the work related to Dili district. However, the building is not prepared to receive dozens of visitors per day. Besides an entry hall where a receptionist registers the name of the visitors, and a row of chairs in front of the director's office, there is no space for clients to wait, leaving them wandering the building.

The building also provides some examples of problems with procurement, planning, and maintenance. Especially in 2010, power cuts were common, some lasting for a few minutes and others for several hours. DNTPSC had a new generator, but it didn't have an automatic switch, so every time there was a power cut it had to be turned on manually. However, only one person had the key to start the generator. Sometimes this person was at work, other times not, and in his absence the entire institution would stop, sometimes for the rest of the day. Throughout 2010 I pushed management to procure an automatic switch for the generator, but the budget for this switch was never approved by the MoJ. Other times the generator could not work because there was no fuel. When I left my job, the generator was broken, due to lack of regular maintenance.

Procurement, access to, and maintenance of vehicles is also problematic. New vehicles figure in most requests for new equipment, and entitlement to a car or a motorbike is a sought-after job bonus and source of heated debates. I recall a meeting where a government member patronisingly explained to DNTPSC staff the importance of periodically checking and replacing the oil of the vehicles. At the end of 2014, more than 20 DNTPSC cars, all now unusable, were lined up in the parking lot to be auctioned as scrap. Computers, printers, and surveyor's equipment are also affected by limited maintenance and replacement. However, maintenance is also affected by very practical problems. For instance, computer software and updates can only be acquired online with credit cards, which DNTPSC and the MoJ do not have.

In conclusion, although DNTPSC produces a considerable amount of work every day (see below), material limitations considerably affect the capacity and quality of that work.

Financial resources

DNTPSC's financial resources come entirely from the MoJ's annual budget. In fact, DNTPSC collects a considerable amount of money from the lease of state land (e.g., 3 million USD in 2015), but it cannot appropriate this

21 I was told that valuable documentation recovered from the wreckage left by the Indonesian troops in 1999 was being stored in these containers, but I never got access to it.

revenue. Each year DNTPSC proposes its budget to the minister of justice, who changes and includes it as part of the MoJ's budget proposed to the government, which is again debated and adjusted in parliament as part of the annual budget. As a result, DNTPSC has little control over which of its activities get funded. Budget execution is problematic throughout government institutions, and DNTPSC is no exception (GoTL and World Bank, 2013: 15). Poorly considered annual plans and interference from MoJ's hierarchy in refusing some of the planned and budgeted activities are some of the explanations for this problem.

In summary, DNTPSC has little incentive to upgrade its services to get more revenues and to streamline its expenses. Little control of its budget, but also problems with planning of activities and execution of the budget, make institutional administration quite difficult.

Internal structure

This section provides a look into DNTPSC organisational design, distribution of formal and informal tasks, administrative procedures, and work methods, showing what DNTPSC does and why, and highlighting the large discretion that its staff have in their work, both at the procedural and decision-making levels. As described above, the DNTPSC is one of the six national directorates of the MoJ, and is composed of the national office located in Dili and 13 district offices located in each district capital, including also Dili (in addition to the national office). This section starts by looking at four of the five departments of the national office, followed by an analysis of the district offices.[22]

Department for Attribution of Land Titles and [coordination of] Land Disputes

The Department for Attribution of Land Titles and [coordination of] Land Disputes (*Departamento de Atribuição de Títulos e Disputa de Terras—DATDT*) is by law responsible for (1) coordinating the process of land titling, and (2) supervising the activities of land dispute mediation in the district offices (art. 10 of Ministerial-Decree 035/2009). However, what this department does in practice is quite different from what is established in law.

Regarding land titling, this department was quite active during the one-year period established by Law 1/2003 for holders of land rights issued by previous administrations to present their land claims (Chapter 6). The department was responsible for receiving, cataloguing, and storing these claims, and relied on the support of the LLP to implement these tasks. With these claims falling into a legal limbo, this activity stopped, and since then they simply store these

22 I skip the Administration Department because it has no direct role in land administration.

documents and search for specific claims when necessary. However, some of these land claims have disappeared from the files. The department's role in land registration has become further limited since 2008 when land registration was delegated to INR and later to SNC.

Regarding disputes, the department staff do not limit themselves to coordinating and overseeing the mediation of disputes in the district offices but also conduct mediations themselves. UNTAET the LLP provided training in dispute resolution and established dispute resolution units in each district office (Fitzpatrick, 2008: 181). But since then many of the trained staff moved to other functions and jobs, and the number of qualified mediators providing mediation services has decreased.[23] Besides the lack of qualified staff, the mediations provided by this department also have a legal issue. Parts of these agreements have to be notarised in order to be valid, but this legal obligation is not followed, which makes these agreements legally void (CES-OPJ and CRL, 2017: 84).[24] I raised this problem a number of times with the chief of department, who was quite aware of it, but despite his worries there was little that he could do to address the issue, due to the very limited number of notaries in the country (Chapter 6).

This department also receives sporadic land claims from individuals. However, these sporadic claims are not part of any legal process, and DNTPSC takes no action after receiving these claims, making them useless. I asked a few times what the basis and purpose of this practice was, but never got a convincing answer. I got the impression that it is, at least, a way of getting rid of demanding and noisy clients, by giving them the illusion that something is happening to their claims.

The most problematic task of this department is the issuing of *recommendations*. This task has no legal basis in the law and fits well in the concept of semi-formal land tenure system debated in Chapter 2. The recommendation is a document issued at the request of individuals, in which DNTPSC attests that, according to the documents submitted by the applicant and occasionally a visit to the site in question, the applicant is the owner of a specific parcel of land. In the document, a disclaimer says that the recommendation is only an 'evidence document' based on what the DNTPSC was able to assess, and it is not a land title.

Although it can sound harmless, the issuing of recommendations is quite problematic, and a good example of the consequences of arbitrary administrative processes not regulated by law. First, these recommendations have no legal

23 For instance, in 2013 this department was able to successfully mediate ten disputes. In 67 other mediations they recommended to take the case to court.

24 By law, any transfer of land rights must be notarised (Chapter 6). Therefore, mediation agreements that involve the transfer of land rights must also be notarised. A law on mediation was drafted by the LLP, but never approved (LLP, 2004: 5).

basis, nor is the process for issuing them regulated by law. Besides the blunt illegality of conducting arbitrary administrative processes, the approach followed can harm other land claimants, considering that the DNTPSC strengthens one party's claim without other claimants being informed of, nor heard during, the process of issuing the recommendation. Second, I cannot remember a single recommendation request in which the right claimed by the applicant was not tainted by legal issues that DNTPSC could not legally address nor overlook. For instance, applicants claimed to have inherited the land, but there was no formal inheritance process, therefore making it impossible to say if he or she was the rightful heir. Another example was land sales without the legally mandated notarised deed (Chapter 6). Third, these recommendations are the perfect ground for rent-seeking. I heard several reports of illegal fees being charged for the issuing of these recommendations. Even if the fees were appropriated by DNTPSC, they would still be illegal, as the law clearly states that fees for services can only be charged when explicitly established by law, which is not the case.[25]

The weakness of the mechanisms for control of legality (Chapter 4) and the possibility of personal gains only partially explains why DNTPSC staff are comfortable with this illegal practice; a deeper look into its origins can explain it further. First, the recommendations are quite similar to the 'declaration letters' (*surat pernyatann)* issued by Indonesian authorities, without any legal basis, attesting that one lives on a specific parcel of land.[26] Therefore, these recommendations are similar to a practice that people were already familiar with. Second, people demand that DNTPSC issues these recommendations or other documents as a way of strengthening their land tenure or justifying their position in a land deal. From what I observed during my time with DNTPSC, most of these requests come from elite members of society that are not interested in 'details' such as lack of legal framework and who use their power and influence to push DNTPSC staff to issue these recommendations. Third, these illegal recommendations are also requested by other government institutions (Nixon, 2011: 241). For instance, the National Directorate of Edifications demands that people obtain these recommendations as part of the process of issuing construction permits. However, the rules of the process for obtaining a construction permit and the criteria to issue them, like DNTPSC's recommendations, are pure inventions of its staff, without any legal basis to support them. A similar thing happens with the notaries; in the few cases that notaries are involved in land transactions, they demand a recommendation from DNTPSC, although both this requisite, and the recommendations themselves, are not established in

25 Art. 8 of Decree-Law 32/2008.

26 In the words of Reerink, 'It is common for people to come to the offices and ask for such documentation. Officials are reluctant to deny such a request, probably also because they can earn some pocket money with it' (2011: 105).

law. All these external factors make it even more difficult for DNTPSC's staff to not issue these recommendations.

I was often approached by staff of this department to give my legal opinion about recommendations, and I repeatedly alerted the DNTPSC National Director about the illegality of the practice. He was concerned about this, and a few times attempted to gather the counterparts from the National Directorate of Edifications and National Directorate of Registries and Notaries to debate the issue. But a lack of replies, a certain inertia that characterises Timorese public administration, and no consequences for illegal practices left the problem unsolved.

Department of Administration of Immovable Property of the State

The Department of Administration of Immovable Property of the State (*Departamento de Administração de Bens Imóveis do Estado*—DABIE) is responsible for DNTPSC's two most visible tasks: (1) the award and administration of lease contracts and (2) evictions from state land (art. 12 of Ministerial-Decree 035/2009). As happens with other departments, these tasks should be conducted by the district offices, with the national office only coordinating and supervising. However, especially in Dili, most of these contracts and eviction processes are done by the national office.

The lease of state land gives this department a central role in the institution. The unclear Timorese formal land tenure system makes lease contracts with the state the safest way of legally accessing land (Chapter 6), which brings many individuals, business owners, CSOs, embassies, and international organisations to this department for obtaining a lease. In 2006 the department was managing around 400 lease contracts (Leigh, 2006: 10); currently it reports managing close to 3,000.[27] However, several problems complicate the work of this department in awarding and managing lease contracts.

The first problem is in the awarding of these contracts. The law provides little guidance on how and to whom these contracts should be awarded (Almeida, 2016: 19). The only clear rule is that contracts for medium and large investments must be preceded by a public tender, but this rule is systematically ignored.[28] The process of awarding lease contracts is totally informal, and can

27 In the first years after independence a Special Lease Programme was created, aimed at regularising the occupation of state and abandoned land since 2000 by national citizens for residential purposes. This program allowed for simplified one-year lease contracts (automatically renewed), with a monthly rent of 10 USD (Sousa, 2005: 7; Leigh, 2006: 10). The programme was later implemented outside Dili, with a rent of 5 USD. A total of 3,030 contracts were signed, 2,903 in Dili. However, this programme was never backed up by any legislation. After the 2006 crisis, a public statement by the Minister of Justice, Lúcia Lobato, was interpreted by the beneficiaries as a suspension of the programme; no more rents under these leases were paid nor contracts signed.

28 To my knowledge there is one single case where the public tender process was followed.

be loosely divided into two main approaches. In some cases, a specific parcel of land is randomly identified by DNTPSC as state land and the occupants are compelled to sign a lease contract with the state, or face an eviction. In other cases, the person interested in leasing a specific land parcel requests DNTPSC to lease it. Without clear guidelines for this process, personal and political connections, status, and means of pressure play a central role in obtaining a lease contract. For instance, it is common that people request meetings with the minister of justice, DNTPSC director, or chiefs of department to push forward their lease process. Others come to DNTPSC claiming to have the support of authoritative figures such as the prime minister or a veteran association, as a way of pressing officials to work on their lease (Chapter 4).

There are cases in which the land requested to be leased is occupied by other people. This results in other arbitrary approaches: sometimes the lease is refused; other times the occupants are evicted, sometimes with some compensation, other times with nothing; there are also cases in which compensation to the occupants is paid by the future tenant.[29] These different outcomes depend on factors such as who the occupants are, the political position and contacts of the future tenant, and the budget and calendar of the project to be implemented on the land. For instance, if the occupant is a war veteran, he or she will likely not be evicted without the payment of a considerable compensation (see below). This arbitrariness is obviously an opportunity for corruption and rent-seeking, but it is also a source of frustration and complications for DNTPSC staff. For instance, one DNTPSC staff member explained to me how their position becomes complicated when, to rush the eviction, future tenants promise land occupants compensation and jobs in the projects to be carried out on the acquired land, but then fail to keep their promises, and later DNTPSC staff are the targets of the complaints.[30]

The negotiation, drafting, and general management of lease contracts are a second set of problems. Regarding negotiation, while the law establishes some limits on lease contract clauses (e.g., the state does not pay any compensation for improvements made to the property), it leaves many other points dependent on negotiation between the parties (e.g., the specific duration of the lease within the maximum limits). This lack of regulation, paired with lack of transparent internal procedures, leave DNTPSC clients exposed to unregulated discretion. For instance, one tenant can get a 30-year lease contract, while the tenant next door only gets a three-year contract, without any justification

29 One director told me that he had instructed the staff to not mediate these transactions between future tenants and occupants, to prevent collection of personal fees. However, he did not report any illegal collection of fees to the public prosecutor.

30 A common practice among Timorese business elites is to use their contacts to secure a lease of state land for a specific investment project, and then try to find an international investor to take over the project. If an investor is not found, there is no incentive to follow through with promises made to those evicted.

for this disparity. Furthermore, this is another open door to rent-seeking and corruption.

The drafting of lease contracts is also problematic. The contracts are drafted in Portuguese, by the department's staff, who copy-paste and adapt previous contracts; when the tenant is an embassy, international organisation, or a foreign investor, the contract is also drafted in English. However, few members of the department speak Portuguese or English to the level required to understand such contracts, and none of them has legal training. The consequence is obvious: the quality of these contracts is low, with gaps, contradictory—and at times illegal—clauses that result in uncertainty and conflict regarding the rights and obligations of tenants and the landlord. To obviate problems in negotiating and drafting contracts, I proposed to develop Tetum contract templates to be formally established as the standard contract, and regulate a process in case of exceptions, but these measures were never implemented.

The administration of these contracts is another difficult problem. The signed paper versions and support documents are kept in individual folders inside cabinets, some in the main room of the department, others in a small archive room. But the capacity of these cabinets has long been exceeded, and unstable piles of folders cover their tops and the floor of the room. There is no digitisation of documents, and the electronic files are scattered through different computers and pen-drives. All the lease contracts and the current status of rent payments are listed in one Excel file that is kept by one staff member. As a result, the loss of documents and the unclear status of leases are regular problems, leading to loss of revenues, disputes with tenants, and uncertainty regarding the status of contracts. Furthermore, administration of leases is another area vulnerable to rent-seeking and corruption. In theory, rent should be paid at the bank, but I heard reports of rent being paid to staff directly in cash (see here Leigh and Nixon, 2005: 11). The authority to sign lease contracts brings a third set of problems that is analysed in the section on leadership.

Evictions from state land is the second task of this department. These evictions are often controversial, raising justified criticism from CSOs, media, and academics. Besides the lack of any social assessment and resettlement alternatives, evictions are often conducted at dawn, without any previous warning about the date and time, and with the use of force and destruction of property. Although DNTPSC staff are often blamed for these harsh evictions, a few limitations, problems, and dilemmas can in part explain them.

As described in Chapter 6, the eviction process was harshly regulated by Law 1/2003, specifically establishing that no compensation due to eviction should be paid, allowing the use of force with no clear restrictions, and providing almost no safeguards except for a weak appeals process.[31] It is the role of politicians, not DNTPSC staff, to establish clear rules and limits on evictions,

31 The Land Law slightly changed the legal framework (Chapter 6).

social assessments, resettlement plans, and compensation. Furthermore, there are no internal guidelines or procedures to guide staff in the eviction process, nor do they receive any training in this regard. When no guidance is provided, it is only normal that staff will follow the paths that they know from Indonesian times and which work easier for them (Chapter 4). I understood this when I asked one DNTPSC staff member why they were doing evictions at 4 or 5 am, and without letting people know that they were coming. His explanation was quite illustrative of how, from the perspective of a street-level bureaucrat like him, this was the logical thing to do. They go early in the morning to make sure that people are at home and therefore can remove their belongings from the house; and they don't give any clear date for the eviction because they experienced several situations in which evictees were prepared to repel them with stones, machetes, and guns, and therefore it is less risky for DNTPSC staff if they arrive by surprise.

With this lack of guidance, the outcome of an eviction process depends on arbitrary factors such as the urgency of obtaining the land, the evictees, and the entity that is getting access to the land after the eviction. Powerful and tenacious evictees are more likely to delay or even stop an eviction or receive a considerable amount of compensation but, in the ambiguous world of DNTPSC's informal processes, the luck of evictees also depends on who is promoting the eviction process. For instance, in my visits in 2016 and 2017, DNTPSC staff told me how they were being pressed by a few ministers to start a large-scale eviction in Tasi Tolu (Dili), to make room for a five-star resort. They told me that many residents in that area were war veterans and members of the police and army, and therefore they were afraid of evicting them. They had been refusing to start the eviction before having enough public political backing, for instance through a decision from the Council of Ministers.[32]

The personal views and feelings of the staff involved also play a role in evictions. I've heard staff complain that DNTPSC should not simply evict people without offering them an alternative, but unfortunately, they must follow the orders of their superiors. On the other hand, I also heard staff bragging about their toughness in applying the law, regardless of the consequences for the affected people, because the law should be followed without question. DNTPSC staff tend to be less accommodating if they suspect that land occupants have already received state compensation in the process created after the 2006 crisis for supporting the return of internally displaced people. Rough eviction processes are also the result of exasperation. DNTPSC staff often talk about cases where land parcels were occupied by new occupants one or two days after previous occupants had been evicted, necessitating yet another eviction by DNTPSC.

32 Regarding disobedience of orders by street-level bureaucrats to avoid dangers and discomfort, see Lipsky, 2010: 18.

As with lease contracts, the lack of qualified staff, such as administrators and jurists, further complicates the evictions process. For instance, the notification given to evictees are copy-pasted versions of previous notifications, with random adaptations made by the staff. Often these notifications do not comply with the general requirements of administrative law, such as clearly stating the legal basis for the eviction and providing information about the redress mechanisms available.[33] Furthermore, it is common that notifications are written in Portuguese, despite the language not being understood by both most DNTPSC staff and the evictees. I suggested, and even prepared, bilingual templates for these notifications, but the need to adapt them to each specific case, and general administrative disorganisation meant that the template system never lasted very long. Legal skills are not, however, the only limitations of the department. For instance, no member of staff has a social-work background, so if any social assessment of the impact of an eviction was even considered, it could not be implemented.

In summary, although this department carries out the tasks given to it by law, it does so with great discretion due to the limitations of resources, some unregulated aspects of the law, but also the lack of consequences for not following legal prescriptions.

Department of Cadastre, Information and Land Valuation

While the law gives an extensive list of tasks to the Department of Cadastre, Information and Land Valuation (*Departamento de Cadastro, Informação e Avaliação*), in practice this department conducts three main tasks (art. 11 of Ministerial-Decree 35/2009).[34] The first is to produce small maps of individual land parcels that are used as attachments in lease contracts, recommendations, and other documents. The quality of these maps varies, and no technical standards or legal basis for their production was ever established, although setting these standards in law is an aspiration of DNTPSC staff.

A second task of this department is what its staff calls 'identification and technical survey' (*identifikasaun no levantamentu tékniku* in Tetum), through which they identify whether a parcel of land belongs to the state, to lease it or allocate it to another state institution. The process for these identifications has no legal basis and is done through a short visit to the site and a talk with occupants, local authorities, and any passers-by, followed by a report summarising the findings. This work is done by land surveyors without any legal expertise. At times, senior staff of other departments with knowledge about the land in question or contacts in that area are included in the team doing an identification. The systematic cadastral survey for collection of land claims,

33 Art. 27 and 42 of Decree-Law 32/2008.

34 Some tasks legally given to this department were taken up by INR and SNC.

established by Decree-Law 27/2011 and now the Land Law, is ignored by this department.[35] The discretion that this informal task gives to the department staff is especially useful for them when the objective is to get access to land for state projects or private investments. With little or no participation of land claimants, the staff of this department quickly define that a piece of land belongs to the state, leaving to those harmed by this decision the very difficult task of fighting it.

The third task of this department is land valuation, which is done for two different purposes. The first is to establish the rent price of leases of state land. The price of rents is, in theory, determined through a formula created in 2005 by the LLP and AusAID (Leigh and Nixon, 2005; Leigh, 2006: 6). Besides the geographical and temporal limitations of this formula—it is only applicable in Dili and was never updated since its creation—it was never formalised, leaving tenants without any information about how their rent value was calculated. The second type of land valuation that, in theory, should be done by this department is valuation for expropriation of land by the state. However, there is no legislation about land valuation nor the profession of land valuer, and the department has no qualified staff members for this task.[36] As described by Leigh, even the staff that worked for the Indonesian BPN did not have any real experience of determining market values, '"value" was the amount of money that the staff were told (by a higher authority) that something was worth' (2006: 4).[37] The same continues to happen today, as the case described in Chapter 9 shows. As in the previously studied department (DATDT), also here the staff members have significant discretion in their work.

Department of Land Management and Development of Spatial Data

The Department of Land Management and Development of Spatial Data (*Departamento de Gestão de Terras e Desenvolvimento de Dados Espaciais*) is located in the much quieter third floor of the building. This department is responsible for larger-scale geographical activities, such as the production of maps and delimitation of national and administrative boundaries. This department had an intense period of work while the land border with Indonesia was being delimited, but now that this task is mostly finished, the department have relatively few activities.

35 In the last few years there were situations in which the department incorporated some of the steps required by this legislation in its process of identification. See the case described in Chapter 9 and the Announcement (*Aviso*) No. 01/GSETP/I/2016 published on 15 January 2016 in the Official Journal.

36 The reduced land market and the lack of a land registry where the value of land transactions can be studied makes land valuation especially difficult. On these problems, see McDermott, 2018.

37 See here Chapter 6 regarding land valuation tables in the Land Law and Expropriation Law.

District offices

David Hicks describes the 'dysfunctional relationship between the capital, Dili, and the rest of the country, its hinterland' (2007). A visit to one of the 13 DNTPSC district offices in each district capital provides a clear example of this dysfunctionality and is enough to understand the disproportionate expectations that politicians especially put on DNTPSC.

The number of staff members in district offices varies, but it is usually a maximum of seven, including the district director. While the position of district director attracts some of DNTPSC's seniors, the rest of the staff members are usually less qualified than their counterparts in the national office. Regarding material resources, while every district office has now a new building, they experience several limitations, such as a lack of computers, generators, fuel, and vehicles (Nixon, 2005: 18). On a good day, a district office has one or two functioning motorbikes to serve the entire district. One district director told me that he was lucky his staff were willing to use their personal motorbikes for work, because otherwise the reach of the office's work would be very limited. For instance, he had not yet gone to an area where a major state infrastructure project was being built because he had no transportation to get there. Regarding budget and expenses, the district offices are dependent on the national office, both to propose and execute the budget, and at least officially because district offices have no source of independent income.

The resource shortages that district offices experience limit the work that they can do, and many activities in their districts are undertaken by the national office, at times not even involving the staff of district offices. Identifications and technical surveys, lease contracts of large parcels of land, and evictions are often planned, negotiated, and executed by the national office. This removes resources and incentives for improving the activities at district level. As a result of these limitations and lack of support, the amount and quality of work produced by the district offices are understandably low, and consist mostly of small-scale surveys, preparation of some small-scale leases, and a few mediations.[38]

Except for the Dili district office, the image I have of DNTPSC district offices is that the staff working there feel less empowered when compared with the staff at national level, and their views of the role of DNTPSC and the state in land administration are much more limited. Generally speaking, I got the impression that their embeddedness in these smaller local communities and the limitations of their offices force them to be more realistic and to negotiate much more their official position with their role as a community member.[39] In some cases, especially if the district director comes from another district, his or her position can be quite isolated. One episode made me particularly

38 See Suara Timor Lorosae, 16 November 2012.

39 On this topic, see the points raised by Crewe and Axelby, 2013: 59.

aware of their isolation. During a visit to a district office, and after a long conversation, I asked the DNTPSC district director where I could go for lunch. He replied that he didn't know, because since he had moved to that district he never went out for lunch or dinner. The reason was quite frightening. He had been advised by other DNTPSC staff that he should never eat out, because in their position they tend to gain enemies, and eating at a restaurant was a good opportunity for these enemies to poison them.

Leadership

This section looks at the DNTPSC's leadership, showing how the way it is structured and the background of its leaders have a clear influence on the work developed by the institution.[40] But before analysing DNTPSC leadership, I should make two clarifications. First, the distinction between street-level bureaucrats and managers made by Lipsky is considerably more diluted in the case of DNTPSC (Lipsky, 2010; see also Wilson, 1989: 27). The relatively small size of the institution when compared with equivalent ones in other countries and the very centralised decision-making exposes its leadership (i.e., chiefs of departments, directors, and at times even ministers) to direct contact with the institution's clients. In other words, although to different degrees, DNTPSC's leadership are also in part street-level bureaucrats that deal with and take decisions about individual cases. Second, the high level of discretion that I describe in this chapter happens throughout the processes conducted by DNTPSC and go all the way from the procedures and criteria invented by the staff on the ground to the final decisions of the leadership.

Regarding DNTPSC's leadership structure, the very hierarchical and centralised institutional design is a source of problems and controversies. Internally, each DNTPSC district office is headed by a *District Director*, and at the national office each department is headed by a *Chief of Department*. Their roles are to coordinate the staff under their supervision, but with little power to take significant decisions. For instance, a chief of department cannot sign a lease nor order an eviction and cannot visit a district office without the travel expenses being approved by the *National Director* of DNTPSC. However, the role of *National Director* of DNTPSC is also difficult. While the director heads DNTPSC, the organisation has been part of MoJ since independence, and therefore under the direct orders of the *Minister of Justice*. The separation of tasks between the director and the minister has always been difficult. Yet, since 2010 the leadership at MoJ has been divided between a minister and *vice minister*, and in 2012 a *State Secretary for Land and Property* (*Secretário de Estado*

40 I follow here Esman's definition of leadership as 'the group of persons who are actively engaged in the formulation of the doctrine and programme of the institution and who direct its operations and relationships with the environment' (1967: 3). See also Blase, 1973: 267.

de Terras e Propriedades, SETP), the latter with the role of politically overseeing DNTPSC on behalf of the minister of justice.[41] The distribution of powers between all of these leaders was never clarified in more detail by law or internal rules, resulting in power struggles and constant confusion regarding who has the power to do what. Interference from other political figures and powerful elites in DTNPSC further confuses the work and leadership of the institution (Nixon, 2011: 241; Nixon, 2012: 158).

The signing of lease contracts of state property is a clear example of this problem with leadership. District directors are not authorised to sign any leases, so all contracts must be sent to the national office to be signed there.[42] At the national office the chief of the department responsible for managing state land is also not authorised to sign any leases. During the entire time I worked with the MoJ, the authority to sign lease contracts was disputed between the minister, vice minister, state secretary, and the director of DNTPSC, sometimes with people claiming this authority for themselves, other times pushing it to others. Several times I suggested that the competency for signing lease contracts should be clarified and formalised through an internal rule, but despite my insistence, this never happened. I even drafted the regulation, only leaving blank the lease periods and land areas above which the lease should be signed by a hierarchical superior, but with no success. The result of this confusion was that leases went unsigned for months and at times were considered invalid and 'recalled' from the tenants after being signed. When I asked around why it was so difficult to solve this problem, a hold on power and personal gains were not the only explanations. Some leaders expressed concerns that they could be later blamed for corrupt activities of their subordinates and therefore had to keep tight control of the signing of these leases. Others expressed a different view: they didn't want to have this power and responsibility and were even scared of being blamed by their superiors for wrongdoing and therefore were avoiding signing these leases.[43] In some cases even people external to the MoJ and DNTPSC contributed to this problem. There was at least one case in which the lease of a large parcel of state urban land to a foreign company was negotiated by the Ministry of Commerce and authorised by the Council

41 The position of state secretary (*secretário de estado*) is not equivalent to political positions with the same name in other countries. In Timor-Leste a state secretary is subordinate to a minister or the prime minister and has a specific portfolio.

42 DNTPSC staff told me that previously that district directors could sign lease contracts, but some of them 'misbehaved', and the Minister of Justice Ana Pessoa took this competence from them.

43 An informant described to me how, during Alkatiri's government (2002–2007), hundreds of lease contracts were piled up for months on the table of the minister of justice, waiting for authorisation from the prime minister to be signed (see Sousa, 2005: 6). The embeddedness of centralised processes of decision became clear to me when, during a meeting, the minister of justice complained about a national director (of another directorate) sending a request to buy new curtains for her office, just days after the minister had sent an internal order delegating procurement powers for smaller expenses on national directors.

of Ministers. When this contract started to raise controversy in the media, the MoJ and DNTPSC did not even have a copy of the signed lease.[44]

Apart from these disputes, a look at the background of DNTPSC and MoJ's leaderships further helps to understand the work of DNTPSC. With one exception, all DNTPSC national directors until now have belonged to the group of people trained by the Indonesian BPN, and most chiefs of department are also from this group, which keep rotating through different leadership positions. Except for a few district directors, all leadership positions are occupied by men. On the other hand, the leadership of MoJ, hierarchically superior to DNTPSC, has been taken mostly by jurists, and already three women have occupied the position of Minister of Justice (Ana Pessoa, Lúcia Lobato, and Ângela Carrascalão). These differences between the leadership of DNTPSC and the MoJ lead to conflicts that I observed in my work and later confirmed in interviews.[45] DNTPSC staff complain that the MoJ's leadership does not understand land administration, especially technical matters. For instance, for many years DNTPSC staff included the acquisition of expensive satellite imagery of the country in the annual budget, but the expense was always refused by MoJ's leadership. On the other hand, the MoJ's leadership complained that DNTPSC staff claim to know everything about land administration, and call themselves 'technicians' and 'experts', but in practice their knowledge is outdated, and their work in land administration far from ideal. In case of disagreements between DNTPSC staff and the MoJ's leadership, a high degree of noncompliance can be expected. By simply ignoring orders or cunningly delaying actions, DNTPSC staff and its leadership make their views prevail (see here Lipsky, 2010: 16).

As the examples above show, these leadership problems result in various inefficiencies and institutional problems that are reflected in DNTPSC's work.

DNTPSC's clients

This section looks at DNTPSC's *clients*, meaning all people and institutions that use its services. This includes ministries and other state institutions, companies, international organisations, embassies, and the general population. As detailed above, the analysis of DNTPSC's clients includes their *interest* and *access* to the institution, as well as DNTPSC's *reach* and *enforcement* capabilities.

Regarding *interest*, there are three main reasons for clients to contact DNTPSC: (1) to obtain legal access to state land (e.g., through a lease), (2)

44 Replying to appeals from evictions is another area where it is not clear if the SETP took over the powers previously given to the minister of justice by Law 1/2003 (art. 7.2). The practical result is that many appeals never get a reply (Timor Post, 28 September 2015).

45 Although I never specifically asked about this topic, it is my impression that the authority of female ministers was received worse by DNTPSC leadership when compared with male ministers.

to attempt to formalise or further secure their land tenure (e.g., recommendations), and (3) to seek help in a land-related dispute resolution (e.g., mediation request). However, there are also situations in which DNTPSC contacts clients: to challenge their land tenure (e.g., claiming that the land belongs to the state), to acquire land (e.g., expropriations), and to systematically collect land claims (see Chapter 6). The capital, Dili, is by far the place where people refer most to DNTPSC, but also where the institution is most active in reaching out to its clients, whereas the populations outside of the capital rely much more on customary systems for land management (Chapter 8).

Regarding *access* to DNTPSC services, physical distance is a problem for those clients that are not located in the district capitals where DNTPSC has its offices. However, due to the very centralised decision-making, physical distance is in many cases a problem for everyone outside Dili. Informal 'fees' further limit clients' access to DNTPSC services. The lower socio-economic status of poor populations, DNTPSC's arbitrary processes, and clients' unclear knowledge about the powers and limitations of the institution further confuse potential clients (see above). In this regard, it is revealing that DNTPSC puts no effort into public information campaigns about its roles and services (ICG, 2010: 10). As with many other Timorese public institutions, DNTPSC is very inwardly focused, with little consideration for the improvement of the quantity and quality of services provided.[46] One final element that further scares potential clients away from DNTPSC is the risk that, by raising awareness about their land tenure situation, potential clients can in fact complicate their land tenure position, for instance, by DNTPSC declaring that their land belongs to the state.

However, and despite the hurdles that clients have to go through to obtain services from DNTPSC, the institution is still approached by a considerable number of people, especially in Dili. The *reach* and *enforcement* of its decisions, or in other words the effective power of the institution, can in part explain this. As detailed in this chapter, the general perception of the institution's mandate is much wider than what is established in law. Therefore, a document issued by DNTPSC strengthening someone's land claim or a decision determining that a parcel of land belongs to the state carries a considerable weight, both among the population and state institutions, even when those decisions are contested. In many situations this brings a value to DNTPSC services that outweighs the lack of legality and the difficulties of obtaining those documents, at least for those that can afford to invest the necessary time, effort, and money. The lack of other alternatives, such as effective courts and legal aid services (Chapter 4),

46 See, for instance, Suara Timor Lorosae, 19 October 2015, regarding public services at the National Directorate of Notaries and Registries. Lack of care for clients is a common criticism for many institutions working on land administration worldwide (Enemark *et al.*, 2015: 98).

further attract people to DNTPSC in search of solutions for their land-related problems.

In summary, despite the problems that DNTPSC's clients have in accessing it, the reach and enforcement of DNTPSC's decisions makes its services attractive to those that can go through these hurdles. The low sense of responsibility for its clients, the little accountability of staff for the work delivered, the low expectations of the Timorese for government services, and the many problems and dilemmas identified above provide little incentive to improve DNTPSC's quality of service delivery (see here Lipsky, 2010: 178).

The following section provides an overview of the external institutions that somehow influence the work of DNTPSC. The final section of this chapter provides some final conclusions about DNTPSC in relation to their role in the Timorese formal land tenure system.

External institutions

As mentioned in the introduction, the implementation of the formal land tenure system is also participated in by a few institutions external to the state. This section provides a brief analysis of the INR and SNC projects, international organisations, and CSOs working on land-related issues.

Ita Nia Rai (INR) and National Cadastre System (SNC)

As summarised in Chapter 3, since 2007 DNTPSC's task of developing a systematic land-claims process was first supported by USAID's Ita Nia Rai project (INR), and later by National Cadastre System (SNC), a project outsourced by the government to a consortium of Timorese and Portuguese companies. This section adds to the points debated in Chapter 3 about INR and SNC, providing a brief look at the relationship of these two projects with DNTPSC, and the work developed by them.

Ita Nia Rai (INR)

The INR project was designed to work inside DNTPSC, in cooperation with its staff, and contribute to the institution's staff training and development of internal processes, but the project was strongly opposed by DNTPSC's senior staff from the national office.[47] The main reason invoked was the methodology used by INR to survey land boundaries. DNTPSC staff argued that, if instead of INR-trained staff, professional land surveyors like them were used in the land-claims process, the accuracy of the surveyed boundaries would be more accurate. INR's argument that more accuracy would cost more time and

47 Haburas Foundation and Rede ba Rai (2013) has a detailed study of INR.

money, and that the trade-off between accuracy and time/money/benefits was much in favour of a survey with less accuracy, did little to stop DNTPSC's criticism (Cullen, 2010).

However, the accuracy argument is only part of the explanation why DNTPSC senior staff of the national office were so strongly opposed to the INR. First, the adopted land-claims process disempowered DNTPSC staff by removing their broad discretionary powers. Through the INR's process they could not simply decide who owned land or who could claim it. Everyone was entitled to present their claims, the state also had to claim its own land, and the results were publicly exhibited, which brought more transparency, public scrutiny, and questions about DNTPSC's decisions.[48] Second, the use of young Timorese staff, briefly trained by INR, and equipped with GPSs, was a clear threat to the authority of the Indonesian-trained DNTPSC senior staff. Accepting the INR's methods meant accepting that their skills learned during the Indonesian administration were obsolete and that the relevant skills could be gained by anyone. Furthermore, the fact that a considerable proportion of INR staff, including very competent members of INR's leadership, were young Timorese women, added another layer of grievances in the male-dominated DNTPSC. Third, the higher salaries, fancier equipment, and the better-resourced work environment of INR staff further contributed to this antagonism. The opposition was so strong that often DNTPSC leadership would state that all work conducted by INR would have to be repeated once the project was finished (Haburas Foundation and Rede ba Rai, 2013: 18).

On the other hand, the project had strong support from the minister of justice at the time, Lúcia Lobato. In an interview she told me how, through the influence of DNTPSC staff, she started her mandate very suspicious about INR, but their staff were able to progressively show how they were doing good work. The district directors of DNTPSC were in general also strong supporters of INR. The project brought new staff, equipment, and also activities and a purpose to the isolated district offices, which made the district directors generally positive about INR. However, and despite this support, the opposition from the national office was strong, and at the national level INR started to work more and more separately from DNTPSC. By the end of the project, INR headquarters was in a separate building from DNTPSC, and collaboration and skills transfer between the two were mostly non-existent. As a result, little technical and organisational knowledge was passed from INR to the national office of DNTPSC.

48 For instance, Rede ba Rai reports that 'during monitoring of evictions [...] [i]n the Timor Plaza case senior DNTPSC officials were filmed stating that DNTPSC had the power to decide what was and was not state land and was not subject to the INR process. (Haburas Foundation and Rede ba Rai, 2013: 18).

National Cadastre System (SNC)

It was evident that little was learned from the INR experience when, in 2014, the government created the SNC (Chapter 3). The SNC headquarters were in the same separate building where INR headquarters was, working with its own staff, and with no close involvement of DNTPSC staff from the national office, except a few coordination meetings with DNTPSC leadership.[49] In the district offices there is also no involvement of DNTPSC staff in the SNC's activities. Even the INR's much-criticised survey methods remain a topic of debate in SNC's work. One of SNC's main selling points was the use of tablets to survey the land instead of the hand-held GPSs used by INR.[50] However, to save time and effort, instead of walking the boundaries of the land, the surveyors often simply drew the boundaries on top of a satellite image on a tablet, based on their observation of the field, which raised problems of accuracy in the definition of boundaries. During one visit to Timor-Leste, some DNTPSC members of staff expressed to me their discontent with this new approach, with one animatedly explaining that 'before we had square meters, now we have imaginary meters!' Moreover, and like what happened with the INR, there were again reports of DNTPSC leadership saying that the SNC work is just a 'census' and that new surveys will be necessary to recognise formal land rights (Rede ba Rai, 2019: 44).

More importantly, SNC has failed to incorporate INR's main lessons regarding the importance of transparency and public information in the process of land-claims registration and the limits of INR's approach to urban centres (Rede ba Rai, 2019: 30, 40). Instead of functioning as a source of knowledge and guidance to DNTPSC, SNC has further promoted a self-centred approach, with no sense of responsibility for its clients, no reflection on its role, nor accountability for the impact of its work. As argued in Chapter 3 and in more detail in Rede ba Rai's research (2019), the nationwide land registration conducted by SNC focused on individual land claims and, by completely disregarding the complex reality on the ground, added yet another layer of problems and difficulties to land tenure in Timor-Leste.

International organisations and donors

As briefly mentioned in Chapter 4, the influence of international organisations and donors in the country has been felt more in overarching ideologies,

49 Even this coordination is limited. For instance in Tibar, where the government plans to build a new port, SNC and DNTPSC conducted two separate land-claims processes over the same area within a couple of weeks of each other, causing confusion among residents.

50 The use of tablets became such a token of SNC that during launching ceremonies, tablets were handed to land surveyors as if they were a trophy (see, for instance, the SNC Facebook page). Unfortunately, much less effort was put into adequately choosing the information to be collected with these tablets.

such as democracy and liberalism, than in specific land-related policies. Their participation in the development and implementation of the formal land tenure system is relatively low, especially when compared with other developing countries more dependent on international aid. Nevertheless, international organisations and donors play a role in the development and implementation of the Timorese formal land tenure system, as this section shows.

There are several examples of this participation. During the first decade after independence, USAID was deeply involved in the development and implementation of the Timorese formal land tenure system, first by sponsoring the two LLP programmes and later the INR project.[51] However, the troubled end of INR, largely due to poor political management of the project by USAID leadership, removed the topic from the organisation's priorities (Chapter 3).[52] The World Bank, through the Justice for the Poor initiative, also had a considerable role in promoting debate and research on the topic of community land (World Bank, 2010). However, after the initial success with this research, and despite a clear request from the MoJ and more than two years of meetings and guaranties that the World Bank would continue to support research on this topic, this much-needed research project was suddenly cancelled by the World Bank, with little explanation. My position with the MoJ was in part sponsored by the United Nations Development Programme. Other donors such as Japanese International Cooperation Agency, the Asian Development Bank, and AusAID also occasionally worked with DNTPSC (see Chapter 5). Other organisations such as the Asia Foundation and Oxfam have also been working on land-related issues, but less directly involved with DNTPSC (Chapter 8).

There are also a few examples where international organisations and donors have spectacularly failed to support DNTPSC at the right time and on the right issues. The example I particularly recall concerns DNTPSC's large-scale eviction in 2011 in the so-called Brimob neighbourhood. Around 175 families were evicted at dawn, after a troubled process of notifications and negotiation, with little compensation, and no pre-warning of the eviction (Matadalan ba Rai and Haburas Foundation, 2010: 62). A few weeks after this eviction, the DNTPSC national director asked me to support him in a meeting about the eviction, requested by some UN staff. This meeting quickly became tense, with two UN staff being quite rough with the director, accusing him of violating several treaties and UN guidelines. The director, not very fluent in any of the languages used in the meeting, was having trouble defending himself, and

51 USAID's involvement of in the land sector was a source of conspiracy theories. I recall a conversation where a foreign person, trying to profit from discrediting INR work, claimed that the project was spying for the CIA.

52 In summary, USAID leadership did little to actively address the institutional difficulties of INR with DNTPSC and the need for careful planning of the end of the project. USAID's political management of INR deserves a separate article.

at some point I intervened to explain that DNTPSC had only followed orders and had acted according to the harsh laws of the country. I also acknowledged that it was clear that DNTPSC had a serious problem of lack of rules and procedures on evictions, as well as lack of training and institutional coordination with other state entities, and support addressing these issues would be very welcome. This UN team replied saying that they could send us copies of documents on best practices on evictions, but they could not offer more than that. During the weeks that followed, concerns about the eviction were raised in several donors' forums in which I participated. In all of them, I outlined the problems with evictions, and said that DNTPSC and the MoJ were willing to receive support in this area, and that I was totally available to work as an entry point to help establish any cooperation in this matter. Ultimately, however, no such support was provided.

While the analysis of the work of international organisations and donors is outside the scope of this book, the explanation I most often heard for why they avoid working on land-related issues in Timor-Leste is that it is a controversial and difficult topic, on which these organisations don't want 'to burn their fingers'. On the other hand, there are also situations in which donors are willing to support the MoJ and DNTPSC, but unresponsiveness, lack of planning, and miscommunication lead to missed opportunities.

Timorese civil society organisations

Finally, this section briefly analyses the Timorese civil society organisations that work on land-related issues.[53] Although Timorese CSOs rarely cooperate with DNTPSC, their work provides some monitoring of DNTPSC's activities and influences choices in the formal land tenure system, making them relevant to this chapter's analysis.

The core of Timorese CSOs formed after independence are modern incarnations of clandestine groups of students and activists that assumed a central role in the fight against the Indonesian occupation, especially in its last decade, when the Timorese armed resistance was weakening (Wigglesworth, 2013: 54).[54] After independence, some of these clandestine groups managed to reshape their scope of work, and several of their members were employed by the many newly formed CSOs, especially incentivised by the influx of

53 The terms 'civil society organisations' (CSOs) and 'non-governmental organisations' (NGOs) are contested. At times the two terms are used interchangeably to refer to voluntary organisations governed by citizens; other times distinctions are made, categorising NGOs as one type of CSO (Candland, 2001; Alagappa, 2004: 27; Tomlinson and AidWatch Canada, 2013: 123). While avoiding this debate, I prefer the term CSOs, since it is the term that is commonly used in Timor-Leste.

54 For instance, the National Resistance of East Timorese Students (RENETIL), the Organisation of Catholic East Timorese Youth and Students (OJECTIL), and the Always United Front of Timor (FITUN).

international funding. Progressively, a few Timorese CSOs included land in their areas of interest.[55]

The shift from the freedom struggle to complex governance problems, ruled by new, intricate, and fairly foreign systems has been a problem for Timorese CSOs (Richmond and Franks, 2009: 100). Generalising, Timorese CSOs are good at activities such as mobilising a protest, being close to the population, and lobbying politicians, but weaker on more technical knowledge such as legal analysis, and in skills such as conducting and publishing sound research (La'o Hamutuk, 2010: 4).[56] There are exceptions, and from my own experience I can see relevant progress in the capacity of CSOs since I first went to Timor-Leste in 2009. For instance, in the last few years, national CSOs produced a few pieces of sound research on land-related issues.[57] Moreover, the commitment from Oxfam to support a multi-year research agenda has helped CSOs to be more organised in planning relevant research and trainings. I participated in some of these trainings and research and was impressed with the progress achieved in the last decade. Nevertheless, Timorese CSOs working on land-related issues still have considerable fragilities in their technical knowledge.

Funding, management, and retention of qualified staff are another set of issues that Timorese CSOs experience. Especially since 2012, when many multilateral and bilateral donors decreased their aid budgets to Timor-Leste, many CSOs had to reduce their activities and became much more dependent on government contributions (Pambazuka News, 1 April 2016; Tatoli, 7 August 2018). Besides making their planning more erratic and difficult, this dependence on government funding constrained their criticisms of government decisions. Furthermore, CSOs' experienced staff members have been poached for advisory and government positions, taking skills from these organisations, and at times putting them in the difficult situation of having to criticise their former colleagues. In summary, while the national CSOs play a relevant role in the development and implementation of the Timorese formal land tenure system, they are not, politically and technically, as strong and powerful as CSOs in other parts of the world, such as Latin America or neighbouring Indonesia.[58]

These limitations of national CSOs have at least two clear impacts on the way they influence the development and implementation of the Timorese formal land tenure system. The first one is relatively limited participation in and contribution to the law-making process (Chapter 5). Once draft legislation is proposed for approval, CSOs tend to be quite active participating in consultation

55 For instance, Haburas Foundation, La'o Hamutuk, Belun, and Rede ba Rai (an umbrella organisation that gathers several CSOs).

56 Regarding examples of CSOs mobilisation, see, for instance, Stead, 2016: 154.

57 Matadalan ba Rai and Haburas Foundation, 2010; Haburas Foundation and Rede ba Rai, 2013; Rede ba Rai, 2019.

58 See, for instance, Lev, 2000: 283–304; Aspinall, 2004.

processes, providing comments, and lobbying politicians. However, their participation is mostly reactive; CSOs often criticise the draft legislation, but rarely present alternative policy options and legal solutions to the problems on the table. Furthermore, their contributions have a strong political inclination, but less technical analysis. As a result, the place of CSOs at the 'law-making table' is smaller than it could be. I saw first-hand how this more political and less technical approach makes CSOs' views easier to dismiss by politicians, who say that *they*—not the CSOs' representatives—are elected to represent the people, so politicians and not CSOs can make political decisions. I don't mean with this point that CSOs' role does not influence law-making; for instance, the 2012 veto of the Land Law Package and its approval in 2017 was in part due to their opposition and later due to their support of the draft-laws (see Cryan, 2015).[59] But the lack of a stronger technical background gives them a weaker position in law-making that they could otherwise have.

The second point where CSOs have a relatively limited impact is in exploring judicial strategies to challenge the legality of political decisions and administrative practices, leaving politicians and state officials less accountable for their actions and decisions.[60] As described above, most of CSOs' work is based on informing citizens, lobbying politicians, protesting, reporting, and monitoring, but almost never recurring to the courts to challenge political decisions and administrative practices. I do not know of a single case where a CSO has started a court case against DNTPSC or the state, and the little legal aid provided to individuals rarely results in a meaningful court decision. Evictions provide a good example here. While CSOs monitor, report, and advocate against these processes, the MoJ, DNTPSC, or any other state institution are not challenged in court, even when the legal arguments to do so are quite strong. In talks with CSO staff, I have shared some ideas of possible legal paths to stop or at least delay most evictions, but because of their lack of expertise and inexperience with courts, litigation is never used. By not using this option, CSOs waste an opportunity to make politicians and state officials accountable for their decisions and, as such, they provide them with little incentive to change and improve their practices.[61]

59 After strong opposition to the Land Law Package in 2012, CSO staff started questioning whether continuing under Law 1/2003 wouldn't be worse than approving a less-than-perfect Land Law Package. In the end, most decided that the law should be supported. I should add that, during the 2012 revisions of the Land Law Package, Timorese CSOs hired an external consultant to provide more detailed technical comments on the proposed drafts, which allowed their deeper involvement in the process. It is interesting to compare the participation of CSOs in law-making with the case of Indonesia (Vel *et al.*, 2017: 7).

60 See here Cotula, 2013: chap. 4, para. 62. Specifically about Timor-Leste, La'o Hamutuk, 2010: 5, Grenfell, 2015. Compare with Indonesia in Lev, 2000.

61 On the consequences of CSOs' weaknesses for the protection of basic rights and political liberalism, see Halliday *et al.*, 2007: 31.

Furthermore, the lack of litigation against the state on land-related issues prevents the development of legal doctrine on these issues (see Bedner, 2013: 262). A judicial strategy is no guarantee of success and can even backfire; but on the other hand, opportunities are wasted by not recurring to this possibility, and even an unsuccessful court case can be another tool for social contestation (World Bank, 2017a: 94). During my time with the MoJ I became seriously convinced that a few judicial decisions against state institutions' malpractice on land-related cases would help to shake things up, but such legal action never materialised.

As pointed out by Borras Jr. and Franco (2010), the interaction between politicians, civil servants, and CSOs is paramount for reforming a land tenure system. Timorese CSOs have had a role in the development and implementation of the formal land tenure system, and some progress can be observed, but they still have limited influence in shaping the laws, institutions, and practices that form this system.

Conclusion

This chapter allows us to better understand how DNTPSC, Timor-Leste's main state institution responsible for land administration, works and why. The Indonesian BPN is a major influence on the DNTPSC, while the LPU from UNTAET left almost no institutional legacy. In part due to this influence, but also due to an unrealistic image of DNTPSC and the state institutions in general, politicians, society, and even DNTPSC staff expect and demand from the institution much more that it can currently deliver, both due to legal and institutional limitations. Among all limitations, the lack of adequate human resources is, in my view, one of the most serious flaws of the institution, with a clear mismatch between the qualifications of the people hired and some of the tasks that the institution must perform. It is perhaps a biased view due to my legal background, but core activities of the institution involve fairly complex legal processes, such as drafting lease contracts and conducting expropriation processes, and therefore the legal component of the institution needs special attention. A lack of other resources further complicates the work of the institution, especially in the districts outside Dili. A visit to one district office is enough to raise serious questions about the capability of the institution to exercise robust land management throughout the country.

External actors to the state have worked with DNTPSC throughout the years, but have not brought considerable changes to the institution. The LLP and INR project were not able to improve DNTPSC, and INR's successor, the SNC project, only exacerbated DNTPSC's self-centred approach, with no attention for the needs of its clients, reflection on its role, nor accountability for the impact of its work. The support of international organisations and donors to DNTPSC has also been far from ideal, often failing to intervene when help is needed, but also hindered by the MoJ and DNTPSC's unresponsiveness, lack of planning, and even miscommunication. While CSOs have played a role in providing some supervision of political decisions and DNTPSC activities, their reach and impact in the way the Timorese formal land tenure system is developed is limited.

The environment in which DNTPSC's staff works gives members of staff a high degree of discretion, both in the different steps of (arbitrary) administrative processes and in the final decision-making. Some discretion in the work of state officials is unavoidable, and the level of discretion that they should have is debatable (Wilson, 1989: 337; Lipsky, 2010: preface para. 25). But factors such as the broad role that is expected from the institution, various external pressures to perform certain tasks, and the weak rule of law and lack of accountability give DNTPSC staff a level of discretion that goes much beyond the limits established in law. The conditions in which the law is implemented create a set of new informal norms; the discretion given to state officials makes them the law-makers of these informal norms that in practice rule the Timorese formal system (Lipsky, 2010: 13). This extreme discretion makes these state officials especially powerful law-makers.

Acknowledging the existence of extreme discretion in the work of these state officials and understanding its causes and consequences is important to comprehending how DNTPSC works. As this chapter shows, this high level of discretion is at times a safety valve to deal with dysfunctional legislation and be able to cope with the hardships of DNTPSC's difficult jobs, but most often it works as a source of injustice, insecurity, corruption, and rent-seeking. As is further debated in the final chapter, curbing this extreme discretion is fundamental to making people, especially the most vulnerable, less exposed to abuses of state power.

Wilson writes that, just like with childhood for adults, the formative years of an organisation can be of most importance in determining its behaviours (Wilson, 1989: 68). This chapter shows that the formative years of DNTPSC have not been the easiest ones. If an institution does not have clear guidance about its goals, and lacks the resources, structure, leadership, and adequate environment to perform its tasks, one cannot expect much from that institution.

This raises a final question: why is DNTPSC not getting a clearer goal and the resources, structure, and leadership it needs to provide the Timorese with better land administration services? Taking one step back, countries like Timor-Leste are trying, in a very short period, to develop institutions that took other countries more than a century to develop (Otto, 1993: 105). Despite this caveat, much needs to change to improve the work of DNTPSC. As many examples in this book show, new laws and technological innovations will have little impact if the core goals of DNTPSC are not clarified, clear processes established, its structure and staff adapted to its real needs, and the leadership of the institution improved (see Blase, 1973: 5). It is easy to blame DNTPSC staff for the problems of the institution, but the truth is that little has been done to politically guide it. Reforming an institution such as DNTPSC is much more than just a technical challenge; it is a serious political exercise that demands political courage and vision (Hillman, 2013: 2). Moreover, this political exercise is dependent on political coherence; DNTPSC will not change if, instead of law obedience, efficiency, and especially respect for people's rights, politicians demand from DNTPSC fast and cheap access to land.

The options for changing the institution are many: redesign the institutional structure, divide DNTPSC into two separate institutions, or establish an independent oversight committee. Nevertheless, some considerable institutional change is needed if the state is serious about implementing a formal land tenure system that is fair and better for its people.

During my last visit to DNTPSC in 2018, my hope that the approval of the Land Law Package would have encouraged some changes in the institution was seriously shaken. Many of the staff complained that, due to the political uncertainty that the country was experiencing, the leadership was not taking any decisions, and therefore most of their work had been pending for months. There was also no clear plan to implement the Land Law Package and, according to their calculation, around 20 regulations were needed before the package could be implemented. I was also told that 14 new temporary staff had been hired, all with geography backgrounds. The general atmosphere was darker; the staff were even more cramped than before between more furniture, files, and colleagues. Instead of blinds, many windows now had newspapers covering them. It was a sadder place.

Chapter 8

Social relationships, ideas, and practices around land tenure and the formal land tenure system

Introduction

This chapter analyses the social relationships, ideas, and practices that regulate land tenure on the ground and the role that the formal land tenure system plays in them. The previous chapters explore different layers of the development of the Timorese formal land tenure system. However, formal land tenure systems have little meaning by themselves; they must work with social relationships, ideas, and practices of people on the ground to have an impact on their lives. As I once heard, Crusoe only became the owner of his belongings once Friday showed up. By looking at what happens on the ground, this chapter provides a picture of the role and value that, in reality, the formal land tenure system has in Timorese society and what people expect from it. In other words, this chapter sheds some light on what the formal land tenure system does in practice.

The study of this layer of social ordering, as defined in Chapter 1, has two caveats. First, social relationships, ideas, and practices can be studied through various methods, from ethnographic descriptions of customary systems and land-related relationships to quantitative research. This range of possibilities raises the issue of determining which method(s) use. Second, there is also the issue of determining which social relationships to study. Ultimately, this analysis could include the study of all relationships that each individual establishes with each piece of land and with every other individual, as well as with formal and informal entities. Considering that this endeavour is beyond the capacity of most researchers, it is necessary to determine how deep the research needs to go to give an adequate account of the roles played in practice by the formal land tenure system.

In this account I have opted for a quantitative approach. A survey on land-related issues in Timor-Leste that I led in 2016 and the main report analysing the findings of this survey are the basis of this chapter (Almeida and Wassel, 2016). Three reasons guided this choice. First, there is already a considerable body of outstanding ethnographic work on customary land tenure systems

DOI: 10.4324/9781003196396-8

in Timor-Leste, especially in rural areas.[1] Besides ethnography not being my expertise, my contribution with new ethnographic findings would be limited. Second, an approach that provides a broader geographical and thematic overview is more in line with the objectives of this book. Third, while other land-related surveys were conducted in Timor-Leste, they were either too old or too narrow to provide the data needed for addressing my research questions.[2]

Regarding the depth of analysis caveat, this chapter focuses on those points where the land-related social relationships, ideas, and practices connect with and diverge from the formal land tenure system. This includes an overview of the prevalence of customary land tenure systems in the lives of the Timorese, and the presentation of a number of findings about the characteristics of land rights claimed by respondents, key numbers about land tenure security, and people's views on land titling and the right of the state to expropriate land.[3] The focus on the land-related social relationships, ideas, and practices, and their connections and clashes with the formal land tenure system, serve the purpose of this chapter by showing what this system is achieving in practice, and how it is cohabitating with other land tenure systems.

As described in Chapter 1, this survey was part of the research project 'Land rights and access to land survey in Timor-Leste: a tool for evidence-based policy and advocacy', implemented by the Van Vollenhoven Institute and The Asia Foundation, of which I was the lead researcher. It consisted of a questionnaire with 126 closed questions about access to land, land use, land tenure security, land-related disputes, and expropriation, mostly regarding the land where the household of the respondent lives.[4] The survey was conducted in three districts; the urban area of the capital Dili where the population density is high and state institutions considerably active, and the districts of Ainaro, Ermera, where most of the population lives in rural areas and state institutions are much less present (Map 8.1). A total of 1,152 interviews were made, 384 in each of the selected districts, by enumerators specifically trained for this survey. The sample size and the target population resulted in a 5 percent margin of error for the results.

Although the survey only covered three of the 13 districts of Timor-Leste, and most questions were focused on residential land only, its results allow some extrapolation regarding other districts and other types of land with fairly similar characteristics. Despite its limitations, this survey provides interesting findings

1 Among others, McWilliam and Traube, 2011. Interestingly, there is almost no ethnographic work on land-related issues in urban areas.

2 See Urresta and Nixon, 2004a; Matadalan ba Rai and Haburas Foundation, 2010; Dale *et al.*, 2010.

3 Further information can be found both in the final report and in the data-set of the survey.

4 Although the questionnaire had 126 questions, many of these were sub-questions. Therefore respondents answered less questions.

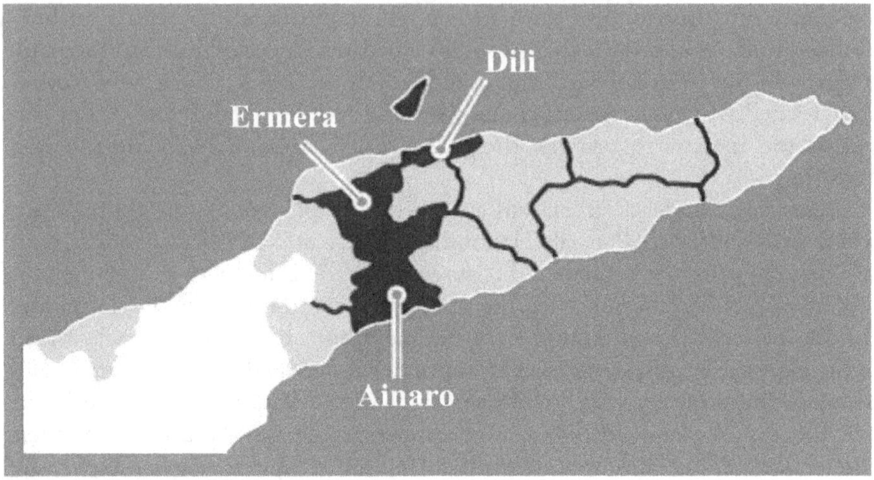

Map 8.1 Survey areas

that help to further understand the social relationships, ideas, and practices of the Timorese regarding land tenure.

The next section discusses how the survey results show the high relevance of customary systems in land administration, followed by findings on customary rules on land rights and their disconnection with state rules. Next, the chapter looks at legal and perceived tenure security, showing that the formal system fails to legally protect the land rights of most Timorese, but their perceived tenure security varies substantially, depending on where respondents live. The following section illustrates the high value that respondents give to land titles and the roles they see these titles playing for them. The subsequent sections look at causes of land-related disputes and respondents' preferences regarding dispute-resolution mechanisms. The final section examines respondents' views on expropriation, showing that respondents perceive this state power very differently from the elite's state-centred developmentalistic views.

Relevance of customary systems

The central role that customary land tenure systems play in the social relationships and practices of the great majority of Timorese is evident throughout the findings of the survey. While respondents do not fully disregard the formal land tenure system, in practice it plays a secondary role in the lives of many of them. These conclusions are not new. Many authors have already concluded that, despite all efforts and intentions of state representatives to territorialise frontier areas with state systems, customary systems continue to serve a great majority of Timorese in land administration and other areas such as conflict prevention and dispute resolution.[5] Customary systems are not totally isolated from the formal one, but in many situations formal rules are unknown, and state institutions too distant and mostly inaccessible. This survey adds to previous studies, providing new findings that further confirm the central role of customary land tenure systems in the lives of many Timorese.

However, showing the relevance of customary land tenure systems in a survey is not so easy. Most respondents would not understand the question if they were directly asked if their land tenure is regulated by customary systems. Nevertheless, the relevance of customary systems comes to light in several findings. For instance, by comparing the great majority of respondents that claimed to own the land where they live, both in urban and rural areas, with the minority of those that reported to have a formal land right (or a 'land title' as it is often called in Timor-Leste), it is possible to assume that those rights derive from customary systems. This is further confirmed when the bundle of rights that respondents claimed to have is quite different from the rights and obligations established in the law. The prevalence of customary systems is also visible in the central role that respondents attributed to local and traditional authorities in the resolution of their land disputes. These findings are discussed in more detail in the following sections and the main report of the survey (Almeida and Wassel, 2016).

However, the central role of customary systems in the lives of most Timorese does not mean that the formal land tenure system is totally disregarded by the respondents, and they are, to a certain extent, keen to be more connected with it, or at least curious about the possibility. The following sections further elaborate on these matters.

Characteristics of land rights

This section looks at the characteristics of the customary land rights that, in practice, regulate land access and avail in Timor-Leste, and compare them with the land rights established by the formal system. The characteristics of rights with customary basis, or even the way formal rights are perceived and applied by their holders, often differ significantly from what is established in state legislation, even when the terminology used is the same. In other words, for the 'same' land right, the customary and formal land tenure systems establish different bundles of rights and obligations (Chapter 2).

The discrepancies between the land rights established by a formal and a customary land tenure system are to a certain extent inevitable. First, there are

5 Among others, Fitzpatrick, 2002: 167; D'Andrea, 2003; Yoder, 2005: 3; Nixon, 2009: 3; McWilliam and Traube, 2011; Jerónimo, 2011; Simões, 2015: 392.

situations in which the formal land tenure system is deliberately used to change land-related customary practices, and therefore explicitly regulates against them (e.g., customary limitations on women's land rights that are forbidden by law). Second, because even when the state intends to integrate customary rules in the formal system, it is impossible to incorporate all the details, nuances, and flexibility of rights in the country's diverse customary systems (Fitzpatrick, 2005: 457; Wily, 2016: 68; Chapter 2).

Nevertheless, the discrepancies between the land rights established by a formal and a customary land tenure system, combined with misinformation and opportunism, can be a great source of conflict and dispossession, especially when the state is doing efforts to expand its formal land tenure system (see Lund, 2008: 15). With this concern in mind, the survey enquired if there were significant differences between the individual, 'Western-like', ownership rights established in the law and ownership of land perceived and applied in practice.

In Timor-Leste, terminology is part of the confusion.[6] Tetum vocabulary does not have a clear equivalent for ownership right (or *direito de propriedade* in Portuguese), but uses the word *na'in* to refer to the 'owner' of something (Klinken, 2008: 119). However, this term is used to refer to clear cases of ownership rights, but also situations in which someone has control or authority over an object or land, but not an ownership right as established by law (Cryan, 2015a: 2). At times people recur to foreign terminology such as Portuguese *propriedade perfeita*, or Indonesian *hak milik* to refer to ownership rights, but these expressions are mostly associated with formal rights. So when someone says that he or she is *na'in ba rai* or *rai na'in* ('owner' of the land, with *rai* meaning land), it is not clear if they are referring to a formal ownership right or a less clearly defined customary-based land right that involves some control of the land. To further complicate this issue, the expression *rai na'in* is also used by some groups to refer to people with special knowledge about customary land rights, with a special land-related function inside a community, or with a special authority position in the customary hierarchy. These problems with terminology raised the issue of determining how questions about land ownership in the survey should be phrased.

The survey assessed the characteristics of land rights by first asking the respondents who is the owner of the land where they live, using term *na'in*, as described above. Most respondents identified the land where they live as privately owned, belonging to themselves individually, together with their spouse, or jointly owned with other family members (87 percent in Dili, 97 percent in Ermera, 100 percent in Ainaro). Only Dili had a relevant number of respondents reporting that they live on state land (7 percent).[7]

6 More generically about this topic see Lund, 2008: 15.

7 Compare with the 2010 census results (GoTL, 2011a: xxiv).

Table 8.1 What are the respondents NOT allowed to do with their land?

	Ainaro	*Dili*	*Ermera*
Sell/give their land to members of their family (%)	81	81	61
Sell/give their land to members of their community (%)	87	87	72
Sell/give their land to people from another municipality (%)	89	92	75
Sell/give their land to foreigners (%)	89	95	76
Rent their land to people of another municipality (%)	74	78	65
Transfer the land as inheritance (%)	8	26	15
Build a house in their land (%)	6	17	8

Next, the survey assessed whether the land ownership claimed by the respondents corresponded to an individualised, Western-like, concept of ownership as established in the Timorese Civil Code (Chapter 6), in which the owner can freely transfer and avail of the owned property. The survey asked a series of questions regarding what respondents were allowed to do with the land they claim to own. Despite claiming ownership of land, most respondents said that they were not allowed to sell, give, and rent their land to family members, other members of their community, people from other districts or foreigners (Table 8.1). By contrast, only a small minority of respondents said that they were not allowed to transfer their land through inheritance, to build a house, or to farm the land.

These results show that the respondents' concept of 'owning' land is very different from the legal concept of ownership right, where the owner can freely transfer the owned property.[8] It shows that there is a network of rights, obligations, and beneficiaries connected to land. The ownership claimed by the respondents resembles more closely a land use right, through which the beneficiary uses the land, but in which transferring land rights to others carries many limitations.[9] This finding raises concerns regarding the implementation of land-related legislation, including the Land Law and the Civil Code, and the impacts of the land registration process implemented by SNC (Chapter 3; Rede ba Rai, 2019). The implementation of a Western-like concept of ownership empowers the land claimant to the detriment of others in these networks of rights, obligations, and beneficiaries, and it is at odds with many Timorese's current understanding of and relation to land. The social changes and potential conflict that can derive from this shift of land tenure paradigm are unpredictable, and can endanger central social links of communities and families.[10]

8 See here Yoder, 2005: 207.

9 Urresta and Nixon, 2004a: 55; Matadalan ba Rai and Haburas Foundation, 2010: 88; Fitzpatrick *et al.*, 2013: 134, 274.

10 See Indonesian example described by Tanya Li (2014).

The differences between the customary and formal land tenure systems are not just on the characteristics of land rights, but also on the ways of acquiring them. The survey assessed the respondents' reactions to adverse possession, which are especially relevant when considering that adverse possession is a fairly new concept in Timor-Leste, introduced by the Land Law and the Civil Code.[11] Pre-existing data indicated that few people considered that by abandoning land the owner would lose rights to it, but there was no data on the possibility of a third party acquiring land through long-term possession (Urresta and Nixon, 2004a: 66).[12]

Two survey questions assessed respondents' receptivity to adverse possession solutions. First they were asked whether, in their opinion, someone who uses an empty parcel of land for a long period of time should become the owner of that land. The opinions were divided, with more than half of the respondents saying that the possessor should become the owner of the abandoned land (47, 65, and 58 percent in Ainaro, Dili, and Ermera, respectively), but many others refused this possibility (49, 29, and 39 percent in Ainaro, Dili, and Ermera, respectively). Second, they were asked a similar question but about a parcel of land that had been abandoned by a third party long ago, rather than about an empty parcel of land. Interestingly, while the results remained similar to the previous question in Dili and Ermera (60 and 53 percent), fewer respondents in Ainaro agreed that the possessor should become the owner of the abandoned land (22 percent). Adverse possession can be a cheap and practical mechanism to provide some legal tenure security to land users (Williams, 2009), but these results indicate that adverse possession solutions are not universally popular or acceptable. Furthermore, they also hint at some differences between customary land tenure systems in different areas of the country.

Land tenure security

Land tenure security is another point where the social relationships, ideas, and practices connect, but also clash, with the formal land tenure system. As debated in Chapter 2, land tenure security is often the reason (or the excuse) for governments to change or further enforce the state's formal land tenure system, while pointing out the uncertainty and insecurity of customary systems. However, at times the state and its system are in reality the main threat and a cause of more insecurity.

While there are various definitions and subdivisions of the concept of land tenure security, especially relevant for this chapter are, (1) the concept of legal tenure security, which refers to the recognition and protection that state law

11 On adverse possession in Timor-Leste see Almeida, 2016: 36; Almeida, 2018.

12 In this study the urban respondents were more in favour of people not losing their rights due to abandonment (62 percent) than the rural respondents (52 percent). See also Yoder, 2003: 5.

Table 8.2 Do you have a formal land title? What kind of land title?

	Ainaro	*Dili*	*Ermera*
Yes, I have a formal land title (%)	16	54	18
No, I don't have a land title (%)	84	45,0	81
Portuguese land titles (%)	6	9	33
Indonesian land titles (%)	91	86	62

gives to land holders from being dispossessed against their will; and (2) perceived tenure security, which refers to land holders' feeling that their land tenure is safe and that they are not at risk of being dispossessed (Chapter 2). The following sub-sections debate the survey results regarding legal and the perceived tenure security, and the relation between them.

Legal tenure security

At the time of the survey, the Land Law had not yet been approved, and Law 1/2003 was the central piece of legislation regulating land rights. As detailed in Chapter 6, this law gave some legal recognition to formal land rights issued by previous administrations, but raised doubts about whether land rights issued by the Indonesian administration were protected. Furthermore, this law left completely unprotected the great majority of Timorese that never obtained a formal land right, and instead accessed and availed of land through customary systems. This lack of legal protection, combined with the loose definition of state land, left the great majority of Timorese with no legal tenure security and exposed to the risk of eviction. Often state officials simply claim that land without a formal land right belongs to the state (Chapter 6; Almeida, 2018a). However, while this generalised lack of legal tenure security was widely known by academic researchers and politicians, there was little information quantifying the dimension of this problem.

The survey asked respondents whether they had a formal land right, more precisely a *land title* (*titulu/sertificadu* in Tetum) as it is commonly called in Timor-Leste, for the land where their household lives. While 54 percent of respondents in Dili reported having a land title, in Ainaro and Ermera a much smaller percentage of respondents reported having one (16 and 18 percent; Table 8.2).[13] Extrapolated to the district populations, this means that around 101,000, 102,000, and 55,700 people in Dili, Ermera, and Ainaro, respectively, did not have a land title, and consequently no legal protection under Law 1/2003 (Table 8.3). However the lack of legal protection was even worse if

13 Compare with the Matadalan ba Rai and Haburas Foundation study (2010), where 77 percent report to not have a land title.

Table 8.3 Estimated number of people WITHOUT legal tenure security

	Ainaro (approx. 68,000 inhabitants)	*Dili (approx. 220,000 inhabitants)*	*Ermera (approx. 121,000 inhabitants)*
Less strict interpretation of Law 1/2003	55,700 (84%)	101,000 (46%)	102,000 (81%)
Stricter interpretation of Law 1/2003	65,300 (96%)	214,00 (97%)	116,800 (84%)

the stricter interpretation of Law 1/2003 that excluded Indonesian land titles is followed, considering that the majority of the respondents reported having Indonesian land titles (Table 8.2).[14] If we add these respondents to those that have no formal land title, considering the average size of households we can conclude that around 214,000 (97 percent), 116,800 (84 percent), and 65,300 (96 percent) people in Dili, Ermera, and Ainaro, respectively, had no legal land tenure security (Table 8.3). This is, however, the best-case scenario, considering that the legal validity of many reported formal land rights can be challenged by the state for several reasons (e.g., lack of formalities, prohibition on transactions with Indonesians from 1999 onwards).

These findings show that, at least until the approval of the Land Law, the formal land tenure system was failing to provide most Timorese with legal tenure security. While in practice, the customary-based land rights are in certain situations recognised by state officials, this recognition is arbitrary and not based on the law (Chapter 9). The lack of legal recognition of customary-based land rights, and the interpretation that all non-formalised land is state land, made the formal land tenure system and the state more of a legal threat than a solution. In theory the approval of the Land Law has changed this level of legal insecurity, but for now the law remains unimplemented, and, depending on legal interpretation, many people can still be excluded from the protections established in this new law (Chapter 6). Furthermore, it is estimated that in Dili at least 28 percent of the people will not have legal tenure security over their houses under the new Land Law (Almeida and Wassel, 2016: 27).

Perceived tenure security

Under such a grim scenario of legal tenure insecurity, one would expect that perceived tenure security is also low. However, the results of the survey show a more complex situation.

14 Three to six percent of respondents reported not knowing if they have a land title, or reported having a land title but not knowing what type.

Table 8.4 Are you afraid of being evicted in the next five years?

	Ainaro	*Dili*	*Ermera*
Yes, I'm very afraid that I will be evicted in the next five years (%)	3	59	5
Maybe, I'm not sure if I'll be evicted in the next five years (%)	8	11	12
No, I'm not afraid of being evicted in the next five years (%)	84	28	73

Around 70 percent of respondents in the three districts thought that the government allows them to reside on or own the land where they live. At first glance this finding could give the idea that, in general, people feel secure with their tenure despite widespread legal tenure insecurity. However, the results become more nuanced once other questions are accounted for. In Dili, where legal tenure security is higher, 70 percent of respondents feared that they would be evicted in the next five years (Table 8.4), with 92 percent of these respondents expecting an eviction to be conducted by the state. This fear of eviction was further confirmed by 50 percent of the Dili respondents reporting that being evicted by the government was their main concern regarding land. On the contrary, in Ainaro and Ermera, where almost no one had legal tenure security, only a few respondents feared being evicted in the next five years, and only a few reported fears of eviction by the government as their main land-related concern (8 and 5 percent in Ainaro and Ermera, respectively).[15]

My experience in the country points me to a few factors that can explain the difference of perceived tenure security between Dili and the other two municipalities, and the mismatch between legal tenure security and perceived tenure security. The lack of traditional connections with the land in Dili, the much higher competition for land, the stronger presence of state officials, and the past experiences with state-led evictions gives Dili residents more doubts about their land rights, and higher awareness of state-led evictions. This shows that for many people, at least in Dili, the state and its formal land tenure system (i.e., norms, institutions, practices) is perceived as a threatening and disruptive force, rather than a protective and stabilising one. In Ainaro and Ermera, two rural districts where customary land tenure systems play a much stronger role than the formal one, people seemed to be more confident about their land rights, despite the lack of legal tenure security. Because of the customary connection to the land, and the lower presence of state officials, the customary systems seem to provide these rural residents with enough security, and the state is seen by them as less of a threat.

15 The survey focused on the land where the household of the respondent lives. This can explain why disputes over coffee plantations in Ermera are not influencing these numbers (see Matadalan ba Rai and Haburas Foundation, 2010: 46).

Nevertheless, the higher perceived tenure security in Ainaro and Ermera cannot be extrapolated to the rest of the rural municipalities. In municipalities like Oecusse and Cova-Lima, where large-scale state-led dispossession for infrastructure projects has been happening in recent years, perceived land tenure security is likely to be much lower.[16] Moreover, the higher perceived tenure security in rural districts does not seem to make people discard the formal land tenure system nor put them completely at ease regarding their rights. The views on land titles described in the following section are a very clear example of this.

Land titling

Land titling is an interesting point of connection and clash between social relationships, ideas, and practices and the formal land tenure system. As discussed in Chapter 2, many politicians and state officials tend to see land titling as their preferred tool of land administration, despite the problems that it frequently causes.

I knew by experience the fascination of Timorese politicians and state officials with land titles, and through the survey we attempted to understand the general population's views on this matter. Almost all respondents claimed that it is important to have a land title (98 percent in all municipalities). Avoiding evictions (94, 63, and 84 percent in Ainaro, Dili, and Ermera, respectively), and to better protect the household's land rights (90, 68, and 82 percent in Ainaro, Dili, and Ermera, respectively) were reported as the main reasons why it is important to have a land title.[17] Furthermore, most respondents also believed that a land-titling programme would reduce land conflict (84 percent). These findings, especially in the two rural districts, raised a few questions: why do people value land titles so much? Why do those with high perceived tenure security nonetheless put so much value on land titles?[18]

The importance given to land titles by almost all respondents, even from those that feel safe with their customary-based land rights, highlights the idea present in all formal land tenure systems implemented in Timor-Leste that formal rights trump, or at least can significantly challenge, any customary-based land rights. This is in line with a previous study that identified a belief that a formal land title is more valuable than a customary-based right, and uncovered strong support for land-titling programmes in Timor-Leste (Dale *et al.*, 2010: 3). In other words, and in line with studies on land registration, people feel that land titles can better protect them against the arbitrariness of the state (see

16 Chapter 9. See also Cryan, 2015a; Yoder, 2016; Almeida, 2018a.

17 In this question more than one answer was possible, therefore the sums are above 100 percent. Compare these results with Batterbury *et al.*, 2015: 636, and Haburas Foundation and Rede ba Rai, 2013: 76.

18 More generically on the topic of desire for a land title see Hall, 2013: chap. 5 para. 7.

Bruce *et al.*, 1994: 259). The current practices and legal interpretations regarding land rights in Timor-Leste that privilege formal rights issued by previous administrations further give people reason to think this way (see here Cullen, 2015: 479). Furthermore, as well illustrated by the enthusiastic reception given to De Soto's theory on land registration (Chapter 2), the assumptions about the benefits of land titling can be quite compelling, not only to politicians and state officials but also to the population in general.[19]

However, as debated in Chapter 2, the bias towards formal systems and land-titling options often overlook their pitfalls, such as the potential for starting conflict, the likelihood of favouring some members of a community or group to the detriment of others, and the risk of promoting a rapid commodification of land.[20] The fact that these problems are usually not immediately visible, get mixed with other social problems, and are primarily experienced by those with less voice in society further limits the awareness about the risks of land titling as a land-management tool. In the specific case of the respondents in Ainaro and Ermera, where perceived land tenure security is high, inexperience with land titling might in part explain the strongly positive views about titles. At the time of the survey very few respondents in Ainaro and Ermera had their land registered by the INR and/or SNC projects, and therefore had little exposure to the problems that might come with land titling (9 percent in Ainaro and 11 percent in Ermera as reported by the survey).[21] In the case of Dili residents, it is probably the weaker perceived land tenure security and the many examples of dispossession of those without formal rights that shape their view of land titles as the main solution for their insecurity.

Regardless of the reasons, it is clear that formal land titles are strongly valued by the respondents, which will make urban and rural populations receive well, if not actively promote, land-titling solutions. However, while land titling might be a solution for some of the land-related problems in Timor-Leste, it has been, and will continue to be, the cause of many other problems (Chapter 3; Rede ba Rai, 2019).

Land-related disputes and dispute-resolution mechanisms

Land-related disputes are, to a bigger or a lesser degree, a given in every society, and providing mechanisms to address these disputes and not let them

19 See Suara Timor Lorosae, 10 February 2014; Suara Timor Lorosae, 3 July 2014; Jornal Nacional Diário, 4 November 2014.

20 As mentioned in Chapter 3, and well-illustrated by the work of Rede ba Rai (2019), SNC's land claim process is a clear example of how can land registration seriously disadvantage considerable parts of the population.

21 By contrast, in Dili 57 percent of respondents claim that they had had their land surveyed by INR and/or SNC projects.

escalate into serious conflicts is one of the main roles of a land tenure system, whether formal or informal. In post-colonial and post-conflict countries such as Timor-Leste, where customary systems play a central role in land administration, determining the level of land-related disputes, understanding their reasons, and identifying the mechanisms that people use to address those disputes are key to understanding land-related social relationships on the ground. Furthermore, dispute resolution is another point where the formal system and customary practices connect, but also clash. While there were already a few studies looking at land-related disputes and dispute-resolution mechanisms, the survey provided new data on these matters (e.g., Dale *et al.*, 2010; The Asia Foundation, 2013; 2015).

Regarding land-related disputes, the findings of the survey were consistent with previous data. Around 10 percent of the respondents reported to have a dispute over the land where they live (12, 8, and 11 percent in Dili, Ainaro, and Ermera, respectively).[22] In all three districts most disputes were with family members, although in Dili close to 40 percent of disputes were with the state. The fact that most disputes are with family members is not surprising, given the high proportion of land that is obtained through inheritance and donation (82 percent in Ainaro, 56 percent in Dili, and 86 percent in Ermera).[23] In light of the history of violence, displacement, and conflict in Timor-Leste, this relatively low number of reported land-related disputes can be surprising at first glance. However, it becomes more understandable when considering the central role and resilience of customary systems in providing permanent or temporary solutions for these disputes, without depending on the state system (Chapters 3 and 4).

The respondents were also asked about who they thought could solve a land dispute fairly. Most respondents in the three areas answered that the most capable actors are elected local authorities in the community, i.e. aldeia and suco chiefs.[24] In Ainaro and Ermera, customary leaders (*lia'nain*) and family members were also seen as highly trusted parties (see here Cummins, 2010: 909). State actors such as DNTPSC officials, police, lawyers, and courts were much less trusted to address land-related disputes (Table 8.5).[25]

22 See here Dale *et al.*, 2010: 5; The Asia Foundation, 2015: 35. INR also reported around ten percent of land disputes (Fella and Boudreaux, 2011: 1).

23 See here Matadalan ba Rai and Haburas Foundation, 2010: 88.

24 As mentioned in Chapter 3, while suco legislation is quite obscure, these elected leaders are considered representatives of the suco and aldeia, not state representatives. Often these positions are co-opted by customary leaders or someone appointed by them, but there are cases were other candidates won the election.

25 It should be noted however, that when asked if courts can fairly address land disputes, 84 percent of the respondents answered affirmatively. However, as detailed in Chapter 4, courts and lawyers are almost inaccessible for the great majority of Timorese.

Table 8.5 In case of dispute over your land parcel, who do you think is able to solve it fairly?[1]

	Ainaro	*Dili*	*Ermera*
Family (%)	75	42	73
Aldeia chief (%)	92	83	94
Suco chief (%)	91	83	87
Lia'nain (%)	94	35	79
Community members (%)	24	13	15
DNTPSC (%)	20	30	10
PNTL (%)	46	18	16
Lawyer (%)	10	6	1
Courts (%)	19	26	14

[1] In this question more than one answer was possible, therefore the sums are above 100 percent.

Regarding the method to address land-related disputes, negotiation and mediation were the preferred approaches (around 44 and 30 percent, respectively), while the courts were the least chosen option (10, 8, and 1 percent in Dili, Ermera, and Ainaro). However, despite the low percentage of respondents indicating a court case as a good method to address land disputes, 82 percent said that a state representative needs to be involved in the resolution process to completely resolve a land dispute (Urresta and Nixon, 2004).[26] While these results may seem contradictory at first, they are in line with previous research on community dispute resolution. Although communities prefer local dispute-resolution methods, the agreements are honoured more consistently when a state official is present to provide authority to the result (Yoder, 2003: 24; The Asia Foundation, 2015).

In combination with the findings described above, these numbers suggest that, despite the prevalence and important role of customary systems, the formal land tenure system still has a role to play in land dispute resolution, even in rural areas. Rather than one system replacing the other, it seems that formal and customary systems have been—and need to—cohabitate.

'Development' and the right to expropriate land

As detailed in Chapter 4, the idea of 'development', mostly focused on infrastructure and private investment, has been a key influence on the evolution—or lack thereof—of the Timorese formal land tenure system. The uncertainty about land rights, the blurred notion of the right of the state to expropriate

26 Compare with Leach *et al.*, 2012: 16. However, it is important to consider that the sample of Leach *et al.*'s study was only secondary school students.

Table 8.6 In which situations can the government take land from individuals and communities?[1]

	Ainaro	*Dili*	*Ermera*
Build a public school (%)	86	79	76
Build a public road (%)	94	75	86
Build a public hospital (%)	80	58	72
Build state building (e.g., suco office) (%)	57	50	50
Build a hotel (%)	14	18	5
Give it to a private party to build a factory (%)	13	16	1
Build a church (%)	25	26	18

[1] In this question more than one answer was possible, therefore the sums are above 100 percent.

land, and arbitrary and informal processes have been frequently used in favour of the state and (some) investors to provide them with quick, easy, and cheap access to large tracts of land.[27] This section focuses on the main findings of the survey regarding expropriation and how they shape social relationships on the ground between individuals and the state, through the power of expropriation.

The survey found that respondents acknowledge the right of the state to expropriate land. Around half of them said that the state is entitled to, in all situations, expropriate land for public purposes upon the payment of fair compensation (55, 46, and 24 percent in Ainaro, Dili, and Ermera, respectively). However, a considerable number of respondents was more cautious, saying that the right of the state to expropriate land depends on the situation (33, 38, and 59 percent in Ainaro, Dili, and Ermera). Fewer respondents believed that the state does not have the right to expropriate land at all (12, 14, and 11 percent in Ainaro, Dili, and Ermera, respectively).[28]

These perceptions about the right of the state to expropriate land get more refined once respondents are asked in which specific situations they consider that an expropriation is fair (Table 8.6). While most respondents agreed that the state could expropriate land for more obvious cases of public purpose such as building a public school, road, or hospital, only around half agreed with expropriation for public administration buildings, such as a suco office. Maybe more relevant, only a small minority agreed with expropriations for private economic activities such as the construction of a hotel or a factory. Also relevant, less than a quarter of respondents agreed that their land could be expropriated for the construction of a church, which is surprising in a country so strongly influenced by the Catholic Church. These findings show that people make a clear distinction between different beneficiaries of an

27 See the case study described in the Matadalan ba Rai and Haburas Foundation study (2010: 61).

28 Compare here Urresta and Nixon, 2004a: 81.

expropriation, and have a fairly restrictive view of the concept of public purpose.

This finding is especially interesting when considering the ideas of development debated in Chapter 4, where the state and investors play a central role. Any ideas of promoting expropriation of private land for private interests, with the excuse that it will bring investors, jobs, and 'development', are contrary to what most respondents consider to be fair (Chapters 5 and 6; Almeida, 2018b). Furthermore, this finding also challenges an assumption common among state officials that any state project automatically fulfils the concept of public purpose (see Chapter 6; Almeida, 2018; Almeida, 2018a).

A final finding about expropriation is regarding the form of compensation. Respondents were asked whether, in case of expropriation, they would prefer to receive a fair monetary compensation or, alternatively, replacement land and a house of equivalent value to those expropriated. Replacement land as total or partial compensation is often used as an alternative or a complement to compensation (Keith *et al.*, 2008: 38). In the survey, the great majority of the respondents said that in case of expropriation they would prefer replacement land and housing instead of monetary compensation (69, 96, and 69 percent in Ainaro, Dili, and Ermera, respectively). It is noteworthy that in Dili almost all respondents would prefer replacement land and housing instead of monetary compensation. At least two factors can explain these results: first, as detailed in the main report of the survey, access to land is difficult and uncertain, so maybe the respondents prefer to leave to the state the burden of looking for land for resettlement (Almeida and Wassel, 2016: 18). Second, the track record of fair compensation in Timor-Leste is not exemplary; there are several cases before and after independence where compensations did not cover all the costs of resettlement. Based on these experiences the respondents might find it safer to obtain land and a house from the state than to receive monetary compensation that does not cover all their resettlement costs.

From these results it is clear that the power of the state to expropriate land makes it a special player in the competition for land. However, while this prerogative is acknowledged by most respondents, their views about these rights are nuanced, and not in line with ideas of development and investment of the political elite described in Chapter 4. As the following chapter shows, these different views clash in practice, and have real impacts on people's lives.

Conclusion

By analysing the social relationships, ideas, and practices that actually regulate land tenure on the ground, this chapter sheds light on the role(s) that the formal land tenure system plays in the lives of the Timorese, and what they expect from it. Although methodological limitations and the scope covered do not allow for a full picture, this chapter still provides the literature with new insights regarding how the Timorese formal land tenure system functions in practice.

This chapter shows that, at least until the approval of the Land Law, the formal land tenure system failed to give any legal tenure security to the great majority of Timorese. Only a few people, mostly in Dili, were able to clearly benefit from the formal land tenure system, through formal land rights issued by previous administrations or lease contracts with the Timorese state, but even in these cases their legal stance was dubious. Others, even in the capital, Dili, depended on informal local norms, institutions, and practices to access and avail of land, as well as to address conflicts. The fact that the Land Law remains unimplemented would suggest that this situation continues. In fact, in line with other studies, this chapter shows the central role of customary land tenure systems in regulating and distributing land rights, and in providing dispute-resolution mechanisms for most Timorese for whom the formal land tenure system is not accessible.

This central role of customary systems does not mean that the formal system is disregarded by, or does not play a role in, the lives of those who live outside of it. The chapter shows how the formal land tenure system is a threat for those that are within its reach but cannot benefit from it, as the case-study in the following chapter exemplifies. For those that cannot benefit from the formal land tenure system, their land problems start when the state—with its arbitrary rules and opaque institutions—shows up. In connection with this point, the chapter shows how, despite the high levels of perceived tenure security in rural areas, almost all respondents, perhaps aware of the risks of being outside the formal system, see land titles as a path to protect their land rights against intervention from the state and other possible threats. Moreover, in the case of land disputes, respondents see a value in the authority of state officials, and view mixing the customary and formal systems as an adequate solution. As debated in Chapter 2, these findings highlight the fact that the territorialisation of the formal land tenure system contributes both to the recognition of the state's legitimacy and of those that manage to see their rights recognised by the state (Lund, 2008: 10). If on one hand people want state recognition, on the other hand part of that desire is to protect themselves against the state.

The power of the state to expropriate land is another threat of the formal land tenure system. On this topic, this chapter shows how the vision that respondents have of the powers of the state to expropriate land significantly differs from the state-centred developmentalistic views of the elite, debated in Chapter 4. While a large majority of respondents agree that their land can be expropriated for projects with clear public purpose, such as roads and schools, only a few agree with expropriations with fuzzy public benefits, such as hotels and factories.

Furthermore, this chapter also provides a few examples of the conceptual differences between the formal and customary systems. Legal concepts inherited from previous administrations, legal transplants, the involvement of foreign legal drafters (Chapter 5), but also a wish to bring 'development' to the country (Chapter 4), introduce to the Timorese formal land tenure system concepts that are at odds with customary norms. The different conceptualisations of ownership and the reluctance to accept adverse possession are just two examples of how the formal land tenure system clashes with customary ones.

The consequences of these findings for the bigger picture of the Timorese formal land tenure system are further debated in Chapter 10.

Chapter 9

The layers in movement—the formal land tenure system and the Suai Supply Base

Introduction

This chapter brings together the five key analytical themes identified in the Land Tenure System Analysis Model described in Chapter 1. Through a case study, this chapter shows how the points studied in each of these themes interact with each other in practice, how these interactions shape the norms, institutions, and practices of the formal land tenure system, and how this system impacts land tenure on the ground.

The case study presented in this chapter is the Suai Supply Base (SSB), which is a part of the larger Tasi Mane Project, a grandiose state-led infrastructure plan envisioned by former Prime Minister Gusmão, through which he hopes to create an oil and gas industry in the south coast of the country. The SSB is a particularly interesting case study because it brings together many of the points raised in previous chapters. It provides a clear example of the practical consequences of colonialism, occupation, and violence on land tenure, and the clash between prevalent customary land tenure systems with the formal state system (Chapters 3, 6, and 8). It showcases the high-modernistic visions of development of the Timorese political elite, centred on state-led infrastructure development and private investors (Chapter 4), and how the formal land tenure system is selectively used to implement this vision, to the detriment of local populations (Chapters 4 and 6). It also illustrates the weaknesses of the Timorese rule of law and legal framework (Chapters 4 and 6), the results of poor law-making processes (Chapter 5), and the effects of the above-described authoritarian temptation (Chapter 4). Finally, this chapter shows the practices and fragilities of the state and non-state institutions working on land-related issues (Chapter 7), and the consequences on the ground for those who cross the path of the state (Chapter 8). Even when the state does not use force to obtain land, the implicit threat of it, combined with little respect for legal process and protection of individual rights, paves the way for land acquisition by the state.

The first part of this chapter focuses on the political environment surrounding this case study, which includes the dispute between Timor-Leste and Australia over resources in the Timor Sea, the creation of the Tasi Mane

DOI: 10.4324/9781003196396-9

Project, and an overview of the geographical area where the SSB is being implemented. The second part of this chapter focuses on the process followed by the government to obtain access to the land they required, and the consequences of this process.

Oil, politics, and 'development'

This section focuses on the geopolitical and economic background in which the ideas of the Tasi Mane Project were developed, and which are relevant to better understanding land tenure in the case of the SSB.

The resource dispute in the Timor Sea

This case study is connected with the oil and gas reserves that lie under the Timor Sea, an arm of the Indian Ocean that separates Australia from the island of Timor. Geophysical exploration of the Timor Sea in the 1960s revealed the existence of these reserves, prompting the negotiation of seabed boundaries. In 1972 Australia and Indonesia negotiated and agreed on these boundaries, including the Indonesian part of the island of Timor. The demarcation was based on the 'continental shelf' principle, which moved the boundary considerably closer to the Indonesian shore than the more-common principle of equidistance would have (Munton, 2006: 47; Dunda, 2007: 16; King, 2013: 3, 6). Portugal, unwilling to follow the same principle, refused to negotiate its maritime boundaries, leaving in the Australian boundary what is now known as the 'Timor Gap' (Map 9.1).

After the 1975 occupation of Timor-Leste, Indonesia and Australia were not able to agree on closing the Timor Gap, leaving the seabed boundary undefined and establishing instead a joint development zone for the area (Munton, 2006: 81). At the time of independence in 2002, Prime Minister Alkatiri agreed with Australia to keep the same approach to the Timor Gap, but the revenue-sharing was changed from 50:50 to 90:10 in favour of Timor-Leste (Bugalksi, 2004: 291).[1] The generosity of the new revenue-sharing formula was contested by many Timorese, who argued that if the equidistant principle was applied, Australia would not have any rights over these reserves, but Alkatiri opted for the pragmatic solution that gave to Timor-Leste access to a source of revenues (Schofield, 2005: 267). Already in 2000 the two countries had approved the specific plans to start the gas extraction in the Bayu-Undan fields, which included the construction of a pipeline from these fields to Darwin (Australia),

1 In 2002 Australia declared that it would not recognise the compulsory jurisdiction of the International Court of Justice in maritime-boundary disputes, nor accept the procedures for dispute resolution established in the United Nations Convention on the Law of the Sea, therefore preventing Timor-Leste from taking the dispute to international jurisdictions (Munton, 2006: 191).

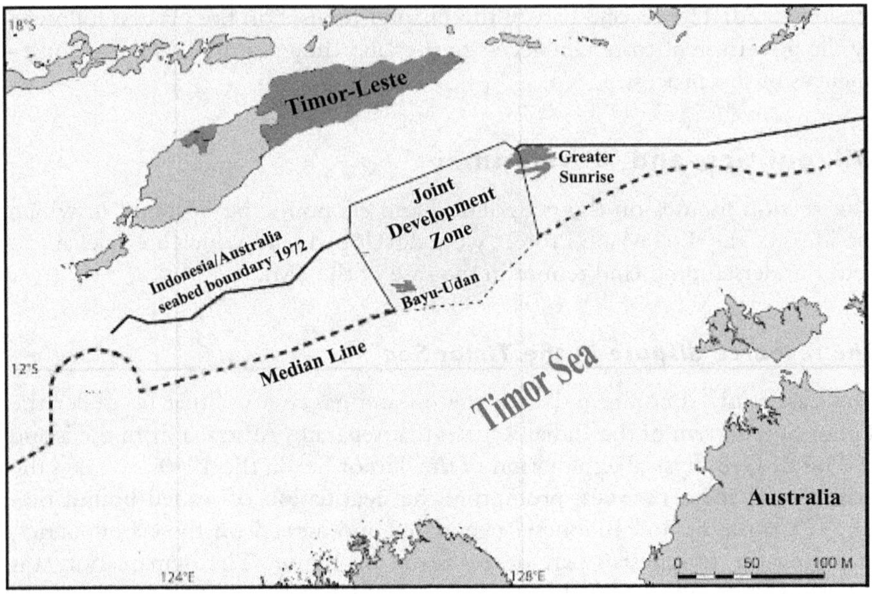

Map 9.1 The Timor Gap in the Australian boundary

where one of the world's biggest plants for processing liquefied natural gas was being built (King, 2013: 34, Munton, 2006: 196).

The exploitation of the Greater Sunrise, a gas field at least three times bigger than the Bayu-Undan and partially located in the joint development zone, became much more controversial. A treaty signed by the two countries in 2006 regulated the exploitation of the Greater Sunrise, but one critical issue remained unresolved: where should the pipeline of this field go to? The Timorese politicians envisioned the pipeline coming to Timor-Leste, as an opportunity for economic and social development, as well as a matter of justice, considering that the Bayu-Undan pipeline went to Australia (Bloomberg, 6 May 2009). Woodside Petroleum, the company responsible for the exploitation of the field, was much more inclined to a floating-facility option, arguing that the costs and technical difficulties of processing the oil and gas in Timor-Leste made this option infeasible (King, 2006: 70).

However, bringing the pipeline to Timor-Leste was a central promise of Gusmão's first election campaign for prime minister in 2007. Through his charismatic leadership, he made this dispute a matter of national pride, leaving the impasse unresolved for the next few years (Reuters, 13 January 2010).[2] In 2012, during the swearing-in of his re-elected government, Gusmão reaffirmed that:

2 ABC's show Four Corners summarises well the tensions created by this process (ABC, 1 October 2012).

> The Government is committed to bringing the pipeline of the Greater Sunrise to the south coast of Timor-Leste. We will prove to the world that the pipeline to Timor-Leste is a viable, and economically safe solution, and that our horizon is in the development of a petro-industry capable of creating direct economic dividends to our population.
>
> (Gusmão, 2012: 8)

The impasse developed further in 2013 when Timor-Leste, led by Gusmão, took the case to the International Court of Justice, arguing that Australia had failed to negotiate the 2006 treaty in good faith.[3] It became public that in 2004 Australian Secret Service had used an Australian aid project to plant listening devices in Prime Minister Alkatiri's conference room, giving Australia an unfair advantage in the negotiations of the treaty (The Australian, 3 December 2013).[4]

Contrary to what many predicted, Gusmão's bold move paid off. In the beginning of 2018, Australia agreed to establish the medium boundary line in the Timor Gap (Inside Story, 8 March 2018). This move gave Timor-Leste full rights over the almost-depleted Bayu-Undan field, and a share of 70 percent of Greater Sunrise if the pipeline goes to Timor-Leste, or 80 percent if it goes to Darwin. However, the impasse regarding a decision on the destiny of the pipeline remained.

The Tasi Mane Project and the SSB

It was under this scenario of dispute with Australia that the Tasi Mane Project was born.[5] The project is the result of a grand vision of Gusmão, through which he intends to build an oil and gas processing industry in the country, and to force Australia and Woodside to bring the pipeline to the shore of Timor-Leste.[6] In line with Scott's definition of high-modernistic, state-planned development (Scott, 1998; Chapter 4), the Tasi Mane Project is proudly classified by politicians as a 'mega project', and consists of three clusters of petroleum industry and support infrastructure, spread along the south cost of the country, connected by a four-lane highway (GoTL, 2011c: 138).

The three clusters are: (1) the SSB; (2) the Betano Refinery and Petrochemical Industry; and (3) the Beaço LNG-Plant (Map 9.2). Besides the logistical and

3 http://www.laohamutuk.org/Oil/Boundary/CMATSindex.htm

4 Australia never confirmed or denied the accusations, but the case became even more complex after the Australian secret services searched and apprehended documents from the residence and office of the Australian lawyer that represented Timor-Leste in the arbitration case (The Australian, 3 December 2013; ABC, 24 March 2014).

5 This project has been called other names, such as South Coast Petroleum Infrastructure Project and South Coast Petroleum Corridor.

6 The idea of building a supply base to serve the oil and gas fields in the Timor Gap was already a point of contention between Indonesia and Australia during the Indonesian occupation (Mboeik and Pellokila, 1996: 4).

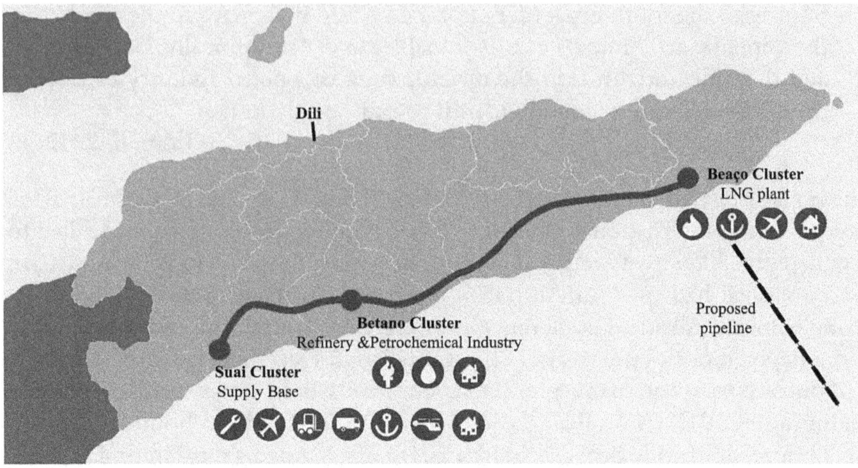

Map 9.2 Tasi Mane Project clusters. Source: GoTL, 2011c: 140

technical infrastructure, the plan also includes the construction, from scratch, of four new cities that will change the rural landscape of the south coast. The estimates regarding the cost of the project—both global and for its individual clusters—have varied significantly, and the initial idea of attracting private investors was progressively replaced by extensive public investment (GoTL, 2011c: 140).[7]

The SSB cluster (hereafter 'Suai cluster') is in the centre of this case study. This cluster is envisioned as a logistics base for the petroleum sector, divided into three main infrastructures: (1) the SSB, composed of a sea port, container park, warehouse, logistics area, office spaces, fuel storage facility, heavy-metals workshop, and shipbuilding and repair facilities; (2) the rehabilitated Suai airport; and (3) the new city 'Nova Suai' (or New Suai, in English; GoTL, 2011c: 140).[8] The Suai cluster is especially symbolic because it is the starting point of this grand vision. Gusmão's visit to the Lamongan shore base in Java (Indonesia) in October 2010 gave the final impulse to move the project from paper to reality. A few months after his trip, several multi-million dollar contracts for the initial preparations were awarded, and the fast implementation of the SSB was declared an 'inescapable national imperative' (Government Resolution 45/2010).[9]

7 See http://www.laohamutuk.org/Oil/TasiMane/13SSBen.htm. See also GoTL, 2012a: 4–26.

8 Some documents state that non-oil related industries such as industrial fishing are also expected to be introduced in the area (Timor GAP, 2013: 26).

9 Lamongan became the example to follow. The same company responsible for the Lamongan shore base received these contracts. In 2011 and 2013 respectively, a delegation of MPs and a group of

Since 2010 much has happened in the Suai cluster. The Suai airport was expanded and inaugurated in 2017 as 'Commander in Chief of FALINTIL Kay Rala Xanana Gusmão International Airport' (Tatoli, 20 June 2017). The section of the highway connecting Suai to Betano was finished, but controversially included no pedestrian or vehicle crossing, cutting off villages from their agricultural fields and causing major floods (Tatoli, 23 February 2018; Sentru Mídia Investigativu, 29 November 2018). The new city 'Nova Suai' has made little or no progress until now. The SSB has seen only difficult and limited progress. The process to vacate the necessary land is mostly finished (see below), and in June 2015 a 720 million USD contract for the design and construction of the SSB was awarded to a Korean company (Sapo Notícias, 25 June 2015). However, this contract—the most expensive contract ever awarded in Timor-Leste—was suspended by the Audit Chamber due to illegalities in the procurement process (Sapo Notícias, 30 October 2015). The government appealed and, in 2017, the Court of Appeal overruled the decision of the Audit Chamber, but by then the company had walked away from the contract (Sapo Notícias, 20 July 2017). At the time of writing the next steps of this project are not yet public.

The Tasi Mane Project has raised serious concerns among national and international observers.[10] First, the project is criticised for putting the cart before the horse. The project is based on the premise that the pipeline will come to Timor-Leste, but there is still no final decision on this matter. Timor-Leste risks spending invaluable resources on an oil and gas industry that will have no oil and gas to process. Second, observers worry about the ever-growing estimated costs of the project, now calculated at around 12.5 billion USD, almost the entire value of the Timorese Petroleum Fund, and about the lack of a public cost-benefit analysis (Scheiner, 2018: 16; Chapter 4). Furthermore, no foreign investors have shown real interest in the project.[11] Third, observers criticise many wrong assumptions and blind spots of the project, and its disregard for social and environmental impacts. For instance, the promised job creation does not take into consideration that the oil and gas industry mostly needs highly skilled workers, of which the great majority will be foreign personnel (Scambary, 2015: 302). Furthermore, the cost of creating these jobs is much higher than the salaries that these jobs will ever create, and estimations

community leaders from Covalima visited the Lamongan shore base (Parlamento Nacional, 2011: 3; Luta Hamutuk, 2014: 1). See also Government Resolution 26/2011 and 19/2014.

10 Among others, see La'o Hamutuk, 2010a: 7; The Diplomat, 17 October 2011; Fundasaun Mahein, 2013; Tempo Semanal, 11 April 2014; La'o Hamutuk, 2015: 5; Bovensiepen *et al.*, 2016: 226; and Scambary, 2017.

11 As mentioned in Chapter 4, also in regard to the Tasi Mane Project, politicians and state officials often refer to construction companies as 'investors'. For instance, a leader of the national petroleum company told me that an 'investor' was going to build the houses of Nova Suai, and the government would then buy those houses.

do not take into consideration the many (self-employed) agricultural jobs that will be lost with the displacement of people.[12] Finally, this investment shows that there is no real effort from the government to diversify the economy from the oil and gas sector.

When considering the uncertainty about the pipeline, the economic, social, and environmental costs of the project, and the difficulties of its implementation, one must ask: why is Gusmão leading the country into such a risky venture, and why are the Timorese following? The nationalistic discourse of independence and sovereignty has been a leading argument of Gusmão to promote the project and elicit support from political elites, war veterans, and the Timorese in general (Bovensiepen and Nygaard-Christensen, 2018).[13] With this project, Gusmão intends to affirm Timorese sovereignty over its national resources and to show Australia, Woodside, and the world that the Timorese are capable of implementing this complex project. The nationalistic value put on the project is such that those who disagree with it are depicted by project supporters as unpatriotic, almost equivalent to those who, before independence, supported integration with Indonesia (Cryan, 2015a: 6; Timor Post, 2 October 2014; Suara Timor Lorosae, 17 March 2016; The Diplomat, 1 June 2019).

However, patriotism and nationalistic views alone do not explain the national commitment to this uncertain venture. This project would not move forward without the strong and mostly unquestioned leadership of Gusmão, his political savviness, and the ambition of—as one of the founding fathers and visionary of the nation—leaving another mark in the independence struggle and development of the country (Chapter 4).[14] Furthermore, bringing the pipeline to Timor-Leste would give Gusmão another tremendous political victory over his eternal political rival, Alkatiri, who was not able to secure the pipeline.[15]

The high-modernistic views of development of the Timorese elite, mostly based on infrastructure and promises of private investment, and the money available in the Timorese Petroleum Fund, further allow them to think big (Chapter 4). Personal benefits for the elite, both through legitimate businesses

12 Based on a PowerPoint presentation by Timor GAP, 300 jobs will be created during the construction and 250 during the operation of the SSB. Another 1,000 to 1,500 will be indirectly created (available at http://www.laohamutuk.org/Oil/TasiMane/2012/SSBIntro25Oct2012.pdf). La'o Hamutuk concludes that each job created will cost almost twice as much as the salaries that those jobs will generate (http://www.laohamutuk.org/Oil/TasiMane/13SSBen.htm).

13 Regarding the elicitation of war veterans' support for the project see Timor Post, 23 October 2013 and 2 October 2014; Jornal Nacional Diário, 20 March 2015; Timor GAP, 2015: 3.

14 The way the project is envisioned and planned resonates with McCarthy's description of the disastrous 'Million Hectare' project in Kalimantan, in which Suharto's decisions totally eclipsed the project's technical aspects (2013: Chapter 6).

15 About this rivalry, see Shoesmith, 2013.

but also through rent-seeking opportunities, can further explain the support they give to this project. In the words of Alfredo Pires, the former Minister of Petroleum and Natural Resources:

> Timor-Leste now has money. So for anyone who has money, it becomes a bit difficult for someone to tell them what to do.
>
> (Tempo Semanal, 1 April 2013)

A national survey conducted at the end of 2016 concluded that 89 percent of respondents were in favour of the Tasi Mane Project (CISR, 2016: 24). The nationalistic discourse, the utopic views of the future, the promises of work and better life, and the co-optation of national and local elites leave little room for those directly affected by the project to negotiate their position. This topic is further debated below.

The Suai and the area of the SSB

Before analysing the land-related issues raised by the SSB, it is important to provide a brief description of the area. Suai, located on the south coast of the country, is one of the sub-districts of the district of Covalima, and the name of the district capital. Despite distancing only around 190 km from the capital, Dili, Suai is quite isolated due to very poor roads, which makes a journey from Dili to Suai 10 to 12 hours long (Tempo Semanal, 11 April 2014). Most residents in the district of Covalima are subsistence farmers (GoTL, 2012a: ES-10; Crespi and Guillaud, 2018: 433).[16] Suco Kamenasa, the most relevant area for this case study, has a population of 3,493 people distributed across 612 households (GoTL, 2011d: 46).[17]

The SSB is planned to be located on the coastal area of the east side of the city of Suai, near the village of Sanfuk, in the flat area between the river Kamenasa and the River Raiketan (GoTL, 2012a: 4–25). The area selected for the SSB has around 1306 ha and comprises land with relatively high agricultural potential (GoTL, 2012b: 15–254).[18] Before the project, the area was mostly used by subsistence farmers to grow a large variety of crops (GoTL, 2012a: 5–79). As the following sections describe, the situation on the ground changed significantly after the land acquisition for the construction of the Suai Suppy Base started.

16 In Suai only 19.5 percent of the population between 15 and 17 attends secondary school, and 32.6 percent of the population never attended school (GoTL, 2011b: 56, 58).

17 Kamenasa is also written as Camenaça, Camanasa, Camenasa, and Camenassa.

18 Like many specificities of the Tasi Mane Project, the SSB area varies considerably in different documents.

Land tenure, land tenure systems, and 'development'

The second part of this chapter focuses on the land tenure situation and the role of land tenure systems in the Suai cluster, with special focus on the SSB.[19] Grandiose infrastructure projects need large tracts of land. After the initial planning of the SSB, at the end of 2011 obtaining access to the necessary land was the next step. At the time, no land registration nor other form of territorialisation of the formal land tenure system had been implemented in the area by the Timorese Government, with land administration being based on customary systems. Moreover, at that time the draft Land Law and Expropriation Law were pending in parliament (Chapter 5). The legal framework was extremely unclear regarding which land rights were recognised by the formal land tenure system, the administrative mechanisms to identify land claims were limited, and there was no legal framework for expropriation (Chapter 6). Moreover, DNTPSC nor any other state institution was prepared for conducting the social assessments and legal procedures necessary for an adequate land acquisition (Chapter 7). Nevertheless, as it happened many times previously at a smaller scale, the government moved ahead with the project.[20]

The next sections analyse the role of the formal land tenure system in the implementation of the SSB. The process used by the government to free land for the project can be roughly divided into four main approaches: it started with (1) an informal approach by an inter-ministerial team, followed by (2) an agreement with the 'community of Kamenasa'. Later, (3) a legislative approach was tried, followed by (4) a contractual approach. These approaches are detailed in the following sections.

The informal approach of the Inter-ministerial Team

The first serious effort to free the land (*liberstasaun rai*, as it was called in Tetum), started at the end of 2011, with the formation of an inter-ministerial team lead by the national petroleum company—Timor GAP—closely directed by the Minister of Petroleum and Natural Resources at the time, Alfredo Pires.[21] The tasks of this team were divided according to the competency of each member:

19 The land acquisition process for the nearby Suai airport happened more or less at the same time and fashion, so in the description of the SSB case I make some references to the airport process.

20 Interestingly, the problems found, and the tactics used to obtain land for this project, have remarkable resemblances with those experienced in Kupang (West Timor), during Suharto's authoritarian regime, for the construction of a supply base to serve the oil and gas activities (Mboeik and Pellokila, 1996).

21 Timor GAP, the national petroleum company, should not be mistaken with the Timor Gap in the Australian maritime boundary mentioned above. The work of this inter-ministerial team is documented in a PowerPoint presentation of the Timor GAP, available at http://www.laohamutuk.org/Oil/TasiMane/2012/LacerdaPresLibertaRai24Oct2012.pdf, and http://www.laohamutuk.org/Oil/TasiMane/2012/Lacerda13Nov2012.pdf. See also Transparency Timor Blog, 15 May 2013.

the MoJ, represented by DNTPSC, was responsible for collecting information regarding land tenure; the Ministry of Agriculture and Fisheries was responsible for collecting information regarding rights over trees, plantations, livestock, and fisheries; the State Secretariat of Environment collected information about the environment and culturally relevant sites; the local authorities, *lia na'in*, and veterans were responsible for helping to identify the owners of land and plantations, and provide witness statements about tenure; and finally the National Police of Timor-Leste, also a member of the team, was responsible for keeping order during the process of freeing land.[22]

After a few coordination meetings, the inter-ministerial team started the so-called 'socialisation' of the project, through one-day public meetings at each of the four relevant sucos (Kamenasa, Matai, Belakasak, and Labarai).[23] Afterwards, DNTPSC started the identification of land rights (hereafter called 'survey'). However, this survey raised a few questions: what land rights were going to be identified? Through which process? And based on what legislation? (Chapter 6).

Ironically, DNTPSC adopted an approach that much resembled the one developed by the *Ita Nia Rai* project (INR), which DNTPSC senior officials had much criticised (Chapter 3 and 7). The area to be surveyed was divided into several collection areas, in which DNTPSC staff collected geographical information of land parcels and claims of land ownership from individuals. In the beginning of 2013, maps with the identified parcels and land claimants were displayed in public places (Fundasaun Mahein, 2013: 2). During the period of the maps' publication, land claimants were expected to come and verify the data in the maps, and present a reclamation if anything was incorrect.[24] Around 1,800 land parcels were identified through this process. However, while this survey was—at first glance—more systematic and transparent than previous processes conducted by DNTPSC, it was quite problematic.

First, the process created by INR was designed for land registration in urban areas, where more individualised land rights, resembling ownership rights, are more prevalent (Chapter 3). The INR process was not designed for areas ruled by complex customary land tenure systems, with multiple overlapping land rights, competing authorities, several material and symbolic roles for land, and flexibility regarding rights and boundaries (Crespi and Guillaud, 2018: 437). By focusing only on individual ownership of land, the survey was much simplified, but to the detriment of those whose land rights did not fit into the established categories (Chapter 2). As later became obvious, the survey seriously

22 Slide 11 of the PowerPoint mentioned in the previous footnote.

23 According to slide 7 of the PowerPoint referred to in footnote 21, information regarding compensation and livelihoods seemed to have been left for the 'questions' part of the session. See also GoTL, 2012a: 5–49.

24 Slide 40 of the PowerPoint referred to in footnote 21.

endangered the livelihoods and social connections of many of those that somehow were connected to that land, but did not, or could not, claim it as owners (see below).

Second, while people without clearly recognised formal land rights were allowed to claim ownership of land and crops in the survey, discretionary restrictions on land claims were imposed by the state officials involved in the process. As described in Chapters 6, 7, and 8, a broad understanding of which land belongs to the state, the unclear concept of abandoned land, and arbitrary administrative processes for identifying land rights left many Timorese at risk of seeing land that they use and depend on, registered as state land. This was exactly what happened in this case. People were barred from claiming land in those cases where the Dili-based state officials decided, on the spot, that land was abandoned or somehow belonged to the state (see Timor Post, 26 January 2012: 15; Cryan, 2015a: 4; Chapter 7). During an interview, a state official even told me how a corn field that was farmed during the beginning of the survey was considered state land because, at the end, the corn had been harvested and therefore there was no proof of occupation. He explained me how the team was afraid that, if they allowed people to claim land without any clear evidence of use or formal rights, they could later be accused of corruption or other crimes. Therefore, and without clear law or guidelines to follow, they adopted an approach that could also protect their own position.

Nevertheless, the high number of people affected, the visibility of the project, and the fact that land belonging to war veterans and politicians was also needed might explain the recognition that the government gave to land claims without formal rights. While this was progress when compared with other cases (Almeida, 2018a; Almeida, 2019), an undetermined number of people was nevertheless excluded from the survey.

Third, despite resembling the land claims process developed by INR, DNTPSC decided to conduct this survey independently, without the technical support of INR staff. At that time, the USAID was starting its phasing-out of the INR project (Chapter 7), and the debate about its continuity was inflaming egos inside DNTPSC. This survey was an opportunity to show the autonomy and capacity of the department in moving forward with such a task. But the copied approach improvised by DNTPSC overlooked key elements of the INR process, such as professional public-information campaigns and carefully designed internal processes, which further contributed to misinformation and confusion.[25]

Fourth, although at first glance this survey seemed more systematic, it was in fact illegal. As described in Chapter 6, at that time the only piece of legislation

25 See, for instance, the very unclear form used for collecting land information. See slide 31 of the PowerPoint referred to in footnote 21.

that provided a legal path for identifying land rights was Decree-Law 27/2011. However, even the very basic legal requirements established in this decree-law, such as the publication of notices about the survey in the Official Journal, and the publication of maps for at least 30 days, were not followed.[26] I, at the time the only legal adviser working with DNTPSC, only came to know about this survey a few months after it was completed; DNTPSC staff did not seek any legal advice regarding the legality of their survey.

Furthermore, even if the survey was legal, the land could not be expropriated because there was no expropriation law. But, as described in Chapter 4, in such a weak rule of law environment the legality of the survey and land acquisition was not a concern of politicians and state officials, who were much more concerned about delivering results for Gusmão's grand vision. Without incentives or pressure to follow the law, the mere appearance of legality was enough to move the project forward.

Despite the problems of the survey, at first the government was pleased with the work of the inter-ministerial team, which was presented as an example to follow in other land acquisition processes (Jornal Nacional Diário, 13 February 2012). However, as the following section shows, these problems soon became visible.

The ten-percent agreement with the 'community of Kamenasa'

For almost one year after the survey was completed, not much happened. Suddenly, in April 2013, it was announced in the media that, in a public ceremony in Covalima, representatives of the 'community of Kamenasa' had signed a declaration in which they temporarily gave the necessary 1,113 hectares of land for the implementation of the SSB to the government. The transfer was for a period of 150 years, and the compensation was 10 percent of the profits of the management of the SSB.[27] The agreement was signed by 15 representatives of the community, all men, and also by the district administrator, the sub-district administrator, the suco chief of Matai, the suco chief of Kamenasa, the former director of DNTPSC of Suai, the district commander of the National Police of Timor-Leste, and a number of war veterans (La'o Hamutuk, 2014: 2).[28] At the time, Alfredo Pires, at the time Minister of Petroleum and Natural Resources, stated that:

26 The publication period only lasted for 12 days (15–26 of May).

27 As detailed below, it remained unclear what this really meant in practice.

28 Rede ba Rai's Facebook account shows photos of this event, where many signatories of the agreement use their fingerprint to sign it, indicating that they are illiterate. Interestingly, the land acquisition process and the composition of this group of representatives closely resembles forestry projects implemented on the south coast during the Indonesian occupation (D'Andrea, 2003: 12).

> The Government promises that it will make a concerted effort [to proclaim] the day of 6 of April the Day of the Heroes of Development in Suai Kamenasa.
>
> (Timor Post, 12 April 2013)

The government explained that the customary rules of that community did not allow for a permanent transfer of land, and therefore they opted for a 'temporary' transaction of 150 years.[29] The distribution of the 10 percent of profits would be done through a foundation, supported by the government, although the nature of this support—financial, logistical, or administrative—remained unclear (Timor GAP, 2013: 27; Fundasaun Mahein, 2013: 4).

A few days later, a new ceremony was organised. In this ceremony one of the community representatives, the *lia na'in*, Jorge Alves, handed over the signed agreement to Gusmão, who thanked the community for their understanding of the importance of the SSB in the process of developing the country (Jornal Nacional Diário, 12 April 2013).[30] However, the text of the agreement was kept secret, and no copy of it was given to the signatories (Cryan, 2015a: 6; Bovensiepen, 2016: 84; Grainger, 2017: 181). As debated below, the text of the agreement became a matter of much speculation, which the government's secrecy did not help to dissipate.[31]

As the legal adviser working on land issues, I was surprised by this agreement. What was the connection between the previous survey and this agreement? How was the collective decision of such a heterogeneous group of people achieved, and how was the community represented in this process? How was the transaction formalised? How legal was this agreement? Answers to these and other questions started to emerge in the following months.

My first insight into more-detailed information about the ten-percent agreement came at an event in May 2013, in which a representative of a national CSO proudly described how their support to the community allowed it to bargain a raise, from 7 to 10 percent, in the share of profits of the project. The questions that I and other members of the audience raised took this CSO representative by surprise: what is the definition of 'profit', and how is the profit calculated? How is the profit equitably distributed within the community? What will happen before the profits start to flow? What happens if there is no profit? Who is 'the community' and how were its representatives selected? What will be the mechanisms for transparency and fair management of the promised profits?

29 See the media release of the Presidency of the Council of Ministers, 22 April 2013. It is not however clear what specific right *in rem* was transferred by the 'community of Kamenasa' to the government.

30 See Timor Post, 12 April 2013a; Presidency of the Council of Ministers, 22 April 2013.

31 I recall a presentation by Timor GAP officials sometime after, where the agreement was proudly mentioned, but its image included in the PowerPoint presentation was blurred to hide the text from the audience.

Puzzled by these questions, the CSO representative defensively answered that the organisation was there to support the community, but was not responsible for their final decision. After this presentation there was a generalised concern among the participants about the quality of the support the community had received during the negotiations, the transparency and legality of the agreement, and the lack of awareness of the difficulties and problems that the implementation of this agreement would bring.

These concerns were later confirmed by reports of other CSOs and news in the press. It became clear that the ten-percent agreement created expectations on the affected people that were far from the announced terms of the agreement. There were expectations that the profit of the SSB would pay 1,000 USD per month to each affected person during the following 150 years (Fundasaun Mahein, 2013: 4).[32] There was the belief that the beneficiaries would get the status of civil servants and have priority over other Timorese and foreigners in accessing future jobs at the SSB (Fundasaun Mahein, 2013: 5, 11; Bovensiepen *et al.*, 2016: 227).

There were reports of disputes between communities, as well as strong opposition to the agreement among individual community members. One of the conflicts between communities was described to me directly by Timor GAP officials, who were looking for a legal solution to it. The SSB was planned to be built in the administrative area of suco Kamenasa (see also Crespi and Guillaud, 2018: 434).[33] Such an area roughly corresponds to what was previously considered the land of the *Liurai* (king) of Kamenasa, and during the Portuguese administration was considered part of the suco of Kamenasa.[34] However, during the Indonesian administration, the population of the Dais village, from suco Belcasac, was moved to suco Kamenasa by the Bupati in order to prevent them supporting the resistance fighters.[35] Since then, the population of Dais village has been living inside suco Kamenasa, using mostly for agriculture a considerable part of the land needed for the SSB.[36] The presence of the Dais population in the area had been always controversial, but

32 See also Jornal Nacional Diário, 13 February 2012; La'o Hamutuk Blog, 1 May 2013. See also GoTL, 2012b: 15–242.

33 Many sucos correspond to areas of customary groups, but in some cases problems such as displacement created mismatches between the administrative delimitations and the claims of customary groups. In practice, the delimitation of sucos is a very heated topic that no government has yet been able to address.

34 Fox reports that in 1999 the concept of a traditional ruler of the kingdom of Kamenasa was still present (Fox, 2003: 17).

35 While Belcasac is a Bunaq-speaking region, the main language of Kamenasa is Tetum Terik. Schapper reports that 'the Bunaq are typically regarded by their neighbours with disdain, frequently characterised as a coarse and aggressive people' (Schapper, 2011: 163). Bupati is an administrative Indonesian position that heads a regency.

36 Figure 15-1 of the environmental impact assessment shows where the Dais population is currently settled inside suco Kamenasa (GoTL, 2012b: 15–228).

the prospect of compensations raised the level of disputes. The population of Sanfuk village, represented by its *lia na'in*, Jorge Alves, one of the main signatories of the agreement with the government, was strongly opposed to the payment of any compensation for land rights to the people from Dais. On the other hand, the people from Dais were opposed to this view, and claimed that their ancestors also had land rights over that area, and they were the ones that, for more than 30 years, had lived there and first cleared and farmed the land (Fundasaun Mahein, 2013: 11; also Crespi and Guillaud, 2018: 438). The fact that a number of people from Dais were members of martial art groups further raised the potential for violent conflict (Fundasaun Mahein, 2013: 11).

Other disputes between the communities also surfaced. La'o Hamutuk reported that people from the Fatu-Isin village were upset because the government paid much more attention to the people of Sanfuk village during consultations (La'o Hamutuk, 2014: 4; Independente, 31 July 2014).[37] Additionally, the *lia na'in* of Fatu-Isin, who was critical of the ten-percent agreement, was simply excluded from its signing (La'o Hamutuk, 2014: 1, 4). To further complicate this dispute, the community liaison person representing Timor GAP was a nephew of the *Liurai*, Jorge Alves, raising questions about his independence (Business Timor, 16 February 2015).

In addition to these conflicts between communities, a number of individual community members were unhappy with the ten-percent agreement: they were not aware of the benefits that such an agreement could bring to them, and they did not feel represented by the signatories, whom they considered to have been manipulated by the government.[38] The lack of access to a copy of the signed document, both by the signatories and the 'represented' community members became the source of much suspicion and distrust (La'o Hamutuk, 2014: 2; Fundasaun Mahein, 2013: 11; Bovensiepen, 2016: 84). Requests from civil society to get access to a copy of the agreement were refused with the justification that such an agreement was not public (La'o Hamutuk, 2014: 2).[39] As often happens in Timor-Leste, refusing access to basic information became another tool of state power.[40]

To further complicate this matter, a few months after the signature of this agreement, Timor GAP took 23 community leaders on a study tour to similar

37 Contrary to this position, the government's press release talks about 'a long process of consultation with the local community over several years' (Presidency of the Council of Ministers, 22 April 2013). Similar problems also happened in the airport project (Suara Timor Lorosae, 18 November 2014).

38 Fundasaun Mahein, 2013: 11; La'o Hamutuk, 2014: 7; Crispi and Guillaud, 2018: 436. On representation of communities more generally, see German *et al.*, 2011: 37.

39 Another point of heated discussions was about who deserved to live in the (future) luxurious new city, Nova Suai. The idea of 'deserve' (*merese*) alludes to the vision of development as a flow of gifts, used by the New Order regime to discipline the population (Li 2014, chap. 1, para. 26).

40 For instance, see the secrecy that surrounds the SNC project (Chapter 3 and 7; Rede ba Rai, 2019: 62).

supply bases in Lamongan, Indonesia and Kemaman, Malaysia (Timor GAP, 2013: 27, Timor GAP, 2014a: 3). This tour was presented by Timor GAP as a way of showing to community leaders the operations of a supply base and the positive flow-on effects for the local community that such a base has. But some of the affected people perceived the tour as a gift to those who had cooperated with the government and as a mechanism to further divide collaborators and opponents to the SSB (Tempo Semanal, 11 April 2014).

These conflicts show that the signatories of the ten-percent agreement were not the legitimate representatives of the so-called 'community of Kamenasa', and their agreement was far from the legitimate collective decision of a close-knit group.[41] When I asked state officials who decided, and how, that those 15 people were the representatives of the 'community of Kamenasa', the answer was always vague, referring to the representatives having been appointed by the community. As the following section shows, representation in the signing of this agreement became an issue.

The legislative approach

After the signing of the ten-percent agreement, the politicians and state officials involved in the process were convinced that the land problem was mostly solved, but reality proved them wrong. In addition to the above-mentioned protests and conflicts, the legality of this agreement was extremely dubious, both due to the legitimacy of the signatories, and the lack of legal formalities of the contract (Chapter 6). Worried with the legal fragilities of the ten-percent agreement, the international lawyers of Timor GAP recommended that measures would have to be taken to strengthen the legality of the land acquisition. The legality of this agreement had two main problems: first, any affected person could easily start a court case against it. While a successful challenge of the agreement in court was not very likely due to the weaknesses of the judicial system, it was nevertheless possible (Chapter 4). Second, with such a weak legal foundation, any diligent private investor would be reluctant to invest in the SSB.[42]

The fact that prospective (foreign) investors were the trigger for politicians' and state officials' concerns about legality is quite revealing of the very limited role that law plays in the Timorese formal land tenure system. For politicians and state officials the law works more as a tool to drive expropriation processes,

41 A few examples of the use of this idea of the 'community of Kamenasa' can be found at Timor Post, 12 April 2013; Timor Post, 12 April 2013a; Independente, 25 August 2014; Timor GAP, 2013: 27.

42 On this matter, the Director of Timor GAP said during a consultation in Suai that 'we need the legal basis for the land […], we need security for investors, we have to protect the investors' (Independente, 11 April 2014). Concerns about investors were also a reason for government officials' appeal for national unity in supporting the project, and for the prevention of internal criticism (Bovensiepen *et al.*, 2016: 229).

applicable on demand and reinterpreted when needed, than as a set of norms that must be followed. The law, or more precisely a vague and partial reference to it, gives the state stronger legitimacy and another tool to claim ownership of land or to bully people into quickly and cheaply leaving their land, but does little to guide and limit state interventions. Although the process had an appearance of legality, there was no real concern regarding due process when dealing with national citizens; only when illegality could scare investors, this became a concern for the government. Furthermore, the fact that the issue of legality was only raised after the signing of the ten-percent agreement is quite revealing of the amateurism that had been guiding the project.

But addressing the identified legal issues was not easy. The draft Land Law and Expropriation Law, at the time again waiting to be debated in parliament, were the more obvious solution to this problem, but waiting for the approval of these draft laws presented several obstacles. First, there was no guarantee when and whether these draft laws and further regulatory framework would be approved, therefore jeopardising the tight schedules that Gusmão had established for the project. Second, it was not certain that some of the purposes that the land was going to be used for would fit in the concept of public purpose (e.g., industrial area), and therefore expropriation would not be possible. Finally, the requirements of those laws would demand various time-consuming administrative processes, such as a new survey, a preparation of a resettlement plan, and the renegotiation of compensation. This would further delay the implementation of the project and show how worthless the ten-percent agreement was, forcing politicians and state officials back to the negotiating table. As such, the solution found by Timor GAP and its lawyers was the approval of specific legislation for this project.[43]

Timor GAP and the Ministry of Petroleum and Natural Resources, in collaboration with an international law firm, began drafting a decree-law specifically designed to provide a legal basis to the already finished land acquisition. The decision of approving a decree-law instead of a law had a tactical objective: it could be easily pushed through the Council of Ministers, while a law would be dependent on the parliament's agenda, and the results would be unpredictable (Chapter 5). However, a decree-law would also have a limitation. The constitution establishes that expropriation must be regulated by a law from parliament or a decree-law with a legislative authorisation from parliament.[44] Therefore, this decree-law would have to perform a de facto expropriation, without ever calling it such.

Before analysing this decree-law, two important notes should be made. First, before the approval of this decree-law, the government had already

43 Approving legislation for a specific land acquisition was a common Indonesian practice during the New Order (Davidson, 2015: 40).

44 Art. 96.1 l) of the Constitution. See also Almeida, 2017a: 181.

approved Government Resolution 20/2014, which established the maximum land values to be paid in the Suai cluster, also including the land necessary for the highway. This resolution says that, considering the difficulties identifying and negotiating the acquisition of land rights, the maximum price to be paid for land is 3 USD per square meter, and it establishes a list of prices for different trees and crops. To the best of my knowledge, this price was established in the Council of Ministers and was decided without any technical study, consultation with the affected people, nor support of any valuation specialist (see also La'o Hamutuk, 2014: 7).[45] This resolution never talks about expropriation, leaving room for two interpretations: one is that these were the maximum values that the state was willing to pay for a negotiated land acquisition and that it would not acquire land where the owner refused this price. Another interpretation is that this is the maximum price per square meter that the state will pay, with or without the agreement of the landowner, therefore through expropriation.[46] Albeit unconstitutional, this second interpretation was the one adopted by politicians and state officials, who often referred to this resolution as the price established by law, and which people had to accept. The low legal literacy of the people affected, the lack of any legal aid available to them, and the pressure put on them by the government and state officials gave them little room to challenge this resolution. Talking about land compensation for the Suai airport, Minister Alfredo Pires said that:

> The Government is ready to pay compensation, but it will have to happen according to the process and the table that was approved by the Council of Ministers.
>
> (Independente, 31 July 2014)[47]

The second note about the draft decree-law is about its law-making process, which presents another example of how legal drafters and the drafting and approval process have a significant impact on the final outcome (Chapter 5). Starting with the legal drafters, the international law firm hired to draft this decree-law attempted the impossible task of, retroactively, providing legal legitimacy to a process that had been conducted without any legal concerns. Solving the legal problems of the land acquisition process, while respecting the rule of law and protecting basic rights of the affected people, was an impossible mission. But it is difficult for a commercial law firm to impose strict limits to

45 According to Timor GAP's 2013 annual report, they 'coordinated the discussions on the drafting of a compensation value table for agricultural crops and trees including land issues with MAP (Ministry of Agriculture and Fishery) and SETP (Secretary of State for Land and Property)' (2013: 28). State officials told me the lack of consultation about the 3 USD per square meter raised protests on the ground. See also La'o Hamutuk, 2014: 5.

46 See Independente, 31 July 2014.

47 Regarding the Suai airport process, see MoJ's press release (Ministério da Justiça, undated).

its client or refuse to continue the drafting, even when the outcome is far from ideal. Furthermore, unlike international organisations, law firms do not have safeguard mechanisms that they can refer to in order to guide their work, and which allow them to refuse to continue when the requested outcome violates those safeguards.[48] I personally know the people involved in the drafting, having worked with them when I provided some comments to the draft, and I know that they are respectable professionals who did their best in drafting this decree-law. But they were in a position in which the client was demanding an impossible product, and in the world of business, 'the client is always right'. Additionally, a law firm only works with lawyers, which are not aware of the intricacies of local communities, and therefore could not take them into account. Timor GAP also made some efforts to involve other relevant ministries, including MoJ, and had at least one consultation session with (some of) the affected people. But despite these efforts, the final draft that was sent to be debated in Council of Ministers was far from satisfactory.[49]

The approval process provides another example of the fragilities of the law-making process described in Chapter 5. According to reports of informants, in Council of Ministers Gusmão tore apart the legal solutions that had been found.[50] Just the month before, the Vice Prime Minister Lasama had explained to people living in the area of the planned Suai airport expansion how Gusmão was feeling about their demands for compensation. The prime minister was angry because other big projects, such as electrification, happened all over the country, cutting people's trees and getting into their gardens, and people didn't ask for compensation; the people from Suai were the only ones asking for it (Independente, 31 July 2014, Timor Post, 31 July 2014; Ministério da Justiça, undated).[51] At the Council of Ministers meeting, the draft was mostly changed on the spot, without consultation, study, or proper control of the legality of those changes, and mostly at the whim of the prime minister.

The result of this law-making process speaks for itself. Decree-law 36/2014 regulating the transaction of rights over immovable property in the SSB, besides being an example of poor legislative writing with several gaps and

48 On the role of safeguard mechanisms in Timor-Leste, see Almeida, 2019.

49 To my knowledge there was at least one consultation session with the population in Suai regarding this decree-law (Independente, 11 April 2014). The only public output of the law-making was the decree-law. There are no other public documents that can help jurists and the people in general to understand the ideas that guided the drafting process (Chapter 5). Regarding the approval of this decree-law, see the press release of the Presidency of the Council of Ministers, 22 August 2014.

50 I, together with other MoJ advisers, provided comments on the draft decree-law, but did not participate in the Council of Ministers meetings. Conversations with informants in January 2015 gave me insights about this debate.

51 This meeting happened because the people affected were demanding being compensated before the construction started (see the press release of the MoJ—Ministério da Justiça, undated). On the land acquisition for the electrification project, see Almeida, 2019.

incoherencies, violates basic principles of law and the Timorese Constitution, and raises the questions about legality to a new level. The following paragraph provides a summary of some, but by no means all, examples.

The few social protections that had been included in the already-weak initial draft were simply removed, such as an option for replacement land as compensation, and a safeguard clause establishing that the living condition of the affected people could not be left worse than before the process. Furthermore, the ten-percent agreement on profits of the SSB (as unclear as that was), initially promised to be in favour of the community and managed by a foundation, was completely subverted. It was converted into 10 percent of the shares of the commercial company that would manage the SSB, in favour of those that claimed land in the (illegal) survey, shared among them proportionately to the land area they claimed.[52] Moreover, this decree-law established preposterous legal solutions such as retroactively addressing the problems of legitimacy of the ten-percent agreement, legalising through decree the illegal survey, and limit any possibility of the affected people taking their case to court. For instance it says that:

> [f]or the sake of this Decree-Law, the community of Kamenasa decided, freely, to be represented before the state and any other third parties, by their community traditional leaders, invested [in that power] according to their uses and traditions, and accepted by the members of that community. (art. 3.2)[53]

Finally, while never using the word, this decree-law establishes a de facto expropriation. This is visible when the legal text fixes a compensation, not a price, imposed by the government and not negotiated with the affected people (art. 13.2). In conclusion, the legislative power was not used to, in conformity to constitutional limits, harmonise legitimate public interests and state powers with the individual land rights of the Timorese, but rather as a tool to cut legal corners and promote fast and cheap dispossession.

It would be expected that in a democratic country the approval of such legislation would cause a wave of protests and public indignation. But despite the incongruities and abuses of this decree-law, its approval prompted almost no reaction in parliament nor civil society. To my knowledge, only the local CSO La'o Hamutuk sent a submission to the president, asking him to not promulgate this decree-law. However, while providing a good description of the facts

52 It is not necessary to be a commercial law specialist to imagine all the ways in which share-holders of ten percent of a company can be cut from any hypothetical profit.

53 Ironically, the lack of mandate of the signatories of that agreement was used by Alfredo Pires to justify the disputes in the SSB and deflect the controversy around the land acquisition. See page 6 of http://www.laohamutuk.org/econ/OGE15/LHKartaOJE15PN28Nov2014en.pdf

on the ground and presenting strong political arguments against the approval of the decree-law, this submission failed to use obvious legal arguments to advocate for its veto (Chapter 7).[54] Despite sitting on this decree-law for almost half a year, the president promulgated it in mid-December 2014.

The contractual approach

Although there were efforts to provide a legal basis for the land acquisition, legality was never a major concern, and even before the entry into force of Decree-Law 36/2014, another strategy for land acquisition was put in place.

At this point in the process the general climate around the project and this land acquisition process was one of confusion, distrust, and fear to speak out against the project, due to its high political profile and the government tactics to convince people to accept it (La'o Hamutuk, 2014: 5, 7; Cryan, 2015a: 6). I was told by state officials how they were entrusted by Gusmão to give a clear message to the local population: if they did not give up their land, the project would be moved elsewhere, so others, more cooperative with the government, would benefit from it (see also Bovensiepen, 2018: 135). I was also told how the government strategically involved local war veterans in public meetings and media appearances, in order to curb any dissent against the project (see Timor Post, 23 October 2013; Jornal Nacional Diário, 20 May 2015). Informants also mentioned that state officials in Suai had been avoiding public meetings where civil society organisations were present (see La'o Hamutuk, 2014: 7). After a meeting of CSOs with affected people, a representative of a war veterans association of Covalima warned the CSOs that they were not allowed to do political propaganda, and they should respect the state and the government (Timor Post, 2 October 2014). Finally, state officials also explained to me how, once the government resolution establishing the price of 3 USD per square meter was approved, their message in public meetings became much simpler: we did not come here to negotiate, we came here to inform you about the price established by government to take your land.

At the end of 2014 contracts for the acquisition of 147 parcels, corresponding to 148 hectares of land for the first stage of construction, were signed between the government and the individuals that had been identified in the survey (Timor GAP, 2014: 31). The people could choose between the 10 percent of profits for 150 years, or a 3 USD per square meter payment for definitive sale of the land (Business Timor, 13 April 2015). The majority, quite confused about the 10 percent option, opted for a definitive sale of the land (La'o Hamutuk,

54 I must highlight the role of La'o Hamutuk, a local CSO that provides an invaluable and, unfortunately, all-too-rare service as a watchdog of government activities. The amount of information gathered for this case study through La'o Hamutuk's website is itself an example of the value of this organisation to Timorese political debate and accountability.

2014: 5).[55] People were asked to open bank accounts to receive the payments of these contracts, but the payments took several months, which was a cause of discomfort and distrust by the signatories (Timor Post, 20 December 2014).

In 2016, when I last visited Suai, these contracts were still being signed.[56] Interestingly, many of those that had chosen the 10 percent solution were now changing to the definitive sale of their land (Timor GAP, 2016: 41). While I did not see these contracts, experience tells me that most probably they have several legal problems. I recall a situation in 2014 when I started receiving phone calls from DNTPSC colleagues, asking me the meaning of certain legal words. After two or three calls, I enquired why they were asking those questions, and they told me that they were in Suai, signing contracts for the acquisition of land for the airport. The draft contract used was based on an old contract, prepared for a completely different situation, and it was totally inadequate for that situation. Furthermore, as in the previous ten-percent agreement, there are reports that people did not receive a copy of the contract they signed (Crespi and Guillaud, 2018: 437).

Months after the signing of these contracts, the compensations for the loss of land started to be paid, and at the time of writing the process of land acquisition was considered mostly finished. After much jostling, the government had managed to free the land from people, although with a quite questionable legality. The effects of these informal and arbitrary processes are debated in the following section.

The effects of land acquisition

The full impact of this project will never be known. As argued by Bovensiepen and Yoder, the mere planning of these mega projects has effects on the ground, and even from the early stages there are many consequences that are not immediately perceived nor anticipated by those involved (2018: 382, 390). To my knowledge the government has no clear information about the impacts of the land acquisition. An initial environmental impact assessment from 2012 recommended a detailed Resettlement Action Plan that could assess the social impacts of the project, but this recommendation was ignored by the government (GoTL, 2012b: 15–266; Cryan, 2015a: 8). However, the partial picture provided by several media articles and academic research provides enough reason to question the way the formal land tenure system was used to free land for the project.

55 The initial draft of Decree-Law 36/2014 established the two as options for compensation, but the approved version of the draft leaves this option unclear (art. 6). These transactions should be registered (art. 9.1), according to a ministerial-decree that was never approved.

56 In 2016 Timor GAP reported to have cleared 348.16 hectares of a total 1,113 hectares (Timor GAP, 2016: 41).

At the end of 2017 the compensation for the land acquisition had been mostly paid. While the values of compensation are not publicly available, different reports talk about compensations of around 10,000 USD or 15,000 USD, with a few cases going as high as 180,000 USD (Business Timor, 13 April 2015; Grainger, 2017: 184).[57] Once people accepted that they were going to lose their land, they attempted to position themselves inside families, clans, and towards the state in a way that would maximise the benefits from their loss (Cryan, 2015a: 12; Bovensiepen, 2018: 131). The increase, reinvention, and adaptation of customary rituals are part of these positioning strategies (Crespi and Guillaud, 2018: 434). In some cases, the compensation for the land was shared between those claiming the ownership of the land and those using it, but in other cases the land acquisition created serious disputes. There are many reports of disputes within families, and within and between customary groups. The mismatch between the individualised identification of land ownership adopted by the government and the complex network of customary-based land rights on the ground, and the lack of solution for grievances caused by forced displacement and colonial injustices are main causes of these disputes (Grainger, 2017: 186; Crespi and Guillaud, 2018: 437).

The prices of land in the private market for those that wanted to replace their land quickly escalated, in some places as much as five times the initial 3 USD per square meter paid by the government (Cryan, 2015a: 10; Bovensiepen, 2018: 131). There are also many rumours that strategically located parcels of land were bought by politicians and state officials, for speculation (Grainger, 2017: 184). Some of the affected people managed to invest their compensation money well, buying land elsewhere or starting new, non-agricultural, activities. But others chose not to, or were unable to, buy new land or wisely invest their money. Instead, they kept living off the compensation they received and were somehow expected to transition from being subsistence farmers to wage workers (Grainger, 2017: 185; Bovensiepen, 2018: 134). In fact, there are many reports that considerable amounts of compensation were spent on goods such as motorcycles, cars, and televisions, and that loans were given based on expected compensations (Business Timor, 13 April 2015; Cryan, 2015a: 10; Crespi and Guillaud, 2018: 443).[58] Gambling in the area is also on the rise (Bovensiepen and Nygaard-Christensen, 2018: 16).

The feelings of people from Suai about the project vary between excitement, expectation, and fear. Some people seem to be hopeful that the

57 To give some perspective, the average national monthly income per capita in rural areas in 2011 was around 50 USD (GoTL, 2011e: 22).

58 Referring to the people affected by the construction of the Suai airport, Alfredo Pires said that the affected people were not victims, but were actually lucky for receiving such compensation, because it enabled them to make investments (Business Timor, 25 May 2015; see also Timor Post, 21 April 2014). Regarding access to land and the use of compensations, see also www.laohamutuk.org/Oil/TasiMane/13SSBen.htm.

project will bring positive changes to the area and improve their quality of life (Bovensiepen *et al.*, 2016; Crespi and Guillaud, 2018: 443). However, at least for now, the jobs and opportunities created have been far below the very high expectations, and there are reports of outbreaks of violence against contractors who employed foreign workers (Cryan, 2015a: 11; La'o Hamutuk, 2016: 5; Bovensiepen *et al.*, 2016: 227; Grainger, 2017: 186). People affected by the project express concerns about the negative effects on their livelihoods, but also on social cohesion and loss of traditions (Fundasaun Mahein, 2013: 10, 14; Business Timor, 16 February 2015a; Bovensiepen, 2018: 131; Crespi and Guillaud, 2018: 436, 443). Also relevant, the nationalistic discourse about the project used by politicians and state officials, and the deliberate involvement of war veterans in the promotion of the project, side-lined most critical voices against the project, especially at the local level (Bovensiepen, 2018: 134). However, as happened during Portuguese and Indonesian times, those local leaders who managed to show the right support and commitment to the project managed to strengthen their position as community leaders to the detriment of those that were not supportive (Crespi and Guillaud, 2018: 436, 440).[59]

Conclusion

What does the SSB case study show about the formation of the Timorese formal land tenure system? First, this case illustrates the political environment that surrounds the formation of the Timorese land tenure system. The SSB is one of the most paradigmatic examples of a vision of development based on high-modernistic, large-scale infrastructure projects, concentrated on the state, fuelled by oil and gas revenues, and envisioned by a very centralised leadership. Securing people's land rights is not a priority of the political elite, and can even be a disadvantage for this kind of project. As I was told by a Timor GAP official, the leading mentality is that people should look at the future benefits of the project, not at the struggles that the project will bring them now.

This case is also a demonstration of the almost-unquestioned power of Gusmão. While a nationalistic sentiment, fuelled by the dispute with Australia, is the motor of this high-risk project, it would probably never happen without the strong and mostly unchallenged leadership and political influence of Gusmão. Furthermore, this case shows how planning, administrative processes, the law, and people's rights have to bend and give way under the weight of Gusmão's vision.

Legality was not a major concern of politicians and state officials, with the law being used as an instrument for state action but not as a source of protection

59 About the appropriation of development by local actors in Timor-Leste, see Shepherd, 2014: 234. A very vivid image of the Tasi Mane Project in 2019 can be found at ABC, 21 July 2019.

of people's rights. Politicians and state officials selectively used and reinterpreted the law as necessary to their intents, but ignored it when inconvenient, showing the weak rule of law and lack of autonomy that marks the Timorese legal system. Legal gaps about land rights and expropriation did not prevent the project from moving forward. New, unconstitutional legislation such as the Government Resolution 20/2014 exemplifies how law is selectively used to promote and impose the project. And while inside the government there were some efforts made to develop a systematic process of land acquisition, the single effort to give real legality to the project was only intended to please eventual investors, not the affected populations, and even in this case these legal concerns were mostly abandoned. Without legal aid, legal knowledge, and a reliable judicial system to challenge the legality of the process, and under pressure to accept the project, the affected people could only try to maximise their compensation.

Furthermore, this case shows that the formal land tenure system did not provide an answer to past land grievances and was not adequate to deal with the complex customary systems on the ground. It is, however, relevant that, despite the problems of the approach adopted, the government recognised land rights that had not been formalised by previous administrations, and were not clearly protected by law. The high number of people affected, the visibility of the project, and the fact that some war veterans and politicians were affected by it might explain why, in this case, some compensation was paid by the state. However, this recognition was based on the discretion of state officials, therefore excluding many without clear legal reason.

The case also shows that the process adopted for law-making has an impact on the final outcome. The choice of the legal drafters and the discussion process have an impact on the legal solutions adopted, and without adequate preparation nor control mechanisms, even carefully studied solutions (although problematic) can be undone in minutes by uninformed politicians. The result was a piece of legislation that was full of gaps, contradictions, and unconstitutionalities. However, this had little impact in practice. This legislation attempted to give an appearance of legality to the process, but there was no real commitment to comply with the law.

The SSB case provides a clear example of the influences, fragilities, and dilemmas of the institutions working on land administration. DNTPSC's staff, without the legal and administrative mechanisms to adequately identify and grant land rights and acquire them, and politically pressured to conduct a quick and cheap land acquisition, did not have the instruments nor the incentive to implement a fair and legal process. Furthermore, discretionary power in deciding who has which rights to land and using pressure to make people relinquish their land have been part of the professional practice of DNTPSC's senior staff since their Indonesian training. Moreover, giving too much protection to people's rights can result in problems for these civil servants, so there is little incentive to provide local populations with an adequate process. The fragilities of civil society organisations, both in supporting communities in understanding their rights, negotiating with government, and challenging the legality of such processes, provide further leeway for these arbitrary and discretionary approaches. While politically vocal, their lack of technical skills prevents them from going beyond political advocacy into legal action against the government when wrongdoings occur.

Regarding those on the ground, this case shows how people have difficulty protecting their land rights when they stand in the path of a state project. The formal land tenure system does not even provide them with mechanisms to address their inter-community and family land-related grievances. If anything, the formal land tenure system can be selectively used by the state against them. Formal defence strategies, such as legal argumentation or court cases, are far realities for most Timorese. Some people manage to adapt and even thrive under the state threat, but many others end up losing more than they gain when they interact with the state.

Finally, the SSB case study illustrates the value of using the Land Tenure System Analysis Model described in Chapter 1 for the analysis of a formal land tenure system. A simpler 'law on the books and law in practice' approach would conclude that the Timorese legal framework has various gaps, and it is used selectively by the government when deemed necessary to justify its actions, and ignored when its application is inconvenient. But such approach would not be able to identify why those gaps in the legal framework exist, nor why state officials have so much discretion in their use of the law. Moreover, it would not allow to anticipate nor understand the clashes that the state's formal system has with the existing informal systems on the ground. The 'law on the books and law in practice' is at times the only approach possible, and one can learn a lot about a social issue from it. But, as debated in Chapter 1, if international organisations and politicians are serious about addressing complex land-related problems, they must invest more on broader studies such as the one proposed by the Land Tenure System Analysis Model.

I would have liked to finish this chapter with a note of hope, saying that the approval of the Land Law and Expropriation Law was bringing changes to the protection that the formal land tenure system gives to the land rights of people on the ground, and the government's approach to land acquisition. However, more than two years after the approval of these laws, little was done to implement them. Moreover, at the time I was revising this chapter, news was circulating about the formation of a new inter-ministerial team for the acquisition of land for another cluster of the Tasi Mane Project, this time the liquefied natural gas plant in Beaço (Tatoli, 16 May 2019). This news made me fear that the same arbitrary and improvised approach for land acquisition will be used again, with similar consequences to those that happen to be on the path of the state.

Chapter 10

Conclusions

Introduction

My last day as the MoJ's legal adviser for the land sector in 2014 coincided with the Ministry's Christmas lunch, to which the staff of all directorates were invited. After five years of working side by side with politicians and state officials, that lunch proved to be the perfect setting in which to talk with colleagues, share a good laugh and some stories, and say goodbye. Later, as I shared a drink with my partner at a bar by the sea, I felt that an enormous weight had been lifted from my shoulders: I was no longer on the frontline of dealing with one of the most complex and intricate topics facing Timor-Leste. But I was also grateful: my time with the MoJ had been one of the most remarkable experiences of my life, which gave me the opportunity to learn so much about Timor-Leste and the Timorese, the chance to see how state machinery works from the inside, and the honour of actively participating in the construction of the country.

In this book, based on my professional experience as land legal adviser and subsequent fieldwork, I analyse the processes, problems, and dilemmas of developing the formal land tenure system in Timor-Leste. Almost 20 years after independence, the country is still grappling with the enormous task of developing a state system that can address the land-related problems caused by colonialism, conflict, and authoritarianism, and at the same time attending to the current and future needs of the country and its people. Taking the perspective of an insider in the state administration, this book examines how political, legal, and administrative decisions about land administration are made, what and who influences them, which problems and dilemmas politicians and state officials face, and how the formal land tenure system works in practice. In other words, from a perspective still unexplored in the literature on Timor-Leste, this book enquires into the role of the state and its systems in addressing and causing land-related issues in the country. Moreover, the debate of the Timorese case provides several lessons that can be relevant to other countries dealing with similar post-colonial, post-conflict, and development land-related problems.

DOI: 10.4324/9781003196396-10

Instead of repeating the conclusions of the previous chapters, this final chapter reflects on the framework of analysis adopted in this book, and how the conclusions of each chapter answer the research question and sub-questions stated in Chapter 1. The following section reflects on the framework of analysis and the study of land tenure systems. Questions 4 and 5 are analysed in the section that follows, and questions 1, 2, and 3 are analysed in the last section, which also provides final remarks on the development of the Timorese formal land tenure system.

Studying land tenure systems—an analytical framework

To structure the study of the Timorese formal land tenure system, this book uses the Land Tenure System Analysis Model described in Chapter 1, which I designed with the objective of avoiding simple dualist approaches like the frequently used 'law on the books and law in practice'. Such an approach would show the gaps in the Timorese legal framework and how the law is selectively used in practice by the government when deemed necessary to justify its actions and ignored when its application is inconvenient. However, it would not identify the reasons why the legal framework has those gaps and inconsistencies, why they are not being addressed, not why state officials have so much discretion in their use of the law (see Benda-Beckmann *et al.*, 2006: 30; Barry, 2015: 30). It would also not allow the anticipation nor understanding of the clashes that the state's formal system has with the existing informal systems on the ground.

By studying five key analytical themes (i.e., political environment; law-making; legislation; institutional framework; and social relationships and practices), the Land Tenure System Analysis Model shows a much broader picture of what influences the design and implementation of the Timorese formal land tenure system. In other words, it helps the reader to better understand why the Timorese formal land tenure system came to be the way it is and why it works in practice so differently from what is established in law, and to anticipate the problems and comprehend the consequences of its implementation.

As discussed above, the 'law on the books and law in practice' is at times the only approach possible, and one can learn a lot about a social issue from it. Limitations of time and resources are common realities, especially in countries like Timor-Leste, and aiming for ideal scenarios regarding research might not be realistic (Chapter 5). Nevertheless, if international organisations and politicians are serious about addressing complex land-related problems, they must invest more in broader studies such as the one proposed by the Land Tenure System Analysis Model.

Importantly, the value of this model goes beyond the study of the formal land tenure system in Timor-Leste, and can also be used in other countries and other socio-legal phenomena, such as family law and criminal law.

What can we learn from Timor-Leste? Factors of success and failure of a formal land tenure system

As debated in Chapter 2, formal land tenure systems play a role in addressing key problems that countries must deal with, such as insecurity, poverty, inequality, destruction of nature, and social estrangement, but these systems can also cause or aggravate these same problems. This section debates the key factors that contribute to the successes and failures of the Timorese formal land tenure system in dealing with these problems, and the lessons that can be drawn from the Timorese case for other developing countries dealing with similar land-related post-colonial, post-conflict, and development issues (research questions 4 and 5). These lessons can also be valuable to specific areas of governance that all countries must deal with, such as the work of state institutions and legislatures. In order to bring this analysis into an organised structure, this section is divided into three key overarching factors: (1) administrative processes, public administrations, and state officials; (2) rule and role of law and law-making; and (3) ideology.

Land tenure and administrative processes, public administrations, and state officials

While public administrations in developing countries are often criticised for being very bureaucratic, less is said about the importance of bureaucracy. The case of Timor-Leste highlights the importance of administrative processes, the principle of legality, and the rule of law in controlling the negative impacts that state institutions can have on people's lives.

The regulation of administrative processes is not a whim of jurists and bureaucrats. Public administrations are entrusted with powers that can seriously harm people's rights. The principle of legality that determines that state institutions can act only based on processes regulated by law intends to tame the use of these powers by the administration, and attempts to provide certainty, fairness, and predictability to administrative processes (Bedner, 2010: 58; Weber, 2013: 979). As extensively exemplified in the description of DNTPSC's work (Chapter 7), when administrative processes are not regulated, or when law is an optional tool that state officials can choose to ignore at their convenience, it is only natural that they will follow the path of least resistance. The administrative processes that state officials arbitrarily create and their selective use of law tend to facilitate their work and provide them with advantages to the detriment of people's rights and defence against administrative decisions.

As argued in the literature, the level of discretion that state officials should have in their work is debatable (Wilson, 1989: 337, 342; Kanstroom, 1997: 721); some level of discretion is unavoidable, and in some cases discretion can be beneficial to the people that state officials serve. A case in point is the selective application of law that at times DNTPSC's officials make to bypass the very harsh rules on evictions, allowing occasional financial compensations to evictees who, under a strict interpretation of the law, should be evicted without any payment.

But the Timorese case also shows that extreme levels of discretion by state officials, both by lack of legislation and selective use of it, more often tend to disfavour the people affected by their improvised administrative processes. Such discretion removes transparency, predictability, and balance between the rights and obligations that should mark the work of the public administration, taking away procedural guaranties, and allowing for rushed and unsubstantiated decisions (Nonet and Selznick, 1978: 65). This is all the more problematic the more powerful the institutions are, the further the people are from the decision-makers, and the weaker the judicial system is. The process used to obtain land for the SSB is a clear example (Chapter 9). State officials, used to employing extreme discretion in their work and politically pressured to provide the state with quick and cheap access to land, claimed a broad power of the state to dispossess people, based on a selective and very biased interpretation of existing legislation and ignored the lack of legal mechanisms for adequate identification of land rights and expropriation. The improvised administrative process they implemented had the appearance of legality, but in practice allowed them to take arbitrary decisions regarding who has which land rights, to unilaterally decide how much compensation would be paid and to whom, and to provide in practice no real mechanisms of contestation to those affected by the process.

One point less discussed in the literature, and clearly highlighted in the case of DNTPSC, is that adequate bureaucracy also provides protection for state officials. The same way that too much discretion opens the door to abuses by state officials, the lack of clear processes also exposes them to unfair allegations of corruption, bribery, and malpractice by third parties, as well as unacceptable political orders. The problems experienced by DNTPSC with the signature of lease contracts over state property is a clear example of how poor bureaucratic processes are open doors for abuses, but also expose those involved to unfounded accusations by disgruntled clients (Chapter 7). Interestingly, even the political leadership that should focus on the regulation of administrative processes at times uses the discretion of state officials to blame them for problems of the administration and disavow themselves of their own responsibilities. This is clear in Timor-Leste: the same ministers and MPs who complain about the work of DNTPSC do not invest the time and resources in regulating its administrative processes.

However, the role that bureaucratic processes play in protecting people rights must not be overstated. The value of bureaucratic processes depends on their design, the objectives they intend to achieve, the capacity of state institutions to implement them, and the mechanisms available to participate in and react against these processes (Wilson, 1989: 342). Moreover, one must be aware that bureaucratic barriers are often used as a way of deriving personal benefits. The case of Timor-Leste provides several examples where useless bureaucratic steps, lack of resources by state institutions to implement them, and de facto exclusion of possible clients are detrimental to the people that the bureaucracy should serve, and open opportunities for abuses by state officials. The haphazard implementation of nationwide land registration by SNC is a paradigmatic example of how poorly designed, intended, and implemented bureaucratic processes can bring more harm than good (Chapters 3 and 7). For instance, the requisite that land claims must include a declaration from two local state officials attesting to the truthfulness of the claim is a clear example of an administrative step that adds no value to the process, contradicts the logic of an open land claims process, put a bigger burden on the people the process should serve, and create more opportunities for corruption and rent-seeking. In these cases a bureaucratic process becomes another problem instead of a solution for those that it should serve. Bureaucracies must have the capacity to keep questioning the purposes of their processes and adjust them when they prove to be inappropriate to serve that purpose.

Moreover, the case of Timor-Leste clearly exemplifies how the value of bureaucracy is constrained by severe limitations of human, financial, and material resources that commonly characterise state institutions in developing countries. Under these circumstances, those involved in the development of the formal land tenure system need to choose their battles, be realistic and pragmatic when designing administrative processes and institutions, and avoid the mesmerising effects of complex technology and large-scale interventions (Enemark *et al.*, 2014). The choices about where, how, and which type of bureaucracy to build, besides carrying an ideological weight (see below), are not free from problems and dilemmas but are nevertheless necessary. Picking the right battles can make the difference between building a formal system that helps to address land-related problems and one which further complicates them. The development of the expropriation process detailed in the Expropriation Law provides a clear example of these problems and dilemmas (Chapter 5). On the one hand, a complex process with several phases that incorporates the participation of several specialists (e.g., resettlement specialists, land valuers) and provides multiple opportunities for public participation is more protective of people's rights. On the other hand, complex processes tend to be more easily disregarded by politicians and state officials with justifications such as the lack of resources and regulatory framework to implement them, as is happening in the case of Timor-Leste. Finding the right balance between ideals like inclusiveness, protection of rights, and equality on one side, and pragmatism on the other leave politicians and state officials with difficult choices to make.

However, some of these dilemmas are also a symptom of a deeper problem in land administration, common in post-colonial states. The case of Timor-Leste adds to the long list of developing countries where the design of the formal land tenure system ignored the perils of past colonial administrations and adopted a 'replacement paradigm', through which the government tried to replace, with little success, deeply rooted customary systems with a new, state-based one (Bruce *et al.*, 1994: 261). For instance, the study of the Timorese case shows how the presence of state institutions outside Dili will likely remain minimal for many years due to the lack of human and financial resources (Chapter 7), and how attempts to create complex administrative processes for land administration outside the main urban areas are likely to fail. SNC's nationwide survey is a clear example of an unrealistic bureaucratic process that takes no consideration of the limitations of public administration institutions, nor respects and works with local land tenure systems. The result is clear: without administrative mechanisms to update land claims, the survey is outdated from day one; and the clashes between the claims collected and the customary-based land rights on the ground are, and will be for decades, a source of many conflicts (Chapter 8).

This example reinforces the support given by many authors to an 'adaptation paradigm' (or 'third way'), in which formal systems rely more on, incorporate, and work with customary systems.[1] Although these systems have their disadvantages, they generally have in practice more legitimacy that state institutions, are much more adapted to local realities, and are known to and participated in by local populations (Chapter 2). Instead of trying to replace these customary systems, state institutions would benefit from looking at their gaps and problems, and addressing them collaboratively. For instance, this book shows that the Timorese value a combination of state officials and customary authorities in dispute resolution (Chapter 8); a fraction of SNC's cost would pay for more, better-trained, and better-equipped state officials in the districts that could support dispute resolution, instead of trying to replace the customary system with land registration that is causing more problems. As the case of Timor-Leste shows, poor attempts to replace customary systems with state ones carry a serious risk of bringing more uncertainty and insecurity to land tenure when they are intended to do the opposite.

Finally, and in line with other studies on bureaucracies (Lipsky, 2010; Tidey, 2012), the analysis of the Timorese formal land tenure system highlights the importance of paying attention to the human side of state institutions that work on land-related issues. To understand the work of these institutions, one must try to step into the shoes of the state officials that work there. Their backgrounds and training, the conditions in which they work, the resource limitations they experience, the personal risks they face, the implicit and explicit pressures they suffer, and the political orders they receive make their roles much more complex and layered than they appear at first glance. The example of DNTPSC state officials is paradigmatic. They were trained during Suharto's regime and were left since independence to address one of the country's most complex issues without clear legislation, judicial supervision

1 Among others, Bruce *et al.*, 1994: 261; Platteau, 1996: 44; Fitzpatrick *et al.*, 2008; Otto and Hoekema, 2012; Wily, 2012.

nor adequate resources. Moreover, they experience constant political pressure to provide the state with quick and cheap access to land, are often targets of threats, and work with no guidance in a sector that is known to be prone to corruption and malpractices. Under these conditions one simply cannot expect that these state officials will be the champions of administrative efficiency and rule of law, nor the defenders of people and communities' land rights. As the face of public administration, state officials are easy targets of critiques and complaints, but under the same conditions, others would probably follow the same paths.

Land tenure and the rule and role of law and law-making

At a minimum, the rule of law implies that a state follows its own rules (Bedner, 2010: 56). However, this book shows how, for several reasons, politicians and state officials have a high degree of discretion regarding following state law (Chapters 4 and 7). As mentioned above, in a weak rule of law environment such as the Timorese, where politicians and state officials can, with a high degree of impunity, decide to not follow the law, it should be no surprise that they will often choose to ignore it. If at times the bending of rules can work in favour of the most vulnerable, too often they will bend or ignore the rules in order to facilitate their lives and promote their own interests, to the detriment of the rights of the people.

This situation might lead some readers to think that, in a weak rule-of-law environment, there is no point in investing time and effort in improving legislation because it will be ignored in practice. I argue differently; although it can be quite frustrating to see important legislation remain unapproved or unimplemented—and I probably let my frustrations seep through in this book—for the reasons stated below, even in a weak rule of law environment, is still worth fighting for better legislation. Although better laws will not solve all land-related problems and promote fairer land tenure, they will help, and are therefore worth investing in.

Those more sceptical about state laws point out that, at the minimum, they are ignored, but most importantly, state laws are also a tool of oppression by the state and the ruling elites (Balbus, 1977: 580, 582; Pashukanis, 1983: 62; Chapter 2). This book adds some nuance to that argument. Indeed, a draconian law such as Law 1/2003—especially as it was interpreted throughout the years—played a role in legitimising state interventions that unfairly disempowered and displaced many Timorese, and allowed the state, and in a less-obvious way the ruling elites, to secure rights over land (Chapter 6). Moreover, even in those cases where the law is more favourable to the people, it is still used by the state and ruling elites to abuse their power, through strategies such as selective use of the law, biased interpretations, and excuses such as the lack of a regulatory framework. The case of expropriation in Timor-Leste is a clear example. Politicians and state officials constantly use the Timorese

Constitution to justify land dispossession in favour of the state, but systematically ignore the obligation to follow a clear process established by law instead of improvised ones (Chapter 6). The same arbitrary processes are still used even after the approval of the Expropriation Law, with the argument that complementary regulations are still missing. Therefore, it is undeniable that the law can be used as a tool of oppression and dispossession by the state and the ruling elites. However, the fact that even good law can be used to oppress people adds a first point of nuance to the debate about the role of law; at times the problem is not the law, but the power to use it in a discretionary and biased way.

The second point of nuance about the role of law is that, like a double-edged sword, the law can cut both ways and even under adverse conditions can play a role in curbing abuses of power of the state and the ruling elites. First, as argued by Thompson, due to its characteristics of universality and equity, even a law that aims to strengthen state power and protect ruling elites can work as tool to curb abuses of power (2013: 205; Halliday *et al.*, 2007: 36; Bedner, 2016a: 13). By using law to legitimise state power and elite privilege, elites become bounded by those same rules, which can later be used against their privilege. This was clear, for instance, in the case of the SSB (Chapter 9). The Government Resolution 20/2014 establishing the price that the state was going to pay for land, besides several problems of legality, was used to legitimise a de facto illegal expropriation. On the other hand, it can be argued that, despite several problems of legality, this legislation fixed the standard of compensation higher than in previous similar processes of eviction (Almeida, 2019: 279), and those that managed to be identified as the owners of land and crops could have a stronger claim for compensation. From an ideal perspective, this regulation would not be approved, and a much more careful process of expropriation and compensation would be followed, but despite not being fair nor legal, this resolution established some boundaries to state behaviour. In summary, although law is often used to justify abuses of power, there is value even in bad legislation that should not be disregarded.

Moreover, the law also provides those who suffer from, and resist against, abuse of power a clear target to fight and an aim to which to aspire (Thompson, 2013: 204; Cotula, 2016: 179). The law-making of the Land Law Package clearly exemplifies this role of law (Chapter 5). This law-making process provided a forum for numerous debates between various actors that otherwise would not have talked to each other; it gave CSOs and society in general clearer aims to fight for; it worked as a reality check on the extreme positions of all stakeholders; and it forced politicians to clarify their own political views on the topic. Although the process of approval and the outcome was not ideal, in the end this law significantly changed the existing legal framework that, once applied, provides a stronger weapon with which to fight against arbitrary state interventions. The fight for fairer laws and their implementation might not be an easy struggle, but provides at least some ground on which to fight.

The Timorese see this value in the law, despite still experiencing several limitations to making it work in their favour. People contest the fairness of existing laws, the legitimacy of law-makers, the implementation of legislation, and the practices of public administration, but they do not call for the end of the rule of law. If anything, they complain that the law is not strong enough, and see some value in formal state systems (Chapter 8). As said by Thompson, 'there is a difference between arbitrary power and the rule of law' (2013: 208). Giving up the fight against bad laws or no laws only leaves the powerless even less equipped against arbitrary power, which highlights the importance of good laws.

However, the example of Timor-Leste also compels me to add some caution in my appeal for investing in better legislation. The focus on law, both by state and non-state actors, can also work as a distraction from more urgent matters, such as the improvement of administrative institutions and the judicial system as a whole. In some situations the search for the perfect law can be detrimental, as even imperfect laws can work in favour of the people if other factors such as institutional capacity are improved. The case of Timor-Leste shows that the 'waiting for the law' approach can be used as a subterfuge to perpetuate unjust state practices. After many years justifying arbitrary state-led land dispossession with the lack of approval of the Land Law and Expropriation Law, now politicians and state officials justify the same behaviour with the excuse that further regulations still need to be approved. The fight for new laws can be a mask to those that want to keep the status quo, and a distraction for those that want to change behaviours.

It is important to note that the role law can have in addressing land-related issues and promoting fairer land tenure is also dependent on what Bedner calls the 'autonomy of law' (2016a). The institutions that form the legal system must be able to autonomously perform their tasks, based on the procedural rules that guide their activity, and to do so without outside (illegal) interference (ibid.: 10; see also Nonet and Selznick, 1978: 54, 59). This autonomy is crucial for enforcing legislation but also to, through legal reasoning of court decisions, address the gaps and contradictions of that legislation, work as a buffer against unjust norms, and promote legal certainty of court decisions. Although only briefly analysed in a few lines of this book (Chapter 6), also in this field the infant judicial system of Timor-Leste still has a lot of room for improvement. Court decisions still miss the depth of legal analysis necessary to engage with the gaps of the land tenure legal framework and to provide citizens with more justice and certainty. The fight for better laws is easier under the protection of a strong judiciary.

Finally, the relevance of good laws links with the importance of the law-making process. As this book shows, the weaknesses of procedural devices of Timorese law-making—such as specialised offices for verification of legal compliance, monitoring and evaluation mechanisms, and translators—seriously affect the coherence of the law-making process and the quality of legislation

(Chapter 5). If one wants to promote better laws in developing countries, the law-making process must be taken into consideration. However, this conclusion must be read with some prudence; law-making in developing countries comes with intrinsic limitations and dilemmas that cannot be easily solved, and aiming for perfection in law-making can result in costly paralysis (Tamanaha, 1999: 155). As highlighted in Chapter 5, there is a need for more research that can help developing countries to improve their law-making processes despite the limitations that they experience.

Land tenure and ideology

One of the points that the case of Timor-Leste most clearly highlights is that land tenure administration is, first and foremost, a political matter, and the formal land tenure system is a political instrument. By deciding who has which rights over land, and by finding a balance between the different uses and users of land, the formal system sets the prevailing ideology about land tenure in the country (Chapter 2). This delivery is done both through actions, such as the approval of legislation, but also through inactions, such as the inertia to approve and implement necessary legislation (Chapter 4). It can also be done through legal and illegal means and, as the Timorese case exemplifies, sometimes it is not even possible to clearly define where legality starts and ends (Chapter 6).

The reason why I choose to highlight this point in the conclusion is because the political dimension of land tenure administration is too often, consciously or unconsciously, ignored and overlooked by politicians, state officials, practitioners, and academics (see Li, 2017: 1248, 1258). It is common for debates on land tenure administration in different arenas—conferences, papers, political debates—to get tangled in the technicalities of land administration, without acknowledging that, in the end, it is all about the politics of distribution. New laws, different institutional arrangements, and innovative technological solutions are neither politically neutral nor operate in a political vacuum, and ignoring their political dimension contributes to masking and promoting hidden agendas that might not be in the best interests of those in need (ibid.: 1258). For instance, SNC's land registration is not politically neutral, as it promotes state claims to land over private ones and individualised land rights as the main form of land tenure. As further argued below, the fact that technical solutions carry a political dimension emphasises the importance of ideology in land administration and the role that all actors play in it.

The political dimension of technical solutions highlights the fact that innovative approaches to land tenure administration are not enough to promote fairer formal land tenure systems. This objective can only be achieved if fairness regarding land rights is a concern of the prevalent ideologies. Defining what fairer means here raises difficulties. However, and following Sen's line of thought in the debate of what justice is (2009: 21), the fact that it is not possible to perfectly define a just formal land tenure system does not prevent us from pointing out injustice when we see it. For instance, the conflicting interests on land tenure in Timor-Leste will never allow a perfect consensus about which land rights should prevail. But the state claiming ownership of land that has been used and managed for centuries by communities, and promoting quick and cheap displacement with the justification that a few—usually the poorest and most vulnerable—should sacrifice their wellbeing and livelihoods for supposed future national development is bluntly unjust. As argued in Chapter 2, land tenure systems need to strike a balance between different roles, uses, and users of land, and sometimes that balance is extremely tilted in disfavour of certain groups. The case of Timor-Leste provides the literature with another example of a post-colonial developing country where this balance is clearly distorted in favour of large infrastructure projects, supposedly targeting economic development, and although less openly stated, favouring elites. And as in many other countries, this approach has not led to more secure land rights of the majority of Timorese nor significant improvements in their life conditions. As highlighted by Li, when economic growth is a priority over everything else, the distribution of eventual benefits is never sufficient to compensate for the livelihoods lost (2014: Conclusion, para. 16). Without minimum fairness in the dominant ideology, there is little chance that a formal land tenure system will deliver a fair balance between different uses and users of land.

But getting the ideology right is not just the task of politicians. While they tend to have a more visible role in the development and implementation of a formal land tenure system, state officials, practitioners, academics, and the general population, through their actions and inactions, also participate in this development and implementation, and are therefore doing politics. I must add that, when criticising anyone's work on land tenure, one must not lose sight of the wicked nature of land-related issues (Chapter 2). Even the best-intentioned and most well-prepared politicians, civil servants, practitioners, and academics have trouble defining the land-related problems they need to study or address, finding the solutions to adopt, and predicting the impacts that those solutions will have. In short, land tenure administration is difficult. But despite these difficulties, the final conclusion is simple: the importance of ideology as the starting point for the construction of a formal land tenure system cannot be ignored, and the actions and inactions of all of those involved ultimately contribute to improving or damaging the livelihoods of many people.

The Timorese formal land tenure system—final remarks

Building on the conclusions of each of the previous chapters, this final section briefly summarises the main land-related problems caused by past colonial administrations, violence, and displacement (research question 1), how the Timorese formal land tenure system has dealt with those problems, and how this system has been used to promote the ambitions and visions of development of the Timorese elite (research question 2). It also reflects on how successful the Timorese formal land tenure system has been in addressing these problems, ambitions, and visions, and what the consequences of its implementation are (research question 3). The chapter finishes with a very brief recommendation.

As described in Chapter 3, the centralised colonial state systems implemented by the Portuguese and Indonesian administrations were designed to favour a strong state control of land tenure and worked mainly in favour of those with close contact with state authorities. The great majority of Timorese were in practice excluded from these formal land tenure systems, which also gave little legal recognition to the customary systems that de facto ruled—and still rule—land tenure throughout most of the country. The forced displacement, violence, corruption, and nepotism experienced in Timor-Leste, especially after the violent Indonesian invasion, were sources of many long-lasting land-related grievances that persist nowadays, and the difficult transition between the Portuguese and Indonesian formal land tenure systems added another layer of confusion about formal land rights. These problems were further increased with the mass displacement and re-occupation of land after the violent withdraw of the Indonesian troops in 1999, and the limited capacity of UNTAET to address land-related problems. At the verge of independence, the post-colonial, post-violence, and post-authoritarianism past of Timor-Leste were the picture of a perfect storm in land-related issues.

Since the independence of Timor-Leste in 2002, the development of the formal land tenure system has been a slow and difficult process. The political environment in Timor-Leste has never been conducive to the development of laws, institutions, and practices that legally recognise and effectively protect people's and communities' land tenure (Chapter 4). A combination of interconnected ideological and contextual factors promotes strong control of land by the state, dissuades politicians from trying to effectively regulate state-led dispossession, and gives little room for contestation to those affected by state interventions. This political environment, combined with weaknesses of the procedural devices of law-making (Chapter 5), have a clear impact on the legislation that shapes the Timorese formal land tenure system.

The legislation that has regulated the Timorese formal land tenure system since independence has been marked by gaps, contradictions, unrealistic legal requirements, lack of regulatory framework, and unimplemented legislation (Chapter 6). Moreover, from 2002 until 2017, Timorese legislation mostly ignored the problems caused by previous colonial administrations, violence, and displacement; it did little to protect people's and communities' land rights; and it did not tame the state's voracity for land. After almost nine years in the making, the approval of the Land Law Package in 2017 considerably changed the legal framework. Although with limitations, the laws of the package filled many previous legal gaps, established legal criteria to address overlapping land rights, recognised customary-based land rights, established a much more protective legal framework for the land rights of people and communities, and tamed the power of the state to claim land and dispossess people. But more than two years after the approval of the Land Law Package, the regulatory framework for its implementation has not yet been approved, and these laws remain mostly ignored in practice.

The success of the Timorese formal land tenure system has been further complicated by the limitations of the institution responsible for its implementation (Chapter 7). DNTPSC, the main state institution responsible for land administration since independence, struggles with resource limitations, including inadequate workspace, equipment, financial resources, and qualified staff for the tasks of the institution, most notably jurists. Several tasks of the institution demand legal skills, but the institution does not have jurists on its staff. The structure of DNTPSC is poorly aligned with the tasks that the institution needs to perform, and its presence outside Dili is minimal, further limiting its capacity to deliver land administration services throughout the country. Unrealistic expectations and demands by politicians, DNTPSC's own staff, and society, and the weaknesses of the judicial system to provide checks and balances further influence how DNTPSC operationalises the formal land tenure system. DNTPSC's work, deeply influenced by the previous work experiences of its senior members with the Indonesian BPN, is marked by a selective use of law, improvised administrative processes, and extreme discretion of its staff. Kafkaesque processes for leasing state land, harsh evictions, and swift arbitrary decisions by state officials about ownership of land are hallmarks of the institution.

Politicians and DNTPSC's staff have been pointing out land registration as the path to address conflicting land claims and promote tenure security, but several problematic land registration attempts have only added new layers of confusion regarding land rights. The land claims process created by Law 1/2003 had several legal and practical issues that put the thousands of land claims made under this law in a legal limbo (Chapter 6). The USAID's INR project (2007–2012) developed a transparent and locally adapted administrative process to collect land claims in the urban areas of the district capitals, but strong opposition to the project's methods by DNTPSC senior staff, and the poorly managed end of the project by USAID meant that most of INR's work was, in practice, wasted (Chapters 3 and 7). From 2014 onwards SNC, the controversial sole-sourced contractor hired by the government to continue land registration, completely ignored INR's main strengths such as transparent processes, well-designed public information, and awareness of the complexity of customary systems. Moreover, SNC's expansion of the land-claims collection process to rural areas without an adequate methodology, a focus on individual and state land claims to the detriment of communal ones, and disrespect for legal criteria created a new layer of problems in the already complex scenario of land tenure in Timor-Leste (Chapters 3, 7, and 8). After three failed attempts, the expansion of land registration has proven to not be the way forward.

Throughout the years, DNTPSC has received support from international organisations, who, although sporadically influencing DNTPSC's work, have also failed to intervene when help is needed. However, unresponsiveness, lack of planning, and even miscommunication from the MoJ and DNTPSC have also limited the intervention of these international actors. Timorese CSOs working on land-related issues are strong in activities such as mobilising a protest, being close to the population, and lobbying politicians, but their research skills, legal knowledge, and use of judicial strategies to challenge the legality of political decisions and administrative practices remain limited. While these CSOs have been improving their skills, they still experience serious limitations that reduce their voice at the law-making table and their capacity to influence the development and implementation of the formal land tenure system.

In conclusion, although some progress has been made, the result is still a formal land tenure system that gives most Timorese almost no certainty about land rights, provides little protection to those who cross the path of the state, is disconnected from the customary systems that de facto manage land throughout the country, and keeps the few formal mechanisms of dispute resolution out of reach for most Timorese (Chapters 8 and 9). Notwithstanding important steps such as the fairly recent approval of the Land Law Package, the land-related problems caused by colonialism, violence, and displacement that the country inherited from previous administrations are far from solved (Chapter 3), and in practice the formal system is still failing to provide a fair recognition of land rights. In fact, this system is often used as a tool of state dispossession, through which only a few can access and secure their land rights. For many Timorese, the contact with the formal land tenure system means the beginning of new problems to their lives. Some people have been able to navigate the inconsistencies of the system and secure their land rights, but uncertainty, arbitrariness, and risk of dispossession are still strong markers of the Timorese formal land tenure system.

When analysing the development of the Timorese formal land tenure system, one must not forget the magnitude of the challenge. If developing a system to address land tenure problems is complicated in any context, when considering the political, economic, administrative, and social situation of the country, we can only conclude that developing the Timorese formal land tenure system is an enormous and extremely complex endeavour that requires time and plenty of trial and error. However, this perspective should not distract us from the fact that the failures of the formal land tenure system have real consequences in the lives of the Timorese today. While the long-term perspective is important, focusing too much on the promises of tomorrow's bright future opens up the risk of exculpating obvious and sometimes opportunistic mistakes and of continuing to leave people's current needs unaddressed.

If those involved in the construction of the Timorese formal land tenure system are serious about creating a formal land tenure system that provides a fairer access to land and tenure security, significant changes must be made to the path that is currently being followed. It is my opinion that the development of the Timorese formal land tenure system needs to focus on strategic, solid, smaller steps that prioritise respect for the basic rights of the Timorese, and which curb the powers of the state to dispossess people of their land. Despite the limitations, the Timorese Constitution and the Land Law Package provide a relatively solid starting point on which these steps can be built. But in my view, a better formal land tenure system can only be achieved with a considerable change to the prevalent visions of development that the Timorese political elite has for the country. The hopes and dreams that fuelled the fight of so many Timorese for the country's independence will not be fulfilled if a fairer land tenure administration is not achieved.

References

Aditjondro, George (1994). *In the Shadow of Mount Ramelau – The Impact of the Occupation of East Timor*, Indonesian Documentation and Information Centre

Alagappa, Muthiah (2004). 'Civil Society and Political Change: An Analytical Framework' in Muthiah Alagappa (ed.), *Civil Society and Political Change in Asia - Expanding and Contracting Democratic Space*, Stanford University Press: 25–57

Almeida, Bernardo (2016). *Land Tenure Legislation in Timor-Leste*, The Asia Foundation

Almeida, Bernardo (2017). 'Navigating Without a Compass: State Transition in Timor-Leste's Formal Land Tenure System' in Rui Feijó, Susana Viegas (eds.), *Transformations in Independent Timor-Leste*, Routledge: 123–141

Almeida, Bernardo (2017a). 'The Main Characteristics of the Timorese Legal System – A Practical Guide' in *Verfassung und Recht in Übersee VRÜ*, 50(2): 175–187

Almeida, Bernardo (2018). 'A aplicação da usucapião em Timor-Leste' in *e-boletim Lei & Justiça*, 1(1): 5–15

Almeida, Bernardo (2018a). 'Expropriation or Plunder? Property Rights and Infrastructure Development in Oecusse' in Judith Bovensiepen (ed.), *The Promise of Prosperity: Visions of the Future in Timor-Leste*, ANU Press: 99–118

Almeida, Bernardo (2018b). 'Hakarak ka lakoi? Os limites da expropriação em Timor-Leste' in *e-boletim Lei & Justiça*, 1(2): 19–35

Almeida, Bernardo (2019). 'With or Without International Institutions? Acquisition of land rights for Infrastructure Projects in the Weak Legal Framework of Timor-Leste' in Susanna Price, Janer Singer (eds.), *Country Frameworks for Development Displacement and Resettlement – Reducing Risk, Building Resilience*, Routledge: 269–287

Almeida, Bernardo; Wassel, Todd (2016). *Survey on Access to Land, Tenure Security and Land Conflicts in Timor-Leste*, Van Vollenhoven Institute and The Asia Foundation

Anderson, Tim (2013). 'Development Strategies' in Michael Leach, Damien Kingsbury (eds.), *The Politics of Timor-Leste – Democratic Consolidation after Intervention*, Cornell Southeast Asia Program Publications: 215–238

Anonymous Author (1991). 'Winner Takes All - East Timorese Convert to Indonesian Land Certificates' in *Inside Indonesia – Bulletin of the Indonesia Resources and Information Programme*, 26: 9–11

ARD Inc. (2006). *USAID-ARD Land Law Program II: Timor-Leste*. Final Report, USAID

Arnscheidt, Julia; Rooij, Benjamin van; Otto, Jan Michiel (2008). 'Lawmaking for Development: An Introduction' in Julia Arnscheidt, Benjamin van Rooij, Jan Michiel Otto (eds.), *Lawmaking for Development: Explorations into the Theory and Practice of International Legislative Projects*, Leiden University Press: 11–22

Arthur, Catherine (2019). *Political Symbols & National Identity in Timor-Leste*, Palgrave Macmillan

Asad, Talal (2004). 'Where Are the Margins of the State?' in Veena Das, Deborah Poole (eds.), *Anthropology in the Margins of the State*, School of American Research Press: 279–288

Aspinall, Edward (2004). 'Indonesia: Transformation of Civil Society and Democratic Breakthrough' in Muthiah Alagappa (ed.), *Civil Society and Political Change in Asia - Expanding and Contracting Democratic Space*, Stanford University Press: 61–96

Aspinall, Edward; Hicken, Allen; Scambary, James; Weiss, Meredith (2018). 'Timor-Leste Votes: Parties and Patronage' in *Journal of Democracy*, 29(1): 153–167

Atwood, David (1990). 'Land Registration in Africa: The Impact on Agricultural Production' in *World Development*, 18(5): 659–671

Aubert, Vilhelm (1967). 'Some Social Functions of Legislation' in *Acta Sociologica*, 10(97): 98–120

Augustinus, Clarissa (2010). 'Improving Access to Land and Shelter' in Klaus Deininger, Clarissa Augustinus, Stig Enemark, Paul Munro-Faure (eds.), *Innovations in Land Rights Recognition, Administration, and Governance* (World Bank Studies), World Bank: 164–179

Aussies, Willem; Duhau, Emilio (2009). 'Land Tenure and Tenure Regimes in Mexico: An Overview' in in Janine Ubink, André Hoekema, Willem Assies (eds.), *Legalising Land Rights – Local Practices, State Responses and Tenure Security in Africa, Asia and Latin America*, Leiden University Press: 355–385

Bachriadi, Dianto; Wiradi, Gunawan (2013). 'Land Concentration and Land Reform in Indonesia: Interpreting Agricultural Census Data, 1963–2003' in Anton Lucas, Carol Warren (eds.), *Land for the People: The State and Agrarian Conflict in Indonesia*, Center for International Studies Ohio University (Kindle version)

Bachriadi, Dianto; Lucas, Anton; Warren, Carol (2013). 'The Agrarian Movement, Civil Society, and Emerging Political Constellations' in Anton Lucas, Carol Warren (eds.), *Land for the People: the State and Agrarian Conflict in Indonesia*, Center for International Studies Ohio University (Kindle version)

Balbus, Isaac (1977). 'Commodity Form and Legal Form: An Essay on the "relative autonomy" of the Law' in *Law and Society Review*, 11(3): 571–588

Banakar, Reza; Travers, Max (2005). 'Law, Sociology and Method' in Reza Banakar, Max Travers (eds.), *Theory and Method in Socio-Legal Research*, Hart Publishing: 1–25

Barry, Michael (2015). *Property Theory, Metaphors and the Continuum of Land Rights*, UN Habitat and GLTN

Barry, Michael; Augustinus, Clarissa (2015). *Framework for Evaluating Continuum of Land Rights Scenarios*, UN Habitat

Barry, Michael; Fourie, Clarissa (2001). 'Wicked Problems, Soft Systems and Cadastral Systems in Periods of Uncertainty' in *Proceedings of CONSAS 2001*, March, Cape Town

Batterbury, Simon; Palmer, Lisa; Reuter, Thomas; Carvalho, Demetrio; Kehi, Balthasar; Cullen, Alex (2015). 'Land Access and Livelihoods in post-conflict Timor-Leste: No Magic Bullets' in *International Journal of the Commons*, 9(2): 619–647

Bedner, Adriaan (2008). 'Amalgamating Environmental Law in Indonesia' in Julia Arnscheidt, Benjamin van Rooij, Jan Michiel Otto (eds.), *Lawmaking for Development: Explorations into the Theory and Practice of International Legislative Projects*, Leiden University Press: 171–198

Bedner, Adriaan (2010). 'An Elementary Approach to the Rule of Law' in *Hague Journal on the Rule of Law*, 2010(2): 48–74

Bedner, Adriaan (2013). 'Indonesian Legal Scholarship and Jurisprudence as an Obstacle for Transplanting Legal Institutions' in *Hague Journal on the Rule of Law*, 5: 253–273

Bedner, Adriaan (2016). 'Indonesian Land Law: Integration at Last? And for Whom?' in John McCarthy, Kathryn Robinson (eds.), *Land and Development in Indonesia: Searching for the People's Sovereignty*, ISEAS-Yusof Ishak Institute: 63–88

Bedner, Adriaan (2016a). 'Autonomy of Law in Indonesia' in *Recht der Werkelijkheid*, 37(3): 10–36

Bedner, Adriaan; Huis, Stijn van (2008). 'The Return of the Native Indonesian Law – Indigenous Communites in Indonesian Legislation' in *Bijdragen tot de Taal-, Land- en Volkenkunde (BKI)*, 164(2/3): 165–193

Belun (2015). *Revista Situasaun Maiu 2015*, Belun

Belun (2016). *Revista Situasaun Abril 2016*, Belun

Benda-Beckman, K. von (2001). 'Folk, Indigenous and Customary Law' in *International Encyclopedia of the Social & Behavioral Sciences*, Elsevier Science Ltd.

Benda-Beckmann, Franz von (2003). 'Mysteries of Capital or Mystification of Legal Property' in *Focaal - European Journal of Anthropology*, 41: 187–191

Benda-Beckmann, Franz von; Benda-Beckmann, Keebet von; Wiber, Melanie (2006). 'The Properties of Property' in Franz von Benda-Beckmann, Keebet von Benda-Beckmann, Melanie Wiber (eds), *Changing Properties of Property*, Berghahn Books: 1–39

Benjaminsen, Tor; Holden, Stein; Lund, Christian; Sjaastad, Espen (2008). 'Formalisation of Land Rights: Some Empirical Evidence from Mali, Niger and South Africa' in *Land Use Policy*, 26: 28–35

Bernard, Harvey (2006). *Research Methods in Anthropology – Qualitative and Quantitative Approaches*, AltaMira Press

Berry, Sara (2002). 'Debating the Land Question in Africa' in *Comparative Studies in Society and History*, 44(4): 638–668

Beuman, Lydia (2013). *Semi-Presidentialism in a New Post-Conflict Democracy: The Case of Timor-Leste*, PhD dissertation defended at the School of Law & Governance of Dublin University

Bexley, Angie (2010). *Youth at the Crossroads: The Politics of Identity and Belonging in Timor-Leste*, PhD dissertation defended at the Australian National University

Blase, Melvin (1973). *Institution Building: A Source Book*. Agency for International Development, U.S. Dept. of State

Blunt, Peter (2009). 'The Political Economy of Accountability in Timor-Leste: Implications for Public Policy' in *Public Administration and Development*, 29: 89–100

Borras Jr., Saturnino (2006). 'The Underlying Assumptions, Theory, and Practice of Neoliberal Land Policies' in Peter Rosset, Raj Patel, Michael Courville (eds.), *Promised Land – Competing Visions of Agrarian Reform*, Food First Books: 99–129

Borras Jr, Saturnino; Franco, Jennifer (2010). 'Contemporary Discourses and Contestations around Pro-Poor Land Policies and Land Governance' in *Journal of Agrarian Change*, 10(1): 1–32

Borras Jr., Saturnino M.; Hall, Ruth; Scoones, Ian; White, Ben; Wolford, Wendy (2011). 'Towards a Better Understanding of Land-grabbing: An Editorial Introduction' in *Journal of Peasant Studies*, 38(2): 209–216

Bovensiepen, Judith (2015). *The Land of Gold: Post-Conflict Recovery and Cultural Revival in Independent Timor-Leste*, Cornell University Press

Bovensiepen, Judith (2016). 'Visions of Prosperity and Conspiracy in Timor-Leste' in *Focaal—Journal of Global and Historical Anthropology*, 75: 75–88

Bovensiepen, Judith; Monis, Filipe; Freitas, Flaviano (2016). 'Expectations of Development: the Tasi Mane Project in Suai-Covalima' in Sarah Smith, Nuno Canas Mendes, Antero da Silva, Alarico Ximenes, Clinton Fernandes, Michael Leach (eds.), *Timor-Leste: Iha kontextu lokal, rejional no global*, Swinburn Press: 220–224

Bovensiepen, Judith; Nygaard-Christensen, Maj (2018). 'Petroleum Planning as State Building in Timor-Leste' in *The Asia Pacific Journal of Anthropology*, 2018: 1–20

Bovensiepen, Judith; Yoder, Laura Meitzner (2018). 'Introduction: The Political Dynamics and Social Effects of Megaproject Development' in *The Asia Pacific Journal of Anthropology*, 19(5): 381–394

Brady, Cynthia; Timberman, David (2006). *The Crisis In Timor-Leste: Causes Consequences and Options For Conflict Management and Mitigation*, USAID

Brama, Naazneen (2012). 'Petroleum, Governance and Fragility: The Micro-Politics of Petroleum in Postconflict States' in Brenda Shaffer, Taleh Ziyadov (eds.), *Beyond the Resource Curse*, University of Pennsylvania Press: 330–439

Bruce, John (1998). 'Review of Tenure Terminology' in *Tenure Brief*; No. 1, Land Tenure Center, University of Wisconsin

Bruce, John (2012). 'Simple Solutions to Complex Problems: Land Formalization as a 'Silver Bullet'', in Jan Michiel Otto, André Hoekema (eds.), *Fair Land Governance – How to Legalise Land Rights for Rural Development*, Leiden University Press: 31–56

Bruce, John (2017). 'Land Tenure Dualism in China: How the Dichotomy between State and Collective Ownership has Shaped Urbanization and Driven the Emergence of Wealth Inequality' in *2017 World Bank Conference on Land and Poverty*, The World Bank, Washington DC, March 20-24, 2017

Bruce, John; Holt, Sally (2011). *Land and Conflict Prevention*, Initiative on Quiet Diplomacy

Bruce, John; Migot-Adholla, Shem; Atherton, Joan (1994). 'The Findings and their Policy Implications: Institutional Adaptation or Replacement' in John Bruce, Shem Migot-Adholla (eds.), *Searching for Land Tenure Security in Africa*, The World Bank: 251–266

Building, Arthur Lewis (2010). *Beyond Institutions. Institutions and Organizations in the Politics and Economics of Poverty Reduction - A Thematic Synthesis of Research Evidence*, DFID-funded Research Programme Consortium on Improving Institutions for Pro-Poor Growth

Bugalski, Natalie (2004). 'Beneath the Sea – Determining a Maritime Boundary Between Australia and East Timor' in *Alternative Law Journal*, 29(6): 290–295

Burns, Tony; Fairlie, Kate (2018). *Framework for Costing and Financing Land Administration Services (CoFLAS)*, UN Habitat, FIG, GLTN

Butterworth, David (2010). 'Expanding State, Expectant Citizens – Local Perspectives on Government Responsibility in Timor-Leste' in *Briefing Note*, 4(2), Justice for the Poor (World Bank).

Candland, Christopher (2001). 'Civil Society' in Joel Krieger (ed.), *The Oxford Companion to Politics of the World*, 2nd edition, Oxford University Press

Campbell, Jeremy (2015). *Conjuring Property: Speculation & Environmental Futures in the Brazilian Amazon*, University of Washington Press (Kindle version)

Cao, Guanzhong; Feng, Changchun; Tao, Ran (2008). 'Local Land Finance in China's Urban Expansion: Challenges and Solutions' in *China and World Economy*, 16(2): 19–30

Castree, Noel; Kitchin, Rob; Rogers, Alisdar (2013). *A Dictionary of Human Geography*, Oxford University Press

Castro, Gonçalo Pimenta de (1944). *História de Timor*, Editorial Atica

CAVR - Commission for Reception, Truth and Reconciliation in East Timor (2005). *Chega!* Full report.

CES-OPJ - Observatório Permanente da Justiça do Centro de Estudos Sociais da Universidade de Coimbra; CRL - Comissão para a Reforma Legislativa e do Sector da Justiça (2017). *Os Tribunais em Timor-Leste - Desafios a um sistema judicial em construção*, CRL

Chesterman, Simon (2005). 'Rough Justice: Establishing the Rule of Law in Post-Conflict Territories' in *Ohio State Journal on Dispute Resolution*, 20(69): 69–98

CISR – Center for Insights in Survey Research (2016). *National Survey of Timor-Leste Public Opinion – November 7–24, 2016*, International Republican Institute

Cliffe, Sarah (2003). 'The Joint Assessment Mission and Reconstruction in East Timor' in *Out of the Ashes - Destruction and Reconstruction of East Timor*, ANU E. Press (2003 Edition): 234–242

Cohen, Michael; March, James; Olsen, Johan (1972). 'A Garbage Can Model of Organizational Choice' in *Administrative Science Quarterly*, 17: 1–25

Conklin, Jeff (2009). 'Building Shared Understanding of Wicked Problems' in *Rotman Magazine*, Winter 2009.

Cordeiro, António Menezes (1997). 'A Usucapião de Imóveis em Macau' in *Revista Jurídica de Macau – Edição Especial: A questão das Terras em Macau*, Gabinete para os Assuntos Legislativos

Costa, Hirdan Katarina de Medeiros; Santos, Edmilson Moutinho dos (2013). 'Institutional analysis and the "resource curse" in developing countries' in *Energy Policy*, 63: 788–795

Cotton, James (2005). 'East Timor in 2004: It Is All About Oil' in *Asian Survey*, 45(1): 186–190

Cotula, Lorenzo (2007). 'Introduction' in Lorenzo Cotula (ed.), *Changes in "Customary" Land Tenure Systems in Africa*, IIED: 5–14

Cotula, Lorenzo (2012). 'Securing Land Rights in Africa – Trends in National and International Law' in Jan Michiel Otto, André Hoekema (eds.), *Fair Land Governance – How to Legalise Land Rights for Rural Development*, Leiden University Press: 57–84

Cotula, Lorenzo (2013). *The Great African Grab? Agricultural Investments and the Global Food System*, Zed Books Ltd (Kindle version)

Cotula, Lorenzo (2016). ''Land Grabbing' and International Investment Law: Toward a Global Reconfiguration of Property?' in Andrea Bjorkund (ed.), *Yearbook on International Investment Law & Policy 2014–2015*, Oxford: 177–214

Cotula, Lorenzo; Berger, Thierry; Knight, Rachel; McInerney, Thomas; Vidar, Margret; Deupmann, Peter (2016). *Responsible Governance of Tenure and the Law - A Guide for Lawyers and Other Legal Service Providers*, Food and Agriculture Organization of the United Nations

Courville, Michael; Patel, Raj (2006). 'Introduction and Overview. The Resurgence of Agrarian Reform in the Twenty-first Century' in Peter Rosset, Raj Patel, Michael Courville (eds.), *Promised Land – Competing Visions of Agrarian Reform*, Food First Books: 3–22

Cowan, Jane; Dembour, Marie-Bénédicte; Wilson, Richard (2001). 'Introduction' in Jane Cowan, Marie-Bénédicte Dembour, Richard Wilson (eds.), *Culture and Rights: Anthropological Perspectives*, Cambridge University Press: 1–26

Crespi, Brunna; Guillaud, Dominique (2018). 'Oil and Custom: Impacts of the Tasi Mane Oil Project on Local Communities in Suai, Timor-Leste' in *The Asia Pacific Journal of Anthropology*, 19(5): 432–449

Crewe, Emma; Axelby, Richard (2013). *Anthropology and Development – Culture, Morality and Politics in a Globalized World*, Cambridge University Press (Kindle version)

CRL – Comissão da Reforma Legislativa de Timor-Leste (2017). *Relatório Especializado "Processo Legislativo a Nível de Governo"*, CRL

Crozier, Michel (1964). *The Bureaucratic Phenomenon*, University of Chicago Press

Cryan, Meabh (2015). 'The Long Haul: Citizen Participation in Timor-Leste Land Policy' in *SSGM DISCUSSION PAPER* 2015/13, Australian Nation University

Cryan, Meabh (2015a). 'Dispossession and Impoverishment in Timor-Leste: Potential Impacts of the Suai Supply Base' in *SSGM DISCUSSION PAPER* 2015/15, Australian National University

Cryan, Meabh (2015b). "Empty Land'? The Politics of Land in Timor-Leste?' in Sue Ingram, Lia Kent, Andrew McWilliam (eds.), *A New Era? Timor-Leste After the UN*, Australian University Press: 141–151

Cryan, Meabh (2016). *Whose Land? Analysis of the Timor-Leste Transitional Land Law*, The Asia Foundation

Cullen, Grant (2010). *Briefing Note on Cadastral Survey Techniques & Standards for Land Rights Registration in Timor-Leste*, Ita Nia Rai

Cullen, Alexander (2015). 'Making Sense of Claims across Institutional Divides: critical PGIS and mapping customary land in Timor-Leste' in *Australian Geographer*, 46(4): 473–490

Cummins, Deborah (2010). 'Democracy or Democrazy? Local Experiences of Democratization in Timor-Leste' in *Democratization*, 17(5): 899–919

Cunha, Ricardo (2018). 'A *Legisprudência* na Construção de Uma Teoria Normativa da Legislação em Timor-Leste' in *e-boletim Lei & Justiça*, 1(2): 122–144

Curtain, Richard; Davies, Robin; Howes, Stephen (2011). *Helping Timor-Leste implement a regional employment strategy: A submission to the Joint Standing Committee on Foreign Affairs, Defence and Trade's inquiry into Australia's relationship with Timor-Leste*. Development Policy Centre, Australian National University

D'Andrea, Claudia. (2003). *The Customary Use of Natural Resources in Timor-Leste*, Oxfam, GTZ, Timor-Leste Directorate of land and Property

Dale, Pamela; Himelein, Kristen; Nikitin, Denis; Bexley, Angie (2010). 'The Lay of the Land: Land Access and Dispute Resolution in Timor-Leste' in *Briefing Note 56006*, 5(3), Justice For the Poor (World Bank)

Dann, Philipp (2013). *The Law of Development Cooperation – A comparative Analysis of the World Bank, The EU and Germany*, Cambridge University Press

Davidson, Jamie (2015). *Indonesia's Changing Political Economy: Governing the Roads*, Cambridge University Press

Davidson, Katharine (1994). *The Portuguese Colonisation of Timor: The Final State, 1850–1912*, Doctor of Philosophy Thesis

De Soto, Hernando (2000). *The Mystery of Capital: Why Capitalism Triumphs in the West and Fails Everywhere Else*, Basic Books

Dehaibi, Lara (2015). 'The Case for an Inclusive Human Right to Property: Social Importance and Individual Self-Realization' in *Western Journal of Legal Studies*, 6(5), art. 5

Deininger, Klaus (2003). *Land Policies for Growth and Poverty Reduction*, World Bank and Oxford University Press

Deininger, Klaus; Enemark, Stig (2010). 'Land Governance and the Development Millennium Goals' in Klaus Deininger, Clarissa Augustinus, Stig Enemark, Paul Munro-Faure (eds.), *Innovations in Land Rights Recognition, Administration, and Governance*, World Bank (Kindle version)

Deininger, Klaus, Selod, Harris; Burns, Anthony (2012). *The Land Governance Assessment Framework – Identifying and Monitoring Good Practice in the Land Sector*, The World Bank

Department of Foreign Affairs – Republic of Indonesia (1984). *East Timor after Integration*. Department of Foreign Affairs – Republic of Indonesia

Dekker, Henri (2005). *In Pursuit of Land Tenure Security – Essays on Land Reform and Land Tenure*, Pallas Publications

Delville, P. (2006). 'Securité, insécurités, et sécurisation foncières: un cadre conceptuel' in *Reforme agraire et cooperatives*, 2006/2, FAO

Delville, P. (2010). 'Registering and Administering Customary Land Right: Can We Deal with Complexity?' in Klaus Deininger, Clarissa Augustinus, Stig Enemark, Paul Munro-Faure (eds.), *Innovations in Land Rights Recognition, Administration, and Governance (World Bank Studies)*, World Bank

Devereux, Annemarie (2015). *Timor-Leste's Bill of Rights: A Preliminary History*, ANU Press

Devine, Joseph (2002). 'Ethnography of a Policy Process: A Case Study of Land Redistribution in Bangladesh' in *Public Administration and Development*, 22: 403–414

DKSPTT - Dingan Kantor Statistik Propinsi Timor (1996). *Timor Timur – Dalam Angka 1996 – East Timor in Figures*, DKSPTT

Direito, Bárbara (2013). *Políticas Coloniais de Terras em Moçambique: o Caso de Manica e Sofala sob a Companhia de Moçambique, 1982–1942*. PhD dissertation defended at the Institute of Social Sciences of the Lisbon University

Direito, Bárbara (2014). 'African Access to Land in Early 20th Century Portuguese Colonial Thought' in José Vicente Serrão, Bárbara Direito, Eugénia Rodrigues, Susana Münch Miranda (eds), *Property Rights, Land and Territory in the European Overseas Empires*, CEHC-IUL: 255–266

Dirlik, Arif (2014). 'Developmentalism – A Critique' in *International Journal of Postcolonial Studies*, 16(1): 30–48

Doraisami, Anita (2018). 'The Timor-Leste Petroleum Fund, Veterans and White Elephants: Fostering Intergenerational Equity?' in *Resources Policy*, 58: 250–256

Dovert, Stephane; Durand, Frédéric (2016). 'Crónica de uma anexação hesitante. A invasão do Timor Português pela Indonésia 1974–1976' in Rui Feijó (ed.), *Timor-Leste: Colonialismo, Descolonização, Lusotopia*, Edições Afrontamento: 329–351

Du Plessis, Jean; Leckie, Scott (2000). *Housing, Property and Land Rights in East Timor: Proposals for an Effective Dispute Resolution and Claim Verification Mechanism*, UN Habitat

Dunda, Nugzar (2007). *Delimitation of Maritime Boundaries Between Adjacent States*, United Nations – The Nippon Foundation Fellow

Durand-Lasserve, Alain; Selod, Harris (2007). 'The Formalisation of Urban Land Tenure in Developing Countries' in *World Bank's 2007 Urban Research Symposium*, May 14–16, Washington DC

Duun, James (1996). *Timor: A People Betrayed*, ABC Books

Edelman, Murray (1988). *Constructing the Political Spectacle*, University of Chicago Press

Ederington, L. Benjamin (1997). 'Property as a Natural Institution: The Separation of Property from Sovereignty in International Law' in *American University International Law Review*, 13(2): 263–331

Eisenberg, Andra (1995). '"Public Purpose" and Expropriation: Some Comparative Insights and the South African Bill of Rights', in *South African Journal on Human Rights*, 11(2): 207–221

Elderton, Cath (2002). 'East Timor – Land Issues and Independence' in *Transforming Land Conflict*, FAO/USP/RICS Foundation South Pacific Land Tenure Conflict Symposium, 10 -12 April

Enemark, Stig; Bell, Keith; Lemmen, Christiaan; McLaren, Robin (2014). *Fit-for-Purpose Land Administration*, FIG and Word Bank

Enemark, Stig; McLaren, Robin; Lemmen, Christiaan (2015). *Fit-For-Purpose Land Administration Guiding Principles*, GLTN

Erp, Sjef van (2015). 'Should English be the Shared Academic Property Law Language?' in *EPlJ*, 4(1): 1–2

Esman, Milton (1967). *The Institution Building Concepts – An Interim Appraisal*, Graduate School of Public and International Affairs, University of Pittsburgh

Fairbairn, Madeleine (2013). 'Indirect Dispossession: Domestic Power Imbalances and Foreign Access to Land in Mozambique' in Wendy Wolford, Saturnino Borras Jr., Ruth Hall, Ian Scoones, Ben White (eds.), *Governing Global Land Deals: The Role of the State in the Rush for Land*, Wiley Blackwell: 141–162

FAO - Food and Agriculture Organization of the United Nations (2002). *FAO Land Tenure Studies 3 – Land Tenure and Rural Development*, FAO

FAO - Food and Agriculture Organization of the United Nations (2009). *Compulsory Acquisition of Land and Compensation*, FAO

Feijó, Rui (2016). *Dynamics of Democracy in Timor-Leste: The Birth of a Democratic Nation, 1999–2012*, Amsterdam University Press

Feijó, Rui (2016a). 'Long and Winding Road: A Brief History of the Idea of a 'Government of National Unity' in Timor-Leste and Its Current Implications', in *SSGM Discussion Paper 2016/3*, Australian National University

Fella, Timothy; Boudreaux, Karol (2011). *An Evaluation of the Strengthening Property Rights in Timor-Leste Project (SPRTL)*, USAID

Fernandes, Francisco Liberal (2015). *Direitos Reais em Timor-Leste: Uma Introdução*, Faculdade de Direito da Universidade do Porto

Fernandes, Luís Carvalho (2009). *Lições de Direitos Reais - 6ª Edição*, Quid Juris – Sociedade Editora, Lda

Figueiredo, Fernando (2011). *Timor – A Presença Portuguesa (1769 – 1945)*, Centro de Estudos Históricos da Universidade Nova de Lisboa

Figueiredo, Fernando (2011a). 'Timor na Viragem do Século XIX para o Século XX: Tipo de Colonização e os Seus Agentes' in *Colóquio Timor: Missões Científicas e Antropologia Colonial*, AHU, 24 and 25 of May 2011

Fitzpatrick, Daniel (2002). *Land Claims in East Timor*, Asia Pacific Press

Fitzpatrick, Daniel (2002a). 'Land Policy in Post-Conflict Circumstances: Some Lessons from East Timor' in Working paper No. 58, UNHCR

Fitzpatrick, Daniel (2004). *Comparative Desk Study of Land Title Restitution Experiences, Strategies and Options*, USAID

Fitzpatrick, Daniel (2005). ''Best Practice' Options for the Legal Recognition of Customary Tenure' in *Development and Change*, 36(3): 449–475

Fitzpatrick, Daniel (2008). 'Mediating Land Conflict in East Timor' in *Making Land Work – Volume Two*, AusAID: 175–197

Fitzpatrick, Daniel; Barnes, Susanna (2010). 'The Relative Resilience of Property: First Possession and Order Without Law in East Timor' in *Law & Society Review*, 44(2): 205–238

Fitzpatrick, Daniel; McWilliam, Andrew (2005). 'Waiting for Law: Land Custom and Legal Regulation in Timor-Leste' in *Development Bulletin*, 68: 58–61

Fitzpatrick, Daniel; McWilliam, Andrew (2013). 'Bright-Line Fever: Simple Legal Rules and Complex Property Customs among the Fataluku of East Timor' in *Law & Society Review*, 47(2): 311–343

Fitzpatrick, Daniel; McWilliam, Andrew; Barnes, Susana (2008). *Policy Notes on Customary Land in Timor-Leste.*

Fitzpatrick, Daniel; McWilliam, Andrew; Barnes, Susana (2013). *Property and Social Resilience in Times of Conflict: Land, Custom and Law in East Timor*, Ashgate Pub Co

Fitzpatrick, Daniel; Monson, Rebecca (2009). 'Balancing Rights and Norms: Property Programming in East Timor, the Solomon Islands and Bougainville', in S. Leckie (Ed.), *Housing, Land and Property Rights in Post-Conflict United Nations and other Peace Operations: A Comparative Survey and Proposal for Reform*, Cambridge University Press: 103–135

Flyvbjerg, Bent (2017). 'Introduction: The Iron Law of Megaproject Management' in Bent Flyvbjerg (ed.), *The Oxford Handbook of Megaproject Management*, Oxford University Press: 1–18

Foucault, Michel (2007). *Security, Territory, Population: Lectures at the Collège de France, 1977–1978*, Palgrave Press

Fox, James (2003). 'Tracing the Path, Recounting the Past: Historical Perspectives on Timor' in James J. Fox, Dionísio Babo Soares (eds.), *Out of the Ashes: Destruction and Reconstruction of East Timor*, ANU E Press: 1–27

Freedom House (2006). *Freedom of the Press 2006 A Global Survey of Media Independence*, Rowman & Littlefield Publishers, Inc.

Freedom House (2017). *Freedom in the World 2017*, Freedom House

FRETILIN – Frente Revolucionária de Timor-Leste Independente (1974). *FRETILIN – Manual e Programa Políticos*, FRETILIN

Fundasaun Mahein (2013). 'Projetu Suai Supply Base: Dezenvolvimentu ka Ameasa?' in *Mahein Nia Lian*, No. 57, Fundasaun Mahein

Ganti, Tejaswini (2014). 'Neoliberalism' in *Annual Review of Anthropology*, 43: 89–104

German, Laura; Schoneveld, George; Mwangi, Esther (2011). 'Contemporary Processes of Large-scale Land Acquisition by Investors: Case Studies from sub-Saharan Africa' in *Occasional Paper*, 68, CIFOR

Goldstone, Anthony (2004). 'UNTAET with Hindsight: The Peculiarities of Politics in an Incomplete State' in *Global Governance*, 10(1): 83–98

Gorjão, Paulo (2004). 'O legado e as lições da Administração Transitória das Nações Unidas em Timor-Leste' in *Análise Social*, 38(169): 1043–1067

GoTL – Government of Timor-Leste (2007). *Relatório de actividades desenvolvidas no âmbito do Orçamento Geral do Estado – Período de Transição 1 de Julho a 31 de Dezembro de 2007*, GoTL

GoTL – Government of Timor-Leste (2010). *Justice Sector Strategic Plan for Timor-Leste 2011–2030*, GoTL

GoTL – Government of Timor-Leste (2010a). *2010 State Budget – Book 1*, GoTL

GoTL – Government of Timor-Leste (2011). *Highlights of the 2010 Census Main Results in Timor-Leste*, Ministry of Finance of Timor-Leste and United Nations Population Fund

GoTL – Government of Timor-Leste (2011a). *Population and Housing Census of Timor-Leste, 2010 - Volume 2: Population Distribution by Administrative Areas*, Ministry of Finance of Timor-Leste and United Nations Population Fund

GoTL – Government of Timor-Leste (2011b). *Census Atlas 2010 – Volume 15*, National Statistics Directorate and United Nations Population Fund

GoTL – Government of Timor-Leste (2011c). *Strategic Development Plan 2011–2030*, Government of Timor-Leste

GoTL – Government of Timor-Leste (2011d). *Hosing Census of Timor-Leste, 2010 - Volume 4: Population distribution by Administrative Areas*, Ministry of Finance of Timor-Leste and United Nations Population Fund

GoTL – Government of Timor-Leste (2011e). *Timor-Leste Household Income and Expenditure Survey 2011*, Ministry of Finance of Timor-Leste

GoTL – Government of Timor-Leste (2012). *Review of Procurement in the Ministry of Infrastructure for the Period 1 January 2009 to 30 June 2011*, GoTL, available at http://www.laohamutuk.org/econ/portal/DeloitteMinInfraJuly2012.pdf

GoTL – Government of Timor-Leste (2012a). *Tasi Mane Project - Suai Supply Base Environmental Impact Assessment - Volume 1 - Main Report Part A*, GoTL

GoTL – Government of Timor-Leste (2012b). *Tasi Mane Project - Suai Supply Base Environmental Impact Assessment - Volume 2 - Main Report Part B*, GoTL

GoTL – Government of Timor-Leste (2015). *Population and Housing Census 2015 - Preliminary Results*, GoTL

GoTL – Government of Timor-Leste; World Bank (2013). *Democratic Republic of Timor-Leste: Public Expense Review*, GoTL, World Bank

Grainger, Alex (2017). 'Land Control, Authority and Political Economy, and Planned Petroleum Infrastructure Project in Timor-Leste' in *Journal of Southeast Asian Human Rights*, 1(2): 173–191

Graziadei, Michele (2017). 'The Structure of Property Ownership and the Common Law/Civil Law Divide' in Michele Graziadei, Lionel Smith (eds.), *Comparative Property Law: Global Perspectives*, Edgar Elgar: 71-99

Greenhalegh, Trisha; Russell, Jill (2009). 'Evidence-Based Policymaking – *A Critique*' in *Perspectives in Biology and Medicine*, 52(2): 304–318

Grenfell, Laura (2006). 'Legal Pluralism and the Rule of Law in Timor-Leste' in *Leiden Journal of International Law*, 19: 305–337

Grenfell, Laura (2013). *Promoting the Rule of Law in Post-Conflict States*, Cambridge University Press

Grenfell, Laura (2015). 'Realizing Rights in Timor-Leste' in *Asian Studies Review*, 39(2): 266–283

Guerreiro, Sara (2012). *Colectânea De Direito Administrativo Timorense Com Comentários De Conteúdo Parte II – Actividade Administrativa Em Timor-Leste*, Provedoria dos Direitos Humanos e UNDP

Gunn, Geoffrey (1999). *Timor Loro Sae: 500 Years*, Livros do Oriente

Gunn, Geoffrey (2007). 'A Ocupação Indonésia de Timor-Leste – Lições e Legados para a Construção do Estado na Nova Nação' in Kelly Silva, Daniel Simião (eds.), *Timor-leste por trás do palco: cooperação internacional e a dialética da formação do Estado*, Editora UFMG: 40–62

Gunn, Geoffrey (2011). *Historical Dictionary of East Timor*, The Scarecrow Press

Gusmão, Xanana (2000). *To Resist is to Win! The Autobiography of Xanana Gusmão with Selected Letters and Speeches*, Aurora Books

Gusmão, Xanana (2012). *Discurso de Sua Excelência o Primeiro-Ministro Kay Rala Xanana Gusmão por Ocasião da Tomada de Posse do V Governo Constitucional*, GoTL

Guterres, Francisco (2006). *Elites and Prospects of Democracy in East Timor*, PhD thesis defended at the Department of International Business School, Griffit University

Haburas Foundation; Rede ba Rai (2013). *Land Registration and Land Justice in Timor-Leste*, Haburas Foundation and Rede ba Rai

Hägerdal, Hans (2012). *Lords of the Land, Lords of the Sea - Conflict and Adaptation in Early Colonial Timor, 1600–1800*, KITLV Press

Hall, Derek (2013). *Land (PRS – Polity Resources Series)*, Polity Press (Kindle version)

Hall, Derek (2013a) 'Primitive Accumulation, Accumulation by Dispossession and the Global Land Grab' in *Third World Quarterly*, 34(9): 1582–1604

Hall, Derek; Hirsch, Philip; Li, Tania (2011). *Powers of Exclusion: Land Dilemmas in Southeast Asia*, University of Hawai'i Press

Halliday, Terence; Karpik, Lucien; Feeley, Malcolm (2007). 'The Legal Complex in Struggles for Political Liberalism' in Malcolm Feeley, Terence Halliday, Lucien Karpik (eds.), *Fighting for Political Freedom: Comparative Studies of the Legal Complex and Political Liberalism*, Hart Publishing Ltd.

Harrington, Andrew (2006). *Ethnicity, Violence, and Property Disputes in Timor-Leste*. B.A thesis, International Affairs of the Norman Paterson School of International Affairs & Faculty of Common Law, University of Ottawa

Harvey, David (2004). 'The 'New' Imperialism: Accumulation by Dispossession' in *Socialist Register*, 40: 63–87

Harvey, David (2005). *A Brief History of Neo-liberalism*, Oxford University Press

Head, Brian; Alford, John (2015). 'Wicked Problems: Implications for Public Policy and Management' in *Administration & Society*, 47(6): 711–739

Heady, Ferrel (1979). *Public Administration: a Comparative Perspective*, Second Edition Revised and Expanded, Marcel Dekker

Herbertson, Kirk (2012). *Will Safeguards Survive the Next Generation of Development Finance?*, International Rivers

Herzfeld, Michael (2001). 'Performing Comparisons: Ethnography, Globetrotting, and the Spaces of Social Knowledge' in *Journal of Anthropological Research*, 57(3): 259–276

Hicks, David (2007). 'Community and Nation-state in East Timor - A View from the Periphery' in *Anthropology Today*, 23(1): 13–16

Hicks, David (2014). *Rhetoric and the Decolonization and Recolonization of East Timor*, Routledge

Hill, Hal; Saldanha, João (2001). 'The Key Issues' in Hal Hill, João Saldanha (eds.), *East Timor: Development Challenges for the World's Newest Nation*, Institute for Southeast Asian Studies: 3–36

Hillman, Ben (2013). 'Public Administration Reform in Post-Conflict Societies: Lessons From Aceh, Indonesia' in *Public Administration and Development*, 33: 1–14

Hoadley, Stephen (1976). 'East Timor: Civil War – Causes and Consequences' in *Southeast Asian Affairs*, 3: 411–419

Hoekema, André (2012). 'If Not Private Property, Then What? Legalising Extra-Legal Rural Land Tenure via a Third Road' in Jan Michiel Otto, André Hoekema (eds.), *Fair Land Governance – How to Legalise Land Rights for Rural Development*, Leiden University Press: 135–180

Hohe, Tanja; Nixon, Rod (2003). *Reconciling Justice - 'Traditional' Law and State Judiciary in East Timor – Final Report*, United States Institute of Peace

Hoops, Björn (2016). 'The Public Purpose Requirement in Expropriation Law: A (Potentially) Rich Source of Safeguards against Arbitrary Expropriation' in *2016 World Bank Conference on Land and Poverty*, The World Bank, Washington DC, March 14–18

Hoops, Björn (2018). *The Legitimate Justification of Expropriation – A Comparative Law and Governance Analysis*, Juta

Human Rights Council (2019). *Visit to Timor-Leste - Report of the Special Rapporteur on the rights of indigenous peoples*, United Nations General Assembly

Ibrahim, Suliman (2017). 'Property Claims in Post-Gaddafi Libya: Political Debates and Justice Seeking in the Aftermath of Law 4/1978' in *Hague Journal on the Rule of Law*, 9: 135–156

ICG - International Crisis Group (2010). 'Managing Land Conflict in Timor-Leste' in *Asia Briefing*, No. 110, 9, ICG

ICG - International Crisis Group (2013). 'Timor-Leste: Stability at What Cost?' in *Asia Report*, No. 246, ICG

IFJ - Federation of Journalists (2018). *Underneath the Autocrats - South East Asia Media Freedom Report 2018*, IFJ

IMF – International Monetary Fund (2017). *Democratic Republic of Timor-Leste – Staff Report for the 2017Article IV Consultation*, IMF

IPAC – Institute for Policy Analysis of Conflict (2015). 'Justice at the Crossroads in Timor-Leste' in IPAC Report No. 22, IPAC

Jerónimo, Patrícia (2011). 'Estado de Direito e Justiça Tradicional – Ensaios para um equilíbrio em Timor-Leste' in *Estudos Em Homenagem Ao Professor Doutor Carlos Ferreira De Almeida - Vol. III*, Almedina

Jerónimo, Patrícia (2017). *Report on Citizenship Law: East Timor (Timor-Leste).* European University Institute, Robert Schuman Centre for Advanced Studies

Joireman, Sandra; Brown, Jason (2013). 'Property: Human Right or Commodity?', in *Journal of Human Rights*, 12(2): 165–179

Jones, Harry (2011). 'A Guide to Monitoring and Evaluating Policy Influence' in *Background Note*, February 2011, Overseas Development Institute

JSMP- Judicial System Monitoring Program (2011). 'The Civil Code and Legislative Dynamics in the National Parliament' in *Justice Update*, JSMP

JSMP- Judicial System Monitoring Program (2014). *Overview of the Justice Sector 2014 – JSMP Annual Report*, JSMP

JSMP- Judicial System Monitoring Program (2014a). *Dismissal of International Officials and Advisors in the Timor-Leste Judicial Sector - An Analysis of the Constitutionality, Legality and Impact of Parliamentary Resolution No. 11/2014 and Government Resolutions No. 29/2014 and 32/2014*, JSMP

Kammen, Douglas (2009). 'Fragments of Utopia: Popular Yearnings in East Timor' in *Journal of Southeast Asian Studies*, 40(02): 385–408

Kammen, Douglas (2016). *Three Centuries of Conflict in East Timor*, Nus Press

Kammen, Douglas (2018). 'Progress and Propaganda in Timor-Leste: Visions of the Future in Comparative Historical Perspective' in Judith Bovensiepen (ed.), *The Promise of Prosperity: Visions of the Future in Timor-Leste*, ANU Press: 29–41

Kanji, Nazneen; Cotula, Lorenzo; Hilhorst, Thea; Toulmin, Camilla; Written, Wray (2005). *Research Report 1- Can Land Registration Serve Poor and Marginalised Groups? Summary Report*, iied

Kanstroom, Daniel (1997). 'Surrounding the Hole in the Doughnut: Discretion and Deference in U.S. Immigration Law' in *Tulane Law Review*, 71: 703–818

Keith, Simon; McAuslan, Paul; Knight, Rachael; Lindsay, Jonathon; Munro-Faure, Paul; Palmer, David (2008). *Compulsory Acquisition of Land and Compensation*, FAO

Kerssen, Tanya (2013). *Grabbing the Power: The New Struggles for Land, Food and Democracy in Northern Honduras*, Food First Books/ Institute for Food and Development Policy (Kindle version)

King, Robert (2013). *Inquiry into Australia's Relationship with Timor-Leste*, Submission No 13 to the Joint Standing Committee on Foreign Affairs, Defence and Trade Foreign Affairs Sub-Committee, House of Representatives, Parliament House, Australia

Kingdon, John (2003). *Agendas, Alternatives, and Public Policies*, Harper Collins

Kingsbury, Benedict (1999). 'Operational Policies of International Institutions as Part of the Law-Making Process: The World Bank and Indigenous Peoples' in E. S. Goodwin-Gill, S. Talmon (eds.), *The Reality of International Law: Essays in Honour of Ian Brownlie*, Oxford University Press: 323–342

Kingsbury, Damien (2007). 'Timor-Leste: The Harsh Reality After Independence' in *Southeast Asian Affairs 2007*, Institute of Southeast Asian Studies

Kingsbury, Damien (2009). *East Timor: The Price of Liberty*, Palgrave Macmillan

Kingsbury, Damien (2014). 'Democratic Consolidation in Timor-Leste: Achievements, Problems and Prospects' in *Asian Journal of Political Science*, 22(2): 181–205

Klinken, Catharina Williams-van (2008). *Word-Finder, English-Tetun, Tetun-English*, Sentru Lingua, Dili Institute of Technology

Klinken, Catharina Williams-van; Williams, Rob (2015). *Mapping the Mother Tongue in Timor-Leste Who Spoke What Where in 2010?,* Dili Institute of Technology

Kolstad, Ivar; Arne, Wiig (2009). 'It's the Rents, Stupid! The Political Economy of the Resource Curse' in *Energy Policy*, 37: 5317–5325

Krishna, Vijesh; Kubitza, Christoph; Pascual, Unai; Qaim, Matin (2017). 'Land Markets, Property Rights, and Deforestation: Insights from Indonesia' in *World Development*, 99: 335–349

La'o Hamutuk (2010). 'Land Justice in Timor-Leste' in *The La'o Hamutuk Bulletin*, 11(1–2)

La'o Hamutuk (2010a). *Submission to Committee C on the Proposed General State Budget from 2011*, La'o Hamutuk

La'o Hamutuk (2014). *Esbosu Dekretu Lei Transmissão de Direitos sobre Bens Imoveis no projecto Suai Supply Base*, La'o Hamutuk

La'o Hamutuk (2015). *La'o Hamutuk Submission to Parliament on 2015 Budget Rectification, 31 March 2015*, La'o Hamutuk

La'o Hamutuk (2016). *Relatóriu peskiza hosi La'o Hamutuk Kona-ba Impaktu hosi Konstrusaun Aero-Portu Suai ba komunidade sira iha Aldeia Lohorai, Suku Matai, Posto Administrativu Maukatar, Munisipiu Covalima*, La'o Hamutuk

Lawless, Robert (1976). 'The Indonesian Takeover of East Timor' in *Asian Survey*, 16(10): 948–964

Leach, Michael; Scambary, James; Clarke, Matthew; Feeny, Simon; Wallace, Heather (2012). 'Attitudes to National Identity among Tertiary Students in Melanesia and Timor Leste: A Comparative Analysis' in *SSGM Discussion Paper 2012/8*, Australian National University

Leach, Michael (2017). *Nation-Building and National Identity in Timor-Leste*, Routledge

Leigh, John (2006). 'East Timor: A Summary of Land and Valuation Issues for a New and Developing Nation' in World Valuation Congress XI - Expanding the Horizon: Re-Engineering the Profession through Innovations, 9–11 May 2006, Kuala Lumpur

Leigh, John; Nixon, Rod (2005). *Dili Rental and Valuation Report*, USAID, AusAID and the National Directorate for Land and Property

Lev, Daniel (2000). *Legal Evolution and Political Authority in Indonesia - Selected Essays*, Kluwer Law International

Li, Tania (2009). 'Tom Make Live or Let Die? Rural Dispossession and the Protection of Surplus Populations' in *Antipode*, 41: 66–93

Li, Tania (2014). *Land's End: Capitalist Relations on an Indigenous Frontier*, Duke University Press (Kindle version)

Li, Tania Murray (1999). 'Compromising Power: Development, Culture, and Rule in Indonesia' in *Cultural Anthropology*, 14(3): 295–323.

Li, Tania (2017). 'After Development: Surplus Population and the Politics of Entitlement' in *Development and Change*, 48(6): 1247–1261

Lindberg, Staffan (2007). 'Institutionalization of Party Systems? Stability and Fluidity Among Legislative Parties in Africa's Democracies' in *Government and Opposition*, 42(2): 215–241

Lipsky, Michael (2010). *Street-Level Bureaucracy: Dilemmas of the Individual in Public Service (Updated edition)*, Russel Sage Foundation

LLP - East Timor Land Law Program (2004). *Final Research Report: An Overview of the LLP's Research Activities*, ARD

LLP - East Timor Land Law Program (2004a). *East Timor Department of Land and Property - Future Action Plan 2004 Onwards*, ARD

Lobato, Manuel (2014). 'Influência política, ocupação territorial e administração (in)directa em Timor (1702–1914)' in José Vicente Serrão, Bárbara Direito, Eugénia Rodrigues, Susana Münch Miranda (eds.), *Property Rights, Land and Territory in the European Overseas Empires*, CEHC-IUL: 197–209

Lopes, Ibere (2008). *Technical Framework for a Transitional Land Law for East Timor*, USAID/ARD

Lopes, Ibere (2009). 'Land and Displacement in Timor-Leste' in *Humanitarian Exchange*, 43, June 2009, Humanitarian Policy Group: 12–14

Lucas, Anton (2013). 'The Cimacan Golf Course Dispute since the New Order' in Anton Lucas, Carol Warren (eds.), *Land for the People: The State and Agrarian Conflict in Indonesia*, Center for International Studies Ohio University

Lucas, Anton; Warren, Carol (2013). 'The Land, the Law and the People' in Anton Lucas, Carol Warren (eds.), *Land for the People: the State and Agrarian Conflict in Indonesia*, Center for International Studies Ohio University (Kindle version)

Lund, Christian (2000). *African Land Tenure: Questioning Basic Assumptions*, International Institute for Environment and Development

Lund, Christian (2008). *Local Politics and the Dynamics of Property in Africa*, Cambridge University Press

Lund, Christian (2011). 'Property and Citizenship: Conceptually Connecting Land Rights and Belonging in Africa' in *Africa Spectrum*, 46(3): 71–75

Lund, Christian (2016). 'Rule and Rupture: State Formation through the Production of Property and Citizenship' in *Development and Change*, 47(6): 1199–1228

Lundahl, Mats; Sjöholm, Fredrik (2005). *Poverty and Development in Timor-Leste - Sida Country Economic Report*, Sida

Lundahl, Mats; Sjöholm, Fredrik (2008). 'The Oil Resources of Timor-Leste: Curse or Blessing?' in *The Pacific Review*, 21(1): 67–86

Lundahl, Mats; Sjöholm, Fredrik (2012). 'Improving the Lot of the Farmer: Development Challenges in Timor-Leste during the Second Decade of Independence' in IFN Working Paper No. 929, Research Institute of Industrial Economics

Luta Hamutuk (2014). *Factus Informasaun No. 113*, Luta Hamutuk

Maine, Henry (1861). *Ancient Law: Its Connection with the Early History of Society and Its Relation to Modern Ideas*, 1920 reprint, John Murray

Marquardt, Mark; Unruh, Jon; Heron, Lena (2002). *Land Policy and Administration: Assessment of the Current Situation and Future Prospects in East Timor – Final Report*, USAID

Marriott, Andrew (2013). 'The Justice Sector: Achievements, Challenges, and Comparisons' in Michael Leach, Damien Kingsbury (eds.), *The Politics of Timor-Leste – Democratic Consolidation after Intervention*, Cornell Southeast Asia Program Publications: 99–120

Martinez, Esmeralda (2010). 'Legislação Portuguesa Para o Ultramar' in *Sankofa. Revista de História da África e Estudos da Diáspora Africana*, Ano III, No. 5

Martinho, José S. (1943). *Timor – Quatro Séculos de Colonização Portuguesa*, Livraria Progredior

Marx, Karl (1887). *Capital – A Critique of Political Economy – Volume I – Book One: the Process of Production of Capital*, Progress Publishers

Massier, Ab (2008). *The Voice of the Law in Transition: Indonesian Jurists and Their Languages*, KITLV Press

Matadalan ba Rai; Haburas Foundation (2010). *Community Voices on the Land: Results of the Consultation by Matadalan ba Rai*. Matadalan ba Rai – Haburas Foundation, UNDP, Trocaire and Oxfam

Mattei, Ugo (1994). 'Efficiency in Legal Transplants: An Essay in Comparative Law and Economics' in *International Review of Law and Economics*, 14: 3–19

Maynard-Moody, Steven; Musheno, Michael (2000). 'State Agent or Citizen Agent: Two Narratives of Discretion' in *Journal of Public Administration Research and Theory*, 10(2): 329–358

Mboeik, Lerry; Yones, Pellokita (1996). 'Timor Gap Base Camp – A Case Study of Oil Drilling in the Indonesian Province of Nusa Tenggara Timor' in Tenth INFID Conference on Land and Development, 26–28 April 1996, Canberra, Australia

McAuslan, Patrick (2010). 'Ensuring Access to Land for Private Investors' in Klaus Deininger, Clarissa Augustinus, Stig Enemark, Paul Munro-Faure (eds.), *Innovations in Land Rights Recognition, Administration, and Governance*, World Bank

McAuslan, Peter (2013). *Land Law Reform in Eastern Africa: Traditional or Transformative?*, Routledge

McCarthy, John (2013). 'Tenure and Transformation in Central Kalimantan after the "Million Hectare" Project' in Anton Lucas, Carol Warren (eds.), *Land for the People: the State and Agrarian Conflict in Indonesia*, Center for International Studies Ohio University (Kindle version)

McDermott, Michael (2018). *Wicked Valuations: People and Landed Property*, Routledge

McWilliam, Andrew (2007). 'East and West in Timor-Leste: Is There an Ethnic Divide?' in Dennis Shoesmith (ed.), *The Crisis in Timor-Leste: Understanding the Past, Imagining the Future*, Charles Darwin University Press: 37–44

McWilliam, Andrew; Traube, Elizabeth G. (eds.) (2011). *Land and Life in Timor-Leste – Ethnographic Essays*, ANU E. Press

Menski, Werner F. (2006). *Comparative Law in a Global Context*, Cambridge University Press

Merry, Sally Engle (2011). 'Measuring the World: Indicators, Human Rights, and Global Governance: with CA comment by John M. Conley' in *Current Anthropology*, 52(S3): S83–S95

Mitlin, Diana; Bicknell, Jane (1994). 'Evictions: Enough Violence; We Want Justice' in *Environment & Urbanization*, 6(1): 3–7

Mosse, David (2005). *Cultivating Development – An Ethnography of Aid Policy and Practice*, Pluto Press

Mosse, David (2006). 'Anti-social Anthropology? Objectivity, Objection, and the Ethnography of Public Policy and Professional Communities' in *Journal of the Royal Anthropological Institute*, 12: 935–956

Morrow, Jonathan; White, Rachel (2002). 'The United Nations in Transitional East Timor: International Standards and the Reality of Governance' in *Australian Yearbook of International Law*, 22: 1–46

Munton, Alexander (2006). *A Study of the Offshore Petroleum Negotiations Between Australia, the U.N. and East Timor.* PhD dissertation defended at the Australian National University

Neves, Guteriano (2013). 'Timor-Leste: The political economy of a Rentier State' in *Timor-Leste Studies Association Conference*, July 2013, Dili: 20–26

Newmann, William (2012). 'Persuasion-Bargaining and Institutions in an Organized Anarchy: Clinton Administration Decisions on China, 1993–1994' in *The American Review of Public Administration*, 43(3): 347–368

Niner, Sara (2011). *Xanana – Líder da luta pela independência de Timor-Leste*, Publicações Don Quixote

Nixon, Rod (2005). *Non-Customary Primary Industry Land Survey: Landholdings and Management Considerations*, USAID/ARD

Nixon, Rod (2006). 'The Crisis of Governance in New Subsistence States' in *Journal of Contemporary Asia*, 36(1): 75–101

Nixon, Rod (2007). 'Challenges for Managing State Agricultural Land and Promoting Post-subsistence Primary Industry Development in East Timor', in Denis Shoesmith (ed.), *Crisis in Timor-Leste: Understanding the Past, Imagining the Future*, CDU Press: 101–105

Nixon, Rod (2009). 'Contracts, Land Tenure and Rural Development in Timor-Leste' in Briefing Note 51884, November 2009, 3(3), Justice for the Poor (World Bank)

Nixon, Rod (2011). 'Timor-Leste – Change, Stagnation and Questions of Political Economy' in Ron Duncan (ed.), *The Political Economy of Economic Reform in the Pacific*, Asian Development Bank: 227–264

Nixon, Rod (2012). *Justice and Governance in East Timor – Indigenous approaches and the 'New Subsistence State'*, Routledge

Nonet, Philippe; Selznick, Philip (1978). *Law and Society in Transition: Toward Responsive Law*, Harper Colophon Books

Norfolk, Simon; Tanner, Christopher (2007). 'Improving Tenure Security for the Rural Poor: Mozambique- Country Case Study' in LEP Working Paper No. 5, FAO

North, D. (1990). *Institutions, Institutional Change and Economic Performance*, Cambridge University Press

Nygaard-Christensen, Maj (2013). 'Negotiating Indonesia: Political Genealogies of Timorese Democracy' in *The Asia Pacific Journal of Anthropology*, 14(5): 423–437

O'Connor, Sue; Spriggs, Matthew; Veth, Peter (2002). 'Excavations at Lene Hara Cave Establishes Occupation in East Timor at least 30,000 -35,000 Years Ago', in *Antique*, 76(291): 45–50

O'Laughlin, Bridget (2007). 'A Bigger Piece of a Very Small Pie: Intrahousehold Resource Allocation and Poverty Reduction in Africa', in *Development and Change*, 38(1): 21–44

Ospina, Sofi; Hohe, Tanja (2002). 'Traditional Power Structures and Local Governance in East Timor: A Case Study of the Community Empowerment Project (CEP)' in *Etudes Courtes No. 5*, Graduate Institute of Development Studies

Otto, Jan Michiel (1992). 'Conflicts between Citizen and state in Indonesia: The Development of Administrative Jurisdiction' in Working Paper No. 1, Van Vollenhoven Institute for Law and Administration in Non-Western Countries

Otto, Jan Michiel (1993). 'Politics, Administration Rural Development in Egypt' in H. Asmeron, R. Jain (eds.), *Politics, Administration and Public Policy in Developing Countries – Examples for Africa, Asia and Latin America*, VU University Press: 103–133

Otto, Jan Michiel (2007). *Some Introductory Remarks on Law, Governance and Development.* Notes for the course of Law, Governance and Development at Leiden University

Otto, Jan Michiel (2009). 'Rule of Law Promotion, Land Tenure and Poverty Alleviation: Questioning the Assumptions of Hernando de Soto' in *Hague Journal on the Rule of Law*, 1: 173–195

Otto, Jan Michiel; Arnscheidt, J.; Stoter, W. (2008). 'Using Legislative Theory to Improve Law and Development Projects' in Julia Arnscheidt, Benjamin van Rooij, Jan Michiel Otto (eds.), *Lawmaking for Development*, Leiden University Press: 53–74

Otto, Jan Michiel; Hoekema, André (2012). 'Legalising Land Rights, Yes But How? An Introduction' in Jan Michiel Otto, André Hoekema (eds.), *Fair Land Governance – How to Legalise Land Rights for Rural Development*, Leiden University Press: 7–30

Palanivel, Thangavel; Mirza, Tasneem; Tiwari, Bishwa; Standley, Scott; Abha, Nigam (2016). *Asia-Pacific Human Development Report – Shaping the Future: How Changing Demographics can power Human Development*, UNDP

Parlamento Nacional (2011). *Info Badak No. 1*, Parlamento Nacional

Pashukanis, Evgeny (1983). *Law & Marxism – A General Theory*, Pluto Press

Pawson, Ray (2011). 'Evidence-Based Policy: The Promise of Systematic Review' in *Evidence-Based Policy*: 2–18

PDHJ – Provedoria dos Direitos Humanos e Justiça (2016). *Relatóriu Monitorizasaun Direitus Umanus no Governasaun Diak Relasiona ho Projetu ZEESM refere liu ba; "Impaktu, Projetu Alargamentu Estrada no Projetu Irigasaun no Barazen Tomo ba Komunidade*, PDHJ

Peake, Gordon (2013). *Beloved Land – Stories Struggles, and Secrets from Timor-Leste*, Scribe Publications (Kindle version)

Peake, Gordon; Kent, Lia; Damaledo, Andrey; Thu, Pyone Myat (2014). 'Influences and Echoes of Indonesia in Timor-Leste' in *SSGM Discussion Paper 2014/8*, Australia National University

Peluso, Nancy; Lund, Christian (2011). 'New Frontiers of Land Control: Introduction', in *The Journal of Peasant Studies*, 38(4): 667–681

Penha, Rui (2012). *Guia de Direitos Reais em Timor-Leste – Sumários desenvolvidos das aulas ministradas ao III Curso de Magistrados e Defensores Públicos no CFJ 2008–2009*, Tribunal de Recurso

Peters, E.; Ubink, Janine (2015). 'Restorative and Flexible Customary Procedures and Their Gendered Impact: A Preliminary View on Namibia's Formalization of Traditional Courts' in *The Journal of Legal Pluralism and Unofficial Law*, 47(2): 291–311

Pikkety, Thomas (2014). *Capital in the Twenty-First Century*, The Belknap Press of Harvard University Press (Kindle version)

Pimenta, Fernando (2014). 'O Estado Novo e a reforma do Estado colonial em Angola: o comportamento político das elites brancas (1961–1962)' in *História (São Paulo)*, 33(2): 250–272

Pinto, Paulo (2014). 'Traders, Middlemen, Smugglers: The Chinese and the Formation of colonial Timor (18th–19th Centuries)' in José Vicente Serrão, Bárbara Direito, Eugénia Rodrigues, Susana Münch Miranda (eds.), *Property Rights, Land and Territory in European Overseas Empires*, CEHC-IUL: 267–279

Pires, Florbela (2005). 'Fontes do direito e procedimento legislativo na República Democrática de Timor-Leste – alguns problemas', in *AA. VV. Estudos em Memória do Professor Doutor António Marques dos Santos*, II. Coimbra

Platteau, Jean-Philippe (1996). 'The Evolutionary Theory of Land Right as Applied to Sub-Saharan Africa: A Critical Assessment' in *Development and Change*, 27: 29–86

Pradurowx, Sabrina (2017). 'Objects of Property Rights: Old and New' in Michele Graziadei, Lionel Smith (eds.), *Comparative Property Law: Global Perspectives*, Edgar Elgar: 51–70

Prata, Ana (2005). *Dicionário Jurídico*, Almedina

Psychas, Ellen (2010). *Building State Failure in Timor-Leste: Patterns of Political Competition & Constraints to Private Sector Development (1999 – 2006)*. PhD dissertation defended at the Johns Hopkins University

Radin, Margaret (1993). *Reinterpreting Property*, University of Chicago

Rede ba Rai (2019). *Land Registration in Timor-Leste: Impact Analysis on the National Cadastral System (SNC)*, Rede ba Rai

Reerink, Gustaaf (2011). *Tenure Security for Indonesia's Urban Poor – A Socio-Legal Study on Land, Decentralization and the Rule of Law in Bandung*, Leiden University Press

Reerink, Gustaaf; Gelder, Jean-Louis van (2010). 'Land Titling, Perceived Tenure Security, and Housing Consolidation in the Kampongs of Bandung, Indonesia' in *Habitat International*, 34: 78–85

Ribot, Jesse; Peluso, Nancy (2003). 'A Theory of Access' in *Rural Sociology*, 68(2): 153–181

Richmond, Olivier; Franks, Jason (2009). *Liberal Peace Transitions – Between Statebuilding and Peacebuilding*, Edinburgh University Press

Riggs, Fred (1964). *Administration in Developing Countries – The Theory of Prismatic Society*, Houghton Mifflin Company

Rittel, Horst; Webber, Melvin (1973). 'Dilemmas in a General Theory of Planning' in *Policy Sciences*, 4: 155–169

Robie, David (2016). 'La'o Hamutuk and Timor-Leste's Development Challenges: A Case Study in Human Rights and Collaborative Journalism' in *Media Asia*: 1–16

Rohland, Klaus; Cliffe, Sarah (2002). 'The East Timor Reconstruction Program: Successes, Problems and Tradeoffs' in *CPR Working Papers*, Paper No. 2, World Bank

Ronen, Yaël (2013). *Transition from Illegal Regimes under International Law*, Cambridge Books Online

Rooij, Benjamin van (2006). *Regulating Land and Pollution in China: Lawmaking, Compliance, and Enforcement: Theory and Cases*, Amsterdam University Press

Rooij, Benjamin van (2008). 'Bargaining about the Land Bill: Making Effective Legislation to Protect Arable Land in China' in Julia Arnscheidt, Benjamin van Rooij, Jan Michiel Otto (eds.), *Lawmaking for Development: Explorations into the Theory and Practice of International Legislative Projects*, Leiden University Press: 145–170

Rose, Michael (2016). 'ZEESM: Destructive 'Development' in Timor's Special Economic Zone' in *State, Society & Governance in Melanesia*, Brief 2016/04

Ross, Michael (2012). *The Oil Curse: How Petroleum Wealth Shapes the Development of Nations*, Princeton University Press

Sahin, Selver (2010). 'Timor-Leste in 2009 Marking Ten Years of Independence or Dependence on International "Assistance"?' in *Southeast Asian Affairs*, 2010(1): 344–364

Saldanha, João (2006). 'Anatomy of Political Parties in Timor-Leste' in Roland Rich, Luke Hambly, Michael Morgan (eds.), *Political Parties in the Pacific*, ANU E-Press: 69–81

Santos, Boaventura de Sousa (1977). 'The Law of the Oppressed: The Construction and Reproduction of Legality in Pasargada' in *Law & Society Review*, 12(1): 5–126

Santos, Boaventura de Sousa (1995). *Toward a New Common Sense –Law, Science and Politics in the Paradigmatic Transition*, Routledge

Santos, Eduardo (2004). *Regimes de Terras no Ex-Ultramar Português: Evolução Política Legislativa até 1945*, Universidade Técnica de Lisboa

Scambary, James (2009). 'Groups, Gangs, and Armed Violence in Timor-Leste' in *Issue Brief*, 2: 1–8

Scambary, James (2015). 'In Search of White Elephants: Political Economy of Resource Expenditure in East Timor', in *Critical Asian Studies*, 47(2): 283–308

Scambary, James (2017). 'The Road to Nowhere: The Rise of a Neo-patrimonialistic State in East Timor' in Marie de la Rama, Chris Rowley (eds.), *The Changing Face of Corruption in the Asia Pacific - Current Perspectives and Future Challenges*, Elsevier: 267–280

Schapper, Antoinette (2011). 'Finding the Bunaq: The Homeland and Expansion of the Bunaq in Central Timor' in Andrew McWilliam, Elizabeth Traube (eds.), *Land and Life in Timor-Leste – Ethnographic Essays*, ANU E. Press: 163–186

Scheiner, Charles (2015). 'Can the Petroleum Fund Exorcise the Resource Curse from Timor-Leste?' in Sue Ingram, Lia Kent, Andrew McWilliam (eds.), *A New Era? Timor-Leste After the UN*, Australian University Press: 73–102

Scheiner, Charles (2017). *As Bayu-Undan Dries Up: Challenges and Opportunities*, La'o Hamutuk

Scheiner, Charles (2018). *After the Oil Runs Dry: Timor-Leste Economics and Government Finances*, La'o Hamutuk

Schlager, Edella; Ostrom, Elinor (1992). 'Property-Rights Regimes and Natural Resources: A Conceptual Analysis' in *Land Economics*, 68(3): 249–262

Schofield, Clive (2005). 'A 'Fair Go' for East Timor - Sharing the Resources of the Timor Sea' in *Contemporary Southeast Asia*, 27(2): 255–280

Schwarzmantel, John (2008). *Ideology and Politics*, Sage

Scott, David (2005). *Last Flight Out of Dili: Memoirs of an Accidental Activist in the Triumph of East Timor*, Pluto Press

Scott, James (1998). *Seeing Like a State: How Certain Schemes to Improve the Human Condition Have Failed*, Yale University

Seidman, Ann; Seidman, Robert (2006). 'Law in Aid of Development: 'Hasty Legal Transplants' and the Fatal Race' in *The Journal of Comparative Law*, 282: 282–320

Seidman, Ann; Seidman, Robert (2008). 'Lawmaking, Development and the Rule of Law' in Julia Arnscheidt, Benjamin van Rooij, Jan Michiel Otto (eds.), *Lawmaking for Development: Explorations into the Theory and Practice of International Legislative Projects*, Leiden University Press: 91–132

Seidman, Ann; Seidman, Robert (2009). 'ILTAM: Drafting Evidence-Based Legislation for Democratic Social Change' in *Boston University Law Review*, 89(435): 435–485

Seidman, Robert (1992). 'The Fatal Race: Law-Making and the Implementation of Development Goals' in *Third World Legal Studies*, 79: 79–98

Sen, Amartya (2009). *The Idea of Justice*, The Belknap Press

Serrão, José Vicente (2014). 'Property, Land and Territory in the Making of Overseas Empires' in José Vicente Serrão, Bárbara Direito, Eugénia Rodrigues, Susana Münch Miranda (eds.), *Property Rights, Land and Territory in European Overseas Empires*, CEHC-IUL: 7–17

Shepherd, Christopher (2014). *Development and Environmental Politics Unmasked – Authority, participation and equity in East Timor*, Routledge

Shipton, Parker (1994). 'Land and Culture in Tropical Africa: Soils, Symbols and the Metaphysics of the Mundane' in *Annual Review of Anthropology*, 23: 347–377

Shipton, Parker (2001). 'Land Tenure' in *International Encyclopedia of the Social & Behavioral Sciences*: 8256–8261

Shivakoti, Ganesh P. (2005). *Land Expropriation Policy Suitable For Timor-Leste -Economic Considerations*, USAID

Shoesmith, Dennis (2012). 'Is Small Beautiful? Multiparty Politics and Democratic Consolidation in Timor-Leste' in *Asian Politics & Policy*, 4(1): 33–51

Shoesmith, Dennis (2013). 'Political Parties' in Michael Leach, Damien Kingsbury (eds.), *The Politics of Timor-Leste – Democratic Consolidation after Intervention*, Cornell Southeast Asia Program Publications: 121–144

Siapno, Jacqueline (2006). 'Timor Leste – On the Path of Authoritarianism?' in *Southeast Asia Affairs*: 325–342

Silva, J. Montalvão (1910). *Mão D'Obra em Timor*, A Editora

Silva, Antero; Pereira, Arsénio; Oliveira, David; Sávio, Lúcio; Junior, Adilsonio; Nunes, Natalício (2009). 'Reforma Agraria no Modelu Dezenvolvimentu: Agenda IFIs ho Donor sira iha Pos- Okupasaun Timor-Leste' in Understanding Timor-Leste Conference, 2-3 July 2009: 8–15

Silva, Kelly (2006). 'Elites Timorenses e a Construção do Estado: Projeções Identitárias, Ressentimentos e Jogos de Poder' in Paulo Castro Seixas, Aone Engelenhoven (eds.), *Diversidade Cultural na Construção da Nação e do Estado em Timor-Leste*, Universidade Fernando Pessoa: 179–192

Silva, Antero; Furusawa, Kiyoko (2014). 'Land, State and Community Reconstruction: Timor-Leste in Search of a Sustainable Peace' in Schinichi Takeuchi (ed.), *Confronting Land and Property Problems for Peace*, Routledge: 212–241

Silva, Teresa (2014). 'Maninhos, baldios e bens do concelho no Algarve medieval' in *Revista do Arquivo Municipal de Loulé*, 14: 53–65

Simões, Fernando (2015). 'Law and Language in Timor-Leste: Bridging the Divide' in *Contemporary Southeast Asia*, 37(3): 381–405

Simonsen, Sven (2006). 'The Authoritarian Temptation in East Timor: Nationbuilding and the Need for Inclusive Governance' in *Asian Survey*, 46(4): 575–596

Smith, Anthony (2004). 'Timor-Leste – Strong Government, Weak State' in *Southeast Asian Affairs 2004*, ISEAS – Yosof Ishak Institute

Soares, Adérito (2013). 'Combating Corruption: Avoiding the Institutional Ritualism' in Michael Leach, Damien Kingsbury (eds.), *The Politics of Timor-Leste – Democratic Consolidation after Intervention*, Cornell Southeast Asia Program Publications: 85–98

Soares, Dionísio Babo (2003). *Branching From the Trunk: East Timorese Perceptions of Nationalism in Transition*. PhD dissertation defended at the Australian National University

Soares, Dionísio Babo (2003a). 'Challenges for the Future' in *Out of the Ashes - Destruction and Reconstruction of East Timor*, ANU E. Press (2003 edition)

Soares, Dionísio Babo (2007). 'Desenvolvimento do sector da Justiça em Timor-Leste' in Kelly Cristiane da Silva, Daniel Schroeter Simião (eds.), *Timor-leste por trás do palco: cooperação internacional e a dialética da formação do Estado*, Editora UFMG: 193–209

Sousa, Pedro (2005). 'East Timor, Land Management – a Long Way to Go, But We Have Started' in *FIG Conference* 2005, January 2005, Bangkok

Stead, Victoria (2014). 'Homeland, Territory, Property: Contesting Land, State, and Nation in Urban Timor-Leste' in *Political Geography*, 45(2015): 79–89

Stead, Victoria (2016). *Becoming Landowners: Entanglements of Custom and Modernity in Papua New Guinea and Timor-Leste*, University of Hawai'i Press

Strohmeyer, Hansjörg (2001). 'Collapse and Reconstruction of a Judicial System: The United Nations Missions in Kosovo and East Timor' in *The American Journal of International Law*, 95(1): 46–63

Tamanaha, Brian (1999). 'A Pragmatic Approach to Legislative Theory for Developing Countries' in Ann Seidman, Robert Seidman, Thomas Wälde (eds.), *Making Development*

Work – Legislative Reform for Institutional Transformation and Good Governance, Kluwer Law International: 145–156

Tanner, Christopher (2002). 'Law-making in an African Context: The 1997 Mozambican Land Law' in *FAO Legal Papers Online #26*, FAO

Taylor, John (1991). *Indonesian's Forgotten War – The Hidden History of East Timor*, Pluto Press Australia

Taylor, John (1999). *East Timor: The Price of Freedom*, Zed Books

The Asia Foundation (2013). *A Survey on Community-Policy Perceptions in Timor-Leste 2013*, The Asia Foundation

The Asia Foundation (2015). *Survey of Community-Police Perceptions in Timor-Leste 2015*, The Asia Foundation

The Asia Foundation (2016). *Timor-Leste 2016 Tatoli! Public Opinion Poll*, The Asia Foundation

The Asia Foundation (2017). *A Survey of the Afghan People – Afghanistan in 2016*, The Asia Foundation

Thompson, Edward P. (2013). *Whigs & Hunters – The Origin of the Black Act*, Breviary Stuff Publications

Thomson, Nigel (2003). *Towards Sunrise – East Timor, the United Nations and the Administration of Public and Private Abandoned Land in the Post-Conflict Environment*. Master thesis defended at the University of Queensland

Tidey, Sylvia (2012). *Performing the State – Everyday Practices, Corruption and Reciprocity in Middle Indonesian Civil Service*. PhD thesis defended at the University of Amsterdam

Timor GAP (2013). *Timor GAP Annual Report 2013*, Timor GAP

Timor GAP (2014). *Timor GAP Annual Report 2014*, Timor GAP

Timor GAP (2014a). *Timor GAP Newsletter No. 1*, January 2014, Timor GAP

Timor GAP (2015). *Timor GAP Newsletter No. 3*, March 2015, Timor GAP

Timor GAP (2016). *Annual Report & Accounts 2016*, Timor GAP

Tomlinson, Brian; AidWatch Canada (2013). *Working With Civil Society in Foreign Aid - Possibilities For South-South Cooperation?*, United Nations Development Programme

Transparency International (2018). *Corruption Perceptions Index 2018*, Transparency International

Traube, Elizabeth (1995). 'Mambai Perspectives on Colonialism and Decolonization' in Peter Carey, G. Bentley (eds.), *East Timor at the Crossroads, the Forging of a Nation*, Cassell: 42–55

Ubink, Janine (2009). 'Legalising Land Rights in Africa, Asia and Latin America: An Introduction' in Janine Ubink, André Hoekema, Willem Assies (eds.), *Legalising Land Rights – Local Practices, State Responses and Tenure Security in Africa, Asia and Latin America*, Leiden University Press: 7–31

Ubink, Janine; Quan, Julian (2008). 'How to Combine Tradition and Modernity? Regulating Customary Land Management in Ghana' in *Land Use Policy*, 25: 198–213

UDT – União Democrática Timorense (1975). *Manual Político da União Democrática Timorense*, UDT

Ufen, Andreas (2008). 'Political Party and Party System Institutionalization in Southeast Asia: Lessons for Democratic Consolidation in Indonesia, the Philippines and Thailand' in *The Pacific Review*, 21(3): 327–350

UN Habitat (2012). *Handling Land: Innovative Tools for Land Governance and Secure Tenure*, UN-Habitat

UN Habitat; UNHCR (2014). *Facts Sheet No. 25: Forced Evictions and Human Rights*, United Nations

UNDP - United Nations Development Programme (2002). *East Timor Human Development Report 2002 - Ukun Rasik A'an/The Way Ahead*, UNDP

UNMIT – United Nations Integrated Mission in Timor-Leste (2011). *Timor-Leste Communication and Media Survey*, UNMIT

UNMIT – United Nations Integrated Mission in Timor-Leste (2012). *Implementation of Laws in Timor-Leste: Summary of Findings and Recommendations*, UNMIT

Unruh, Jon (2012). 'Eviction Policy in post War Angola' in *Land Use Policy*, 29: 661–663

Urresta, Edwin (2004). *Report on Research Findings, Policy Options and Recommendations for Compliance with the Constitution by Non-National Land Claimants of Pre-Existing Freehold Rights in East Timor*, USAID

Urresta, Edwin; Nixon, Rod (2003). *Report on Research Findings and Policy Recommendations for State Property Administration / Lease of Government and Private Property*, Centro Nacional de Investigação Científica da Universidade Nacional de Timor-Leste.

Urresta, Edwin; Nixon, Rod (2004). *Report on Research Findings and Policy Recommendations for A Legal Framework for Land Dispute Mediation*, USAID

Urresta, Edwin; Nixon, Rod (2004a) *Report on Research Findings, Policy Options and Recommendations for a Law on Land Rights and Title Restitution*, USAID

USAID – United States Agency for International Development (2007). *East Timor – Complex Emergency Fact Sheet*, USAID

USAID – United States Agency for International Development (2009). *Corruption Assessment – Timor-Leste*, USAID

Vandergeest, Peter; Peluso, Nancy (1995). 'Territorialization and State Power in Thailand' in *Theory and Society: Renewal and Critique in Social Theory*, 24(3): 385–426

Veerman, Gert-Jan (2015). *The Political Context of Law-Making*. Unpublished paper, on file with the author

Vel, Jacqueline (2008). *Uma Politics: An Ethnography of Democratization in West Sumba, Indonesia, 1986–2006*, KITLV Press

Vel, Jacqueline; Zakaria, Yando; Bedner, Adriaan (2017). 'Law-Making as a Strategy for Change: Indonesia's New Village Law' in *Asian Journal of Land and Society*, 4(2): 1–25

Vlies, I. van der (2008). 'Legislation in a Global Perspective' in Julia Arnscheidt, Benjamin van Rooij, Jan Michiel Otto (eds.), *Lawmaking for Development: Explorations into the Theory and Practice of International Legislative Projects*, Leiden University Press: 133–144

Waldorff, Pétur (2016). '"The law is not for the poor": Land Law and Eviction in Luanda' in *Singapore Journal of Tropical Geography*, 37: 363–377

Waldron, Jeremy (2006). 'Principles of Legislation' in Richard Bauman, Tsvi Kahana (eds.), *The Least Examined Branch – The Roles of Legislatures in the Constitutional State*, Cambridge: 15–32

Warren, Carol; Lucas, Anton (2013). 'Indonesia's Land Titling Program (Lap)—The Market Solution?' in Anton Lucas, Carol Warren (eds.), *Land for the People: The State and Agrarian Conflict in Indonesia*, Center for International Studies Ohio University (Kindle version)

Weatherbee, Donald E. (1981). 'The Indonesianization of East Timor' in *Contemporary Southeast Asia*, 3(1): 1–23

Weber, Max (2013). *Economy and Society: An Outline of Interpretive Sociology*. Guenther Roth, Claus Wittich (eds.), University of California Press

Whittal, Jennifer (2014). 'A New Conceptual Model for the Continuum of Land Rights' in *South African Journal of Geomatics*, 3(1): 13–32

Whittaker, Sean (2017). 'The Right of Access to Environmental Information and Legal Transplant Theory: Lessons from London and Beijing' in *Transnational Environmental Law*, 6(3): 509–530

Widman, Marit (2015). 'Joint Land Certificates in Madagascar: The Gendered Outcome of a "gender-neutral" Policy' in Caroline Archambault, Annelies Zommers (eds.), *Global Trends in Land Tenure Reform: Gender Impacts*, Routledge: 110–126

Wigglesworth, Ann (2013). 'The Growth of Civil Society in Timor-Leste: Three Moments of Activism' in *Journal of Contemporary Asia*, 43(1): 51–74

Williams, Charlotte (2009). 'Reaching Back to Move Forward: Using Adverse Possession to Resolve Land Conflicts in Timor-Leste', in *Pacific Rim Law & Policy Journal Association*, 18(3): 575–607

Wilson, James (1989). *Bureaucracy*, Basic Books

Wily, Liz Alden (2012). 'From State to People's Law: Assessing Learning-by-doing as a Basis of New Land Law' in Jan Michiel Otto, André Hoekema (eds.), *Fair Land Governance – How to Legalise Land Rights for Rural Development*, Leiden University Press: 85–110

Wily, Liz Alden (2016). 'Communities and the State – Rethinking the Relationship for a More Progressive Agrarian Century' in *Environmental Forum*, July/August 2016, Environmental Law Institute

Wily, Liz Alden (2017). 'Customary Tenure: Remaking Property for the 21st Century' in Michele Graziadei, Lionel Smith (eds.), *Comparative Property Law: Global Perspectives*, Edgar Elgar: 458–478

Wisborg, Poul; Rohde, Rick (2005). 'Contested Land Tenure Reform in South Africa: Experiences from Namaqualand' in *Development Southern Africa*, 22(3): 409–428

Wolford, Wendy; Borras Jr., Saturnino; Hall, Ruth; Scoones, Ian; White, Ben(2013). 'Governing Global Land Deals: The Role of the State in the Rush for Land' in Wendy Wolford, Saturnino M. Borras Jr., Ruth Hall, Ian Scoones, Ben White (eds.), *Governing Global Land Deals: The Role of the State in the Rush for Land*, Wiley Blackwell: 1–22

World Bank (1975). *Land Reform – Sector Policy Paper*, World Bank

World Bank (2003). *Cities in Transition: Urban Sector Review in an Era of Decentralization in Indonesia*, World Bank

World Bank (2006). *Strengthening the Institutions of Governance in Timor-Leste*, World Bank

World Bank (2010). *Policy Options for Regulating Community Property and Community Protection Zones in Timor-Leste*, World Bank

World Bank (2015). *Democratic Republic of Timor-Leste Public Expenditure Review: Infrastructure*, World Bank

World Bank (2017). *Doing Business 2017 – Equal Opportunity for All*, World Bank

World Bank (2017a). *World Development Report 2017: Governance and the Law*, World Bank

Woude, Maartje van der (2015). *Chain Reactions in Criminal Justice - Discretion and the Necessity of Interdisciplinary Research*, Eleven International Publishing

Yoder, Laura Meitzner (2003). *Custom and Conflict: The Uses and Limitations of Traditional Systems in Addressing Rural Land Disputes in East Timor*, Regional Workshop on Land Policy and Administration for Pro-poor Rural growth. German Technical Cooperation, and Directorate of Land and Property of East Timor

Yoder, Laura Meitzner (2005). *Custom, Codification, Collaboration: Integrating the Legacies of Land and Forest Authorities in Oecusse Enclave, East Timor*. PhD dissertation defended at the Faculty of the Graduate School of Yale University

Yoder, Laura Meitzner (2015). 'The Development Eraser: Fantastical Schemes, Aspirational Distractions and High Modern Mega-events in the Oecusse Enclave, Timor-Leste' in *Journal of Political Ecology*, 22: 299–321

Yoder, Laura Meitzner (2016). 'Oecusse's Special Economic Zone and Local Governance' in SSGM *in Brief 2016/5*, Australian National University

Yoder, Laura Meitzner (2018). 'Piloting the Experimental ZEESM Megaproject: Performing the Future in the Oecusse-Ambeno Enclave' in Judith Bovensiepen (ed.), *The Promise of Prosperity: Visions of the Future in Timor-Leste*, ANU Press

Young, Brigitte (2011). 'Neoliberalism' in Bertrand Badie, Dirk Berg-Schlosser, Leonardo Morlino (eds.), *International Encyclopaedia of Political Science*, SAGE Publications

Zoomers, Annelies (2013). 'A Critical Review of the Policy Debate on Large-scale Land Acquisitions: Fighting the Symptoms or Killing the Heart?' in S. Evers, C. Seagle, F. Krijtenburg (Eds.), *Africa for Sale? Positioning the State, Land and Society in Foreign Large-Scale Land Acquisitions in Africa*, Brill: 55–78

Zoomers, Annelies (2018). 'Plantations are Everywhere! Between Infrastructural Violence and Inclusive Development' in *Geoforum*, 96: 341–344

Zoomers, Annelies; Noorloos, Femke van; Otsuki, Kei; Steel, Griet; Westen, Guus van (2017). 'The Rush for Land in an Urbanizing World: From Land Grabbing Toward Developing Safe, Resilient, and Sustainable Cities and Landscapes' in *World Development*, 92: 242–252

Media articles and press releases

ABC 01/10/2012. *'Taxing Times in Timor-Leste'*, http://www.abc.net.au/4corners/stories/2012/09/27/3599022.htm

—24/03/2014. *'Drawing the Line'*, http://www.abc.net.au/4corners/stories/2014/03/17/3962821.htm

—21/07/2019. '*Oil and Gas is Timor-Leste's Ticket to Prosperity. Is This Impoverished Nation Blowing Its One Chance?*', https://www.abc.net.au/news/2019-07-22/timor-leste-builds-giant-infrastructure-to-process-gas-onshore/11318924

BBC 20/01/2017. '*East Timor Punished for Changing Birth Certificates to Hire Brazilian Players*', http://www.bbc.com/sport/football/38687669

Bloomberg 06/05/2009. *'East Timor Says It Won't Approve Woodside LNG Plan (Update2)'*, http://www.bloomberg.com/apps/news?pid=newsarchive&sid=agitymAdRqLM

Business Timor 28/12/2012. *'Governu Fo Kompesasaun Ba Uma Kain 11 Aitarak-Laran'*, http://www.jornalbisnistimor.com/lalenok-sidade-dili/208-governu-fo-kompesasaun-ba-uma-kain-11-aitarak-laran

—16/02/2015. *'Aeroportu Suai afeta ba sadan istóriku Sorun Tolu, Sasadik ida ba Lia-na'in Kamanasa no Governu'*, http://www.jornalbisnistimor.com/notisia/politika/2324-aeroportu-suai-afeta-ba-sadan-istoriku-sorun-tolu-sasadik-ida-ba-lia-na-in-kamanasa-no-governu?highlight=WyJhZXJvcG9ydHUiLCJzdWFpIiwiYWVyb3BvcnR1IHN1YWkiXQ==

—16/02/2015a. *'Efeitu konstrusaun Aeroportu Suai, Loro tama sadan Sorun Tolu, Kamanasa bele sai kiak'*, http://www.jornalbisnistimor.com/notisia/politika/2325-efeitu-konstrusaun-aeroportu-suai-loro-tama-sadan-sorun-tolu-kamanasa-bele-sai-kiak?highlight=WyJhZXJvcG9ydHUiLCJzdWFpIiwiYWVyb3BvcnR1IHN1YWkiXQ==

—13/04/2015. '*Projetu Nova Suai, Deputadu Adriano: "Hau ta'uk ema sira iha hau nia aldeia la iha rai"*', http://www.jornalbisnistimor.com/notisia/ekonomia/2546-projetu-nova-suai

-deputadu-adriano-hau-ta-uk-ema-sira-iha-hau-nia-aldeia-la-iha-rai?highlight=WyJhZXJvcG9ydHUiLCJzdWFpIiwiYWVyb3BvcnR1IHN1YWkiXQ==

—25/05/2015. *'Timoroan barak involve projetu Aeroportu Suai'*, http://www.jornalbisnistimor.com/notisia/politika/2641-timoroan-barak-involve-projetu-aeroportu-suai?highlight=WyJhZXJvcG9ydHUiLCJzdWFpIiwiYWVyb3BvcnR1IHN1YWkiXQ==

Diário de Notícias 08/05/2017. *'Primeiros certificados de registo de propriedades entregues em Timor-Leste'*, https://www.dn.pt/lusa/interior/primeiros-certificados-de-registo-de-propriedades-entregues-em-timor-leste-7585446.html

—04/11/2017. *'CNRT, segundo partido timorense, reúne domingo conferência nacional'*, https://www.dn.pt/lusa/interior/cnrt-segundo-partido-timorense-reune-domingo-conferencia-nacional-8893999.html

Independente 11/04/2014. *'SETP Husu Apoiu Komunidade ba Implementasaun Baze Suplai'*

—31/07/2014. *'Supply Base - Kultura no Kompensasaun impede Konstrusaun Baze Suplai Suai'*

—25/08/2014. *'Dekretu Lei Baze Suplai Suai: Osan Millaun $4.7 Harii Bairru Foun ba Komunidade'*

Inside Story 17/02/2016. *'Of Paintballs and Power'*, https://insidestory.org.au/of-paintballs-and-power/

—08/03/2018. *'Timor-Leste: architect of its own Sunrise'*, http://insidestory.org.au/timor-leste-architect-of-its-own-sunrise/

Jornal Nacional Diário 13/02/2012 – *'Sekretáriu Estadu Rekursu Naturál sira Alfredo Pires: "Governu Hakarak Dezenvolvimentu Hafahe ba Kosta hotu iha Timor-Leste"'*

—12/04/2013. *'Suai Entrega Rai Hektares 1113 Harii Supply Base'*

—15/04/2014. *'Adriano Nascimento; "Lei Tolu Prioridade ba PN"'*

—04/11/2014. *'Presiza Estatutu Rai Hodi Kria Kreditu'*

—20/03/2015. *'Timor GAP Fahe Informasaun Ba Veteranus'*, http://www.jndiario.com/2015/03/20/timor-gap-fahe-informasaun-ba-veteranus/

—20/05/2015. *'Timor GAP Fahe Informasaun Ba Veteranus'*

—22/06/2016. *'Rai Igreja Nian Barak la iha Títulu'*,http://timoragora.blogspot.com/2016/06/rai-igreja-nian-barak-la-iha-titulu.html

La'o Hamutuk Blog 01/05/2013. *'Suai Supply Base: Benefit or boondoggle?'*, http://laohamutuk.blogspot.nl/2013/05/suai-supply-base-boon-or-boondoggle.html

Ministério da Justiça (undated). *'Konstrusaun Airoportu Suai Paradu, Vice PM-SETP husu labele impede Desenvolvimentu'*, http://www.mj.gov.tl/?q=node/733

Pambazuka News 01/04/2016. *'Governo de Timor-Leste assina Memorando de Entendimento com a Sociedade Civil para 2016'*, https://www.pambazuka.org/pt/democracy-governance/governo-de-timor-leste-assina-memorando-de-entendimento-com-sociedade-civil

Petroleum Economist 28/02/2013. *'Timor-Leste Facing Problems with Spending'*, https://www.petroleum-economist.com/articles/politics-economics/asia-pacific/2013/timor-leste-facing-problems-with-spending

Presidency of the Council of Ministers 22/04/2013. *'Government and Community celebrate agreement on land use for Suai Supply Base'*, http://timor-leste.gov.tl/?p=8060&lang=en

—22/08/2014. *'Extraordinary Meeting of the Council of Ministers from August 22nd, 2014'*, http://timor-leste.gov.tl/?p=10580&lang=en

Reporters Without Borders 03/05/2005. *'Government Harasses Daily Newspaper Suara Timor Lorosae'*, https://rsf.org/en/news/government-harasses-daily-newspaper-suara-timor-lorosae

Reuters 13/01/2010. *'UPDATE 2-East Timor Rejects Woodside Sunrise LNG Plans'*, http://uk.reuters.com/article/2010/01/13/timor-woodside-idUKSGE60C0AL20100113

SAPO24 13/01/2017. '*Debate sobre lei das terras e propriedades em Timor-Leste 'emperra' nos direitos secundários*', https://24.sapo.pt/noticias/internacional/artigo/debate-sobre-lei-das-terras-e-propriedades-em-timor-leste-emperra-nos-direitos-secundarios_21762445.html

Sapo Notícias 25/06/2015. '*Construtora sul-coreana ganha contrato de 720MD para projeto em Timor-Leste*', http://noticias.sapo.tl/portugues/lusa/artigo/19408120.html

—30/10/2015. '*Câmara de Contas timorense 'chumba' maior contrato da história do país*', http://noticias.sapo.tl/portugues/lusa/artigo/19914163.html

—20/07/2017. '*Tribunal de Recurso timorense dá razão ao Governo sobre megaprojecto na costa sul*', http://noticias.sapo.tl/portugues/info/artigo/1508855.html

Sentru Mídia Investigativu 29/11/2018. '*Tan Auto Estrada, Uma-Kain 50 Resin Hetan Inundasaun*', https://www.smi-tl.org/notisia/breaking-news/815-tan-auto-estrada-uma-kain-50-resin-hetan-inundasaun

Suara Timor Lorosae 15/06/2009. '*Governo Identifika, Problema Rai Bo'ot Tebes*'

—21/10/2010. '*Familia Boot Pe. Sequera Entrega Rai Hektares Ida ba Igreja*'

—03/02/2011. '*MJ Ejiji PN Aprova Lei Rai. Borges: Debate Presiza Qourum*'

—16/11/2012. '*DNTPC Hakarak Hadia Failhansu Servisu*'

—22/11/2012. '*DNTPSC Entrega Servisu ba Direitur Distritrais*'

—12/12/2012. '*2013. Lei Rai Sai preoridade MJ*'

—20/02/2013. '*Prosesu Lei Ba Rai, Abril Komesa halao Diskusaun Iha Plenaria*'

—10/02/2014. '*Asesu Finanseru iha TL, Sai Problema Bo'ot*'

—03/07/2014. '*Atrai Investidor Presiza Lei Rai Klaru*'

—18/11/2014. '*Estrangeirus Domina Projetu Aeroportu Covalima, Komonidade Kesar ba PR*'

—19/10/2015. '*PM Rui: "Halo Atendementu Ba Publiku Laos Ho Sabraut"*', http://suara-timor-lorosae.com/pm-rui-halo-atendementu-ba-publiku-laos-ho-sabraut/

—17/03/2016. '*Xanana: Deskonfia Timor Oan Balun Faan Timor*', http://suara-timor-lorosae.com/xanana-deskonfia-timor-oan-balun-faan-timor/

—10/1/2017. '*Parlamentu Nasional Budu Lei Rai*', http://suara-timor-lorosae.com/parlamentu-nasional-budu-lei-rai/

Tatoli 28/04/2017. '*Governo 'Aprova' Lisensa Konstrusaun Timor Fortuna*', http://www.tatoli.tl/2017/04/governu-aprova-lisensa-konstrusaun-timor-fortuna/

—20/06/2017. '*Aeroportu Suai Sarani ho Naran XANANA GUSMÃO*', http://www.tatoli.tl/2017/06/aeroportu-suai-sarani-ho-naran-xanana-gusmao/

—06/08/2017. '*Inaseitável Xanana Demite hosi Kargu iha CNRT*', http://www.tatoli.tl/2017/08/inaseitavel-xanana-demite-hosi-kargu-iha-cnrt/

—23/02/2018. '*Auto Estrada 'Dificulta' Komunidade Kovalima*', http://www.tatoli.tl/2018/02/auto-estrada-difikulta-komunidade-kovalima/

—07/08/2018. '*Governu Kontinua Hametin Relasaun Ho Sosiedade Sivil*', http://www.tatoli.tl/2018/08/governu-kontinua-hametin-relasaun-ho-sosiedade-sivil/

—18/10/2018. '*Veteranus Labele Impede Dezenvolvimentu*', http://www.tatoli.tl/2018/10/veteranus-labele-impede-dezenvolvimentu/

—16/05/2019. '*Ekipa Interministeriál-Timor GAP Hahú Diskute Projetu Konstrusaun LNG*', http://www.tatoli.tl/2019/05/ekipa-interministerial-timor-gap-hahu-diskute-projetu-konstrusaun-lng/

Tempo Semanal, 23/10/2012. '*Dili Portaun Ba Droga Futuru Jerasaun TL Iha Perigu*', http://temposemanaltimor.blogspot.nl/2012/10/dili-portaun-ba-droga-futuru-jerasaun.html

. —01/04/2013. '*Timor-Leste Proven It's Suspicious of Australian Woodside Company*', http://www.temposemanal.com/nasional/timor-leste-proven-it-s-suspicious-of-australian-woodside-company

—11/04/2014. *'Cova Lima: Successful Megaproject or National Disgrace?'*, http://www.temposemanal.com/opiniaun/cova-lima-successful-megaproject-or-national-disgrace

The Australian 03/12/2013. *'Lawyer 'raided over East Timor spying case''*, http://www.laohamutuk.org/Oil/Boundary/2013/AustralianLawyer3Dec2013.pdf

The Diplomat 17/10/2011. *'Timor-Leste's Tasi Mane Project'*, http://thediplomat.com/2011/10/timor-lestes-tasi-mane-project/

—24/05/2016. *'Timor-Leste's Dangerous Political Union'*, https://thediplomat.com/2016/05/timor-lestes-dangerous-political-union/

—17/04/2017. *'The Alarming Nature of Corruption in Timor-Leste'*, https://thediplomat.com/2017/04/the-alarming-nature-of-corruption-in-timor-leste/

—19/07/2017. *'Timor-Leste: Failing State or Missed Opportunity?'*, https://thediplomat.com/2017/07/timor-leste-failing-state-or-missed-opportunity/

—01/06/2019. *'The Looting of Timor-Leste's Oil Wealth'*, https://thediplomat.com/2019/05/the-looting-of-timor-lestes-oil-wealth/

The Guardian 25/05/2017. *'Timor-Leste's Big Spending: A Brave Way to Tackle Economic Crisis or Just Reckless?'*, https://www.theguardian.com/world/2017/may/25/timor-leste-spending-big-economic-crisis

The New Internationalist 01/05/2005. *'Hungry Season in Timor-Leste'*, https://newint.org/columns/essays/2005/05/01/east-timor

The New York Times 01/10/2015. *'Success is No Longer Foreign to East Timor, but the Players Are'*, https://www.nytimes.com/2015/10/02/sports/soccer/how-did-east-timor-soccer-improve-so-much-brazilians.html?_r=0

Timor Post 26/08/2011. *'Problema Rai Motael, Desizaun Ministeru Justisa'*

—05/10/2011. *'Lucia: Rai Karketu Partensia ba Estadu'*

—26/01/2012. *'Hanoin Didiak Bainhira Oferese Rai'*

—05/10/2012. *'Lamentável Estranjeiru Deklara Na'in Ba Rai'*.

—16/02/2013. *'Sidadaun Estranjeirus Hetan Dokumentu TL'*

—08/04/2013. *'Problema rai Balide-Dioseze Díli – Labele Rezolve Ho Emosaun'*

—12/04/2013. *'Supply Base – Povo Kamanasa Hetan Pursentu 10'*

—12/04/2013a. *'"Governu Sai Sasin": Asian Deklarasaun Katuas Lia Na'in Kamanasa Ba SSB'*

—23/10/2013. *'Supply Base importante, Veteranus Kria Estabilidade'*

—21/04/2014. *'Problema Holbelis Seidauk Iha Solusaun'*

—29/04/2014. *'Xanana Impede Debate Lei Rai'*

—28/06/2014. *'Lei Rai Seidau Iha – Hatauk Empreza Investe iha TL'*

—31/07/2014. *'Konstrusaun Aeroportu Suai - Governu Sei Rekompensa Povu Suai'*

—15/09/2014. *'Lei Kadastru Impende Rejistu ba Propriedade'*

—02/10/2014. *'Labele Impede Mega Projeitu iha Suai'*

— 02/10/2014a. *'Governu Impede Diskusaun Projetu Lei Rai'*

—11/11/2014. *'Xanana: Direitu Ita Nia Dever La Iha Atu Impede'*

—01/12/2014. *'SETP Ofisialmente Lansa Programa Kadastrais'*

—20/12/2014. *'Kompensasaun ba Komunidade Afetadu iha Suai Seidauk Hala'o'*

—10/01/2015. *'Lei Rai Difikulta Investidores'*

—28/09/2015. *'Advogadu Jose Ameasa Lori MJ Ho SETP Ba Tribunal'*, http://www.diariutimorpost.tl/berita-advogado-jose-ameasa-lori-mj-ho-setp-ba-tribunal.html#

. —14/10/2015. *'PN Eziji Lei Rai no Ordenamentu. Xanana Sei Estuda'*.

Transparency Timor Blog 15/05/2013. *'Suai Supply Base - Konsultasaun Kommunidade nian (Confidential)'*, http://transparencytimor.blogspot.nl/2013/05/suai-supply-base-konsultasaun.html

Films and documentaries

Brandenburg, Heidi; Orzel, Mathew (dirs.) (2016). *When Two Worlds Collide*, Yachaywasi Films

Websites

https://dicionario.priberam.org/baldio
https://dicionario.priberam.org/propriedade
https://dle.rae.es/?id=UOknpDg
http://laohamutuk.blogspot.nl/2015/10/bobby-boye-sentenced-to-six-years-in.html
http://reliefweb.int/report/timor-leste/untaet-daily-briefing-25-oct-2000
http://timor-leste.gov.tl/?p=14275&lang=en
http://timor-leste.gov.tl/?p=21909&lang=en&n=1
http://timor-leste.gov.tl/?p=17298&lang=en
https://www.cia.gov/library/publications/the-world-factbook/rankorder/2147rank.html#tt
https://www.mapsland.com/maps/asia/east-timor/detailed-map-of-timor-leste-with-relief-roads-and-cities.jpg
http://www.cne.tl/
http://www.crl.gov.tl/pt
http://www.etan.org/et2009/07july/19/09land.htm
https://www.facebook.com/moises.dasilva.3591/videos/2507213009504723/
https://www.laohamutuk.org/
https://www.laohamutuk.org/Agri/land/RedeRecom10Jun09En.pdf
http://www.laohamutuk.org/econ/OGE15/LHKartaOJE15PN28Nov2014en.pdf
http://www.laohamutuk.org/econ/OGE17/LHSubPNOJE2017-7Nov16en.pdf
http://www.laohamutuk.org/econ/SDP/10SDPindex.htm
http://www.laohamutuk.org/Oil/Boundary/CMATSindex.htm
http://www.laohamutuk.org/Oil/TasiMane/13SSBen.htm
http://www.laohamutuk.org/Oil/TasiMane/2012/Lacerda13Nov2012.pdf
http://www.laohamutuk.org/Oil/TasiMane/2012/LacerdaPresLibertaRai24Oct2012.pdf
http://www.laohamutuk.org/Oil/TasiMane/2012/SSBIntro25Oct2012.pdf
https://www.larousse.fr/dictionnaires/francais/propri%C3%A9t%C3%A9/64421?q=propri%C3%A9t%C3%A9#63694
http://www.mj.gov.tl/files/Grupo_de_Trabalho_Opcoes_Terras.pdf
http://www.mj.gov.tl/files/Relatorio_MinJusticaPortugal.pdf
http://www.tribunais.tl
https://www.youtube.com/watch?v=kA4z2sOugJY

Index

For Product Safety Concerns and Information please contact our EU representative GPSR@taylorandfrancis.com
Taylor & Francis Verlag GmbH, Kaufingerstraße 24, 80331 München, Germany

www.ingramcontent.com/pod-product-compliance
Lightning Source LLC
LaVergne TN
LVHW011116300926
849160LV00008B/398